The English Armada

The English Armada

The Greatest Naval Disaster in English History

Luis Gorrochategui Santos

Translated by Peter J. Gold

Bloomsbury Academic
An imprint of Bloomsbury Publishing Plc

B L O O M S B U R Y
LONDON · OXFORD · NEW YORK · NEW DELHI · SYDNEY

Bloomsbury Academic

An imprint of Bloomsbury Publishing Plc

50 Bedford Square	1385 Broadway
London	New York
WC1B 3DP	NY 10018
UK	USA

www.bloomsbury.com

BLOOMSBURY and the Diana logo are trademarks of Bloomsbury Publishing Plc

First published in Spanish by Ministerio de Defensa as *Contra Armada: La mayor catástrofe naval de la historia de Inglaterra*, 2011

© Luis Gorrochategui Santos, 2011, 2018

English language translation © Peter J. Gold, 2018

Luis Gorrochategui Santos has asserted his right under the Copyright, Designs and Patents Act, 1988, to be identified as Author of this work.

British Library Cataloguing-in-Publication Data

A catalogue record for this book is available from the British Library.

ISBN: HB: 978-1-3500-1697-2
PB: 978-1-3500-1941-6
ePDF: 978-1-3500-1699-6
eBook: 978-1-3500-1698-9

Library of Congress Cataloging-in-Publication Data
Names: Gorrochategui Santos, Luis, 1960– author. | Gold, Peter, translator.
Title: The English Armada : the greatest naval disaster in English History /
Luis Gorrochategui Santos ; translated by Peter J. Gold.
Other titles: Contra Armada. English
Description: London ; New York : Bloomsbury Academic, 2018. |
Includes bibliographical references and index.
Identifiers: LCCN 2017040894 (print) | LCCN 2017052722 (ebook) |
ISBN 9781350016996 (PDF eBook) | ISBN 9781350016989 (EPUB eBook) |
ISBN 9781350016972 (hardback : alk. paper) | ISBN 9781350019416 (pbk. : alk. paper)
Subjects: LCSH: Anglo-Spanish War, 1585–1604–Naval operations, English. |
Anglo-Spanish War, 1585–1604–Campaigns. | Great Britain–History,
Naval–Tudors, 1485–1603. | Armada, 1588. Classification: LCC DA356 (ebook) |
LCC DA356 .G6713 2018 (print) | DDC 942.05/5–dc23
LC record available at https://lccn.loc.gov/2017040894

Cover design: CYAN Design
Cover image © Naval Museum, Madrid. Capture of Lisbon by the Duke of Alba and Álvaro de Bazán.
Palace of the Marquis of Santa Cruz, El Viso del Marqués, Spain.

Typeset by Newgen KnowledgeWorks Pvt. Ltd., Chennai, India
Printed and bound in Great Britain

To find out more about our authors and books visit www.bloomsbury.com.
Here you will find extracts, author interviews, details of forthcoming events
and the option to sign up for our newsletters.

To Demetrio Díaz Sánchez
My philosophy teacher,
My generous and wise friend,
Who showed me the path of the winged horses.

It was great providence and a miracle of the Lord
that the enemy came not directly to Lisbon without first attacking Corunna
for they would otherwise certainly have taken the town.[1]

[1]   *Relación de la venida de Don Antonio de Portugal prior de ocrato con la Armada de la Reyna de Inglaterra en el año de 1589.* BN mss 1749, fol. 226.

Contents

List of Figures   ix
Acknowledgements   x
Note on Dates   xi
Note on Translation   xii

Introduction   1

PART 1 The Spanish Armada

1   The Vicious Circle   7

2   In Corunna   13

3   In the Channel   19

4   Carrick na Spania   23

PART 2 The English Armada

5   Preparations in England   31

6   Preparations in Corunna   43

7   Landing   53

8   The Capture of Pescadería   61

9   To the Walls   67

10 The Oath   73

11 The First Attacks   77

12 The Mined Turret   85

13 María Pita   91

14 San Antón and El Burgo   99

15 Full Sail to Lisbon   109

16 Heading South   117

17   Landing in Peniche   125

18   The March Begins   133

19   In Loures   141

20   On the Outskirts of Lisbon   147

21   *Encamisada*   153

22   The Awakening of Saint George   159

23   The Trojan Horses   167

24   Counteroffensive   173

25   Turning Point   179

26   Two Banners   185

27   Essex, Cárdenas and the Windmills   195

28   To the Sea   205

29   Battles at Sea   215

30   Port of Call in Vigo   231

31   Return to England   237

PART 3 The War Goes On

32   A Glove, a Lion and El Dorado   253

33   The End of Drake and Hawkins   263

34   Cádiz and the North Wind   269

35   Crimson Taffeta   277

36   Peace   283

Epilogue   287
Bibliography   301
Index   307

Figures

6.1 Juan Martínez de Recalde   49

6.2 Contemporary view of the castle of San Antón, Corunna   50

7.1 Map 1, 4 May, Corunna   57

7.2 Model of Corunna as seen by the English, made in 1989 for the
exhibition of the fourth centenary of María Pita   60

8.1 Map 2, 5 May, Corunna   64

9.1 Map 3, the capture of Pescadería, Corunna   69

11.1 Map 4, 6–13 May, Corunna   83

12.1 Medieval wall and turret of Corunna   86

13.1 María Pita   95

15.1 Map 5, 14–19 May, Corunna   113

15.2 Engraving of Fernando Ruiz de Castro, Count of Andrade   115

16.1 Map of the Lisbon Estuary   120

26.1 The English banner captured by Sancho Bravo on 5 June 1589 during
Norris's withdrawal from Lisbon to Cascais   187

26.2 The second banner captured by Sancho Bravo on 5 June   188

26.3 Map 6, 2–5 June, Lisbon   190

27.1 Don Pedro Enríquez de Acevedo, Count of Fuentes   197

29.1 Engraving of the galley of the Adelantado of Castile   218

29.2 Map 7, 25 May–20 June, Lisbon   221

30.1 Small English iron cannon   234

30.2 Second English small cannon preserved intact but badly eroded   235

31.1 Map 8, sea route   240

31.2 Sir John Norris (also spelt Norreys)   242

33.1 Sir Francis Drake   268

37.1 Book cover of *Breve compendio de la sphera y del arte de navegar* first
published in Seville in 1551   288

37.2 Book cover of the 1584 English translation of *Breve compendio*
published under the title *The Art of Navigation*   289

(Please note: Maps 1–8 were drawn by the author. Maps 4 and 5 are referred to in Félix Estrada Gallardo, 'Datos para la confección de un atlas histórico de La Coruña', *Revista del Instituto José Cornide de Estudios Coruñeses*, No. V–VI, Corunna, 1960–70.)

Acknowledgements

There are several people, companies and institutions that have assisted me in the long process that has culminated in this book.

For the Spanish version, I would like to thank the Ministry of Defence as joint publishers; the Institute of Naval History and Culture in Madrid, especially Captain José María Madueño Galán for his perseverance; the historian José Cervera Pery, member of the Royal Academies of History and of the Sea, for his prologue; the staff of the Simancas Archive in Valladolid, the National Library, the Royal Academy of History and the National Library of Portugal, who all placed their professionalism at my disposal to assist me with difficult searches; the historian José Luis Casado Soto, former director of the Cantabrian Maritime Museum in Santander, for his inspiration and support from the outset; Colonel José Navas Ramírez-Cruzado, former director of the Military Museum in Corunna, for his enthusiasm and the magnificent model of the galleon *San Juan*; Felipe Peces, Canon Archivist at Sigüenza Cathedral in Guadalajara, for showing me the banners captured in combat; José Antonio Solís Miranda, of the publisher e-lector, for the joint publication of the book; to my sisters Beatriz, Raquel and Marta for their technical and graphic support; the Museum of Lisbon (Gabinete de Estudos Olisiponenses); the Palace of El Viso, Ciudad Real; the Cerralbo Museum, Madrid; the Naval Museum, Madrid; the Royal Palace Library, Madrid; the Rijksmuseum, Amsterdam; the National Trust Collections and the National Marítime Museum, London; Bilbao council; Corunna council; the council of Monforte de Lemos; the University of Seville; Kronos Servicios de Restauración (Kronos Art Restoration Service); Yago Abilleira Crespo; Carlos Fernández-Cid, Carlos Picallo, José Martínez Rodríguez and Wikimedia Commons for the illustrations.

For the English edition, I would like to thank Bloomsbury Academic Division and especially Emily Drewe and Beatriz López for their courage and judgement in accepting the values of the text even though it challenges well-established conventional positions; Lorcan McNamee, Ana Eiroa, Manuel del Campo and Antón Corriente for their advice and enduring friendship; Professor Peter Gold, for tackling with precision and energy the difficult task of translation.

And of course to all my family, especially Ana and our daughters Nerea and Diana, who for ten years have stoically endured life with someone who has been permanently living in the spring of 1589.

Note on Dates

There is a discrepancy of ten days between the dates on the original English documents and the Spanish ones. This is due to the fact that England had not yet adapted its calendar at this period. The current Gregorian calendar is used throughout this work.

Note on Translation

The translator is responsible for the translations into English of quotations from Spanish or Portuguese sources.

Introduction

Between July 1588, when the Spanish Armada (the so-called Invincible Armada) set sail from Spain, and July 1589, when the remnants of its English counterpart (the little-known English Armada) returned to England, there occurred two of the greatest naval catastrophes in history. Since the time of the Spanish Armada until the present day, much attention has been paid to this event and over time it has become one of the defining moments in the history of Europe. However, no attention has been given to the English Armada, or rather, the attention that has been given to it has been to conceal it and as a result it has completely disappeared from history. Yet, remarkably, the English disaster of 1589 was greater than the Spanish one that took place the year before. Such a puzzling situation leads us to consider the nature of such defining moments in history. How do they happen? How do they develop? What is their purpose? And especially, how is it possible that two such similar episodes have received such unequal treatment?

The attention paid to the defeat of the Spanish Armada was entirely commensurate with the fear that was generated in England (still a relatively minor power) by the threat of a substantial invasion by the leading power of the age. This threat came not only from the sizeable army that the Spanish Armada was transporting, but also because it was under orders to escort the Tercio[1] regiments from Flanders and take them to Kent. If that operation had been successful, there would have been little that Queen Elizabeth could have done on land to avoid defeat.[2] Philip II had no imperialist ambitions to conquer and annex England; his intentions were to defeat Elizabeth and put an end to her zealous – and specifically anti-Spanish – Protestantism.[3] His aim in deposing Henry VIII's daughter was to end the pirate attacks that she sponsored, to put a stop to the aid she was giving the Dutch, who had rebelled against the legitimate king, and to ensure religious tolerance for the Catholics. In general terms, there was no such serious or palpable threat to Spain at that time. That is why during the summer of 1588 England concentrated on

---

[1] A former unit of Spanish infantry with command of up to 3,000 soldiers [translator's note].

[2] See Colin Martin and Geoffrey Parker. *The Spanish Armada* (London: Hamish Hamilton, 1988), Ch. 14.

[3] In this sense, this initiative by Philip was not very different from the one led exactly a century later in 1688 by the Dutchman William of Orange. William attacked and invaded England with a fleet whose size exceeded that of the Spanish Armada. In his case, the objective was the overthrow of the Catholic James II, which he achieved and he became the new king of England, thereby providing a victory for the Protestants in the religious confrontation that ran throughout the century in England. In contrast to the Dutchman, one century earlier the Hapsburg Philip went to the aid of the Catholics. For more on this subject, see José Alcalá-Zamora y Queipo de Llano. *La Empresa de Inglaterra (La 'Armada Invencible': fabulación y realidad)* (Madrid: Real Academia de la Historia, 2004).

preventing the much feared landing at all costs. And the landing never happened. The intercepting fleet managed to stop the progress of the operation, which was never likely to be feasible without a deep-water port in Flanders to provide a starting point. The effort required of that English fleet was considerable. But afterwards, when Elizabeth pinched herself to make sure she wasn't dreaming and was still on the throne, she was overcome by boundless excitement and confidence. That was not surprising. Against all predictions and against the prevailing morale and reputation, she had stopped the all-powerful Philip in his tracks. However, the triumph was not celebrated with fireworks. Instead, England set out on a substantial propaganda campaign and, together with the rest of the Protestant world, it was flooded with pamphlets, popular songs, poems, engravings, paintings, coins, medals and so on. In September, the Queen's adviser, Lord Burghley, published a pamphlet which ended with: 'So ends this account of the misfortunes of the Spanish Armada which they used to call INVINCIBLE.'[4] Burghley highlighted the word by putting it in capital letters, but it was an invention that no Spaniard would have used to refer to the Spanish Armada. Translations into French, German, Dutch and Italian immediately appeared, ridiculing the term 'Invincible Armada'. Thus Burghley won a lasting propaganda coup. For his part, Charles Howard, first Earl of Nottingham, commissioned a series of tapestries representing a great all-out naval battle fought at close quarters. But the Spanish Armada was neither called 'Invincible' nor was it involved in the battle. The impact of Howard's propaganda victory lasted as long as Burghley's. The great body of propaganda created an alternative reality which over the centuries turned into "the defeat of the Invincible Armada", the great defining moment of English nationalism, with its litany of related clichés.

The English Armada was England's counteroffensive. The size of it is striking given England's limited resources at the time. But Elizabeth was aware that it offered a unique opportunity. In order to take advantage of it, she put the crown in hock and signed up ship-owners, noblemen and merchants in that ill-fated venture. The strategy was quite clear: exploit to the full Philip's temporary weakness, given that twenty-eight ships had been shipwrecked off the coasts of Scotland and Ireland on the Armada's return journey. In addition, most of the 102 ships that returned needed a complete overhaul.[5] Hence Spain was left comparatively defenceless if faced with a large-scale attack. So Elizabeth assembled her fleet, by far the largest ever put together by England to date. The mission had three objectives: to destroy the bulk of the Spanish fleet which was being repaired in Santander; to take Lisbon, detach Portugal from Spain and place on the throne the bastard

---

[4]   Martin and Parker, *Spanish Armada*, p. 261. It would appear that this resolved the question of the origin of the term 'Invincible', replacing earlier hypotheses that pointed to Italy, as proposed in Cesáreo Fernández Duro, *Armada Española*, III (Madrid: Museo Naval, 1972), p. 23.

[5]   This figure includes the ships which were withdrawn before reaching the Channel and which returned. José Luis Casado Soto, *Los barcos españoles del siglo XVI y la Gran Armada de 1588* (Madrid: Editorial San Martín, 1988), pp. 242–57. See also Antonio Luis Gómez Beltrán, *La Invencible y su Leyenda Negra* (Málaga, 2013), pp. 412–14, 645–73.

Portuguese pretender, Dom António, Prior of Crato, who had offered to install a satellite English government in Lisbon and open up Philip's Portuguese empire to English pretensions; and to intercept the Spanish fleet in the Azores on its return from the West Indies and satisfy England's great unfulfilled dream. This would lead to the collapse of Philip's huge empire and enable England to take over the ocean routes discovered by Spain.

The English Armada failed, but the treatment that its failure received was, from the outset, totally different. Neither country viewed the defeat of the other as one of the greatest triumphs in its history. No one went from terror to euphoria, because in 1589 Spain was suffering from grief and frustration. At that time there was no prominence given to the Spanish victory in Corunna, the first port attacked by the English Armada and where part of the Tercio regiment returning from the Spanish Armada had been stationed in order to defend it. It is true that the English had been mercilessly driven out and had suffered thousands of casualties, both dead and wounded. But once they had left, all that could be seen was that the lower part of the small city was nothing more than a smoking ruin and that the population had endured great suffering. Victory in Lisbon was merely a great city's resistance to a brief attempted siege, with the besieged army later repelling the attackers themselves and forcing them to take to their ships again with considerable losses. The victories at sea were brilliant and particularly humiliating and damaging for an English Armada routed and in retreat. But they were only minor victories, because there were no all-out battles – nor could there be, with the Spanish naval fleet still under repairs (albeit well-advanced) following the storm-ridden return of the Spanish Armada. Philip's spies promptly reported on the major disaster that Elizabeth had suffered and the King breathed a sigh of relief after having overcome those difficult months in 1589 when Spain was virtually devoid of deployable ships. Philip vigorously re-engaged in war and strengthened his navy so that it reached an unprecedented level of power in the Atlantic. Drake's raids were dealt with once and for all, for when he tried to undertake them once more with a powerful fleet, all he encountered was defeat and death. However, no one embarked on a propaganda campaign, no one tried to highlight the fact that the Spanish project had survived a moment that was as critical as England's months earlier. No one talked up the fact that the Hispanic presence in the world had just been born again.

In order to spare Drake and Norris from the wrath of the Queen over their responsibility for the English Armada's defeat, a new propaganda campaign was undertaken which was almost as significant as the earlier one. If in the first case the aim was to talk up and idealize a success, this time it was in order to conceal a failure. Anthony Wingfield published a small pamphlet that created a new alternative reality by replacing the military operations with a story that frequently substitutes verisimilitude with brilliance. For the last four centuries, this piece of writing has been the main source used to reconstruct the fate of the English Armada.[6]

---

[6]   Of the several Anthony Wingfields of note in the sixteenth century, Captain Anthony Wingfield saw much service in the Netherlands and went on the expedition in 1589 against Spain, of which he wrote an account. See *Dictionary of National Biography, 1885–1900*, Volume 62 (New York and London: Macmillan, 1900), pp. 182–3 [translator's note].

Other pamphlets were published – in English for domestic consumption and in Latin for external use – with resounding success. Added to this was the typical exculpatory or eulogistic character of English documents, in contrast to the sober and descriptive style that Philip's bureaucratic machine demanded. And so the English Armada gradually disappeared from the collective memory until it evaporated. It did not turn into a myth. This asymmetry contributed in turn to the distortion of history. The reasons for this distortion are complex and multiple and have passed through the centuries to the present day. It is no coincidence that the historiography on this subject was written and published in the nineteenth and twentieth centuries, a period when Spain ceased to carry any weight in the international order as it fell behind materially and intellectually, only to become mired in internal wrangles. This was precisely the period when Great Britain reached its peak and sought out myths from the past in order to create its identity.

To summarize, the aim of this book is to present the English Armada in a systematic way based on appropriate documentation, to contextualize it within the Anglo-Spanish war of which it was a part, paying particular attention to problems of health and logistics. The first part considers the story of the Spanish Armada and refutes some long-established myths. The second part recounts for the first time the story of the much neglected English Armada on a day-by-day basis. The third part briefly relates the later development of the war and its aftermath. The epilogue attempts to explore the nature of the historiography that, over the centuries, has dealt with this controversial and fascinating subject.

PART 1

The Spanish Armada

Chapter 1

The Vicious Circle

A hundred years before the English Armada, in 1489, the Treaty of Medina del Campo was signed, confirming the fruitful understanding between Spain and England, which lasted for seventy years. In fact, during the 1520s, Henry VIII preferred a closer relationship with Charles I of Spain than with France. The axis Castile–Flanders–England seemed to work, and although the Act of Supremacy was signed in 1536, establishing the beginnings of the Church of England, good relations and profitable exchanges continued. Philip II of Spain persevered in this political legacy of friendship with England and in 1554 sailed to London to marry Queen Mary I of England, daughter of Henry VIII and of Catherine of Aragon, thereby becoming co-monarch of England. Thus the *entente* of decades earlier was reconfirmed. Following her accession to the throne, the Catholic Mary proposed to abolish the reforms of Henry VIII and Edward VI. She was supported in this by her husband, Philip, the papacy and a large proportion of the senior clergy and English society who were tired of religious and political to-ing and fro-ing, although the Protestants were among her enemies and they closed ranks in their opposition to such a union. However, the marriage could not work in the face of Philip's early absence on royal duties, which caused such melancholy in his wife that it had a considerable bearing on her untimely death. On Mary's death, her younger half-sister Elizabeth I acceded to the throne in 1558 and Philip again tried to maintain the dynastic union with England by offering himself once more in marriage. It is known that Elizabeth was attracted to him, but having been brought up with the reformist ideals of her father, she decided to return to them.

A year later, in 1559, Henry II of France died during the tournament held to celebrate the Treaty of Cateau-Cambrésis, which put an end to a long Spanish–French confrontation, and France embarked upon the regency of Catherine de Medici. Under these circumstances, navigation through the English Channel started becoming unsafe, both on account of the French pirates, who took advantage of the indecisiveness of the regency, and also of the English, who used the excuse to attack papist ships. For its part, the English government turned a blind eye to such attacks rather than keeping watch over the channel. In 1563, the Spanish government in Flanders broke off communications with England, using the plague that was ravaging London as an excuse. The intention was to teach Elizabeth a lesson for her connivance with the pirates. But it was 1564 and 1565 that saw the outbreak of iconoclastic rage that was to change the political map of Europe. Bands of Calvinists who had been expelled from England began to sow terror in Flanders, breaking into Catholic churches and destroying images. In the face of the passivity of local authorities, Philip found himself obliged to send the Duke of Alba to head a Catholic army. This was happening precisely at the time of the bipolarization between the Catholic bloc that had recently left the council of Trent and the growing fanaticism of the Protestants. Flemish uprisings were put down and so the rebels turned to England in search of support, although at that time Elizabeth did not pay much attention to them. But the tension was increasing. In 1568, English ships seized a cargo of money that Italian bankers had sent to the Duke of Alba, while in Spain reprisals were taken against English goods. As the tension increased, the first clear *casus belli* occurred. England attacked Spanish towns in Latin America. While this sequence of murder, robbery, burning and rape was taking place in the Caribbean, Philip made a clear distinction between the wheat and the chaff and confronted the Turks at the Battle of Lepanto, the greatest naval battle in history. Some 484 vessels and 173,000 men, including galley slaves and sailors, engaged with each other in a fight of Homeric proportions. The four hours of combat produced 61,000 casualties, either killed or wounded, at a rate of over four per second. It was a case of Catholics holding back Islam. It was more than ever clear that what was required was Christian unity, but the victory was exclusively Catholic. The Protestant world kept itself out of the fight in order to continue with its reforms, although the resonance of such an enormous victory meant that Catholicism gained in confidence while Protestantism became more distrusting. A consequence of this was the terrible slaughter of Huguenots in France on Saint Bartholomew's night in 1572 or, following Elizabeth's congratulations to Philip for such a victory, the renewal by England of its friendship with Spain in 1573 and the exchange of ambassadors. After Lepanto, Philip acquired a new standing in his role as guarantor of the world order.

During the course of these events, violence was on the increase in the Low Countries, a legitimate part of Philip's inheritance from his father and one of which he was particularly fond. It was an important region of Europe, of strategic significance in geopolitical and economic terms, and in addition a supplier of masts, sails, tar and other resources necessary for the maintenance of the West Indies' fleet. But the Virgin Queen was concerned about the presence of the army of Alexander Farnese, Duke of Parma, on the other side of the channel, and in 1585 sent a contingent of 7,000 men to fight in support of the Dutch rebels. At that point, Philip realized that England was the rearguard of the Flemish rebels and that the defence of his inheritance meant a confrontation with Elizabeth. The resistance was swept aside by the Tercio regiments of Flanders. The experienced soldier Sir Roger Williams reported that he 'had never before seen an army surpassing that of the Duke of Parma in discipline and good command' and, after fighting in vain, Lord Burghley recognized that 'they are, today, the finest soldiers in the Christian world'.[1]

On the other hand, the Catholic Monarchy[2] dominated Africa as well as the Americas and Oceania after the union of the Spanish and Portuguese crowns. If England wanted to

---

[1]   Geoffrey Parker, 'Si la Invencible hubiese desembarcado ...' *Historia 16*, No. 140. 1987, pp. 38–9.

[2]   The term 'Monarquía católica', also known as the 'Monarquía hispánica' or 'Monarquía de España', was used from 1479 (following the union of the crowns of Castile and Aragón) until the beginning of the eighteenth century [translator's note].

expand, it could do so only on Philip's territory. It was keen and impatient, but unable to generate sufficient resources to build and maintain a navy that could stand up to Spain, and so it chose to plunder Philip's extensive and vulnerable empire. For years Philip ignored such provocation until his customary prudence led him irretrievably to prepare for the English Enterprise,[3] the Spanish Armada. The letter from Juan de Idiáquez, the royal secretary to the Duke of Medina Sidonia, makes this quite clear: 'The English are so ubiquitous in the Indies and the sea that there is no way that it can all be defended. It gives us no choice but to start a conflagration at home and make it so intense that they have to attend to it and withdraw from everything else.'[4] The fleet that Philip proposed to put together 'was as much concerned with the safety of the Indies as the restoration of Flanders'.[5]

Paradoxically, while the English Enterprise was being prepared, the Spanish coasts appeared to be very vulnerable, for 'Drake is to be found off Cape St. Vincent, as much at his ease as he would be in London'.[6] A number of plans were discussed regarding the invasion and conquest of England. Álvaro de Bazán, the Marquis of Santa Cruz, proposed a huge fleet consisting of 150 war ships, 40 supply ships, 320 auxiliary vessels, 86 rowing boats, 200 landing craft, 16,612 crew, 55,000 infantrymen and 1,200 cavalry, which would take control of the Thames estuary, seize London and conquer England.[7] Somewhat later, in the summer of 1586, it was decided that not everyone would go from Spain, but a fleet would set sail from Lisbon with the mission to escort the Tercio regiments from Flanders, which would cross the English Channel in barges. Part of the Spanish forces would go with the fleet and the other part would cross the channel in the barges under the fleet's protection. For the sixteenth century, it was a complex amphibious operation.

Meanwhile, with the sense that war was imminent, work started in Corunna on a long-standing project to build a castle on the small rocky island opposite the walled town. In addition to being built on an impregnable bastion, the castle of San Antón would not allow any enemy vessel to approach the town. Never was a construction in Corunna ever started at a more opportune moment. Never did a construction have so much influence on the subsequent development of that crucial war.

It was a very long process to assemble the troops in Lisbon, coming as they did from far-flung parts of the empire, and to prepare the fleet, which consisted of vessels from numerous different places. Many men had to wait for months on board. The wait resulted in outbreaks of illness, which caused delays and associated problems of supplies and new delays that prompted more illness. It completed what has been called

---

[3]   This was the title ('Empresa de Inglaterra' in Spanish) that Philip II gave to his plan to overthrow Elizabeth I from the English throne [translator's note].

[4]   Carlos Gómez-Centurión, 'Los motivos de La Invencible', *Historia 16*, No. 148, 1988, p. 39.

[5]   Antonio Domínguez Ortiz, 'La Armada de Inglaterra en la política de Felipe II', ibid., p. 30.

[6]   Contratación Archivo de Indias, 5108. Quoted in Domínguez Ortiz, 'La Armada', p. 32.

[7]   Cesáreo Fernández Duro, *La Armada Invencible*, Vol. I, Madrid, 1884, pp. 250–319.

'the vicious circle of cause and effect',[8] and claimed thousands of sick and dead. The Marquis of Santa Cruz, an experienced sailor who was charged with the successful completion of such a complicated undertaking, died in Lisbon on 9 February 1588, struck down by a 'pestilential fever'. He was sixty-three years old, had a great past behind him and was an irreparable loss. A few weeks later, the Duke of Medina Sidonia reluctantly arrived in the Portuguese capital to replace him. He increased the artillery personnel and also the number of cannonballs per weapon from thirty to fifty, as well as adopting other measures that improved the performance of the fleet. Finally, once the vessels from Castile had been incorporated at the end of April, the fleet was ready to set sail. However, persistent bad weather prevented it from leaving the Tagus estuary for a further month, with the terrible problems that this brought with it in terms of the wastage of supplies. After considerable loss of goods and men, the expedition finally sailed on the morning of 30 May 1588. Thousands of men breathed a sigh of relief that they were finally off to sea.

For the first three days, unfavourable winds meant that the fleet advanced only five miles; then it changed direction but the ships were inevitably driven southwards. From the outset the sailing conditions were appalling for the unwieldy hulks or supply ships[9] of the Spanish Armada – Flemish, German and even English cargo vessels, typical of the North Sea and the Baltic. The fact that eleven days after setting sail the Armada had only reached as far as Cape St Vincent, a hundred miles further from its destination than Lisbon itself, is difficult to explain when viewed from the present day. But in the sixteenth century, sailing on the high seas was determined by the direction of the wind. The West Indies fleet went out via the Canaries and returned via the Azores. The Manila Galleon was swept along by the countertrade winds – an amazing discovery by the cosmographer Andrés de Urdaneta – which blew from the north of the Philippines towards the Californian coast, and returned to their starting point at Acapulco. It was a case of 'sailing into the wind at full sail'. It was ineffective and complicated to sail close to the wind against a headwind, particularly for the numerous squadrons with large and heavy ships. It was a time that was more suited to smaller fleets, ships sailing on their own, small vessels that were easy to manoeuvre and quick to get away. Sailing techniques seemed to make piracy easier than the founding of empires. For that reason, leaving to one side the excessively centralized economy and the uncontrolled flood of gold and silver from the Americas that practically put paid to Spain's productive activity, the organization of the West Indies fleet, which had been in operation for 217 years, was no mean achievement.

On 10 June, Medina Sidonia wrote to the King from the Gulf of Yeguas:[10]

---

[8]   Manuel Gracia Rivas, *La sanidad en la jornada de Inglaterra (1587–1588)* (Madrid: Editorial Naval, 1988), p. 91.

[9]   The supply ships (*urcas* in Spanish) were also known in English as 'hulks'. They were slower than other ships of the fleet and therefore more vulnerable.

[10]   The Gulf of Yeguas was the former name for the sea that lies between the Canary Islands and the Iberian Peninsula.

The voyage with so many ships inevitably delayed, both because of the weather and because of the need to wait for each other, about which there is no choice, especially for the supply vessels that are so unwieldy and difficult to sail as I have previously described to Your Majesty. Also, because the provisions have been on board for so long they have gone bad, rotten and stale, I find myself in a lot of difficulties with the men without being able to do anything about it, and a large part of the supplies has had to be thrown overboard, otherwise it will only make the men ill.[11]

Shortly afterwards the Duke sent a small boat – a patache – to the Marquis of Cerralbo, captain general and governor of Galicia, instructing him to send as much salted meat, bacon, cheese, fish and lard as he could lay his hands on. The fleet, it was later decided, would wait by the Sisargas Islands, off the northern coast of Galicia.

The decision to hold the fleet alongside the Sisargas Islands and await what little help the Marquis of Cerralbo could provide in such circumstances was very surprising. A glance at a map is enough to confirm that the fleet was sailing along the Costa de la Muerte from Finisterre, with the dilemma at that point of either heading east towards Corunna or clearly moving away from the coast by going north. No one felt this dilemma more intensely than Alonso, Duke of Medina Sidonia, a member of the highest Spanish nobility, who had not managed to escape from the enormously heavy burden that his king had imposed upon him. He was very reluctant to leave his residence in Sanlúcar de Barrameda: 'I do not feel well enough to go on board, because I am aware of the little experience I have of being at sea, which I find is a torture for me because I have a lot of humours.'[12] He had sent a reply to the royal command, but in vain. In a second letter Philip gave him no choice.

The Duke found himself between a rock and a hard place, or more precisely, between his monarch, who was constantly pressing for his English Enterprise to be carried out, and the urgent problems that the Spanish Armada presented. Among them, and by no means the least of them, was that a large part of the water supply had been lost and

[11] Medina Sidonia to the King, Galleon San Martín, 10 June 1588. Cesáreo Fernández Duro, *La Armada Invencible*, Vol. II, pp. 111–12. Quoted in Gracia Rivas, *La sanidad*, p. 245.

[12] Fernández Duro, *La Armada Invencible*, I, p. 415, instead of putting the equivalent of 'which I find a tor-ture' ('que me mata'), transcribed it as 'which makes me sea-sick' ('que me marea'). This gave rise to Hume, and other foreign historians after him, translating the sentence thus: 'I have not health for the sea, for I know by the small experience that I have had afloat that I soon become sea-sick, and have many humours.' This translation gave rise in turn to the rumour that the Duke of Medina Sidonia suffered from seasickness. For its part, the rumour caused Philip to be criticized for being insensitive, unwise or capricious for handing com-mand of the fleet to someone who got seasick. The fact is that the Duke did not suffer from seasickness, and moreover had a deserved reputation as an organizer. The King, in turn, was not capricious, unwise or insensi-tive in appointing him to lead the expedition. This transcription error and the consequent mistaken conclusions are a fine example of how such errors can give rise to mistaken interpretations. See José Ignacio González-Aller Hierro et al. *La batalla del Mar Océano en documentos*. Article published in 'The Spanish Armada', British–Hispanic Symposium, London, June 1988, Madrid, November 1988. *Cuadernos Monográficos del Instituto de Historia y Cultura Naval*, No. 3, Madrid, 1989.

many barrels had split open in the storms. By stopping in Malpica (opposite the Sisargas Islands), he thought that he would be able to take on food and water without the inconvenience of having to disembark. To do so would involve the danger that, with so many adverse circumstances and above all the terrible state of the food that had been on board for months, many soldiers and sailors would opt to desert and escape.

But the Marquis of Cerralbo was unable to meet such a substantial order in such a short space of time. On the morning of 18 June, after waiting for three days in the Sisargas Islands, the stocks of sardines and octopus had finally been thrown into the sea and the bacon was 'rapidly going off'.[13] The only food left was vegetables, hardtack (unleavened bread that could keep for a long time and was a fundamental part of any diet on sea voyages) and insufficient quantities of tuna and cod. Then the Duke wrote to the King informing him of his decision to set sail for England 'with much regret at not having received the supplies despite three days of waiting and the need I have of them'.[14] Nevertheless, he carried on waiting all that day for the arrival of supplies. As evening fell, the sky clouded over, and off the dangerous Costa de la Muerte the following morning the sea had the ugly appearance of an impending storm. The Duke called all his commanders together and, having taken their advice, changed his mind from the day before and decided to head for the harbour at Corunna 'because of the bad weather and the lack of water and supplies'.[15]

It is likely that this sudden change of mind was a ruse so that he could present his arrival in Corunna to the King as something unavoidable and contrary to what he would have wished.[16] Whatever the case may be, these uncertainties were disastrous. In the afternoon of 19 June, as the gale intensified, the fleet headed with some urgency for the Galician capital. But by nightfall it had got worse and many ships, among them the supply vessels, did not have time to reach the port. In the darkness of the night, a powerful storm stirred and scattered all the ships that had not reached the protection of the harbour waters. By the inclement and distressing morning of 20 June 1588, more than half the fleet had disappeared and the hopes of continuing with the journey seemed to have totally vanished in the depths of misfortune. But now it was Corunna's turn.

---

[13] Fernández Duro, *La Armada Invencible*, II, p. 109. Quoted in Gracia Rivas, *La sanidad*, p. 247.
[14] Ibid.
[15] Ibid.
[16] Fernández Duro, *La Armada Invencible*, II, p. 119. Quoted in ibid.

Chapter 2

In Corunna

When Medina Sidonia became fully aware that more than half his fleet had been lost rather than finding refuge in the port, he was completely overcome with despair. One document to that effect is the letter he sent to the King, dated 24 June 1588, on account of which he has been accused of being defeatist:

> The fleet has been divided and has suffered, and as a consequence it is so lacking in strength that it is inferior to the enemy by far, according to all those who know about these things. For many of the most powerful ships, including two galleasses, are missing and on the ships that are here the men are sick and will continue to get struck down very quickly because of the state of the provisions ... this puts us in a very poor position; do not allow Your Majesty to be deceived by anyone who tells him otherwise.[1]

Meanwhile, eighty ships had scattered, including the supply vessels, the Levantine ships, the galleasses (Mediterranean ships with huge artillery power propelled by sails and oars), most of the squadron of Juan Martínez de Recalde, admiral and second in command of the Armada and so on. Juan Gómez de Medina, captain of the convoy of supply ships, decided to continue the voyage to England, accompanied by eight other vessels, since he thought that because of the storm they had fallen behind and the Armada was sailing ahead of them.

Everyone was aware of the punishment that Philip had planned for those captains who abandoned the English Enterprise by returning to Spain. It meant nothing less than the loss of their estate and their lives. Despite this, some ships set off for the Spanish coasts owing to the difficult currents caused by the bad weather. Others went on to England and in fact reached the Isles of Scilly, where they seized two English ships whose crew informed them of the latest defensive preparations.

Meanwhile on board the *Ark Royal*, Lord Howard, the commander-in-chief of the interception fleet, complained bitterly to Walsingham about his uncomfortable and dangerous situation in Plymouth. He would have preferred to attack the Spanish and he would have liked to have been accompanied by Dom António, the pretender to the Portuguese throne currently occupied by Philip II (about which more later), with the intention of attacking Portugal. This was something that the Queen had explicitly refused, as she did not want anything to distract from the objective of defending the

---

[1]   Medina Sidonia to the King, Corunna, 24 June 1588. Fernández Duro, *La Armada Invencible*, II, pp. 136–7.

English coast. He also complained about the lack of supplies and their cost, stating that the Spanish were delaying their arrival in order to make the English use up their provisions while waiting in vain for them in Plymouth.[2]

The ensign Esquivel set sail on 27 June from Corunna in a pinnace (a small but long naval craft) to the Scillies, where Medina Sidonia had previously arranged for scattered ships to meet. On the morning of 30 June, he managed to locate the ships and ordered them to return to Corunna: 'On arrival I spoke to them and showed the order from the Duke to the military commander Don Diego Luzón in his ship and to Juan Medina in his, and I also spoke to the Portuguese who were in the Florentine galleon, and in compliance with the Duke's order they all set course for Corunna.'[3]

Among those ships that had to do the journey to England twice was the supply ship carrying women, for although women were not allowed to be part of the expedition, some of them accompanied their husbands. The same stormy winds from the south-west that were driving the ships towards England were preventing the English from getting close to the Spanish coasts, which might otherwise have resulted in an encounter. Other ships were arriving at Santander, Gijón, Laredo, Santoña, Mugía, Vivero ... slowly but surely, the fleet was coming back together again.

Meanwhile, although some of the noblemen lodged in the San Francisco monastery, the vast majority of the men remained on board. A lot of the sick had to be brought ashore and a field hospital was added to the hospitals of Corunna. Two of the lost supply ships, the *Casa de Paz Grande* and the *San Pedro el Mayor*, which had had to seek refuge on the Cantabrian coast because serious leaks had left them in a bad state, were the very ships that were carrying the excellent hospital and the fleet's store of medication, thereby making the health problems even more complicated.[4]

On 11 July, the Marquis of Cerralbo wrote to the King: 'Since last week meat has been provided and I think it will be sufficient. I anticipate that by the time we set sail we shall have on board 1,000 sheep, 500 cattle and all the chickens we can get hold of.'[5] The fleet were also given 2,000 barrels of wine, 4,459 *quintales* (220 tons) of salted pork, cheese, tuna and sardines that the Marquis had managed to round up, 1,000 *arrobas* (about 16,000 litres) of Andalusian olive oil (as much as they could lay their hands on), and all the salt and firewood they needed. The coopers, who were a typical type of craftsmen in Corunna, repaired all the barrels that had been damaged due

[2] Howard to Walsingham, on board the *Ark*, Plymouth, 24 June 1588. State Papers, Dom. Eliz., CCXI, 18. Quoted in John Knox Laughton, *State Papers Relating to the Defeat of the Spanish Armada*, Vol. I, pp. 199–202. Anno 1588, London, Navy Records Society, 1894–5. For the refusal by the Queen to allow Dom António to take part in the 1588 expedition, see Antonio de Vega to Bernardino de Mendoza, London, 29 June 1588. AGS, E-Francia, leg. K-1568–82. Quoted in Martin A. S. Hume, *Calendar of Letters and State Papers Relating to English Affairs Preserved in, or Originally Belonging to the Archives of Simancas*, Vol. 4, doc. 357, London, 1899. Published in Spanish in José Ignacio González-Aller Hierro et al., *La Batalla del Mar Océano*, Vol. 4. T. 2, doc. 5483, pp. 614–15, Madrid 2013.
[3] *Relación del viaje que ha hecho el Alférez Esquivel*. Fernández Duro, *La Armada Invencible*, II, p. 164.
[4] Gracia Rivas, *La sanidad*.
[5] AGS Guerra Antigua. File 225, fol. 75. Quoted in ibid., p. 259.

to the rough weather. A large number of repairs were carried out to the ships in little or no time and the *nao Santa María de la Rosa* had to be completely re-masted. The Pescadería (the lower part of the town) was bustling with the comings and goings of the shipwrights, carpenters and sailors. The order was given to remove all the cabins that had been built for the voyage but which were taking up space needed for the artillery. It must be remembered that the Spanish Armada was in reality nothing more than a heavily escorted troop-carrying convoy.[6] The hulls of the numerous ships were caulked and ballasted so that their sides rose out of the water. For this task they used stone that was already stacked up on the small island of San Antón, which was ready to be turned into a famous fortress.

But this was by no means the end of the role played by the small island, where the castle of San Antón was to be built once the fleet had sailed, for the men of the English Enterprise had to go to confession and receive communion in a makeshift chapel. In a letter on the 15 July, a week before setting out to sea, Medina Sidonia informed the King:

> In order that all the men could leave after they had been to confession and received communion, and because there was nowhere suitable that they could do so without losing this benefit, I ordered the monks and confessors who were with the fleet to disembark on an island in the port and to set up some awnings and altars to attend to it. And I ordered men to guard the island while each squadron of the companies disembarked. The people of the sea and land have done the same thing and the confessors have told me than to date 8,000 men have gone to confession and received communion.[7]

If for one moment we believed that history is determined by divine providence, we would accept without hesitation that God did not allow this place, where such a devout ceremony had been held, to be seized only ten months later. But we shall leave it to the men of the sixteenth century to confer such a divine omnipresence on events. In fact, Medina Sidonia saw in the rough weather that lashed the fleet close to Corunna a sign sent by God himself to cancel the English Enterprise: 'It appears that what has happened is the better to serve Him, for some good reason that only He knows.'[8]

But Philip was not so easily defeated in matters of faith: 'If this were an unjust war, the storm could be taken as a sign of the will of Our Lord to call off the offense; but as it is just, it should not be thought that He will not protect it, but rather help us more than we could wish for.'[9] By way of corroboration of the King's judgement, at least twenty-six new priests went on board at Corunna, making a total figure of some two hundred. In addition to 'preaching and hearing confession and urging Christian behaviour and

---

[6]   González-Aller Hierro et al., *La Batalla del Mar Océano*, Vol. 4. T. 2, doc. 5483, pp. 614–15. Many of the cabins were built for the adventurers and young gentlemen who travelled with their servants.

[7]   Fernández Duro, *La Armada Invencible*, II, p. 193.

[8]   Ibid., p. 135.

[9]   Quoted in Martin and Parker, *Spanish Armada*, p. 162. See also Fernández Duro, *La Armada Invencible* II, p. 151.

fear of God in the soldiers and other people of the fleet, as well as curing the sick and tending to their needs',[10] the priests also had another mission. The general of the Order of the Dominicans gave his men some very clear instructions: 'Where there are or have been monasteries of our order ... try to convert these monasteries to the state they were in before, by taking possession of them and the temporal goods and property they contain.'[11]

The two companies in Corunna consisting of some three hundred men were put on board the Spanish fleet to replace those who were sick and had to remain on land. Captain Troncoso was ordered to re-form the garrison with the sick men as they recovered. In the end, the sicknesses that Corunna suffered were slight, mostly fevers, with only nine dead. Fresh food helped to reduce such problems: 'Bread and fresh meat help them to get better ... it has all been due to the bread and fish they have here.'[12] With such preparations completed, but which left the town and its environs completely exhausted, the fleet was ready to set sail.

Thanks to an extraordinary collective effort, Corunna had been able to provision, feed, cure, repair and – in a word – re-establish the Armada and its men. After thirty-three days of painstaking care, the Spanish Armada once more put out to sea, and its progress was one of the most moving spectacles ever seen from the Galician port.

The four galleys in the fleet – magnificent Mediterranean warships with highly stylized lines and large pointed rams, leading vessels at the Battle of Lepanto together with the galleasses but ill-suited to sailing on the high seas – inevitably went off course during the crossing towards the English Channel as they got blown by the winds towards the Bay of Biscay, where they met different fates.

At four o'clock in the afternoon of Friday, 29 July – much later than the ideal, due to the approach of autumn; the fleet had already tried to set sail from Lisbon in April – the Armada sighted the English coastline. The ensign Juan Gil was despatched in a *zabra* (a small two-masted ship, similar to a pinnace) together with twenty soldiers to the coast. On his return with four fishermen, it was learned that Drake and Howard had 120 vessels at the ready and that a further 40 were sailing in the channel. Medina Sidonia's men prayed for the blessing of victory and raised the royal standard atop the mast of the flagship, the galleon *San Martín*.

Finally, after more than a year since forces began to assemble in Lisbon, the moment of truth was fast approaching. The most formidable fleet that had ever sailed the Atlantic aimed to enter into total and decisive naval warfare against everything that the English and the Dutch could set against it, clear the sea of enemy ships and later escort Farnese's barges carrying the Tercio regiments from Flanders to the Kent coast. With such hopes, the fleet began to line up along the coast.

---

[10] AGS Contaduría del Sueldo, segunda época. File 281, fol. 703. Quoted in Gracia Rivas, *La sanidad*, p. 208.

[11] Ibid., p. 210.

[12] Ibid., pp. 253–4.

During the afternoon of 30 July, Lord Charles Howard of Effingham's squadron set sail from Plymouth. As Howard himself reported: 'The next morning, being Sunday, all the English that were come out of Plymouth recovered [gained the advantage of] the wind of the Spaniards two leagues to the westward of the Eddystone.'[13] A squadron on the windward side – the side the wind is blowing from – has a clear strategic advantage. First, it can decide the distance it wishes to keep, since the opposing formation has to sail against the wind in order to move towards it. In addition, it has a greater ability to manoeuvre if it changes course towards the enemy fleet. To be on the windward side in a naval battle is like controlling a ridge in an engagement on land. In other words, once the light English vessels, laden only with the essentials for combat, had sighted the enormous Spanish fleet, they sailed close to the wind and managed to get in behind it, or 'recover the wind'. The Armada consisted of large ships, most of them merchant vessels fitted with artillery, but it had twenty galleons and four galleasses, which were terrifying ships of war. They had on board everything required for a prolonged sea-crossing, conquest and establishment in England and were undoubtedly slower and heavier than the English fleet.

As Pedro Valdés had indicated in a letter to the King written from Corunna, the Spanish fleet was sailing in three groups. The vanguard was led by Alonso de Levya on board the *nao* from the Levante *La Rata Santa María Encoronada*. The middle group, which included the transport ships, was led by Medina Sidonia on his flagship, the galleon *San Martín*. Closing up the rear in the galleon *San Juan* was Juan Martínez de Recalde. The fleet was sailing east, close to the English coast and in the direction of Flanders. There was a westerly wind and the English, on the windward side, were grouped into two squadrons and were following in the wake of Recalde's *San Juan* from a distance.

With the enemy's approach, the armada changed its position from 'ahead' to 'combat', in accordance with measures successfully used with the large West Indies fleets. Thus Leyva formed the northern flank, close to the coast, Medina Sidonia occupied the centre and Recalde the southern flank. Howard attacked Levya while Drake attacked from the south.

Howard's attack on the northern flank was driven back by the artillery from *La Rata, La Ragazzona* and other ships from the Levantine squadron, and he withdrew. Meanwhile, Recalde's ships had manoeuvred towards Medina Sidonia's positions near the centre of the Armada, but the galleon *San Juan* had become separated from its squadron and was left isolated. Drake's *Revenge*, Hawkins's *Victory*, Frobisher's *Triumph* and four other English galleons attacked what they saw as a guaranteed and important quarry, to judge by the pennants and flags flying atop its mastheads. The *San Juan*, which was leeward from its own squadron, appeared lost.

---

[13]   Quoted in Garrett Mattingly, *The Defeat of the Spanish Armada* (London: Jonathan Cape, 1983), p. 251. First published 1959.

In fact, it was a master stroke by Recalde who, surrounded by seven enemy ships, aimed to engage in close-quarter combat in the knowledge that other ships would soon arrive to attempt a skirmish that could finish off the English fleet in one fell swoop. As the English vessels approached, a deadly hail of musket and artillery fire rained down upon them and because the Spanish galleons were approaching from the windward side with the wind behind them, the English had to escape before they fell into the trap laid for them by Recalde. And so the first encounter ended with an English withdrawal for, as Howard himself acknowledged, 'We durst not adventure to put in among them, their fleet being so strong.'[14] According to Captain Venegas, Spanish casualties were seven dead and thirty-one wounded. There is no data for the English.[15]

The Duke exchanged artillery fire without Howard deciding to accept the challenge. For four hours he tried to 'recover the wind', for that was how he could sail against Howard and force him to fight. But with a large and diverse fleet and the ships fully laden, he did not succeed in doing so.

Howard expressed surprise at the sight of the majestic enemy fleet and its perfect, impregnable formation.[16] The Spanish Armada sailed onwards towards Flanders, following its orders to make contact with the Tercio regiments of Alexander Farnese and facilitate their crossing. Meanwhile, the people of Corunna, who felt exhausted but with a sense of duty well done, waited impatiently for news of what, in one sense, they considered to be *their* armada. They were right to see it in that way, for each and every one of the vessels carried some keepsake from them, rather like knights and their ladies' kerchiefs. What they did not yet know was that a few months later it would itself become the most powerful galleon that sailed the seas in the sixteenth century.

---

[14]   Quoted in Mattingly, *Defeat of the Spanish Armada*, p. 258.
[15]   Mariano González-Arnao Conde-Luque , 'La Aventura de La Armada', *Historia 16*, No. 148, 1988, p. 77.
[16]   Ibid.

Chapter 3

In the Channel

After the first English withdrawal near Plymouth and while the Spanish Armada was manoeuvring in order to try and give chase to the vessels that had turned tail, two accidents occurred, the first misfortunes in an endless series outside the field of combat that defined the fate of the voyage. The *nao Nuestra Señora del Rosario* (1,150 tonnes, 46 cannon and 422 men) collided with the *Santa Catalina*. As a consequence, it broke its bowsprit – the diagonal spar that stems from the prow – and the foremast or prow mast spar. While the damage was being repaired, the foremast itself gave way, bringing with it the spar of the main mast, leaving the *nao* with only the mizzen sail, no steering and trailing behind. The beauty of the rigging and the fully distended sails of those great ships is matched only by their relative fragility. To his great regret, Medina Sidonia had to leave the magnificent vessel behind for the sake of the common good.

The misfortunes of that ill-fated day, 31 July, did not end there, for the magazine where the gunpowder was stored on the *nao San Salvador* (900 tonnes, 40 cannon, 350 men) exploded accidentally and blew the ship to pieces, with almost 200 casualties. The Duke, with the galleon flagship *San Martín*, swiftly went to where he was most needed and did not stop for an instant either to rest or to eat. Meanwhile, far from such terrible nightmares, the Marquis of Cerralbo made sure that the people of Corunna received due recompense for the property and the services provided in the repair of the fleet that had left ten days earlier. More importantly, he oversaw the fortification of the Galician coast, especially Corunna and Bayona, given the possibility that Queen Elizabeth might order a counter-attack if the Spanish Armada failed.

After a day following the English coastline without further mishaps, the Duke rejected the idea of a comfortable landing on enemy territory, much to Howard's relief, but he did discover some good anchorage where he could land, such as Torbay. Pillaging was not his style and his only treasure was to fulfil the orders of the King. English commanders considered it dishonourable not to fight to defend the channel (just as an army would defend a gorge or a pass) and let the Spaniards through. However, they restricted themselves to following them at a distance and abandoning the English coast to its fate. Fortunately for Howard, the Spaniards' mission was conquest and settlement in England. Medina Sidonia then sent the ensign Juan Gil in a patache to let the Duke of Parma know his position, for the Duke was waiting with the Tercio regiments of Flanders in Dunkirk. As soon as he received the news, Alexander Farnese ordered 'everyone who is some distance from the quay to get there as quickly as they can'.[1]

---

[1]   Letter from Farnese to the Spanish Consul in Venice. Fernández Duro, *La Armada Invencible*, II, doc. 183. Quoted in Ricardo Cerezo Martínez, *Las Armadas de Felipe II* (Madrid: Editorial San Martín, 1989), p. 357.

At dawn on 2 August, off Portland Bill, the south-easterly wind veered to a north-easterly, the armada turned, sailed close to the wind towards the coast and, with the wind in its sails, launched itself at the English, who failed in their desire to reach the coast first and had to flee southwards in haste. The sudden manoeuvre left seven English vessels, including the Queen's ship, the *Triumph*, between the coast and the Spanish vanguard. The latter was joined by the powerful galleasses of Hugo de Moncada, which attempted to board the enemy ships. The objective was aborted due to the currents which separated the two squadrons to the south of the bill.

Meanwhile, as he was sailing away, Howard found himself right in the middle of the armada and Martín de Bertendona, head of the squadron of Levantine ships and later bastion of the defence of Corunna, decided that the time had come to fight at close quarters. Both fleets moved towards each other until they were within easy musket range, and a ferocious exchange of artillery fire began. The English, with their less heavily laden vessels, withdrew sufficiently so that none of the Spanish grappling hooks managed to sink into the wood. Suddenly the wind veered towards the south-south-west, giving Howard with his eight large vessels the opportunity to go over to assist those that had been isolated off the coast. The Duke realized his intentions and rowed over with the aim of intercepting him. It then became clear that Juan Martínez de Recalde's *San Juan* had been left leeward of the armada and was again surrounded by English ships, amongst them Drake's *Revenge*. For a moment, the air seemed to have become motionless and a dense cloud of smoke enveloped the *San Juan*, which was spitting fire from all of its cannons, while a penetrating smell of gunpowder impregnated every patch of rigging of the valiant galleon, which stubbornly was still trying to engage in close combat. Medina Sidonia then headed towards the *San Juan*, followed by the vanguard squadron. The *San Martín* rowed over to Howard and exchanged broadsides with the English ships as they passed by. Using its powerful bronze cannons – the best and most expensive of their day– it spat fire and destruction ceaselessly for an hour, creating a terrifying din. Finally the Guipúzcoa squadron arrived, captained by Miguel de Oquendo, and the English, as usual, gave up the fight.

Over 5,000 cannon balls were fired by the Spanish in the fierce skirmish off Portland Bill. It was a bitter fight, with both sides being hit a significant number of times – the *San Juan* alone received over fifty strikes. Its reinforced hull, which gave it extraordinary resistance, did not give way. Although none of the ships of the armada was lost, there were fifty men dead and sixty wounded. Nothing is known about English casualties; at least one small two-masted ship, the *Plaisir*, went under and another ship, the *Swallow*, was set alight.[2] This was the start of the systematic concealment of casualties and damage; Queen Elizabeth forbade on pain of death the divulging of figures concerning the English. It is surprising, because it is so early, that Elizabeth engaged in the

---

[2] The captain of the *zabra Plaisir*, called Cock or Cope, died when the ship sank. In the case of Richard Hawkins's *Swallow*, the fire was put out. Fernández Duro, *La Armada Invencible*, I, p. 89.

clever use of war propaganda, for she was largely responsible for the historical falsification that surrounded this Anglo-Spanish war from the outset. But on the Catholic side, news was plentiful . . .

The Spanish ambassador to France, Bernardino de Mendoza, wrote from nearby Rouen with first-hand information. Philip replied and congratulated the Duke on his triumph and indicated his hope that the amphibious operation would end successfully. But they were pyrrhic victories in the Armada's English Enterprise. Lord Howard urgently demanded the despatch of more munitions. In the south of the country, stores were emptied; London sent all the gunpowder and cannon balls that it could get hold of. The damaged English vessels, with dead and wounded on board, and especially those with their gunpowder magazines empty, could return to their ports and set off to sea again with more munitions and their men refreshed. As if that was not enough, there was a steady flow of new ships joining Howard's fleet.

For their part, the Spanish ships had to ration their stocks of munitions. Medina Sidonia began to realize that he could not stay long in the theatre of operations because the English had an enormous logistical advantage. Without the widespread boarding of opposing ships and the major destruction of the enemy fleet, any victory had no more strategic relevance than continuing on towards the rendezvous with Farnese but without having ensured the essential control of the sea. There was no guarantee of success for the fragile landing craft that were intended to carry the most formidable military force of the day up the Thames estuary. In fact, the strategies of both sides had clear antecedents: on the one hand the usual English privateering practice that could be called guerrilla warfare at sea, consisting of attacking straggling ships and sailing away when the 'defensive curtain' came into action. On the other hand, the remarkable discipline and power of the great escorts of the West Indies fleet and the organization into squadrons that years earlier Álvaro de Bazán had successfully tested.

As it grew light on 3 August, Drake, who was leading the chasing fleet, noticed that the supply ship *Gran Grifón*, lead ship of the supply squadron and commanded by Juan Gómez de Medina, had got left behind. He set off with several other ships in pursuit, but the quarry defended itself well and made up time, for they did not dare to board her. Recalde, who was in charge of the rearguard at the extreme south of the 'defensive curtain' with two galleons and two galleasses, came to its assistance and struck up a lively close-to exchange of artillery with Drake. That was when one of the cannon shots from the *San Juan* took out the main mast of *Revenge*. So the *Gran Grifón*, which looked like easy spoils, turned the tables on its attackers. While Drake was out of action and had to withdraw, his hatred and desire for revenge grew towards Recalde's arrogant and daring *San Juan*. He knew that as soon as his ship was repaired, he would face it again in the very near future.[3] It was the task of the formidable Portuguese-built galleon, as the

---

[3]   The temporary repair on the coast kept Drake out of action for two days. Harry Kelsey, *Sir Francis Drake: The Queen's Pirate* (New Haven, CT and London: Yale University Press), 1998, p. 332.

admiral's ship, to protect the rearguard and to challenge any ships that came too close, something in which Drake's *Revenge* often led the way.

It was at this point that the Duke manoeuvred with the vanguard in search of another naval battle that the English prudently set about avoiding by withdrawing once again. After this clash, the council of admirals of both fleets held a meeting. The Spanish decided to strengthen the rearguard and press forward in order to make contact with Alexander Farnese, bypassing the conquest of the Isle of Wight, which was a secondary objective suggested by Philip. The English, who had never assembled a fleet of this size, quickly learnt about a superior tried-and-tested strategy and ipso facto replaced their rudimentary system of attack in a pack by the organization of their fleet into Spanish-style squadrons.

At dawn on 4 August, the lack of wind meant that the galleon *San Luis* and the hulk *Duquesa Santa Ana* had fallen behind. Hawkins's squadron, which was being towed by oar-powered boats, tried to isolate them, but three galleasses, supported by Leyva's *Rata* and other vessels, rescued them before other English ships could get there. Howard, who felt emboldened by the number of ships – 150 – that he now had, took advantage of the gap left by Leyva's squadron by slipping through on the left of the formation and attacking the vanguard that included the flagship, Medina Sidonia's *San Martín*, plus the merchant ships. Finding themselves at close quarters, harquebuses, muskets and the heaviest artillery of the lower decks were brought into play. Oquendo and Recalde got involved and the battle broadened out so that, according to the Duke, 'it was felt certain that we would board them that day, which was the only way to victory'.[4] But in the end, they did not board them this time, either, with Howard's flagship 'hit by Oquendo's cannon fire, with the Duke ordering his men to fire at it as well and Juan Martínez de Recalde doing the same. It was in a very tight spot, but the wind got up and it managed to slip through their hands.'[5] The day's casualties rose to fifty dead and seventy wounded, with 3,000 cannon balls having been fired. As usual, there were no figures for the English side.

Nothing would now prevent Medina Sidonia from crossing the channel and that same day he sent a new despatch to Farnese urging him to unite his forces with the Armada without delay. On the morning of 5 August, he sent a patache to ask for cannon balls and forty flyboats – light ships with a low draught – for battle in coastal waters where galleons would run aground. Meanwhile, the English fleet sailed at a prudent distance from the Spanish rearguard.

At five o'clock in the afternoon of 6 August, the Spanish Armada achieved the first part of its mission and, having crossed the English Channel, it weighed anchor in the tiny and dangerous roadstead of Calais. Losses had been minimal, although the use of cannon fire had been considerable. It was now the turn of the Duke of Parma, Alexander Farnese. The moment of truth was approaching.

---

[4]   *Diario de Medina Sidonia* in Fernández Duro, *La Armada Invencible*, II, p. 237.
[5]   *Relación de lo sucedido a la Armada de S. M.* (anonymous). Ibid., p. 259.

Chapter 4

Carrick na Spania

The prevailing winds and the sea currents in the English Channel are westerlies and so in order to avoid the risk of sailing too far, Medina Sidonia found himself obliged to anchor the armada outside Calais, despite the fact that the ships had no protection there from the winds and were flanked by dangerous shoals and reefs. The reason he went against naval logic in this way is because the small French town lies twenty miles to the west of Dunkirk, where the Tercio were stationed awaiting an escort, and there was nowhere else, not even Dunkirk itself, that would allow large ships to get anywhere near the coast. This was a difficult stretch of coastline plagued with sandbanks and treacherous rocks.

The Duke anticipated the use of fireships – unmanned incendiary vessels – launched at full sail towards the Armada from the agile and increasingly numerous English fleet which had anchored two miles upwind. He ordered the preparation of a force of pinnaces equipped with grappling irons and ropes which under oar-power could change the course of such fireships. He then sent his secretary Jerónimo de Arceo with a message for Alexander Farnese, the Duke of Parma, telling him of his arrival, regretting the lack of any correspondence from him and informing him that the armada was expecting the Tercio regiment to set sail so that the two fleets could immediately embark on their joint route.

At daybreak on 7 August, Captain Rodrigo Tello brought a letter to Medina Sidonia from Farnese informing him that his invasion force would be ready to set sail within six days. Tello added that when he left Dunkirk the previous day, the embarkation of the troops and the provision of the munitions requested earlier had not yet begun.

It was clear that there was a lack of understanding between the Medina Sidonia's Spanish Armada and the Duke of Parma's Tercio regiments of Flanders. It is worth considering the causes of this strategic failing at such a crucial point in the English Enterprise, which consisted simply in an amphibious operation in which the Spanish Armada was to escort Parma's landing craft to the Thames estuary.

The original invasion plan which had been carefully designed by Álvaro de Bazán was tactically very simple: assemble a huge fleet against which the combined forces of England and Holland would be unable to do anything, and land in Kent in order to launch the conquest of England. Later, Philip believed that rather than assemble a fleet of that size it would be simpler to divide the expedition into two groups and take advantage of the strength of the Tercio regiments who were well settled on England's doorstep. To judge by the words of Farnese's emissary and later the historian Cabrera de

Córdoba and his repeated warnings to the King, the Duke of Parma was doubtful from the outset that such an operation was feasible:

> Your Majesty, the Duke of Parma's ships could never join up with the Armada. The Spanish galleons have a draught of twenty-five to thirty feet, and such a depth is not to be found anywhere near Dunkirk. The enemy ships have a lesser draught and can easily place themselves in a position to prevent anyone from leaving Dunkirk. Bearing in mind that the joining together of the Flanders barges with the Armada is the central point of the enterprise and that it is highly unlikely to happen, why not abandon the plan and save much time and money?

Alexander Farnese proposed the conquest of the large port of Flushing (Vlissingen), where everything could have been organized differently.

Without apparently being fully aware of the complexity of the operation, Philip did not pay enough attention to the choice of the key locations and the preparation and supervision of the landing fleet in Flanders. The responsibility for this was given to one Alexander Farnese who, in contrast to Medina Sidonia, realized that such a fleet was only intended to provide transport and should have no military function. The King assumed – an assumption that the English made sure was seen as totally outdated – that, as in Lepanto, the enemy would face them gallantly in a decisive battle, when the Spanish Armada would mercilessly crush the English fleet.

The wind got up in the afternoon of Sunday, 7 August. Howard anxiously sensed that the amphibious operation was about to begin. He knew that if the Tercio regiments succeeded in crossing the channel, England was lost and so he called a meeting of the commanders of his fleet where it was decided to use the fireships. They had to bring old vessels from Dover, which meant that the fire attack would be delayed until Tuesday. Feeling under pressure, given the imminence of the invasion, Howard decided to sacrifice newer ships so that he could attack that night. Drake offered the 200-tonne *Thomas* from Plymouth; Hawkins followed suit and others, impassioned by a sense of patriotism, handed over their vessels until a flotilla of eight ships was put together ready for the blazing sacrifice. The preparations had been so hasty and so pressured that one of the ships went up in flames while still loaded with its provisions, as was later reported.

'At midnight we saw two fires lit among the English fleet and they grew to eight in number.'[1] The pinnaces made ready for the purpose began their anti-fireship manoeuvres and the first two were rendered harmless. The wind strengthened, as did the tide and the currents, which made it impossible to divert the remaining six and these rushed together, like a giant ball of fire, towards where the Spanish ships were anchored. Plan B was put into operation, consisting of weighing anchor, dodging the fireships and dropping anchor again. The fireships passed 'the same position as our flagship and fleet, without doing any harm to anyone as they moved so swiftly'.[2] Medina Sidonia's *San Martín*, Recalde's *San*

---

[1] *Diario de Medina Sidonia* in Fernández Duro, *La Armada Invencible*, II, p. 240.
[2] *Relación de lo sucedido a la Armada de S.M. en la expedición contra Inglaterra en 1588 por el capitán Alonso Vanegas.* Ibid., p. 389.

Juan, *San Marcos*, *San Felipe* and *San Mateo*, all powerful galleons close to the English fleet, plus some other ships, managed to weigh anchor again nearby. But the rest of the fleet, carried by the wind towards the shallows of Gravelines, manoeuvred in order to get away from the danger of the coast and to avoid colliding with each other, without being able to drop anchor again. The *San Lorenzo* (762 tonnes, 45 cannons and 415 men), flagship of the galleasses, collided with the *San Juan de Sicilia*, lost its rudder and drifted to the shallows of Calais castle, and there was nothing that the efforts of the galley slaves could do about it.

At dawn on Monday, 8 August, Howard discovered that the armada had been dispersed and that only the vessels mentioned were to be seen. An incredible battle then took place between 160 English ships organized in five squadrons and the galleons which, having taken in their sails, took them on in order to protect the rest of the fleet until they managed to regroup. Each one of those ships deserves a separate mention.

Hugo de Moncada's galleass *San Lorenzo*, which had run aground and was listing below Calais castle and with its cannons out of action, watched Howard's squadron with its thirty ships coming towards it. Lord Howard organized a flotilla of vessels and set about preparing for the invasion of the galleass. This gives us an idea of what the English thought about the Spanish ships. They were not far wrong. The landing craft filled up with the dead and the wounded, for de Moncada's men defended themselves heroically, keeping the squadron of the commander of Elizabeth's fleet away from the battle in the channel. Finally a musket shot went through Hugo de Moncada's head and the survivors decided to abandon ship and get on to the beach. Shortly afterwards, the governor of Calais had to open fire from the castle to drive the English vessels away from the coast as they were planning to sack the *San Lorenzo*.

The *San Mateo* (750 tonnes, 34 cannon, 397 men) was totally surrounded on two occasions by enemy ships, and in both instances it managed to avoid being captured by fighting its way out of trouble. Its advantages, like the rest of the Spanish galleons, lay in the solidity of its reinforced oak hull, its bronze cannons, the quality of its harquebusiers and musketeers, and above all, in having on board men who were used to winning. Later the *San Martín* went to assist, but Don Diego de Pimentel refused to leave the ship and abandon the wounded. He ran out of cannon balls, and when Seymour's *Rainbow* dared to approach and invite it to surrender; a musket shot killed the English officer who had the audacity to make such a proposal. Later it ran aground on the sandbanks of Blankenberge and offered fierce resistance for two hours against the Dutch.

The *San Felipe* (800 tonnes, 40 cannon, 520 men) experienced a similar fate. With the galleon badly damaged and surrounded by its enemies, its captain, Francisco de Toledo, released the grappling hooks so as to challenge the English to board, but even then the English did not dare to accept. That was when he ordered the decks of the attackers to be raked with musket and harquebus fire. 'As soon as the enemy saw this, they withdrew. Our men called them cowards, and made known their lack of courage in coarse language, calling them Lutheran chickens.'[3] This is the reason why not a single

---

[3] *Relación de Pedro Coco Calderón*. AGS Guerra Marina, File 221, fol. 190, 3rd v. Quoted in Kelsey, *Sir Francis Drake*, p. 406.

Spanish ship was boarded, even in such an unequal combat. Toledo also refused to abandon ship, and once the attack had been repelled, he managed to put in at Nieuwpoort, which was in Spanish hands, where the Tercio regiment came to his assistance. With the fighting over and out of sight of the enemy, the ship from Biscay *María Juan* (665 tons, 24 cannon, and 276 men) sank after transferring part of its personnel.

For its part, Drake's *Revenge,* which had now been repaired, took part in only the first hour of the battle, something for which he was heavily criticized by Frobisher, who called him a 'cowardly knave or a traitor', but there was time for him to take several hits, among them two in the captain's cabin: one went right through it, the other destroyed the bed.[4]

The large English fleet then furiously pursued the scattered merchant ships before the armada managed to recover its formation. But the *San Martín* of Medina Sidonia, always in the middle of the action, the *San Marcos*, the *San Juan* and other ships mentioned, drove back the massive attack until the galleons from Portugal and Castile, Leyva, Oquendo and others managed to come alongside and join the action. After such tenacious resistance, the *San Martín*, with the Spanish Armada in formation once again, took in its sails in a challenge to a fight but the English ordered the retreat, and for the fourth time the armada watched the English slip away. The impotence and the anger from which Captains Recalde and Oquendo suffered as they watched the English ships sail away left them marked for life.

On the Spanish side, losses rose to over six hundred dead and eight hundred wounded. The *San Martín* fired 300 cannon balls and was hit by 107. On the English side, there is a despatch taken from a fluyt that was seized on 26 August after Howard had definitively abandoned the fight. The Queen regretted that 'only twenty-eight very badly damaged vessels' had reached London and 'thirty-two had arrived in Flushing, in an even worse state and with few survivors, with many others killed, in particular their chief pilot; and the Queen had published an edict that no one in the whole country should dare to say that the armada had been a success, or to allow ships to leave its ports'.[5]

The English ships were in large part left damaged and mastless, although none was sunk within sight of the enemy. Only the galleon *Elizabeth Jones*, one of the largest, lost over two hundred men from combat and also a contagious illness that began to wreak havoc in the fleet. Many others had to withdraw from the campaign. In subsequent days, the Spanish Armada only saw 109 of the 160 ships that took part in the battle of Gravelines and on each of the three occasions that the Duke tried to engage them in a fight, they refused. England was to a certain extent defenceless, but the armada did not know the facts and also had problems of its own.

On Tuesday, 9 August, Medina Sidonia found himself in the most serious of all the situations he had had to face in the English Enterprise, because the north-easterly wind

---

[4]   Kelsey, *Sir Francis Drake*, pp. 407–8.

[5]   Alonso Vázquez, *Los Sucesos de Flandes y Francia en tiempos de Alexandre Farnese*, quoted in *Colección de Documentos Inéditos para la Historia de España*, Madrid 1879, vol. 73, p. 352. Fernández Duro, *La Armada Invencible*, I, p. 139.

was pushing his ships inexorably towards the sandbanks of Zeeland. When the ships were about to run aground, the wind veered to the south-west and took them away from the danger. The Duke called a meeting of his commanders to decide what should be done, given 'the state of the Armada and the lack of cannon balls'. They had to decide if 'it was a good idea to go back to the English Channel or return to Spain via the North Sea, since the Duke of Parma was not yet ready to fight'. They all agreed to return to the channel 'if the weather' – in other words, the wind – 'made it possible'.[6] The winds were westerlies, just as they were in the channel, and the Spanish Armada was still heading north, followed at a distance by the English fleet. The armada challenged the English fleet on three occasions, but the English took in their sails in order to keep their distance.

By 12 August, the English expedition was exhausted and, unable to continue, it headed for the coast. To justify his withdrawal, Howard obliged his captains to sign a memorandum in which they gave their agreement to call off their pursuit.[7] He was not mistaken regarding reaction in London to this course of action. Walsingham, the Queen's secretary, regretted in a letter dated 18 September: 'I am sorry the Lord Admiral was forced to leave the persecution of the enemy through the wants he sustained. Our half-doings doth breed dishonour and leaveth the disease uncured.'[8]

The Spanish Armada was never defeated. It never shied away from fighting the English. It continued to rule the waves after each of the four battles that were fought in the channel. But the English strategy of avoiding proper confrontation ended up by exhausting the capacity of the Spanish fleet to remain in the theatre of operations. Having left Dunkirk behind and with persistent westerly winds frustrating the amphibious operation, it had to return to Spain. Once the ships had left the North Sea and entered the Atlantic, the old seafaring problems of the supply ships reappeared, the same problems that caused the Spanish Armada to scatter outside Corunna and forced it to spend a month in the city. But then came terrible gales and headwinds, especially on 6, 19 and 22 September, in Scottish and Irish waters, where up to twenty-eight vessels[9] perished, with their crews suffering a variety of fates.

The worst incident occurred in Sligo Bay, where three ships 'in a great storm ran into a beach lined with huge reefs, and it was like nothing ever seen before, for in the space of an hour all three ships were ripped apart. Three hundred men escaped and almost a thousand drowned.'[10] There is a huge rocky promontory there that the locals

---

[6] *Diario de Medina Sidonia* in Fernández Duro, *La Armada Invencible*, II, p. 246.

[7] Kelsey, *Sir Francis Drake*, p. 411.

[8] Walsingham to the Lord Chancellor, 18 September 1588. John Knox Laughton, *State Papers Relating to the Defeat of the Spanish Armada, anno 1588*, London 1894, vol. 2, p. 69.

[9] Specifically: one galleon (*San Marcos de Portugal*), one galleass (*Girona*), four Cantabrian naos, nine Mediterranean ships, ten supply ships (*urcas*) and three pataches. Casado Soto, pp. 249 et seq. Ken Douglas, *The Downfall of the Spanish Armada in Ireland* (Dublin: Gill & Macmillan, 2009), pp. 175 et seq.

[10] *Carta de uno que fue en la Armada de Inglaterra y cuenta la jornada*. Francisco de Cuéllar, Antwerp, 4 October 1589. Rah. Col. Salazar, 7, fol. 58. Reproduced in Fernández Duro, *La Armada Invencible*, II, pp. 337–70. This letter has been translated and published with a critical study in Jim Stapleton, *The Spanish Armada 1588: The Journey of Francisco de Cuéllar* (Ireland: Sligo, 2001). It can be found in English in

call *Carrick na Spania* or Rock of the Spaniards. Curiously, the great galleons that sailed round England without the English daring to get too close – the real warships that fought on every occasion – *did* return. And of all of them, the *San Juan*, the most valiant, returned to Corunna with Recalde, bringing with it a sense of bitterness and an unbearable feeling that an opportunity had been lost.

www.celticfringefest.com/epicjourney. This is the famous account of Francisco de Cuéllar, probably the best-known shipwreck survivor in the Spanish Armada. Having been shipwrecked off Streedagh beach on the north-east coast of Ireland, Cuéllar, wounded and naked, managed to hide and began a series of adventures worthy of Homer's *Odyssey*. After several months in Ireland with eight other Spanish survivors and tired of living in penury, they decided to defend Rosclogher castle, a difficult building to take by storm, in the face of an imminent English attack. McClancy, who had given the castle up as lost considering the size of the invading army, offered them food and weapons, and withdrew. But the Spaniards, against expectations, managed to resist. For such deeds they gained the friendship of the Irish noble, who offered Cuéllar the hand of his daughter, but Cuéllar declined and eventually managed to return to Spain. The actions of the shipwreck survivors left a deep mark of gratitude in Ireland and many of them stayed in the Emerald Isle, perpetuating their lineage to this day, and every year their epic is commemorated. Cuéllar also has a tourist trail that traces his adventure and also a symphony, *The de Cuéllar Suite*, composed and published by Michael Rooney in 2012. See www.celticfringefest.com/decuellar; www.draiochtmusic.com/about-us/michael.

PART 2
The English Armada

Chapter 5

Preparations in England

With the Spanish Armada disappearing from view on 12 August 1588, the anxiety felt in England during the preceding months turned into a sense of comparative relief. But there was no reason to rejoice. In fact the armada had not been destroyed and remained extremely powerful. What had happened was that the English had ceased to pursue it. The Royal Navy knew that there was nothing enviable about the Spanish position, but no one could foresee with certainty what their next move would be. On 18 August, Howard gave a serious warning that, with others, would keep England on a war footing for over a month: 'God knoweth whether they go either to the Naze of Norway or into Denmark or to the Isles of Orkney to refresh themselves, and so to return.' Drake appeared to be of the same view.[1] On 19 August, Burghley, possibly the wisest of Elizabeth's advisers, rejected the idea that the armada might return to England and proposed the launching of a flotilla to harry them near Ireland, take up their pursuit again and defeat them in their own ports.[2] The Spanish Armada was seen for the last time on 20 August in the Orkney Islands, where Scottish fishermen saw 'monstrous great ships, being about 100 in number, running west-wards before the wind'.[3] For her part, Elizabeth, given her serious financial problems after the cost of the intercepting fleet,[4] decided to go on the counter-offensive immediately. Her expectations were overpoweringly aroused by the idea of finding herself with the seas open and free in pursuit of revenge, glory and, above all, incalculable booty. Dazzled by the irresistible dream of seizing the West Indies fleet, she ordered her ships to sail immediately to intercept it in the Azores.

She then revealed that she was not fully aware of what had actually happened at sea. The English fleet was also crippled and exhausted. The ships needed a complete overhaul, and the men needed to recover. After three months at sea with poor nutrition, a violent epidemic raged among them. On 30 August, Howard wrote to the Privy Council from

---

[1] Martin and Parker, *Spanish Armada*, p. 251.

[2] 'I am not of opinion that the Spanish fleet will suddenly return from the north or the east, weakened as they are, and knowing that our navy is returned to our coast where they may repair their lacks and be as strong as they were afore. And without a north or east wind the Spanish fleet cannot come back to England. I wish if they pass about Ireland, that four goods ships, well manned and conducted, might follow them to their ports, where they might distress a great number of them, being weather-beaten and where the number of the gallants will not continue on shipboard.' Burghley to Walsingham, 19 August 1588. R. B. Wernham, *The Expedition of Sir John Norris and Sir Francis Drake to Spain and Portugal, 1589* (London: Temple Smith for the Navy Records Society), 1988, pp. 4–5.

[3] Martin and Parker, *Spanish Armada*, p. 252.

[4] Wernham, *Expedition*, p. xii.

Dover to report that there were so many men sick on the 'foul and unsavoury' ships that there were not enough crew to weigh anchor. On 1 September he added: 'The infection is grown very great. Those that come in fresh are soonest infected; they sicken one day and die the next.'[5] Lord Howard continued to defend his men in the face of the Queen's indifference: 'It would grieve any man's heart to see them that have served so valiantly die so miserably.' Burghley, revealing his most ruthless side, expressed the hope that 'by death, by discharging of sick men, and such like ... there may be spared something in the general pay'.[6] The men were dying in their thousands, while others lay on their sickbeds. The officers adamantly refused to do the impossible.[7] And if Elizabeth could clearly see the possibilities offered by her triumph over Philip in 1588, she had scant regard for the men who had achieved it. She was too busy celebrating. But her coffers were empty. The cost of the defensive operation against Spain had risen to £4 million.[8] In any case, this lack of concern for her own men would be in evidence again one year later.

This scourge was made worse by the fact that, despite the Queen's wishes, England kept the army mobilized until definite news was received regarding the fate of Medina Sidonia and his ships. Even as late as early September, Drake justified the mobilization and warned of the possible movements of the Duke of Parma over the following three weeks, even if the Spanish Armada did not return. Paradoxically, that was when Parma abandoned all hope of continuing with the English Enterprise and demobilized the landing flotilla. But given the appalling state of the troops after so long at sea, this extension of English mobilization would have disastrous consequences. In a letter of 14 September, a month since there was any news of the Spanish Armada, a troubled Hawkins wrote to Burghley: 'The companies do fall sick daily. It is not fit for me to persuade in so great a cause, but I see no reason to doubt the Spanish fleet; and our ships utterly unfitted and unmeet to follow any enterprise from hence without a thorough new trimming, refreshing, and new furnishing with provisions, grounding, and fresh men.'[9] But it was not until 18 September that an urgent letter brought the first definite news about the Spanish Armada from Dublin.[10] Hence, as Mattingly summarized, 'the ships were kept fully manned and vigilant until the news began to come in from Ireland. In consequence men sickened and died at Harwich and Margate, at Dover and on the Downs.'[11] The fact is that while the troops and seamen were kept mobilized, the ships were not properly ready to sail the

---

[5]   Howard to Burghley, 30 August 1588. Howard to Queen Elizabeth, 1 September 1588. Quoted in Kelsey, *Sir Francis Drake*, p. 339.

[6]   Martin and Parker, *Spanish Armada*, pp. 253.

[7]   'Sir, Upon your letter I sent presently for Sir Francis Drake and showed him the desire that Her Majesty had for the intercepting of the King's treasure from the Indies. And so we considered of it and neither of us finding any ships here in the fleet anyways able to go such a voyage before they have been aground, which cannot be done in any place but at Chatham, and now that this spring is so far past it will be 14 days before they can be grounded.' Howard to Walsingham, 6 September 1588. Wernham, *Expedition*, p. 5.

[8]   Martin and Parker, *Sir Francis Drake*, p. 254.

[9]   Hawkins to Burghley, 14 September 1588. Wernham, *Expedition*, pp. 5–6

[10] Martin and Parker, *The Spanish Armada*, p. 256.

[11] Mattingly, *The Defeat*, p. 334.

oceans. In fact it was the very urgency of the alarm that prevented them from being ready for action. When the troops were demobilized, there was nothing for them – no money, no clothes, no food, not even somewhere to stay. The emaciated, weak, half-naked men lay down and died in the streets of Dover and Rochester.[12] The final tally of casualties was devastating, and it is no exaggeration to state that half the men who took part in the English interception fleet in 1588 did not survive to tell the tale.[13] It is worth remembering that the number of casualties in the Spanish fleet was less than 50 per cent.[14] Although England achieved a victory in seeing off the Spanish Armada, it suffered the tragedy as much as Spain. Its advantages were of a moral order and fleetingly a naval one. And the Queen was totally convinced that she had to make the most of them.

While the vast majority of the Spanish Armada's ships returned to Spain, Elizabeth and her advisers continued to reflect on how best to take advantage of that extraordinary opportunity. Drake went to London to explain to the Queen the state the fleet was in and to consider what possible action to take. This is where Dom António, the Prior of Cato,[15] comes into the story – a character who played a very important role in the fate of the English Armada. Since it is essential to fully understand who he was, it is important to consider the situation in Portugal at this historic moment.

Thanks to Portugal's constant discovery of new lands and the opening of trade routes, the country had created a vast empire. Lisbon had become a large, wealthy city that attracted merchants from across Europe to come and buy exotic goods. However, just as was to happen in Spain, decadence was never far away. Riches from Africa, from the East, from Brazil lured many people away from work, created inflation (in Holy Week in 1568 the currency was devalued to one-third of its value), brought people away from the countryside; everything was imported, hardship grew, huge trade debts were created with Holland and England. Alongside opulence came rampant poverty. It was in these circumstances that Sebastião I came to the throne, with great hopes invested in him. But the new king was blond, had blue eyes and a thick lower lip (he had Habsburg blood through his mother, Joanna of Austria, daughter of Emperor Charles V), and suffered from delusions of grandeur and ancient phantasies, to such an extent that there were clear pathological tendencies in his mental state. His appearance was that of a true Habsburg, who, anticipating Don Quixote, dreamt of reviving ancient glories in a state close to schizophrenia.[16] In 1576, he received a call for assistance from the Moroccan Sultan Abu Abdallah Mohammed II, who had been defeated with Ottoman assistance by his uncle, Sultan Abd al-Malik I. In exchange for Portuguese help in Morocco, Mohammed

[12] Mattingly, *The Defeat*.

[13] Of the '16,000 men crowded about the English ships', not more than half will have survived. Martin and Parker, p. 253–4.

[14] Gracia Rivas, *La sanidad*, p. 320.

[15] The term *Prior* denotes the head of the Knights of St. John, a Catholic military order; *Crato* is an area in central Portugal [translator's note].

[16] Joaquim Pedro Oliveira Martins, *Historia de Portugal* (Lisbon, 2004), pp. 263–74.

promised the restoration of Portuguese territories in North Africa. Sebastião thought that this was the right time to restrain Ottoman influence in the Maghreb and restore the former Portuguese presence in the region. His uncle, Philip II, who hoped that one day Sebastião would become his son-in-law, tried to dissuade him when they met at the monastery of Guadeloupe. Prince Henry, the widowed Queen Catherine and counsellors Cristóvão de Távares, João de Mascarenhas and Francisco de Sá also tried, but without success. Faced with the inflexible determination of a king, Philip promised to help, with 2,000 experienced soldiers under the command of Alonso de Aguilar, seven galleys and sixty other ships.

A huge, heterogeneous army of 17,000 men assembled in Lisbon, including 3,000 Germans and 600 Italians and the cream of Portuguese nobility. The expedition committed one mistake after another. Sebastião ignored the advice of Francisco de Aldana and the other commanders and boldly entered hostile territory, and it came to the point where the leading figures considered putting him in prison in order to avoid a catastrophe. But on 4 August 1578 they failed to do so on the plains of El-Ksar el Kebir. At the height of the battle Sebastião was killed, along with the two Muslim rulers and a large number of Christian forces, including Spanish, and Alonso de Aguilar and Francisco de Aldana. Portugal's weakness and wretchedness reached a low point, made worse by having to pay ransoms (to which Philip generously contributed) for the survivors. These included Dom António, the Prior of Crato.

The death of Sebastião I without an heir set in train Portugal's complex dynastic problem. King John III had died in 1557, two weeks after the sudden death of his only son, who would have become John IV. As a result, John's three-year old only son, Sebastião, had inherited the throne. Following his death at El-Ksar el Kebir, the throne was taken in 1578 by the aged Cardinal Prince Henry, brother of John III, with the title Henry I, having previously occupied the regency while Sebastião was a minor. Henry, whose advanced age precluded him from having children, summoned the court in 1579 to find a new king. With no descendants from John III, the throne should have gone to a descendant of one of his brothers. There were three pretenders: Philip II, son of Isabella of Portugal; Emmanuel Filiberto of Savoie, son of Princess Beatriz; and Catherine, Duchess of Braganza, daughter of Prince Duarte. Although António was also the son of one of John III's brothers, Dom Luis, Duke of Beja, the fact that he was a bastard son weighed heavily against him, and in addition his father had also been Prior of Crato, which had meant that he could not marry. In fact, faced with António's insistence that he be made king, Henry withdrew Portuguese nationality from him in 1579 and had him exiled. The Cardinal King Henry then revealed his intention to appoint Philip II as King of Portugal but he died shortly afterwards in 1580, leaving a council of five governors. Four of these – Archbishop Jorge de Almeida, Francisco de Sá, Diogo Lopes and Joao de Mascarenhas – also favoured Philip, as did the main representatives of the nobility and the clergy.

In summary, Philip was not only endorsed by dynastic right but also by the ruling classes who were highly aware that he was the best option for Portugal, given his close familiarity with the country, its extreme weakness after El-Ksar el Kebir and the strong greed of the emerging powers that had begun to show itself in earlier decades. The only disadvantage of Isabella's son was that he came across as a Spanish monarch and that, with his ascendancy to the Portuguese throne, the country would be joined in political union with Spain. Dom António continued to pursue his claim, supported by popular nationalism that was protective of Portugal's independence and looked with suspicion at the union of the peninsula. In such circumstances, and with a clear power vacuum,[17] Philip assembled forces on the Portuguese border and prepared to take Lisbon from Cascais, following the very route that later Drake would not dare to try. While Dom António prepared the defence in Santarem castle, he was acclaimed there as king. However, aware that such acclamation was totally illegal, he hastened to say that he was not the king but the regent and defender of the realm. Three weeks later, and with scarcely any resistance, Philip II exercised his right and entered Lisbon.

Dom António then fled to France with the crown jewels and through the control of his supporters only retained some of the Azores, where news was received that France and England would support the islands in their fight against Philip. No one was in any doubt that the Azores were the 'key to the New World', as the Spanish poet Juan de Tassis would later call them. In fact, the West Indies fleet necessarily had to return via the archipelago, which thereby became potentially the greatest source of riches in the world. In addition, everyone was aware of the immense power that Philip wielded and therefore fighting for Dom António seemed to be the best way of confronting him. Thus first France and then England would be dragged into the Prior's intrigues. France was defeated in 1582 in the naval battle of the Isle of Terceira, where France had sixty ships against the twenty-five that the Spanish and Portuguese had, and this was concluded in the amphibious operation in 1583. England would follow the same path in 1589. Thus the English Armada can be seen as the culmination of the European struggle against peninsular union.

After this long but essential clarification we can return to the main narrative, which found Dom António in London, where his task was to get the English offensive to aim at Lisbon. During his stay in the capital, Drake considered at length the prospects that Dom António had to offer. The content of these conversations generated so many stories and rumours that on 5 October, Mendoza, a Spanish agent in London, confessed that 'no-one knows what to believe'.[18] But Dom António was already in talks with Mulay Ahmed, king of Morocco, who had offered to help him, and so the Anglo-Moroccan coalition against Spain was already under consideration. This is confirmed among other

---

[17] 'The Prior of Crato's government in Lisbon was a tyranny of extremists. The nobles and the rich had abandoned the capital and a crazed rabble took over their posts and the arsenals. It was the rule of demagogues. Lisbon seemed like an ancient city and Dom António an ancient tyrant of the masses. Fugitives and those lacking enthusiasm for their new masters were hunted down, and once caught they were bound, dragged through the streets, pelted with stones and insulted, and forced to enlist in the disorderly conscript armies of Lisbon.' Oliveira Martins, *Historia de Portugal*, p. 277.

[18] Kelsey, *Sir Francis Drake*, p. 342.

items in the letter of 15 August from Walsingham to Henry Roberts, an English agent in Morocco. In this interesting communication, Walsingham had ordered Roberts to encourage the King of Morocco to later fulfil his promise to help Dom António, by informing him of the defeat of the Spanish Armada in its attempt to conquer England and by announcing that this fleet was so big and powerful that 'he [the king of Castile] will be unable to reassemble it in three years or perhaps in this lifetime, especially seeing that Her Majesty is resolved to exploit the victory both by sea and land if the other Princes neighbouring Spain ... are willing to play their part'. He also informed Roberts of the imminent departure to Morocco of Dom Cristóvão, Dom António's son, as security for Moroccan assistance to the Portuguese pretender.[19] On 20 September, when the first news of the fate of the Spanish Armada was received from Ireland, it was Elizabeth herself who hastened to write to Mulay Ahmed. In this letter she informed him that Philip II sent against England 'the most powerful Armada ever sent on the sea', but 'has been sent back so mauled and in such disorder that they cannot claim any success and they remain in such a state that the enterprise, in which we concur, to restore the King Dom António to his estate, will be so much the easier for us ... chiefly because of this loss that he has suffered'.[20] In fact the intrigues by Dom António in England and the English in Morocco had been going on for some time, but the disaster of the Spanish Armada ended up activating long-cherished plans.[21]

Thus at the end of September, the objectives of the English Armada began to appear. On 30 August Burghley noted the three main ones: (a) To attempt to destroy the ships of the Spanish Armada in Lisbon and Seville (it was still thought that they would return to these ports). (b) To take Lisbon. (c) To take the Azores.[22]

His plan consisted of preparing a large Anglo-Dutch fleet that would set sail in February. The first thing it would do would be to destroy the Spanish Armada which, it was thought, would be repaired in Lisbon and Seville. Then they would conquer Lisbon and place the Prior of Crato on the throne. Later, in the name of Dom António, they would take the Azores and, with that, capture the West Indies fleet, thereby causing the collapse of the Spanish Empire. Elizabeth could then claim the whole globe for England. But the last of the Tudors had no resources. Drake and Norris came up with a solution. They would take it upon themselves to prepare the fleet. All the Queen had to do was to let them proceed, provide them with six royal galleons and contribute in a limited way to the costs that would be taken on by private investors looking to profit from a massive amount of booty. Elizabeth agreed, and Drake and Norris set to work. They had to find investors, assemble ships, call up conscripts, purchase provisions and

---

[19]   Walsingham to Henry Roberts, 15 August 1588. In Wernham, *Expedition*, p. 6. Dom Cristóvão would be held in Fez for three years. For this subject and, in general, the attempts to rise to power by Dom António and his family, see João Pedro Vaz, *Campanhas do Prior do Crato 1580–1589. Entre Reis e Corsarios pelo trono de Portugal* (Lisbon, 2005).

[20]   Elizabeth to Mulay Ahmed of Morocco, 20 September 1588. In Wernham, *Expedition*, pp. 7–8.

[21]   Ibid., p. xv.

[22]   Notes from Burghley, 30 September 1588. In ibid., p.11.

munitions ... In their favour, they had the patriotic fervour of the times ... and the promise of turning anyone who took part in the enterprise into a millionaire. But the example of what had recently happened with the men who took part in the defence of the channel was not a good advertisement. They found it difficult to get the enterprise off the ground.[23] Although once it was up and running, the growing number of participants encouraged new ones to join in, which led to a progressive increase in the number of recruits, which in the end led to the problem of having to deal with the size of a huge fleet that far exceeded the original plans.

But the invitation was not simply about amassing recruits with an assortment of military training – or hardly any training at all – especially not for fighting against Spain. The best English soldiers were required, but the best were in Holland, defending England by assisting the anti-Philip Flemish rebels. When Elizabeth tried to repatriate her troops stationed in Holland, she encountered opposition from the rebels. They refused to send the soldiers back unless she sent replacements, and they wanted to limit the time during which they would have to do without them. Elizabeth got very angry with the Dutch rebels. Not only did they impose these obstacles, but they also continued to trade with Spain and in addition refused to provide ships and men for the enterprise. The Queen put an end to the matter in drastic fashion. She *ordered* the troops to return.

For her part, the urge to support Dom António in seizing the Portuguese throne proved irresistible, for Crato invited her to turn Portugal into an English protectorate or a vassal English state. In that way Portugal and its empire would be split off from Philip's crown and Elizabeth would be free to engage in unlimited expansion in Brazil. Her dream of having her own empire in the Americas was taking shape. Thus the desires of Crato to reign in Portugal at any price coincided with those of Elizabeth to have her own empire. And so at the end of December, when Dom Cristóvão was already in Morocco seeking assistance from the south, the following clauses were signed between Dom António and Queen Elizabeth:

1. First, Her Majesty the Queen of England undertakes to provide a fleet of one hundred and twenty ships and twenty thousand men, 15,000 soldiers and five thousand sailors and officers for both services, in order to restore Dom António to the kingdom of Portugal.
2. Dom António undertakes that the whole kingdom of Portugal will submit to him within eight days of his arrival with the fleet, in accordance with the letters he has received from the main leaders of the kingdom.

---

[23] Norris complained about the lack of enthusiasm from the clergy and the court: 'I was sorry to understand that my Lords of the Council and the clergy were loth to put themselves to charges. The one might take example by the nobility of Spain who all did send either brothers, sons, or nephews, well appointed, for the Enterprise of England.' Norris to Walsingham, 20 September 1588. In Wernham, *Expedition*, p. 38. Quoted in María José Rodríguez Salgado, *La Guerra hispano-inglesa 1585–1589* (Corunna: Memoria Centenario María Pita, 1990), p. 26.

3. Item: that having arrived in Lisbon, the city will be rendered defenceless, and any Spaniards in it will be destroyed and slaughtered, and for this act of friendship in helping him to recover his kingdom, he agrees to fulfil the following:

4. First, within two months of his arrival in Lisbon, he will give Her Majesty the sum of five million in gold as a contribution towards the costs of the fleet.

5. Item: in recognition of this act, he will pay her every year in perpetuity the sum of three hundred thousand gold ducats, lodged and paid in London at his expense.

6. Item: the English should be free to trade and have dealings in Portugal, as well as the Portuguese Indies, and the Portuguese should be able to do the same in England.

7. Item: if the Queen wishes to prepare a fleet to set against the king of Spain, she may do so in Lisbon and receive all necessary assistance.

8. Item: the castles of Sao Gián, Cascais, Torre de Belem, Capariza, Oton, Sao Felipe, Oporto and Coimbra and the other fortresses in Portugal may permanently include English soldiers at Dom António's expense.

9. Item: there shall always be peace between Her Majesty the Queen and Dom António, and they shall always offer each other assistance whenever required without any excuse.

10. Item: all bishoprics and archbishoprics in Portugal shall be filled by English Catholics and Monsignor de la Torques shall immediately be appointed as Archbishop of Lisbon.

11. Item: On arrival in Lisbon every infantryman shall receive twelve payments, plus three more as a bonus, and they shall be permitted to sack the city for twelve days, provided that no one of any rank or involved with the fleet shall for any reason venture to do harm to any Portuguese, or go to any temples or churches or houses where maidens live. And if they should be in need of anything while they are there, they should pay for it with their own money. Her Majesty duly ordered this to be carried out. Dated in London, the last day of December 1588.[24]

---

[24] *Relación de lo subçedido del armada enemiga del reyno de Inglaterra a este de Portugal con la retirada a su tierra este año de 89.* BN mss 18579, pp. 12–13. There are other documents and books that reprint these clauses. The following have been consulted: *Relación de la venida de Don António de Portugal prior de ocrato con la Armada de la Reyna de Inglaterra en el año de 1589.* BN mss 1749, fols. 225–36. The clauses are included in folios 233–4. Luis Cabrera De Córdoba, *Historia de Felipe II Rey de España*, III (Salamanca: Junta de Castilla y León, 1998), p. 1249. Cesáreo Fernández Duro, *Bosquejo Encomiástico de Don Pedro Enríquez de Acevedo. Conde de Fuentes.* Vol. X of *Colección de Memorias de la Real Academia de la Historia* (Madrid, 1884), pp. 517–18. Martin A. S. Hume, *The Year After the Armada* (Dallas 1970), pp. 19–20 (a summary of the clauses from Spanish). Mariano González-Arnao, *Derrota y muerte de Sir Francis Drake* (Santiago de Compostela 1995), p. 55. González-Arnao gives the date of 25 February as the day when the agreement was signed between Drake and Norris on behalf of the Queen and Dom António.

In March Elizabeth pressed for the preparations to be speeded up. She knew that a large number of the ships from the Spanish Armada were to be found in the ports of the Cantabrian Sea. She then gave quite specific orders: the fleet's objective first and foremost, to which all others were to be sacrificed, was the destruction of the Spanish ships under repair. She warned Drake and Norris that if they failed in this mission, England would be in grave danger, for no-one was in any doubt that Philip would try to attack again. It was only once this objective had been achieved, and it did not appear to be excessively difficult, that thoughts could be turned to Lisbon, the Azores or gold from the Indies ... For his part Philip was in no doubt that Elizabeth would attack the ships under repair, which were therefore in great danger. So he asked Alexander Farnese to organise some distracting manoeuvre that would divide or delay the English forces. But the Duke of Parma did not have a naval force that was capable of satisfying the King's needs. Meanwhile Philip prepared the coastal defences by using some of the troops that had returned on the Spanish Armada. In any event the Spanish situation was becoming quite serious due to the lack of a naval interception force. There was no doubt that this was Elizabeth's great opportunity. However, the English Armada was not yet in her hands, but in those of her commanders, who were after all the guarantors of the investors' interests. But the investors had not offered their scant resources to sink empty ships, which in the short term did not produce the slightest profit. In the medium term it would have resulted in the emergence of England as a world power, with unlimited growth for its trade. But that is not what attracts a business man with cash-flow problems.

The real answer to England's economic problems was the conquest of Lisbon and as a consequence the whole of Portugal, or put another way, of a vast global empire. And England had never had a better chance to have such a major impact on world economic geography. In fact, Crato gifted Portugal to England so that he could have his puppet kingdom. In these circumstances there was a disconnect between the Queen's plan, whose primary objective was to do away with the ships of the Spanish Armada, and that of the commanders of and investors in the English Armada, whose first target was Lisbon. The outcome of a tussle between Santander and the Portuguese capital was somewhere in the middle: Corunna. A stop-off in this small city enabled the Queen's objective of attacking a Spanish port where there were ships back from the Spanish Armada to be achieved without risk and without deviating from Lisbon as the target.

During the last few weeks before setting sail, one of the problems that the organizers of the expedition had to face was the growth in the number of men who wanted to join on the grounds that, given its enormous size, the expedition looked likely to end in certain victory. On 26 March, the bulk of the expedition was assembled in Dover, but the number of men had surpassed the capacity of the fleet to carry them. It was then that sixty Dutch fluyts (flyboats) were sighted in the channel heading to the west of France for salt.[25] 'A better fleet for transporting men could not be found in all of Europe,' wrote Drake, and finding that some of them bore copies of letters of safe passage from the

---

[25]   Wernham, *Expedition*, p xxxi.

Duke of Parma, Drake swiftly seized them all. With this important increase in the fleet's capacity, the numbers of men wanting to take part in the apparently lucrative enterprise grew even faster. On 13 April, Drake and Norris wrote to the council from Plymouth describing the situation, which could be seen as good news but brought with it new problems concerning supplies:

> Whereas now fifteen days past Her Majesty's army under our charge having remained here in readiness to depart in the service intended and been all that time, and yet still is, detained from setting to sea by means the wind hath hitherto held contrary and not served to set sail in our course and to bring unto us our munition and some shipping, by reason whereof and chiefly for that since our first assembly of the determined number of men for this service the army hath been almost double increased, especially of late since the bruit of the taking of the flyboats, by repair of many gentlemen and divers companies of voluntary soldiers offering to be employed in this action, whom both for their satisfaction and the advancement of the service we could in no sort refuse to entertain, we have been forced, the country not being able, by far to furnish the daily expense of victuals.[26]

The 'determined number of men' referred to by the commanders was 12,000 soldiers, which by 13 April had reached almost double. In another document dated 18 April, ten days before the fleet sailed from Plymouth, two different figures are given for the number of those participating in the expedition. The first is 23,375 men, including sailors. This figure is the one used by several writers, like Fernández Duro more than a century ago.[27] However, at the end of this document, the total number had risen to 27,667 men. An analysis of how the figure of 23,375 was arrived at will serve to explain this difference within the same document. On the one hand, each of the fourteen colonels of the army had, independently of the number of companies, a number of men under their command in multiples of a hundred (Drake, Norris, Roger Williams, Thomas Sidney, Ralph Lane) or at least ten (the remainder). However, the companies varied between 158.33 men on average in the case of Norris or Drake and 133.33 for Ralph Lane. This suggests an approximate or ideal distribution rather than an empirical counting of men. In the case of the English (3,200) and Dutch (900) sailors, it is clear that the possibilities that both numbers were multiples of a hundred is 1 in 100,000. This strengthens the hypothesis that these calculations were all approximate, and this imprecision in the rounding up or down reflects a lack of precision in the overall figures. In the case of the ships' captains and the gentlemen who accompanied them, the approximate nature of the figure given is clear. The document reads: 'The captains of the ships, being about 120, with the gentlemen that do accompany them, being of good quality, with their servants, amount unto, by estimation: 1,500.' It becomes obvious that when working out the total number of men in the English Armada, there is only sufficient information

---

[26] Norris and Drake to the council, 13 April 1589. In Wernham, *Expedition*, p. 118.
[27] Cesáreo Fernández Duro, *Armada Española*, III (Madrid: Museo Naval, 1972–73), p. 42.

to enable an approximate number to be extrapolated. It is symptomatic that the document refers to 120 ships' captains, when the total number of vessels was, in principle, 180, as the document itself shows. On this issue it would appear that there has been an increase of 50 per cent on the initial estimate. It should be remembered that the patriotic fervour and enthusiasm that spring, reinforced by the expectation of sizeable profits and the last-minute news of sixty new supply ships, brought about the addition of all kinds of men at the eleventh hour, which meant adjusting and even delaying the preparation and departure of the English Armada. The specific nature of this figure of 23,375 is, after all (and as the document makes clear), purely illusory. By clear contrast, at the end of the document signed by Drake and Norris and confirmed by Burghley, we find the following postscript: 'The numbers of men for the army, and of ships and at foot at end in his hand 27,667.' This, then, is the real number of men who set sail from Plymouth, assuming more did not join them between 18 April when this number was given and 28 April when the English Armada finally set off, which seems more than likely. Compare this figure with the number of men who set sail from Corunna nine months earlier on the Spanish Armada: 25,696.[28] This confirms that in terms of numbers of participants, the two great fleets were similar, with the English fleet containing two thousand extra men.

As far as the number of participating ships is concerned, the document of 18 April gave the number as 180. It is also interesting to compare the documents of 19 April and 15 September.[29] In the 19 April list, there are eighty-four ships divided into five squadrons of sixteen or seventeen vessels. Each squadron is accompanied by 'near about 15 flyboats', which would give us an approximate number of seventy-five small ships and an overall figure of about 160. But in the list of payments of 15 September there are thirteen ships (not flyboats) that took part in the expedition but were not on the 19 April list. Therefore at least thirteen boats have to be added to the 160. But this is without counting possible ships that were not on the 19 April list and did not return, or small vessels that, in addition to the thirteen referred to, joined the expedition, over and above the seventy-five mentioned. In a document sent to the person in charge at the treasury, the number of ships was set at '180 and other ships'.[30] There were probably at least 200 ships that took part in the expedition, compared to the number of 137 that sailed from Corunna in the opposite direction nine months earlier. However, although in terms of the number of ships the English Armada was larger, the size of the Spanish Armada ships was on average significantly greater in terms of tonnage. In any event, on 28 April 1589 the largest naval expedition in English history set sail from Plymouth. The fleet was divided into five squadrons, under the command of five of the Queen's ships: Francis Drake's *Revenge*, now fully repaired; John Norris's *Nonpareil*; Thomas Fenner, vice-admiral of the fleet, in *Dreadnought*. The fourth squadron sailed without its flagship, *Swiftsure*

---

[28] Gracia Rivas, *La sanidad*, p. 320.
[29] Names of ships and captains of the fleet, 19 April 1589. In Wernham, *Expedition*, pp. 336–38. List of ships and payments, 15 September 1589. In ibid., pp. 338–41.
[30] Note to the Treasury in England, 25 February 1591. In Wernham, *Expedition*, p. 297.

for, as will be seen, Roger Williams had set sail in order to help the Queen's favourite, Robert Devereux, to get away; and finally Edward Norris, in command of *Foresight*. A sixth royal ship, the *Aid*, under the command of William Fenner of the army, was not leader of a squadron. In total there were 27,667 soldiers and sailors and over 180 ships aiming to put an end once and for all to Iberian hegemony and to open up the world to England.

Chapter 6

Preparations in Corunna

While fear of the Spanish Armada continued to kill men in England, the Spanish ships began arriving in Spain. Bearing in mind that eventually the English Armada would attack Corunna, it is important to consider at the outset how the vital defence of the city was organized, including the fact that the defensive preparations were carried out all the way along the Atlantic coast of the Peninsula. The defence of Corunna fell to the companies and the weaponry of the few ships of the Spanish Armada that had returned to Galicia. The Marquis of Cerralbo, governor of Galicia, took charge of re-establishing and distributing such forces along the Galician coast in case the English counteroffensive decided to land there.

It is worth remembering that the Spanish Armada was a highly complex operation and Philip knew that he would need additional support and provision fleets to maintain his position in England and to supply and consolidate the expeditionary force. For this purpose, when the Spanish Armada reached Corunna, reinforcements, ships, arms and food supplies were being prepared at different places around Spain, in addition to the provisions that the Marquis of Cerralbo was able to obtain. It was not essential for these reinforcements to arrive in time for the Spanish Armada's departure, but rather that Corunna would act as the support base for the fleet. Hence once the Spanish Armada had left, the Galician city would continue to store provisions for later reinforcement fleets, as well as provide a place for the sick who had been left there to recuperate.[1] When the Spanish Armada failed, these provisions were used for the relief of those who were in a poor condition when they returned, as well as for the reinforcement of Galician coastal cities – mainly Corunna and Bayona – in order to defend themselves from any future English attack, and for the preparation of new fleets. So frenetic activity continued in Corunna over the ensuing months.

For his part, the Marquis of Cerralbo was aware of the strategic importance of the Islet of San Antón that overlooked the Bay of Corunna and the urgent need to fortify

---

[1] The treatment of the sick from the Spanish Armada who remained in Corunna was dealt with through the use of medical supplies carried by the supply ship *La Paz Grande* and brought in by several Breton ships chartered for that purpose, with the assistance of the San Andrés Hospital in Corunna. The Archbishop of Santiago also helped by sending resources and medicines and getting those who had contagious diseases admitted to the city's hospitals. The gathering of provisions was also important. Between October and December 1588, Cerralbo managed to obtain 6,000 casks of wine (25,000 hectolitres), which months later – because they were stored in the lower part of the city – would, to the surprise of the English, fall into their hands, or rather stomachs. More food supplies were obtained, so that between October 1588 and May 1589 stores held in Corunna were of the value of 80,000 ducats (approximately US $12 million today). Fernando Urgorri Casado, 'Hombres y navíos de la Invencible. Los que volvieron a La Coruña'. *Revista del Instituto José Cornide de Estudios Coruñeses*, No. 23, 1987.

it. In order to erect the artillery platform of the castle that was to be built there they used some of the galley slaves from the *Diana*, one of the four galleys in the Spanish Armada that had to abandon the expedition before reaching the channel owing to the bad weather. The ship *Diana* was the first to leave it, for two days after sailing from Corunna on 24 July it had to put in at Vivero in a very sorry state. After several surprising turns of events, the other three galleys ended up in Pasajes de San Juan. Cerralbo asked the *Princesa* to join the *Diana* in Corunna for the construction work, which it did on 15 November. At the same time, the Marquis strengthened the defences at Bayona in case the enemy attacked there and in fact ordered the completion of the construction of the castle wall that protected the port.[2] With the news of the failure of the Spanish Armada the work was speeded up. Cerralbo asked the King to allow the Spanish Armada infantry returning to Corunna to stay there.[3] We now need to consider the ships and companies concerned.

At 5.00 pm on 28 September, the *nao San Bartolomé* (a type of ship having a dual function of being both a fighting ship and a transporter)[4] entered the port after sailing round the British Isles. It was built four years earlier in Cantabria and was one of the best ships of the period. Proof of the great quality of the Cantabrian *naos* is the fact that only four out of the twenty-five that tried to return to Spain by sailing round the British Isles were lost.[5] It weighed 976 tons, had twenty-seven cannons, and belonged to the Andalucía squadron. Before its arrival, Cerralbo wrote: 'Although I was expecting great and successful events, I have been consoled for the lack of them by the arrival of the ship that has put an end to the long and anxious wait we have had.'[6]

The pilot of the *San Bartolomé* reported that on 6 September, off the east coast of Scotland, it got separated from the rest of the fleet because a storm broke its main topsail. Several ships were sighted before 14 September when the wind enabled it to sail in a south-westerly and then a southerly direction. On 21 September they reached Vivero, and spent from then until 28 September sailing close to the wind to Corunna. After a week it reached Corunna, on 28 September. The pilot assumed that the fleet was following on behind, that it had stopped to fix some rigging and that it was about to arrive. The *San Bartolomé* had on board several companies of veteran Tercios infantry regiments: the company of Captain Antonio de Herrera, with sixty-nine men, from the Tercio of Sicily, was detailed to Betanzos. Cerralbo reported: 'The company of Don Antonio de Herrera is amongst those that came from Sicily with Don Diego Pimentel. He has been a Captain for three years and previously did his duty for his military order in Malta. He has always served aboard this ship.' The company of Jerónimo de Monroy,

[2]   Urgorri Casado, 'Hombres y navíos', p. 206.
[3]   AGS Estado. File 165, fol. 288. Quoted in ibid., p. 169.
[4]   Antonio Luis Gómez Beltrán, *La Invencible y su Leyenda Negra* (Málaga: Arin Ediciones, 2013), p. 586.
[5]   José Luis Casado Soto, *Los barcos españoles del siglo XVI y La Gran Armada de 1588* (Madrid: Editorial San Martín, 1988), pp. 119–31, 248.
[6]   Urgorri Casado, 'Hombres y navíos', p. 211.

with fifty-eight men from Extremadura, was also detailed to the Galician capital. The Marquis wrote about this company:

> It is from Don Diego Pimentel's Tercio regiment, one of those sent by the city of Mérida. Don Fernando de Vera was its captain and Don Jerónimo de Monroy its ensign. The company was entrusted to him in Corunna by the Duke of Medina that year. He is a sound chap and did his duties for his military order, the order of San Juan, in Malta.[7]

The company of Captain Cristóbal de Peralta, with sixty-seven men, from the Tercio regiment of Naples, was detailed to Bayona.

The next ship to arrive – two days later, on 30 September – was the supply ship (*urca* in Spanish) *Sansón*, built in Germany and weighing five hundred tons, with eighteen cannon. Of the thirteen German and Baltic supply ships in the Spanish Armada, six sank. They were transport ships of Nordic design. They had a low draught, a broad hull and a large hold. They were no use for fighting and they did not sail well, as already indicated. In addition, they were old ships. But it was essential to seize them from their Northern owners to use as cargo vessels. They became a real burden for the Armada.[8] Cerralbo said of them: 'The men who have arrived on this ship and on the *San Bartolomé* are sick and in need ... They have no clothes and the greatest problem has been the cold. These two ships have more than a hundred sick men, according to what the doctors have said.'[9] On board were the Portuguese companies of Captain Manuel López Valladares with eighty-one men and Captain Domingo Bugallo with sixty-one men, stationed in the area of Ferrol and Puentedeume, who were to form part of the reinforcement troops sent to Betanzos.

On 2 October, the galleon *San Bernardo* entered Corunna. It had been built two years earlier in 1586, it weighed 352 tons, had twenty-one cannons and was one of the smallest ships of the Portuguese squadron. There had not yet been any news of Leyva or Recalde and the arrival of two new ships gave rise to hopes of their return. After various changes of fortune, the *San Bernardo* brought the company of Juan Trigueros, 111 men, which would also be stationed in Ferrol and Puentedeume. But the sailors on board announced that they were the last ones to arrive. That created great anxiety in Corunna since it was thought that no more ships would return and that the rest must have been wrecked.

Five days later, on 7 October, and to its great delight, Corunna watched the arrival, escorted by the pataches *Isabela* and *San Esteban*, of the flagship of the Spanish Armada, the giant galleon *San Juan* of Portugal, Juan Martínez de Recalde's ship, weighing 1,050

---

[7] AGS Guerra Antigua. File 244. Copied from the collection Sans de Barutell, 4th art., Vol. 6, No. 390, f. 209. Quoted in Urgorri Casado, 'Hombres y navíos', p. 167. Also quoted in Miguel González Garcés, *María Pita, Símbolo de Libertad de La Coruña* (Corunna: Fundación Caixa Galicia, 1989), pp. 310–12.

[8] Casado Soto, *Los barcos españoles*, pp. 218 and 249.

[9] Letter from Cerralbo on 1 October. Herrera, doc. CLXX. Quoted in Urgorri Casado, 'Hombres y navíos', p. 215.

tons. It had completely exhausted the large supply of cannonballs for its fifty guns and it only had enough tuna, bread and wine for three or four days.

On board the *San Juan* was the company of harquebusiers of Captain Juan de Luna with sixty-eight men. It was a company on its own stationed in Corunna. Cerralbo reported:

> Captain Juan de Luna's company of harquebusiers is not part of any of the Tercio regiments, but one of the ones that came from Sicily to the Portuguese expedition. The Captain has spent many years in Flanders and Portugal as a soldier. He set out on the same galleon and spent the whole of the expedition on it. He showed himself to be a very brave soldier at all times.

Months later and after a hard struggle, Juan de Luna would become the most distinguished of the prisoners taken in Corunna.

There was also the company of Captain Pedro Manrique, with eighty-four men from the Tercio regiment of Agustín Mexía, stationed in Betanzos. Cerralbo wrote:

> The company of Don Pedro Manrique is from the Tercio regiment of Don Agustín Mexía, sent by the town of Carmona, and was formed a year earlier. He is the brother of the Count of Paredes, and is so well known that all I need say is that he spent the entire expedition on this galleon and at the post to which he was appointed.

The company of Captain Gómez de Carvajal, with seventy-four men, the Tercio regiment of Sicily, stationed in Corunna. Cerralbo said of it: 'Don Gómez de Carvajal and his company came with the companies brought from Sicily by Don Diego de Pimentel. He has been Captain for six years and previously was standard-bearer and soldier. He spent the whole expedition in the same galleon and was always at his post. He is honest, able and of good understanding.'

The company of Captain Juan de Soto, with thirty-two men, probably became part of Bazán's company. The company of Captain Félix Arias, with fifty-four men, stationed in Vigo. The company of Captain Diego de Bazán's harquebusiers, with fifty-six men, from the Tercio regiment of Agustín Mexía, stationed in Corunna. Cerralbo comments:

> The company of Captain Diego de Bazán's harquebusiers is from the Tercio regiment of Agustín Mexia, which was raised by order of Your Majesty in Extremadura in the year '86. He is the son of the Marquis of Santa Cruz, was always with him and has been a Captain for two-and-a-half years. He set off in the *San Juan Bautista* in the Diego Flores squadron and moved to the *San Juan* when the ship he came on foundered off the coast of Ireland. Very few men survived who could report on him, but we can be sure that Don Diego de Bazán did his duty, because he had a reputation in the infantry as a brave soldier.

The company of Diego de Bazán had embarked on the *nao San Juan Bautista*, of the Castile squadron. When this was wrecked, he transferred to the galleon the *San Juan*.

The company of Captain Diego Suárez, with thirty-nine men, was picked up from the *San Esteban*, a patache from the Basque squadron, and joined other companies.[10]

There is no report that the company of Juan de Monsalve, another of the defenders of Corunna, returned in any of these ships, but we do know that it also took part in the Spanish Armada, because we find it in Lisbon, incorporated into the Tercio regiment of Nicolás de Isla and as the crew of the supply ship *San Pedro Menor*.[11] It is likely that it was later sent to reinforce the garrison at Corunna. In any event, the Galician city once more did its duty and gave the soldiers shelter in private lodgings, food and medical attention. They soon recovered, and five hundred of them stayed in the city, which months later would give them the opportunity for revenge.

But Juan Martínez de Recalde, the greatest sailor of the Spanish Armada, returned to Corunna 'at the end of his career', according to his doctors and, just like Oquendo in San Sebastián, 'was inconsolable at seeing how such a glorious victory has slipped between our fingers'. Following the death of the Marquis of Santa Cruz, Recalde had asked the King if he could lead the English Enterprise in a letter dated 13 February 1588 in Lisbon: 'I can say that in those waters Your Majesty has no-one else of my quality, who is more practical and who has sailed them more.'[12] Recalde felt indescribably powerless at not being able to command the Spanish Armada, knowing that he would have made a better job of it than Medina Sidonia (who also knew it and for that reason asked Recalde to stay at his side on the *San Juan*). And so once his men had been saved, together with his remarkable ship, his noble spirit sank into despair. He wrote a brief letter to the King:

> The bearer of this letter, Miguel de Esquibel, will inform Your Majesty what you may wish to know, for I am unable to perform the task myself. I wished to go tomorrow to shut myself in a cell at San Francisco, and then if I die it will be less trouble to bury me. I was very pleased to hear from the Duke; may God provide what we need, which is certain to be great. I am concerned for Don Alonso de Leyba; I kiss your hands,
>
> *Juan Martínez de Recalde*[13]

A few days later, on 23 October 1588, in a cell in the San Francisco monastery, far from his family and without knowing that Alonso de Leyva had gone down with his ship off Ireland, Recalde, Drake's scourge, passed away. But the formidable struggle between Recalde and Drake continued after his death, with 1589 as its epilogue. For Corunna was defended basically by the men who were saved thanks to Recalde's skill and courage during the return journey on the *San Juan*, without whom the city

---

[10] Urgorri Casado, 'Hombres y navíos', pp. 220–25.

[11] Fernández Duro, *La Armada Invencible*, II, p. 38.

[12] AGS Mar y Tierra, File 235. Published by Enrique Herrera Oria, in his *Felipe II y el Marqués de Santa Cruz en la Empresa de Inglaterra* (Madrid: Instituto Histórico de Marina, 1946), p. 167.

[13] AGS Estado, File 165, fol. 317. Published in ibid., p. 169.

would have been lost. Recalde picked up survivors of the shipwrecks of other vessels, gave Marcos Aramburu the cables he needed and showed enormous comradeship, solidarity and seamanship. He thus succeeded in bringing to Corunna more than four hundred soldiers from the veteran infantry Tercios regiments, which later made up the nucleus of the defence of the city. He also brought Sergeant Major Luis de León, who under Cerralbo's orders turned the defenders into a Tercio regiment. Their triumph had consequences that were worthy of the distinguished departed sailor. In a sense Recalde, like El Cid on his horse Babieca, gained his greatest victory after his death (see Figure 6.1).[14]

The huge Venetian ship *Ragazzona*, the flagship of the squadron of Levantine or Mediterranean vessels, arrived in Muros in mid-October. It was the largest ship in the Spanish Armada, weighing 1,249 tons, but it was a merchant ship leased from Venice, not a galleon, and it only had thirty mounted cannon. Admiral Martín de Bertendona arrived with the *Ragazzona* in a very poor state and it ran aground in the Ferrol estuary attempting to reach port in Corunna. Several of its cannon and an anchor now lie in the deep waters opposite the inlet of Cariño. It carried the companies of Captain Pedro Ponce de Sandoval, which was stationed in Betanzos and took part in its defence; of Diego Camacho, with ninety men stationed in Vigo and of Juan de Céspedes, with seventy-six men, stationed in Bayona.

As far as munitions were concerned, the city was well stocked: 'In the city and the surrounding area there was a large quantity of powder, a reasonable amount of cannonballs, lead and cord – reasonable because after eight or nine days of the siege these munitions began to run out and it became necessary to use up what tin there was and make balls out of crushed iron and cord.' There was no shortage of weapons either: 'There were many harquebuses and muskets and pikes, for only a few days earlier a ship had arrived from the Basque country with weapons and had unloaded many of them.' There were also numerous artillery pieces:

At that time there was a good deal of good quality bronze artillery in the city and in Pescadería, both belonging to the city itself and brought back by the galleons and by a Levantine [Mediterranean] ship that was lost near the port of Ferrol, [this refers to the Ragazzona] such that some of it was spare, although all of it would have been used had there been enough space for it.

Also, the city was fortified in readiness for the attack:

A few months earlier, the Marquis had ordered the construction of a small fort next to the new fortress on the beach, where two cannon were placed ... Another

---

[14] Rodrigo Díaz de Vivar, a Castilian nobleman of the eleventh century, was given the name El Cid (equivalent to Sir or Lord) by the Moors, who were still occupying most of Spain. After his death in 1099 he became a national hero of Castile and the subject of the epic poem, *El cantar de mio Cid*, probably written in the latter half of the twelfth century. His warhorse, Babieca, is said to be buried at the monastery of San Pedro de Cardeña [translator's note].

Figure 6.1 Juan Martínez de Recalde, by Álvaro Alcalá Galiano, Biscay Council Office, Bilbao.

was built on an islet off the shore called San Antón. Here very fine artillery pieces of different kinds were placed which proved very effective, for they kept the fleet away from the beach and forced it to move landwards, which gave them trouble enough.[15]

---

[15] *Diario del capitán Juan Varela*. BN MSS 3790, pp. 145–7. Although much used by Enrique de Vedia (Enrique Vedia y Gossens, *Historia y descripción de la ciudad de La Coruña*, Corunna 1845), the journal was thought to have been lost until recently. At least two copies remain, one in the Biblioteca Nacional, manuscript 3790, pp. 137–93. Another was found by Santiago Daviña Sáinz in the Archivo de la Real Academia Gallega and, with a critical study, was published in *La Coruña: Nuevos relatos sobre el cerco* (Corunna: Librería Arenas, 1997), pp. 71–105. For the cannon of the *Ragazzona*, see Luis Gorrochategui Santos, 'Cañones de la Invencible a flor de agua', *Restauro. Revista Internacional del Patrimonio Histórico*, No. 2, 2008.

Figure 6.2 Contemporary view of the castle of San Antón, Corunna, following various alterations during the seventeenth and eighteenth centuries. Photo by Carlos Picallo.
In May 1589, the two long curtain walls joining the main gate with the artillery battery were unfinished, as was the demi-bastion of the tenaille at the gate that faces the city.

These defences, especially the one at San Antón, greatly reinforced the port and the bay of Corunna (see Figure 6.2).

In summary, the infantry that returned to Galicia with the Spanish Armada gave protection to the Galician coast, specifically around Corunna, which was faced with the imminent counteroffensive from England. In addition to the five hundred soldiers bil-leted in the city there was the regular company of Álvaro de Troncoso, with some 150 men. Apart from the professional soldiers, there were also 560 inhabitants of Corunna who made up the local militia (220 harquebusiers and 340 pikers) formed into four com-panies under the command of Francisco de Meiranes, Lorenzo Montoto, Juan Sanchez Cotrofe and Pedro del Lago. Thus the total garrison of the city awaiting the possible arrival of the English amounted to around 1,200 men.[16] This was nowhere near the 27,667 men brought by the English. This difference can be explained by the fact that Drake did not have orders to attack Corunna, but had much greater designs. His squad-ron was appropriate for such an undertaking, but not to take on a city with a total popu-lation of 4,000 inhabitants. But Drake preferred surprise attacks and guaranteed booty rather than large naval or land battles with hand-to-hand fighting, as he showed in the 1588 campaign in the waters of the channel and would show again that summer in the estuary of the Tagus.

---

[16] Among them was Jerónimo de Ayanz, an inventor and military man from Navarre who, with a little historiographic marketing, would occupy a prominent place in the world history of engineering. This is no place to consider his achievements at length, but suffice to mention that, among his forty-eight inven-tions, he built steam engines to drain mines, a submarine, a diving suit and an oven to distil sea water. On this subject, see Nicolás Garcia Tapia, *Un inventor navarro: Jerónimo de Ayanz y Beaumont (1553–1613)* (Pamplona: Gobierno de Navarra, 2010).

Chapter 7

Landing

On the afternoon of 3 May 1589, eight months after the return of the Spanish Armada to Spain, the English Armada was sighted in the distance from the lookout at Estaca de Bares. The news gathered by Philip's spies was accurate: the fleet put together in Plymouth was getting inexorably closer to the Spanish coast. There remained the possibility that the English were heading towards Bayona near the Portuguese border. That seemed more logical bearing in mind that the Prior of Crato, the pretender to the Portuguese throne, was travelling with the expedition. That same day, the Marquis of Cerralbo received news of this first sighting. At dawn on 4 May, a huge bonfire could be seen from the city, lit by the lookouts on Cape Prioriño. Their mission was to light a fire for each enemy ship that was sighted. If there were a lot of them then only one large fire would be lit. Soon a bright bonfire was lit at the Tower of Hercules, the ancient Roman lighthouse, summoning everyone to the city. The news spread like wildfire. Once the gates to the town were open, the labourers from the whole region began to arrive, but the clamour did not seem to disturb in the slightest the *Real Audiencia* (Appellate Court) presided over by Juan Pacheco, the second Marquis of Cerralbo, who seemed to be more concerned with his aristocratic lifestyle than to the terrible threat that was looming over Corunna. Ignoring the growing mob and perhaps believing it was the best way to disregard the enemy, he took his time with a verdict on a court case. He may have thought that resolving the case all in good time was an expression of an inviolable order about which the 'heretics' could do nothing. Or perhaps he believed that the English landing would take so long that there would be plenty of time to get ready.

Cerralbo's lack of a sense of urgency exasperated the messengers who were waiting patiently for the Governor to make a decision. He held both political and judicial, as well as strictly military power. Once he had taken the decision on the court case, he finally turned his attention to his military command. He then ordered Pantoja and Palomino, the captains of the galleys *Diana* and *Princesa*, to set sail and inspect the fleet and, on their return, report on their nature and composition. When the galleys returned, Captains Juan de Luna and Pedro Manrique ordered their companies on board and placed themselves between San Antón and Las Ánimas rock with the objective of preventing any movement of the English fleet via that flank: there would be no point in defending Pescadería if the English attacked via the east. Captain Diego de Bazán was ordered to embark with his company in the *San Juan*. Martín Bertendona was in command of the galleon and his mission was to place himself opposite the hill of Santa Lucia, closing off by sea the line of fire from the Malvecín fort and preventing access to Pescadería from the south. The defence of San Antón was in the hands of Captains Jerónimo de Monroy and Francisco de Meiranes. Theirs was a crucial mission, for if the islet were taken by the English, the city would inevitably be lost. For Jerónimo de Monroy, this was a new task in his professional life. But for the captain of the militia Francisco de Meiranes and for his company of Corunna men it was more than that: it was their families who were at risk. The remaining companies remained in their usual places at the wall of Pescadería and in the city.[1]

The slow passage of the English Armada off the Mera coast was reminiscent of the fleet that one year earlier had sailed in the opposite direction. The English were about to achieve something that had been denied the Spanish: landing on enemy soil. The crew of the *San Juan* recognized Drake's *Revenge*, and in his turn the Englishman once again looked upon Juan Martínez de Recalde's galleon. Shortly afterwards there was work to do for the artillerymen in San Antón castle and the air resounded with the violent roar of cannonballs arching high over the Bay of Corunna. Two powerful culverins – long-range cannons – from the *San Bartolomé* had been mounted in the castle. There was a substantial supply of fuse, powder, projectiles and pistols, and the fortress which was still unfinished performed well. The cannon fire provoked a sudden manoeuvre in the formation's vanguard that caused two ships to run aground on the beach of Santa María de Oza. The English ships that had already dropped anchor were forced to manoeuvre quickly to find a safer place to do so further away. They then had to stay in close formation and close to the coast opposite Mera and Santa Cruz in order to avoid the broadsides from the castle. But the fleet's incursion far into the estuary proved unstoppable and at one o'clock in the afternoon of Thursday, 4 May, without meeting the slightest resistance, the English began to disembark on the sands of Santa María de Oza with fourteen launches.[2] In the first wave, the troop colours of seven companies were brought to shore and as they skirted the coast under the protection of nearby ships, they reached the hill. In successive waves, several thousand men were landed and they soon took control of the Monte de Eirís and the roads to Santiago and Betanzos. The Marquis of Cerralbo sent a message to the companies he had ordered to come from Betanzos to try and gain access to the city via the Bergantiños road. He also ordered the Corunna captain, Álvaro de Troncoso, and Sergeant Major Luis de León to take 150 harquebusiers to defend the

[1]   *Papeles Tocantes a Felipe II.* Vol. II. BN mss 1750, fols. 241–8. This account has been quoted with a critical study by Daviña Sáinz in *La Coruña: Nuevos relatos sobre el cerco*, pp. 107–18. Daviña called it *Relación del cerco por el Rey Don Felipe*. See also *Diario del capitán Juan Varela*. BN mss 3790, pp. 148–51.

[2]   Cerralbo, in a letter to the King on 4 May, justified such passivity arguing that he could not leave to prevent the landing on Oza because it would leave Corunna unprotected: 'Because the fleet was stretched and most of it was close to the weakest part of this city, it was not possible to go out to the quay.' AGS Guerra Antigua. File 248, fol. 78. This letter was quoted by Andrés Martínez Salazar on the occasion of the tercentenary of the English Armada, in the book *El cerco de La Coruña en 1589 y Mayor Fernández Pita* (Corunna: Editorial La Voz de Galicia), 1889, pp. 68–9. Also by González Garcés, *María Pita*, p. 321. However, in the *Diario del capitán Juan Varela* such passivity is criticized, making it responsible for the absence in Corunna of more reinforcements that were sent there later. BN mss 3790, pp. 152–3.

hill of Santa Lucía and put a stop to the enemy advance. Should it be necessary, the Marquis himself would cover their retreat.

With the expert harquebusiers perfectly organized into firing lines, they laid an ambush for the English, who started to suffer casualties, for 'some were seen to fall',[3] and they had to withdraw. Following the punishment the English received as they tried to take the promontory, they chose to surround it, and given their overwhelming superiority in numbers they threatened to leave the Spanish isolated. Troncoso and his men began a risky withdrawal from the hill of Santa Lucía, which was totally successful as they continued skirmishing and firing in echelon until they reached Garás beach. Soon they were protected by the four artillery pieces of the small fort of Malvecín, situated on the southern end of the wall of Pescadería, by the harquebusiers on the wall itself and by the cannons of the *San Juan* and the *San Bartolomé* which were anchored nearby. The Marquis, who was on horseback and squeezed into his armour, received them at the foot of the wall. The determination of Troncoso's daring harquebusiers had a positive effect on the morale of the city, while the English had to start evacuating their dead and wounded.[4]

As night fell, the Pescadería wall remained relatively well protected. The bay was also defended due to the distance that the artillerymen of San Antón castle had covered and the presence of the Spanish Armada ships, *San Juan, San Bartolomé, Sansón, Diana* and *Princesa*, that formed a protective arc around the long Marina beach. Under cover of darkness, the English spread out around Corunna and set up detachments at strategic points: the hill and bridge of Gaiteiro, Castiñeiras, Nelle, Payo-Mouro and Labañóu. The city was therefore totally surrounded on land while the carriages took away the families of the Marquis and other Appellate Court officials. Apparently their departure took so long that only the bravery of Troncoso's harquebusiers, who delayed the siege of the city, prevented them from falling into the hands of the enemy. To judge by the effectiveness of the few harquebusiers, perhaps it would have been better to have sent a larger detachment to prevent the landings from the outset before the English could secure a bridgehead and set themselves up. In any event, it looked impossible to have prevented the landing at Oza, given the size of the garrison, the absence of batteries or coastal barricades, the accessibility of the estuary and the threat of a direct attack on the port. But it was not only the families of the members of the court who were travelling that night. In fact

when night fell something remarkable happened, which was that two companies of soldiers billeted in the city of Betanzos, under Captains Don Juan Monsalve and Don Pedro Ponce, having been ordered to help, were on their way and arrived when the city was already surrounded, short of supplies, with neither powder nor

---

[3]   The Marquis of Cerralbo to the King, Corunna, 4 May 1589. AGS Guerra Antigua. File 248, fol. 78.
[4]   *Diario del capitán Juan Varela.* BN mss 3790, pp. 153–4.

shot. They were confused and, so they said, thinking of returning, when Captain Varela, from Corunna and a veteran soldier of Flanders, came by.[5]

The troops quartered in Betanzos, who were carrying out Cerralbo's orders, arrived in Corunna to help.[6] But as they approached, they found that thousands of men had surrounded the city on land and that was when they came across Captain Varela. Faced with the complaints from Monsalve and Ponce about the lack of powder, Varela replied with pithy remark: 'The Spaniard's real powder in times of need is the sword.'[7]

From then on the men were led by the veteran Galician soldier until the crucial moment of their encounter with the English guards. Captain Varela wrote about this encounter in his journal:

And near the town they came across the enemy, and although they were wary because of their large numbers, nevertheless Captain Juan Varela and the others attacked them, and breaking through the enemy they killed some and captured two others. When they found it harder to advance, they killed the captive Englishmen in order not to be hampered by them and to scare many more; killing and wounding and clearing the way with their swords, they reached the city carrying as a sign of their victory the weapons and clothes of the English, and were received with great delight.[8]

Despite the use of the third person and other details, there is no reason to question (as Santiago Daviña has done recently in his book, listed in the bibliography) the authorship of Captain Varela here. It may well be a case of literary licence or a question of style. Various details in the diary indicate that it was written by the captain himself. In any event, even if the author of the diary was not the veteran soldier it was someone very close to him. The entrance of the Betanzos companies served to reinforce the garrison. But that night was filled with bad omens. Many residents living in the prosperous neighbourhood of Pescadería must have wished they had the 380 year-old walls of the high town which they looked upon as an ancient symbol of protection.

And while Corunna spent an anxious night, no one slept in Santiago either, where all of its resources were brought into play to save the besieged city. Like what happened 219 years later during the Peninsular War, the students tried to raise the university flag:

Word came to the Archbishop in Santiago on Friday 5 May at two o'clock in the morning, when the alarm was sounded, and at five o'clock the Count of Altamira,

---

[5]   *Diario del capitán Juan Varela.* BN mss 3790, p. 155.

[6]   Not only the troops, but the noblemen of Betanzos and other places nearby also got to Corunna before the siege was completed. Among them was Cristóbal Díaz, a public notary from Betanzos's council. This courageous man distinguished himself defending the city to such an extent that he received several votes of thanks and the rank of captain. See José Garcia Oro, 'El Capitán Cristóbal Díaz y la invasión de La Coruña', *Anuario Brigantino*, No. 19, Betanzos 1996, pp. 123–8.

[7]   *Papeles Tocantes a Felipe II. Tomo II.* BN mss 1750, fol. 242.

[8]   *Diario del capitán Juan Varela.* BN mss 3790, p. 156.

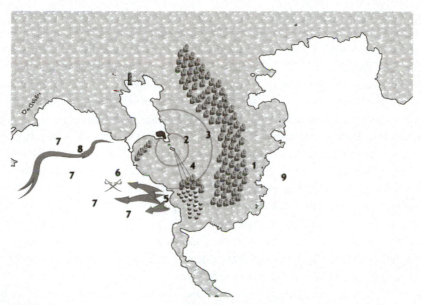

Figure 7.1 Map 1, 4 May, Corunna.

1. Entrance and anchorage of the English Armada, consisting of 180 ships and 27,667 men.
2. Area within range of the precision firing of the culverins from the castle of San Antón (500–600 metres).
3. Maximum range of the culverins (1,500 metres).
4. The castle bombards several ships that have anchored too close, forcing them into a hurried manoeuvre and resulting in two of them running aground.
5. Oza beach where the launches bring the first men onshore.
6. Skirmish on Santa Lucía hill between the English and 150 harquebusiers under the command of Captain Troncoso and Sergeant Major Luis de León.
7. English detachments besiege Corunna.
8. On the night of 4 May, Captain Juan Varela breaks the siege and brings in two companies (150 men) from Betanzos as reinforcements.
9. The coast of Santa Cruz and Mera is defended by 600 men under the command of Juan Rodríguez Suárez, councillor from Betanzos, preventing landings on this side of the estuary.

Don Lope Osorio de Moscoso, left with some infantrymen and horsemen. At six o'clock up to 200 well-equipped men left, and many more left later in stages. At three in the afternoon the Archbishop's bailiff left with one hundred and thirty students who were willing if not well-armed and who had voluntarily come forward to assist.[9]

That same night, the Archbishop also 'sent word to all the ports in Galicia as far as Vigo and Cangas, telling them to be prepared and ordering that no-one should leave until

---

[9]   *Relación de cómo y quando llega la Armada inglesa a la ciudad y puerto de la Coruña y lo qué después ha suçedido.* AGS. Guerra Antigua. File 248, fol. 95. Quoted in Martínez Salazar, *El cerco de La Coruña*, pp. 71–7 and in González Garcés, *María Pita*, pp. 326–8.

further word came'. This was to ensure that people would not come to the defence of Corunna and leave the other Galician ports unprotected.

By dawn on Friday 5 May, the wall of Pescadería had become a genuine frontier between Spain and England. The Marquis reinforced the parapet as much as he could, to the detriment of the garrison in the high town. Some captains, who were aware of the size of the opposing army and the weakness of the four-metre-high wall, decided that it was sensible to transfer provisions, equipment and valuable objects from Pescadería to the rocky promontory on which the old walled city was situated. This was to prevent them being stolen or used by the enemy, like the artillery from the small galleon *San Bernardo*, which was careened on the beach. Later it would be necessary to dig in for protection by the old wall. However, the four cannons of the Malvecín fort were brought into action against the buildings closest to the isthmus wall where the English had set themselves up, and fired a 'few good shots' that kept the English busy. The Spanish ships also started firing their artillery at the English fleet, which returned fire in lively fashion, although they kept such a cautious distance that they did not inflict any damage. The noise in the Bay of Corunna that morning was terrifying.

In the middle of this artillery exchange, the English sent four launches into the water and loaded them with three heavy bronze cannon directly from their ships. Their intention was to set them on cliffs level with the Gaiteiro Bridge and bombard the wall of Pescadería and the ships defending it. The launches began to sail along the beach of Santa María de Oza and headed towards the end of the bay. At the same time, several companies marched by land protecting their advance. The cannon balls fired from San Antón could not reach them and the guns from Malvecín were not effective either. The galleons anchored in the bay could not go out to meet them, for they were heavy sailing ships dependent on the wind and without sufficient crew. If they drifted in a southerly direction it would inevitably have taken them to the opposite end of the estuary, where the English were waiting. But there was a solution. The rowing ships, the galleys *Diana* and *Princesa*, close to San Antón, could row directly towards the enemy launches. Encouragement came from the walls of the high town for Captains Pantoja and Palomino to take the decision to cross the bay to intercept the launches that were coming dangerously close to their objective. Realizing the galleys' intentions, the English began firing frantically at them, but their artillery did not trouble the galleys because they had to keep at a distance in order to keep out of the range of the San Antón castle cannons. The fragile galleys went further into the bay, which was filled with English ships at the southern end, but when they were close to the launches their courage deserted them. Instead of attacking they settled for firing a few tame shots that achieved nothing, before returning towards San Antón and heading to Ferrol, apparently in search of reinforcements. The captains – who were only in Corunna because shortly after setting sail they had abandoned the Spanish Armada the year before – were severely criticized for unworthy conduct at not having prevented the English launches from placing the cannons so close to the city. Juan Varela himself wrote of this episode with great bitterness:

And after some time had passed and they had been shouted at many times, they began to row towards where the launches were heading, and when the enemy ships realised that the launches were under attack, they began to fire a good deal of artillery at the galleys. But none of the cannonballs hit them, and the closer they got to the launches, the further and safer they got from the artillery. And so sailing safe and free from any danger, when they got to where the galleons were and were expected to continue, they stopped and were content to fire a few shots at the launches from a distance. It is clear that the captains of these two galleys could have won no small honour that day by taking those launches and preventing a great deal of harm. But the harm did come to pass by their not taking them, for it may quite fairly be said that the beginning of all the harm that came to Corunna stemmed from not preventing these launches from achieving their objective … Pantoja felt inclined to flee, and to order the other captain to do the same, and the other captain must have felt obliged to obey, as later became clear. They had already turned back from the English Enterprise, and in both instances made it clear that they did not have it in them to fight. If His Majesty were to give them new coats of arms for their exploits, on the border it should read, as it says in the Gospel: *Beati pacifici quoniam ipsi possidebunt terram* [Blessed are the peace-makers, for they shall inherit the earth.][10]

Be that as it may, the English succeeded in setting up their three cannons. Moving such weapons by land must have been extremely difficult, given their weight and the problems with the beach and the paths. But very quickly the *San Juan* and the *San Bartolomé* were being struck, and although they fired some good shots from the ships and two of the cannons were put out of action, the English didn't miss a shot because they had such an easy target. Finally Drake enjoyed one of his most keenly anticipated moments. The recently repaired *San Juan*, the pride of Philip's navy, was ignominiously shot down from the land.

Because of the difficulties of withdrawing it towards San Antón, it was decided on the following day to set fire to it. But before the men abandoned ship, they cunningly "forgot" some barrels of gunpowder that had been strategically placed. The English soldiers, spurred on by Drake, went to rush on board in order to seize the banners, but the *San Juan* drove them back with a deadly explosion and fifteen of them lost their lives in the attempt.[11] Drake looked on as his dream of seizing the most valuable of

---

[10]   *Diario del capitán Juan Varela.* BN mss 3790, p. 161. Varela appears to have combined two verses from the Book of Matthew (5:5 and 5:9): '*Beati pacifici quoniam filii Dei vocabuntur*' ('Blessed are the peacemakers, for they shall be called the children of God') and '*Beati mites quoniam ipsi possidebant terram*' ('Blessed are the meek, for they shall inherit the earth') [translator's note].

[11]   Martín de Bertendona relates the episode thus: 'I wanted to embark with them setting fire to the galleon first so that the enemy would not take it, and so I did and fourteen or fifteen Englishmen who boarded the ship to take its banners died, for by the time they got to the topsails a mine of powder kegs I had prepared for that purpose caught fire.' Martín de Bertendona to the King, Corunna, 19 May 1589. AGS. Guerra Antigua. File 248, fol. 92. Quoted in González Garcés, *María Pita*, pp. 334–5.

Figure 7.2 Model of Corunna as seen by the English, made in 1989 for the exhibition of the fourth centenary of María Pita.

trophies evaporated, while the galleon blazed in the bay like an enormous funeral pyre. Such a sight left the besieged feeling devastated. They then realized that Corunna had reached the most momentous crossroads in its history, for it was abundantly clear that the moment of give way had arrived.

Chapter 8

The Capture of Pescadería

When the ships defending the bay were abandoned and the galleys fled to Ferrol, Pescadería was left totally unprotected by sea. The loss of the *San Juan* was bad news for the besieged. The city was now on its own, leaving the open Marina beach and the tranquil waters of the bay to anyone who dared to disembark under cover of darkness. The castle of San Antón only offered protection from a distance and from one flank. At the other end, the small fort of Malvecín, like the whole of the Pescadería wall, was clearly made to look insignificant and almost ridiculous compared to the size of the invading army. That afternoon, Friday 5 May, Pescadería was enveloped in a dreadful racket from cannon, muskets and harquebuses. But three lads, carried away by their youth, their desire to match each other and their wish for glory, spent a good while planning a strange act of heroism, for they planned to leap over the wall from the small fort of Malvecín and head for the shrine of the tower of Abajo, with the aim of rescuing its fine cross. These three were Juan Vásques de Neira, councillor for the town of Betanzos and native of Lugo, who happened to be in Corunna and did not want to miss the siege; Luis da Vila, servant to Don García Sarmiento, Squire of Salvatierra, who was in the city to settle a particular case in the appellate court[1] and González, servant to Judge Luis de Padilla. Armed with a harquebus and a sword, the three young men jumped from the fort and ran towards the shrine. From the wall, the defenders realized what they were up to and began firing their harquebuses to protect the reckless adventurers. The three lads reached the shrine and soon came out bearing the large cross. The firing began again from the wall at the same time as some strong friendly arms helped them to scale it quickly and bring the relic to safety. This story shows the great reverence felt by the Spaniards for their religious symbols.[2]

Later, when the Marquis anticipated a massive attack on the wall that night, he ordered the building of an earth barricade of the gate to the tower of Abajo. In order to set an example, he threw the first few shovelfuls of earth at the gate to make it inaccessible. Then he assigned duties to the companies. The defence of the fort of Malvecín was allocated to Captain Álvaro de Troncoso with his company of regular soldiers and to Vasco Fernández and Francisco de Meiranes with their militiamen. The centre of the wall was given to Don Juan de Monsalve and Don Pedro Ponce, the captains who had been guided by Don Juan Varela the night before, supported by Captain Montoto and

---

[1] Salvatierra is at the other end of Galicia; Philip II was right when he insisted on transferring the Appellate Court (*Real Audiencia*) in order to boost Corunna's population.

[2] *Diario del capitán Juan Varela*. BN mss 3790, p. 167.

his company of men from the city. In Caramanchón, the area of the wall closest to the beach of Orzán and perhaps the most at risk, there was the company of Don Juan de Luna. In order to prevent a night landing in the middle of the Corunna peninsula, the companies of Antonio Herrera and Gómez de Carvajal took on the defence of the high town and the Marina.

For their part, the English lost no time and busied themselves digging trenches at the foot of the Pescadería wall, which would allow them to attack by using ladders at night. Cerralbo then ordered that provisions should be brought into the high town, as he contemplated – apparently for the first time and rather late in the day – the possibility of losing Pescadería. That was one of a number of actions, or rather omissions, that Captain Juan Varela criticized in his diary:

> The supplies our Lord the King ordered to be gathered in this year of '89 were in the district of Pescadería, including a lot of biscuit, *pescado cecial* [fish dried in the open-air], tuna, bacon, cured meat, chick peas, oil, local wine[3] and clothing for the soldiers.[4] Of these supplies, when Pescadería was taken on the second day of the siege, some of the biscuit was moved into the city with great difficulty, one hour before they broke through and attacked, and it was so useful that it ran out on the very day the siege was lifted. It was just the right amount, even though there was not a lot of it. Some complained when they saw that so many supplies had been lost, saying that they had said it should be taken into the town, but they had not been listened to.[5]

Dusk fell, presenting a terrible threat for the defenders, who were too few to protect the whole side of the bay. Four English ships then attacked the castle of San Antón 'and got so close that the shots from their muskets reached the fort, which responded with such a volley that they were forced to return to their fleet, throwing launches overboard, which then towed them in.'[6] This episode makes clear the decisive role played by the protecting castle, which prevented the galleons from moving closer to Corunna and making the siege extraordinarily difficult. Álvaro de Troncoso noticed that although

---

[3]   The local wines were of rather poor quality. In fact, the sale of any wine from elsewhere was not allowed as long as any remained from the local harvest, for otherwise the local produce would not be sold. In a report dated 14 June 1564, these local wines were described as 'rough, crude, vile, and the cause of a few illnesses, especially for those accustomed to good wines'. The preference by the people of Corunna for wines from the south of Galicia or elsewhere in Spain was well known by that time, and the laws protecting local wines were less stringent. On this subject see Ismael Velo Pensado, *La vida Municipal de A Coruña en el siglo XVI* (Corunna: Editorial Diputación Provincial, 1992), pp. 112–15.

[4]   The clothes for the soldiers were new, for the men of the Spanish Armada had returned half naked due to their tough journey. The clothes were not, as some have suggested, the cause of the plague which would later decimate the expedition. As will be shown, the plague had other causes.

[5]   *Diario del capitán Juan Varela*. BN mss 3790, p. 144.

[6]   *Relación Anónima*. BN mss 3790, p. 205. We know of three copies of this document. One is kept in BN mss 3790, pp. 195–228. The other two have been found by Santiago Daviña in the Archivo de las Madres Capuchinas of Corunna, and quoted in *La Coruña: Nuevos relatos sobre el cerco*. For a critical study of this document, see Daviña Sainz, *La Coruña*.

there were people on the wall of Pescadería and also a small number on the Marina, the fountain of Sierpe, to the north of the high town, was defenceless in the face of a landing by launches under cover of darkness. A few men were sent there to deal with it. Night fell on such precarious defences.

A number supported the idea of sacrificing Pescadería: 'The opinion of almost all the captains was to abandon [Pescadería] because it was impossible to defend it, and in trying to do so many people would be killed; the Marquis responded that we should not surrender any land to the enemy and they should have to fight for every inch.'[7] Cerralbo was inspecting the scattered guards when from the fort of Malvecín boats could be heard rowing in the direction of Pescadería. Immediately, cannon and harquebus fire thundered blindly in the darkness, and some of the soldiers from Malvecín entered Pescadería from the shore. The English realized that they had been discovered and moved away from the beach once more. Meanwhile, the assailants from the wall launched a major attack, including artillery support, for 'under cover of darkness the enemy took some weapons which they used to attack the gate'.[8] The noise from the artillery, harquebuses and muskets meant that the silent English launches were not heard again as they took a detour and ended up behind the church of San Jorge close to the high town. This time they arrived without warning, for a serious battle was going on at the same time on the wall, with great danger for the defenders, who were being as stubborn as the attackers, and turning it into a very bloody battle: 'Those who were outside tackled the wall with ladders and climbed up the Caramanchón. And although our men killed many of them,[9] they did not turn back, but rather kept coming and tried to get through, as did our men to defend themselves.'[10] The English were beginning their strategy of attacking two flanks at the same time.

When the Spaniards became aware of the new English attempt to land, it was already too late to drive them back. When the Marquis realized the seriousness of the situation if the English turned the Marina into a stronghold and caught the defenders of the Pescadería wall between two lines of fire, he started fighting with the few men he had in reserve and valiantly tried to drive back the landing forces. Faced with 1,500 enemies on land, they soon had to draw back as far as the high town, which was completely unprotected and could easily have fallen while the Spanish soldiers were trying in vain to defend the isthmus:

> The men who had come in by sea then turned around and went overland towards the Puerta de la Torre to assist the men on land and make it easier for them to

---

[7] *Diario del capitán Juan Varela*. BN mss 3790, p. 158.

[8] *Relación de cómo y quando llega la Armada inglesa*. AGS Guerra Antigua. File 248, fol. 95.

[9] Tenacious resistance was offered on the Pescadería Wall by the veteran Spanish soldiers. The priest Jácome Labora, who was later taken prisoner and ransomed for two hundred ducats, stated that 'more than five hundred English were killed taking the gate'. Although this figure may be an exaggeration, they give an idea of how solid and effective the entrenched Spanish infantry was. *Relación de cómo y quando llega la Armada inglesa*. AGS Guerra Antigua. File 248, fol. 95.

[10] *Diario del capitán Juan Varela*. BN mss 3790, p. 170.

Figure 8.1 Map 2, 5 May, Corunna.

1. Four English launches transported three cannon to rocky outcrops situated in the Gaiteira and close to the bay.
2. The two galleys, *Diana* and *Princesa*, failed to intercept them and decided to leave Corunna for Ferrol.
3. Once the cannons had been set up, they bombarded the three ships from the Spanish Armada anchored off Pescadería: the *San Juan*, the *San Bartolomé* and the supply ship *Sansón*.
4. The Spanish ships replied by firing on the Gaiteira battery, putting two cannons out of action, but they were such an easy target that the English could not miss. The following morning the decision was taken to abandon them and set them ablaze. Martín de Bertendona strategically placed powder kegs on the *San Juan*, and the explosion killed fifteen of the Englishmen who attempted to board the abandoned galleon.
5. The English dug in close to the Pescadería Wall.
6. The fort of Malvecín with its four cannon plus the harquebuses and muskets at the Wall made digging in difficult.
7. Three harquebusiers rescued the cross from the shrine near Malvecín.
8. At nightfall, four English ships attempted to storm the castle of San Antón and get close enough for their musket fire to hit the target, but they were ruthlessly driven back and had to be towed to safety by small boats.

break through and seize our soldiers who were defending the middle of the wall. And although this worked well, it would have been even better if they had headed for the city. For if truth be told, it could have been taken very easily as there were no men there. Almost all of them, and the best, were defending the wall at Puerta de la Torre, and all its gates were open and without enough guards.[11]

[11] *Diario del capitán Juan Varela.* BN mss 3790, p. 170

But the English were unaware of how desperate the situation was in Corunna. They did not realize that the higher town was defenceless, and although a few English soldiers reached as far as the Puerta Real itself, which was defended by a mere four harquebusiers, they paid for their daring with their lives. The English strategy was not to attempt an attack on the high town with a knock-out blow but to catch the defenders of the Pescadería wall between two lines of fire, wipe them out and then take control of this large quarter of Corunna where the majority of the population lived at that time. When the defenders of the wall discovered that the enemy had landed on the beach and were engaged in hand-to-hand fighting, when they realized to their horror that they had fallen into a trap and into a pincer movement that had left them surrounded, they gave up all resistance at the wall. They then rushed across a Pescadería full of invaders towards the high town, their last hope of salvation, although in the middle of total confusion there were rumours that it had already been taken.

The tragedy that then enveloped Pescadería is one of the saddest episodes in the history of Galicia. That night, 'although many were made prisoner, many atrocities were committed, with many men, women and children killed, some burned, others tortured'.[12] A good number of men plunged into the sea in desperation,[13] others headed for the interior of the peninsula and found safety in the Old Castle (the Tower of Hercules). Most of them had to battle their way to the high town, street by street, in total disarray, the companies without their captains. The troops from Betanzos, who had seen their honour rescued the night before by Captain Varela, struggled to withdraw from Caramanchón towards Marina. They fought their way through the English soldiers to reach the wall and safety, but not without sustaining losses. Captains Monsalve and Ponce, accompanied by two soldiers, started their own difficult journey through the winding streets. Monsalve, who was wounded, was suddenly overcome by weakness when they reached the San Andrés hospital, and in order to avoid falling into the hands of the enemy, he hid in an attic in a nearby house, where he was stabbed to death while his companion could only jump out the window into the darkness of the street, reach the high town later on and relate the sad end of his captain.

Gradually the remaining defenders of Pescadería arrived in the high town. 'In this invasion over seven hundred men died or were captured or fled out to sea ... anyone can see what their loss would mean for the defence of the city.'[14] Considering how critical Captain Juan Varela was regarding the defence of the Pescadería wall and given his support for the creation of strongholds behind the walls of the high town, it is likely that the figures given in his journal are exaggerated. When compared with other sources, a more acceptable number would be around four hundred. In any event, from then on the people of Corunna became the leaders of the resistance.

[12] *Diario del capitán Juan Varela*. BN mss 3790, p. 174.
[13] 'Some soldiers jumped into the water at the part they call the Orzán and arrived naked in Santiago, where the Archbishop gave them clothes and weapons and they returned to the field.' *Relación de cómo y quando llega la Armada inglesa*. AGS. Guerra Antigua. File 248, fol. 95.
[14] *Diario del capitán Juan Varela*. BN mss 3790, p. 172.

During that time of terror, death and chaos there was scarcely anyone to organize the defence of the walls. But once they had conquered Pescadería, the English took their time to enjoy the plundering and pillaging. 'In Pescadería the enemy finally found everything they could wish for. They found very nice houses with comfortable beds, plenty to eat and drink, clothes for those who did not have any, weapons for those who were unarmed, and many other items.'[15] In this way they allowed the besieged some essential time to organize the defence of the ancient wall, even though they did not have time to recover from the terrible events and were in the middle of the most appalling suffering.

On that occasion Drake and Norris, together with their commanders, celebrated the easy spoils with great jubilation. The prosecution of war seemed to be going extremely well and everyone felt that the surrender of Corunna was imminent, which would represent a glorious stage on the speedy road to Lisbon. The clinking of high-quality glasses in the house of Canon Labora in the Calle Real, where they had gathered[16] to celebrate the expedition, rang out between loud peals of laughter. Filled with the spirit of resistance, however, the sound of the glasses symbolized the possibility that those plunderers would come to head the long list of warriors who, on one of the great occasions of history, were profoundly and totally mistaken.

---

[15] *Diario del capitán Juan Varela.* BN mss 3790, p. 176.

[16] Norris lodged in the house of Canon Labora, Dom Manuel (Dom António's son) in the house next door, and Drake in the house of Tonquín, close to the San Jorge Plaza. Dom António remained on Drake's *Revenge*, which he left only once. Francisco Tettamancy Gastón, *Apuntes para la Historia Comercial de La Coruña* (Corunna: Ayuntamiento de La Coruña, 1900) (facsimile edition, 1994), p. 119.

Chapter 9

To the Walls

Corunna lost its innocence on the night of Friday, 5 May 1589. The most terrible symphony of anguish, sadness, bewilderment and fear could be heard in every corner of the high town. Women wept and cursed as they desperately looked for their husbands. Children, who were somehow aware of the tragedy, wept inconsolably as they sensed their grandparents' despair. No one knew if the English had already breached the walls of the high town, for in view of the size of the invading army everything seemed to indicate an imminent break through that very night. False alarms, collective terrors, horrendous ascents up the old winding streets as people fled imaginary ghosts, contagious panic, powerful cries that rose to the heavens, all of these swept away any rational attempt to escape. For 'a rumour went around the town that the enemy had already entered, causing many to jump from the walls near Santa Bárbara, and they were all captured'.[1] The regular soldiers were stunned by the disaster and aware that the numbers of the enemy forces could lead to their annihilation. They were unable to organize any resistance in such circumstances and so 'not much was done to get the men ready at the wall, for there was still much confusion. They were adamantly refusing to go and told the townsfolk to go and defend their homes.'[2] Many of the men who had defended the wall of Pescadería in vain were captured in their attempt to reach the high town towards the Old Castle, amongst them Don Juan de Luna and his company, who had to withdraw from the Caramanchón and were severely depleted. The captain had to hand himself over to the enemy,[3] for the boatman of the Old Castle was concerned about the idea of carrying more people in his launch than prudence would dictate and decided to transport only those who could swim. Time seemed to stand still that endless night, as if dawn would never again come to Corunna, but eventually the sun, that inscrutable symbol of hope, rose on Saturday 6 May. Daylight brought with it new terrors, for there was another false alarm and some residents rushed towards the Old Fortress or the Casas Reales, guided by their inherited instinct to seek out the safest place in order to get away from danger. The Marquis then sent word to the judges of the *Real Audiencia* to 'leave, for it was not fitting for the service and reputation of His Majesty for them to be captured or killed by the enemy'.[4] The judges, however, refused to leave the city without Cerralbo. Several professional captains were aware of the fact that, given the

---

[1] *Diario del capitán Juan Varela*. BN mss 3790, p. 173.
[2] Ibid.
[3] Later he was rescued for 600 ducats and he had to swear that he would no longer act as a captain. *Relación de cómo y quando llega la Armada inglesa*. AGS Guerra Antigua. File 248, fol. 95.
[4] *Diario de capitán Juan Varela*. BN mss 3790, p. 180.

size of the forces they faced, the town was hopelessly doomed and they wanted to evacuate their wives and children by sea. Apparently the judges changed their minds about sailing away a few hours later but the opportunity to leave had gone.

That was when the true size of the infantry and the English army became clear, for 'there must have been between ten and twelve thousand men'.[5] It also became clear that once their enemies had been killed or captured, most of the men who had landed had spent the night searching for food and wine and creating the greatest drunken binge the town had ever seen. However, those who remained sober 'set about making wooden parapets that would enable them to enter the monastery of Santo Domingo that was right next to the outside of the city wall, next to the gate of Puerta de los Aires. They managed to plant six banners inside, although they continued to be fired on from the wall with artillery and harquebus fire.'[6]

That was when the besieged touched rock bottom and that very morning they turned themselves into a group to be feared, bringing together the mayor, the councillors, captains, ensigns and sergeants, as well as tailors, coopers, shipwrights, fishermen, innkeepers, barbers ... and, in addition, over a thousand women 'who would shirk at nothing'.[7] They were all grim-faced; they all wanted to take up arms and prepare defences. They had a task to perform. The angry fishermen and the emotional inhabitants of the high town were now all possessed by one and the same spirit. The latter opened their doors wide and offered their rooms, their food stores and words of hope. 'Everyone was charitable towards everyone else, and those who had more gave more and distributed it among the needy.'[8] Each accepted his share of certainties and hopes about relatives or friends who were dead or captured, or those who had fled to safety by sea. From the total shock to the people of Corunna that sad night, there emerged by contrast the spirit of resistance. Humble peasant women were comforted in the living rooms of the old houses of the high town, and grand ladies must have rested their sorrowful heads on the laps of fishwives.

From then on an imposing peace came over the monasteries and the cries were replaced by silent prayer. 'And it was striking and a great consolation to witness the tranquillity in the churches, the tears that were shed and how after each person had taken communion they went straight to their post at the wall.'[9] Panic and consternation gave way to quiet bravery and mutual solidarity. The extreme nature of the situation produced prayers to God on whose behalf they were ultimately fighting: 'In terms of human forces it was impossible for us to defend ourselves, and so we sought victory in heaven, but not forgetting human means, and all did our best to make peace with God so that our sins

---

[5]   *Relación Anónima*. BN mss 3790, p. 208.
[6]   Ibid., p. 209.
[7]   Ibid., p. 211.
[8]   *Diario del capitán Juan Varela*. BN mss 3790, p. 182.
[9]   Ibid., p. 181.

Figure 9.1 Map 3, the capture of Pescadería, Corunna.

1. The defence of Malvecín fort and the gate of La Torre was entrusted to Captain Álvaro de Troncoso and his company and to Captains Vasco Fernández and Francisco Meiranes with their militiamen.
2. Captains Juan de Monsalve and Pedro Ponce, together with their companies from Betanzos, and Captain Montoto with his militiamen, were the mainstays in the centre of the wall.
3. Juan de Luna was responsible for the most dangerous area, the Caramanchón.
4. The companies of Antonio Herrera and Gómez de Carvajal were stationed on the sands in the bay.
5. Under cover of darkness and the noise of the assault on the Pescadería wall, the English set off in launches towards the sands of Cantón.
6. The first attempt to land was discovered and the attackers left the beach.
7. They managed to land on the Marina. Cerralbo, with his few reserves, could not prevent 1,500 English from landing after a bloody battle.
8. The men who landed head for the Caramanchón, where those attacking the wall redoubled their efforts to take it.
9. The Spanish were caught between two stools and fighting as they went, they withdrew towards the high town.
10. The defenders barricaded themselves in the high town.
11. The English spent the night looting Pescadería and drinking too much wine.
12. The English made use of the magnificent San Andrés hospital, the pride of the Guild of Fishermen.
13. The following day the attackers occupied the monastery of Santo Domingo.

would not prevent us from receiving the grace we hoped for from his blessed hand.'[10] Fortunately for the Spanish, there was a large quantity of arms and munitions in the

---

[10] *Diario del capitán Juan Varela*. BN mss 3790, p. 182.

city, and although some of them (as well as several cannon, including those from the *San Bernardo*, which was in dock) fell into the hands of the English, they had sufficient weapons.

At last Cerralbo decided to use his authority from the King and bring some serious organization to the somewhat improvised defence of the place. All able-bodied men of any age were then strategically placed along the walls. The protection of the perimeter near the Puerta de Aires was entrusted to Captain Álvaro de Troncoso. Captains Pedro Ponce and Francisco de Meiranes, together with Ensign Luna, were stationed along the rest of the wall as far as the Old Fortress. The defence of the Old Fortress, which was now incorporated into the walls, was the responsibility of Ensign Robles. The Parrote area was given to Sergeant Lobo. The rest of the wall as far as Puerta Real was in the charge of Captain Lorenzo Montoto and Don Payo Mariño. Finally, Puerta Real, up to the area defended by Captain Troncoso, fell to the Ensigns Antonio Barrera and Gómez de Carvajal.[11] Not only was a good number of the commands in the hands of townsfolk, but the militiamen, in a great strategic move, were distributed around the whole of the perimeter, so that professional soldiers and the civilian population were united in discipline and courage.

While Corunna was facing such difficulties, the rest of Galicia was preparing to help. The first to respond to the Marquis' letters were Pedro de Andrade, Squire of San Saturniño, and Pedro Pardo from Betanzos, who together with other gentlemen and two Portuguese companies,[12] managed to assemble 1,400 men who settled in El Burgo the day after the English landed. Pedro de Andrade sent a letter to Cerralbo informing him of their arrival, of the little amount of training the recruits had had at such short notice, and the total lack of officers and military supplies. The Marquis ordered them to remain in El Burgo, appointed as generals Fernando Ruiz de Castro, Count of Andrade, and Martín de Ayala, knight commander of Puertomarín and veteran soldier of Flanders, and regretted not being able to send them the supplies they had requested.[13] Those who played an important role from the outset were the well-equipped squadron of six hundred men led by Juan Rodríguez Suárez, councillor for Betanzos. Captain Jacome Colmelo de Sevil was his second in command. The squadron 'marched along the shore in full view of the English fleet, and were so organised and achieved such good results that they never let a single launch disembark on the land of Las Mariñas, even though they attempted to do so'.[14] As a result, the districts of Oleiros, Sada and Betanzos were well protected from

[11] *Relación Anónima*. BN mss 3790, pp. 210–11.
[12] The two Portuguese companies were those of Martín López de Valladares, who had returned in the supply ship *Sansón*, and Juan Trigueros, who had come back in the galleon *San Bernardo*. They had both been stationed by Cerralbo in Ferrol-Puentedeume. The Marquis of Cerralbo to the King, Bayona, 10 June 1589. AGS Guerra Antigua. File 249, fol. 106. See Chapter 6.
[13] Cerralbo thus turned to the existing military structure in Galicia and previously used by Philip II, according to which the great Galician feudal houses exercised military commands. On this subject, see Emilio González López, *La Galicia de los Austrias* (Corunna: Fundación Barrié de la Maza, 1980), I, Chap. LXXVII.
[14] *Diario del capitán Juan Varela*. BN mss 3790, p. 185. César Vaamonde Lores, 'El capitán Colmelo', *Boletín de la Real Academia Gallega*, No. 36, 1910.

the outset and the invaders were unable to get through. This is even more impressive considering that the English fleet was anchored right opposite them.

With Pescadería now taken, new troops arrived the following day, Saturday, 6 May. The Count of Altamira came with two companies of raw Asturian recruits brought from Santiago and others from his land. Don Francisco de Menchaca, Squire of Cayón, brought three more companies. Altogether more than 2,400 men arrived and set up their headquarters in the Monte de Arcas, at the summit of la Zapateira.[15] Up there they could be seen from Corunna, conveying in equal measure hope to the besieged and anxiety to the besiegers, many of whom were still under the influence of drink. Admittedly they were not only vastly superior in numbers, but also protected by the wall of Pescadería.[16] So from the town they could see the silhouette of 'people on horseback', although apparently they were not hardened in a thousand battles but were rather 'rustic riders', who hardly looked like real cavalry. Recruitment was so undiscriminating and the conditions of the army so dreadful that Don Pedro de Sotomayor proposed a selection and a regrouping in order to arm

> four-hundred to six-hundred nobles in the field, and of the other younger men of better appearance, no more than 1,400. Weapons for them would be procured from all those who had come, or at least pikes, and although there was not enough gunpowder for the harquebuses, it would be better to give it to the few, and a squadron of 2,000 men would be formed that could face the enemy and even break through. The remaining men could be used in some more distant place in order to scare and intimidate.[17]

But for some reason or another, such a reasonable strategy was not put into effect.

Another major drawback was the absence of captains with experience of reinforcement troops. This is important, given that 'the labourers were frequently telling us that when they saw the enemy they would willingly go out to them and even die if there was someone leading them'.[18] Despite such a situation, on the morning of Saturday, 6 May, most of the reinforcement troops began a manoeuvre that consisted of 'slowly approaching the city until they took a hill above the hermitage of Santa Lucía, opposite the gates of Pescadería, and dig in there, although they said that it was a rash thing to do because so few of them were armed'. But without a general who could give orders to noblemen and captains, and impose essential order on the army, the three companies of Francisco de Menchaca and the two from Portugal commanded by Captain Luis Ferreira, 'advanced without receiving orders, either thinking that they would gain all

---

[15] *Diario del capitán Juan Varela.* BN mss 3790, pp. 185–6.

[16] In addition to digging in at the wall and in order to ensure communication over land between the besiegers and their fleet, which could not be done by sea owing to the cannons of San Antón, 'they had three cannons placed on the bridge they call del Gaiteiro'. *Relación de cómo y quando llega la Armada inglesa.* AGS Guerra Antigua. File 248, fol. 95.

[17] *Diario del capitán Juan Varela.* BN mss 3790, pp. 187–8.

[18] Ibid., p. 189.

the honour or out of ignorance'.[19] In fact the plan was very daring, because the hill of Santa Lucía was on the route connecting the besiegers with their fleet, and therefore right in the middle of English territory, so to speak. Mechaca with his three companies reached the top from the Bergantiños road and surrounded it by way of the slope falling towards Corunna. Ferreira's Portuguese in turn approached Santa Lucía from the flank near the coast. There followed a skirmish that caused the English to withdraw towards Pescadería and to wonder whether the isthmus wall would be sufficient to hold back the Spanish forces.

When those in the high town saw the reinforcements were so close, 'thinking there were more, and that they had all arrived, there was great joy and the bells were rung'.[20] Since they were now convinced that a real rescue operation was under way, Diego de Bazán sent out a patrol into Pescadería from the fortress with his company and others, making the English withdraw so as to avoid being caught in the firing from both sides. Some of them, 'feeling quite fearful, quickly began to embark.'[21] But it did not take long for the English to realize how small the Spanish 'army' was, and having reinforced the wall of Pescadería they started firing at Santa Lucía from Malvecín fort. They then did a full break out, dislodging the three companies of Menchaca plus Ferreira's two. After having contacted the rest of the forces, they returned to the Zapateira headquarters. By then the Portuguese captain had suffered the reproaches of the Count of Altamira, 'because they had left without waiting and without receiving orders.' Diego de Bazán, as disappointed as the rest of the besieged, was reduced to depending once more on his own forces and on the strength of the old walls for their survival. In the words of Captain Varela, although the reinforcements 'had cheered us up, they left us feeling even more sad'.[22]

[19]   *Diario del capitán Juan Varela*. BN mss 3790, p. 190.
[20]   Ibid.
[21]   Ibid., p. 191.
[22]   Ibid.

Chapter 10

The Oath

Once the available troops had been spread out along the wall, the Marquis retained fifty additional men, officers, councillors and assistants from the *Real Audiencia* in order to 'provide gunpowder and munitions for the posts and to go wherever they were needed'. In principle, the women were responsible for providing food and water so that the men could stay at their posts on the walls at all times. Later on they would also be the ones to distribute gunpowder, rope and projectiles, which in the end were made from any metal object they could find.[1] In addition to this constant supply, a period of frenetic comings and goings began that ultimately would save Corunna. The perimeter wall was reinforced from the inside, its turrets and gates were packed with earth, providing a solidity that the walls did not have previously and that made it possible to place artillery on them. The children, and the elderly with limited mobility, kept the candles lit in the churches. On that Saturday, 6 May, there was another particularly important job to do, for 'all the available biscuits were taken out of the stores that were joined to the outside of the wall, and the stores were burned with whatever was left in them, for it would have been a real problem to leave them standing for the enemy, who had shown signs of their intention to attack at that point'.[2]

By dusk, after a day of intense activity and tears, including tears of joy and the tolling of bells when the meagre reinforcements briefly appeared, the situation in the high town had changed. Meanwhile, a good number of the English were still struggling between a high state of drunkenness and the most horrendous hangover, and their generals were incapable of bringing some order to the large number of drunkards. This was their famous 'inordinate drinking'.[3] Several of them paid with their lives in these circumstances. This may have been one of the causes for the health problems that were visited on the invaders after their defeat, and led to unprecedented disaster. In any event, that night passed more peacefully than any other night of the siege.

At dawn on Sunday, 7 May, the English managed to get a small cannon to the top of the bell tower of the Santo Domingo monastery and used it to threaten the company of

---

[1] Because of this makeshift ammunition, 'the number of them that exploded was a sight to see', Cerralbo later wrote to the King to inform him of the need for more firearms. The Marquis of Cerralbo to the King, Santiago, 5 July 1589. AGS. Guerra Antigua. File 250, fol. 131.

[2] *Relación Anónima*. BN mss 3790, p. 211.

[3] This 'inordinate drinking' mentioned by Hume, *The Year After the Armada*, p. 33, occurred beyond Pescadería: 'Spending too long in the wine cellars, where our men found many of them lying down and they killed them.' *Relación de cómo y quando llega la Armada inglesa*. AGS. Guerra Antigua. File 248, fol. 95. Hume also states that many of the drunkards were unaware of the danger and were then killed.

Troncoso, the defender of the Puerta de Aires. They quickly filled one of the flanking turrets with earth and set upon it two cannon that blew off part of the bell tower. But the English continued to reply from the windows, although there was just as much 'continuous harquebus fire against anyone who showed themselves' coming from the square. The castle of San Antón not only made the English keep their distance but also put the port out of action as far as transport was concerned, because it was within the range of its powerful culverins. Despite the constant exchange of artillery fire, it was a day of preparations for both sides.

In the high town, work progressed at a steady pace; 'Fascines [very tight bundles of small branches] and sacks to be filled with earth were got ready to use for repairs.' Meanwhile the English were not only keeping watch over the Pescadería wall, thereby preventing a new attempt by the Spanish to send reinforcements overland, but they were also consolidating their position by bringing materials for an attack, 'and all that night they could be seen doing carpentry in the chapel of the monastery, although it was unclear whether this was to prepare props and boxes for tunnels, or ladders and *mantas*[4] for the wall'. In fact the attackers wasted no time that night, for on Monday, 8 May, 'when dawn broke the street from Santo Domingo to the orchard where the enemy placed their artillery was fortified, and the walls in between had been taken down as necessary for the task. They began to make the platform and its trench, always keeping it protected by the orchard walls.'[5] The English built a bulwark between the Santo Domingo monastery and the adjacent street. Such a position, which was very close to the Puerta de Aires wall, was of vital importance for poliorcetics, or the art of defending and attacking strongholds, at the end of the sixteenth century. The attackers were offered different options. One of them was to propose surrender but offering something in return. Another was to set up a battery of cannons and pound the wall from a short distance before knocking it down and getting through. Another possibility was to climb the wall using ladders, while the defenders were distracted by a powerful bombardment of artillery, harquebuses and musketry. But as far as tactics were concerned, that was not all. Another formidable scheme was to construct a tunnel underground and arrive like moles at the base of the wall, place a huge amount of gunpowder there and blow it up in a powerful explosion. Every trick, plus others involving incendiary devices, was tried in Corunna. They started with the most obvious, for

> that day they began to land the artillery and bring it to Santo Tomás [the district where the monastery of Santo Domingo was located] along a safe and protected route away from our artillery, which together with the harquebuses never stopped firing on those who were working on the platform, and also on those who were putting themselves at risk by walking across Pescadería.[6]

---

[4] Metal-plated boards for protection against firearms.
[5] *Relación Anónima*. BN mss 3790, pp. 212–13.
[6] Ibid., p. 213. The walls of the high town, due to their elevation, were a good place from which to clear the streets of Pescadería with gunfire. Captain Young, for example, died from an accurate shot while he was walking in the streets. List of captains slain or died, 1589. Wernham, *Expedition*, p. 213.

Once the English had set up some artillery on the still small platform of the bulwark that was under construction, and after a significant skirmish which enabled them to tighten the siege while the besieged established a clear line that could not be crossed, the English sounded a drum to call for a parley. Cerralbo sent Sergeant Major Luis de León with the message that they would only parley if they were going to talk about prisoners. Faced with the insistence by the English emissary to hand over the letter to the Marquis, Luis de León ordered him from the top of the walls to convey his message aloud. Then the English spokesman announced that

> the generals claimed this city for the Kingdom of England, and that if it surren-
> dered they would show clemency, putting to one side the harm that our Armada
> had tried to do them a year ago. If it did not surrender, they would use all the rigour
> of war, and even if all the power of Spain be in it they would take it in two days.

Luis de León answered that 'the Marquis would defend it against the whole world with the men who were holding it, and that he should be gone'.[7] In these circumstances, a harquebusier on the wall, unable to stop himself, fired at the emissary who had been allowed in for a parley, and in turn one of the attackers fired back. The governor, aware that he was responsible for guaranteeing discipline and with a strict sense of honour, offered to hand over the harquebusier who had broken the truce and the parley in exchange for the man who had fired back. The English answered that they would forgive the Spaniard if the Marquis pardoned the Englishman. Juan Pacheco answered that he would punish his harquebusier appropriately, that they could do as they wished with their man, 'and preparing ourselves for within a half an hour they were told that they could then start'.[8]

The afternoon wore on amid increasing tension, with occasional shots and cannon fire that frequently ended up as frenzied skirmishes against enemy positions. Meanwhile men continued to join the reinforcement troops, and so 'on Sunday 7 May up to four or five thousand men came together, and they put the veterans in squadrons, and at sundown they set up near the enemy'.[9] But it was impossible to arm the men or for the few actual soldiers to turn them into some kind of army. For their part, the English continued to transport materials and to work on their bulwark at the Santo Domingo monastery. As night fell, the anxiety was almost palpable, with the efforts of the English turned into a formidable threat. Pescadería, Molinos de Viento, la Sierpe, the rest of the Corunna peninsula and the outskirts were packed with Englishmen. The English camp, which was several times larger than the city of Corunna itself, seemed to be concentrating its power on launching a brutal assault against a single point in the old walls of the city. Corunna had already been warned. It was dwarfed by the attacking force and

---

[7] *Relación Anónima*. BN mss 3790, pp. 213–14.
[8] Ibid., p. 214.
[9] *Relación de cómo y quando llega la Armada inglesa*. AGS Guerra Antigua file 248, fol. 95.

frighteningly outnumbered, a stranger in its own land. Meanwhile, the embers of the galleon *San Juan* were still burning in the bay as a precise portent of what was hovering over the besieged.

As darkness fell, it became clear through countless fires and lamps within the houses how substantial the English war machine was and how remote were the possibilities of salvation, which seemed to vanish and yet had to be believed in, given the English threat to 'use all the rigour of war'. This could only mean the worst, given the cruelty shown the year before to the shipwreck survivors of the Spanish Armada who fell into their hands. That night, the besieged swore the oath of the Guildsmen of Our Lady of the Rosario or the Oath of Corunna, the content of which has survived to this day:

> In the city of Corunna on the 8th of the month of May of the Day of St. Michael in the year of our Lord 1589, we, the dwellers and residents of this city, signing here in our name and in the name of most of those who live and reside here, do solemnly swear to Our Lord God that on the day of Our Lady of the Visitation, which falls on the 2 July of each year, if Our Lord God should free us from the siege under which we now find ourselves by order of the Queen of England, from which we do not expect to be delivered by human hands, on the said day in the monastery of Santo Domingo in this city the masses, vespers and sacrifices usually offered by the Guildsmen of Rosario will be offered, and all of those in this profession will confess and take communion: and instead of the meal and other secular expenses usually incurred on that day we shall marry 15 maidens giving 20 ducats for each, 300 in all, which are to be distributed among the townsfolk taking this oath, and the administrator of the aforementioned guild must give alms to all the poor that should come to visit his home, as well as bread, wine, meat, and fish on the said day of Our Lady instead of the meal usually given by him to the guildsmen; furthermore, if it should please God to lift the siege, a general procession of penitents will take place the day it is lifted or the next, and since at present we are unable to extend this document further, we pledge with our persons and property to keep our word and sign it with our names.[10]

It is worth noting that the signatures of the mayor, the councillors, the Marquis and the judges are missing, although it must be said that this was a particular oath of a representative group of townsfolk. It was a private promise made in haste in an extreme situation. This oath has survived until today and is still celebrated in Corunna. Having concluded this simple but solemn act, those who signed it returned to their posts at the wall. The sounds of the English carpenters could still be heard in the Santo Domingo monastery throughout the night, but meanwhile the harquebusiers at the wall did not sleep, either. Shots rang out from time to time when someone, lit up by the torches, took aim and fired.

---

[10]   Martínez Salazar, *El cerco*, pp. 92–3.

Chapter 11

The First Attacks

During the days following the oath, both sides continued working resolutely on their projects. The English worked on their small-scale works of military architecture, which in this case also involved some engineering. On the one hand, in the orchard and the narrow street next to the Santo Domingo monastery, close to the Puerta de Aires, they were completing their small raised bulwark, which had a well-protected platform for artillery pieces to bombard the wall. That involved the slow process of embanking and transporting materials. On the other hand, they persevered with the entirely different task of digging a tunnel at least twenty metres long from the monastery orchard. This tunnel would allow them to get under the nearest of the hollow turrets, the one at the northern corner. These medieval-style turrets with a semi-circular base abutted straight stretches of the wall. Corunna had seventeen 'old-style small round turrets',[1] plus the six of the Old Fortress. The intention of the English was to blow up one of them using a large amount of gunpowder in a tremendous underground explosion. For their part, the defenders were aware of everything that the invaders were up to. Their tasks were also clear and no less arduous. They had to embank, prop up and reinforce the turret that the English were trying to mine, as well as the part of the wall that was going to be bombarded by the guns from the platform that the English were constructing. They had to strengthen the walls from inside, even using stone taken from the houses. In addition, they constantly disrupted the work of the English, firing at them with cannon and harquebuses wherever they were in range, and the San Antón castle continued to block the port thanks to the culverins. The blockade was so troublesome that on Wednesday, 10 May, the English launched a second attack on San Antón, this time using large launches equipped with cannon. It was no mean attempt by the attackers, but once again they had to face not only the powerful bronze guns of the castle, but also another four placed on the fortress: 'They were met with such a discharge of firepower that they withdrew very quickly whence they had come, having suffered a good deal of damage, as later became clear.'[2]

Meanwhile, the reinforcements based at Monte de Arcas tried to make some forays and killed many English soldiers in various places where they had strayed from their camp. So, on 10 May, Norris ordered a first operation against them: 'At dawn on Wednesday while the Count of Andrade was with his men, and many from the land towards El Burgo, and other companies towards the part near the road to Santiago

---

[1]   As described by Tiburzio Spanocchi in José Ramón Soraluce Blond, *Castillos y fortificaciones de Galicia* (Corunna: Fundación Pedro Barrié de la Maza, 1985), p. 30.

[2]   *Relación Anónima*. BN mss 3790, p. 215.

formed into another squadron, a detachment of musketeers and harquebusiers came to attack them.'³ However, the Spanish saw the English detachment coming, prepared themselves to deal with them and laid 'an ambush of over 1000 men in the ryegrass'. Initially the English musketeers had to withdraw, 'and our men killed some of them, with the Archbishop's bailiff in the vanguard with fifteen or twenty harquebusiers.' But the English got back into formation and prepared to face up to them, so 'in order to draw the squadron into the ambush and having been seen by them, they withdrew towards El Burgo, where the Count of Andrade awaited'. By withdrawing towards the bridge of El Burgo, the Spanish vanguard lured half of the English detachment into another ambush, where '*arcabuceros diestros*' [sharpshooters] were ready for them. And so 'they killed thirty of them, brought back their arms and clothes, and the heads of five of them.'⁴

Following this major skirmish, the English abandoned El Burgo and so this strategic stronghold of the reinforcement troops took on its significant role. Nothing, however, could prevent the other half of the English detachment from advancing in the opposite direction, 'killing and burning whatever they found'. On one side, we see the savagery of making off with the heads of the enemy killed in combat, like hunting trophies. This atrocious practice, however, apart from showing the newly recruited men that the English were not invincible, was seen as fair retaliation for their treatment of the civilian population. What we also see here is that the role of the reinforcements, which would have been impossible in a larger operation, consisted of wearing down the English forces, who had to balance between spreading out far enough so as to gain as much booty and destroy as much as possible, and staying close enough together to avoid becoming the prey rather than the predator. This task, combined with the resilience of the defensive system formed by the high town and the castle of San Antón, would soon wear down this first, furious onslaught from the colossal raging bull of the English forces. By the time this beast of bronze, wood and men set sail for Lisbon, it would have lost much of its strength and courage due to the blood it had shed here. But meanwhile, 'from the time they took Pescadería until Wednesday, all day, they have been looting it and carrying their booty aboard'.⁵ A large column of bearers, laboriously skirting the bay from the town to Oza, where the fleet was, took all the valuable property from Pescadería that they could carry, leaving the houses empty.

Martín de Ayala, the Count of Andrade's second in command, took the decision to move the headquarters of the reinforcements to El Burgo, since in La Zapateira there was nowhere they could lodge overnight. That same day, Wednesday, the Count of Andrade acted very wisely and 'called the knights and captains to a council at which they decided on two things: one, that the Count of Altamira should go to Santiago accompanied by Ensign Olivera, who is a very fine soldier, to encourage the people and make sure certain necessary things were done in case the enemy decided to go there, if Corunna were

---

³   *Relación de cómo y quando llega la Armada inglesa.* AGS. Guerra Antigua. File 248, fol. 95.
⁴   Ibid.
⁵   Ibid.

lost'.[6] In fact, in Santiago de Compostela (at the time a larger city than Corunna), fear of the English was consistent with the riches that Drake could steal or destroy there, and there were a good many of those. Above all there was one whose loss would have meant at the very least a real propaganda coup for the Anglican 'heretics': the desecration of the legendary body of the Apostle St James. Compostela, an inland town and therefore safe from the incursions of pirates, and in addition far removed from the frontlines of a Reconquest concluded two generations before, had no solid walls to defend it. In this sense, the words of Andrade himself in a letter to the King are sufficiently clear: 'There was such fear in the city of Santiago that I decided to send the Count of Altamira there to raise their spirits and from there provide what was necessary for this place.'[7]

Returning to the meeting convened by the Count of Andrade, we have not yet mentioned the second, equally important agreement that was adopted: 'Since the Marquis could not be helped by land but of necessity only by sea, and in that case it would have to be with the galleys, which they risked losing, it was decided to send help in spite of the risk to the galleys.' Andrade had only to contact the Marquis for his plan to send reinforcements by sea to be carried out, 'and so he sent Miguel Izquierdo, a very fine soldier, in a launch, who on reaching the port met with musket fire from the fort and had to turn back'.[8]

There were serious communication problems at that time, for although there was no difficulty about sending a boat at night to the city, which the English had not blockaded, 'on two nights the boat tried to get there, and on both occasions those at the fort thought it was the enemy and shot at them with harquebuses and muskets, so that they had to withdraw'. Andrade's plan could hardly have been more timely, but until he got authorization from the Marquis of Cerralbo, the introduction of reinforcements by sea in Corunna had to be postponed. The Galician nobleman must have felt highly frustrated in the face of such an infuriating obstacle. He was the main person responsible for sending reinforcements to the besieged and was well aware of how urgently they were needed.

During the morning of Thursday, 11 May, the English decided to bombard the arch of Puerta de Aires and succeeded in damaging the shield with the royal arms that was set atop it. Meanwhile, work continued on the construction of the raised bulwark in the monastery of Santo Domingo and on the slow excavation underneath the turret that had been chosen for the explosion. Later they tried their luck with Puerta Real:

> In the afternoon, having gathered in the main street of Pescadería, they attacked Puerta Real, and when the companies came out from their cover they were met with a hail of artillery and musket fire. They all withdrew, leaving a dead ensign in the Market Square with his banner and a ladder they had brought for the attack, and they only managed to come back for them after dark.[9]

---

[6] *Papeles Tocantes a Felipe II*. Vol. II. BN mss 1750, fol. 245.

[7] The Count of Andrade to the King, Bridge of El Burgo, 13 May 1589. AGS. Secretaría de Estado. File 166. Quoted in González Garcés, *María Pita*, p. 330.

[8] *Papeles Tocantes a Felipe II*. Vol. II. BN mss 1750, fol. 245.

[9] *Relación Anónima*. BN mss 3790, p. 216.

That the same day, while the English flag bearer lay opposite the Puerta Real and the harquebusiers were ready to shoot anyone who tried to retrieve him, the English finished making their raised bulwark. The battery they intended to use to breach the wall near Puerta de Aires was ready. Before they began the constant and concentrated artillery fire on the same spot, the besiegers again called for a parley with the aim of finding out if the besieged, who were fearful of the imminent battering and aware that the old defences would not withstand the concentrated pounding of the cannons and sooner or later would collapse, were now willing to surrender the city.

This time the attackers had no opportunity to parley: a harquebusier killed the drummer with a well-aimed shot from the wall. Cerralbo, who may have been worried about possible reprisals against Spanish prisoners, and in any case as mindful as ever of questions of honour, immediately ordered that the harquebusier who had fired the shot be hanged without mercy.

> After their drummer was killed, the enemy brought down the wall covering their artillery and trench and began shooting very rapidly and firing many muskets. After an hour they sent word that they wanted to know why that man had been hanged, for if he was one of theirs they wanted to do the same to all of our men they held prisoner.[10]

It was in this situation that the Marquis ordered that the customary paper placed on the chest of the harquebusier be handed over to them so that they knew the cause of his death. The English, knowing that 'justice had been done to that man, said they would be content to accept our surrender if we agreed to give up the city'.[11] They were told to get out and finish what they had started.

After the thwarted attack on Puerta Real and the castle of San Antón, and once the furious battering of the wall had begun, the forces of both sides increasingly concentrated on the two places where the attackers intended to break through the wall. There followed a terrible and stubborn duel. On the one hand, the English tried to bring the wall down, and on the other, the Spanish were intent on strengthening it from the inside, clearing away the rubble as they did so. 'Inside they cleared everything they could, which kept the women very busy, and it cost us some of our best men.'[12] The constant din of the artillery fire must have had an effect on the minds of the besieged, for whom every shot was a sign that the wall was becoming weaker, and a reminder of the inexorable approach of the impending final assault. Only during the short night did the horrendous pounding of the cannons stop. That was the night that Miguel Izquierdo's launch was driven back for the second time.

On the same day, 11 May, the Archbishop of Santiago de Compostela wrote a letter to the King full of boundless optimism regarding Corunna, saying that 'with God's

---

[10] *Relación Anónima.* BN mss 3790, pp. 216–17.
[11] Ibid., p. 217.
[12] Ibid., p. 218.

help the enemy shall not pass, for the Marquis is well supplied with men, munitions and provisions'. The letter also said that he had advised Andrade, 'since they have so many men, over eight thousand in the field, that he should form a squadron of the best of them to break the enemy's guard at Puerta de la Torre and put reinforcements into the city'.[13] The Archbishop seemed to be unaware of the actual situation and of how few regular soldiers there were,[14] and above all, how few weapons the Count had at his disposal.[15] Perhaps his optimism was a response to the resolve of Cerralbo's words on appointing Andrade ('and so has ordered that the Count of Andrade be told to take his [the Marquis'] role out here in the meanwhile, and that those inside will do their duty'), or to the fact that reinforcements from all over Galicia were converging that day upon Santiago.[16] But the Archbishop, inexperienced in military matters, had no idea how powerful the English Armada was, nor, therefore, how alarming the situation was in Galicia. In any event, his optimism would turn to despair a few days later, when the shadow of Drake threatened the holy city. In Santiago Cathedral, the precaution had been taken two days earlier to hide its most valuable treasures in case the English decided to plunder it.[17]

The following day, Friday 12 May, at four in the afternoon following a long morning filled with thunderous noise, there was a suspicious gathering of troops at the monastery of Santo Domingo. The Marquis ordered the defending companies to be ready both

[13] The Archbishop of Santiago to the King, Santiago, 11 May 1589. AGS. Guerra Antigua. File 248, fol. 94. Quoted in Martínez Salazar, *El cerco*, pp. 70–1 and González Garcés, *María Pita*, pp. 325–6.

[14] On 10 June, with the English Armada in Portugal, the Marquis of Cerralbo, who had been ordered by Philip II to send reinforcements from Galicia, informed him that 'the salaried infantry Your Majesty has in this kingdom are about 900 men'. The Marquis of Cerralbo to the King, Bayona, 10 June 1589. AGS. Guerra Antigua. File 249, fol. 106.

[15] 'And although the Count of Andrade put together all he could during the recent events in Corunna, and the whole kingdom came very willingly to help, the men came without arms, and so were told to leave.' Ibid.

[16] '200 harquebusiers and 20 pikemen are now arriving in good order from the city of Orense with their Captain Pedro Pardo de Ribadeneira, councillor, and a few knights on horseback. Another 600 harquebusiers and well-armed pikemen sent by Don Diego de Sarmiento, son of Don García, Squire of Salvatierra, came and went. Captain Puebla also sent some veteran soldiers with 10 quintals of gunpowder, rope, and lead. From the County of Monterrey came men with 11 quintals of gunpowder and other ammunition.' The Archbishop of Santiago to the King, Santiago, 11 June 1589. AGS. Guerra Antigua. File 248, fol. 94.

[17] On 9 May the Chapter, 'conscious of the danger posed by the presence of the enemy of our holy faith, Draque the Englishman, who is upon the city of Corunna with a very large fleet, and of what might happen, may God neither will it nor permit it, if he came to this city, with the risk to the books of the heritage of this great Apostle, the ornaments and precious objects that there are in this sacred church for his holy service, and wishing to prevent that which God does not wish to happen, ordered Diego Xuarez Tandil and Rodrigo Alemparte, archivists, to remove all the documents, cartularies, privileges, testaments, and books that are the property of this holy church, and any other documents and papers relating to it, to a safe place ... They also ordered García Álvarez, sacristan of the treasure or the custodian of the ornaments of this holy church to take most and the best of them and keep them under the same person's care. They also ordered Don Antonio García and the sacristans of the choir and sacristy of the high altar to bring the books and most valuable things and for all to be kept and put in a safe place.' Antonio López Ferreiro, *Historia de la Iglesia de Santiago de Compostela*, Vol. VIII, Chapter XI, *La Iglesia compostelana en el siglo XVI* (Santiago de Compostela, 1905), Appendices, pp. 202–3. This precautionary removal was probably the cause of the loss of the relics attributed to Saint James the Greater, which remained in an unknown location until 1879.

for an assault with ladders – even though the breach was still small and high up in the wall – and also for what was considered more likely, an explosion under the wall. At that moment

> they blew up the tunnel they had dug from inside the monastery, and either because it fell short or was too weak, it exploded next to the wall on the outside. Not even the stones that flew over the wall and fell into the city did us any harm. Two soldiers were hit on the head, but were not killed.[18]

The cannon then fell silent, although the noise continued ringing in the ears of the defenders after such a bombardment.

This was the first failure of the English tunnelling strategy. As a consequence they did not risk launching the large-scale attack for which they had gathered their forces at the monastery of Santo Domingo, but also because it did not stop the defenders from firing back with harquebuses and muskets and the four cannon they had placed on two turrets facing the monastery.

Meanwhile, the women continued frantically with the repair of the wall, shoring it up with earth and stones that served as a counterweight so that it would not collapse inwards. That would have been the worst thing that could happen to the besieged, for then the way would be clear for the English, and the city would inevitably be invaded. While hundreds of these women kept up their courageous efforts to repair the wall, night fell once more upon Corunna.

At dawn on Saturday, 13 May, after two nights of failed attempts to row silently across the estuary, the brave Miguel Izquierdo, a soldier from the company of Don Juan de Luna who had escaped by sea the night that Pescadería was taken, managed at last to reach Corunna. This time he waited, not without risk, until first light so that the defenders could recognize him, and so 'he entered Corunna and gave the Marquis the Count's message'.[19]

Cerralbo, who fully agreed with Andrade regarding the need to reinforce the garrison immediately and knowing the troops he (Andrade) had, 'sent word to him to give him the Portuguese companies, one of the Asturian ones, and some supplies.'[20] In his journal, Captain Varela increased the number of reinforcements to 'two Portuguese companies and 400 Asturian musketeers'.[21] It seems logical to have wanted to bring at least five hundred men into Corunna. These troops would probably be the best Andrade had to offer, experienced and well-equipped soldiers. Miguel Izquierdo left immediately, this time in broad daylight, and took the letter to the Count. But the Count, anticipating what the Marquis would request and judging quite accurately how urgent it was to send the galleys, had ordered Don Diego de Las Mariñas to 'load them with biscuits in

---

[18]   *Relación Anónima*. BN mss 3790, p. 218.
[19]   *Papeles Tocantes a Felipe II*. Vol. II. BN mss 1750, fol. 245.
[20]   Ibid.
[21]   *Diario del capitán Juan Varela*. BN mss 3790, p. 193.

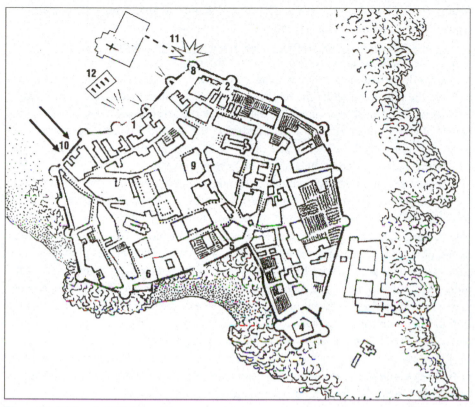

Figure 11.1 Map 4, 6–13 May, Corunna.

1. From Saturday, 6 May, the defenders remained on permanent watch on the walls. The front on the Santo Domingo side, from Puerta Real as far as the mined turret, was under Captain Troncoso, Captain Gómez de Carvajal and Ensign Antonio Barrera.
2. Pedro Ponce's Company.
3. Francisco de Meiranes's Company.
4. Ensign Luna's Company.
5. Ensign Robles's Company.
6. Sergeant Lobo's Company.
7. The Company of Lorenzo Montoto and Payo Mariño.
8. Women embanking and shoring up the wall and the mined turret.
9. The people of Corunna met during the night of 8 May and took their famous oath asking for the protection of the Virgin of the Rosary.
10. On the afternoon of 11 May, the invaders launched an attack with ladders at the Puerta Real, but they were driven back.
11. The English dug a tunnel to end underneath the mined turret. On 12 May, they detonated the mine for the first time, but because the tunnel did not go far enough it caused little damage.
12. The English finished off their raised bulwark on 11 May and began their non-stop bombardment until they breached the wall on 14 May.

Betanzos and bring them to Sada'.[22] Thus that night he was able to put on board the men requested and give orders for the galleys to transport the aid from Sada.

The orders from the Marquis of Cerralbo included another important element, which was for the Galicians under Andrade's command 'to approach the city in order to attack the enemy from within and from without'.[23] The Marquis' idea was for the relief troops to leave the high town while the English were busy repulsing an attack on the wall of Pescadería. It seems that his intention was to make the invaders experience a pincer the people of Corunna had suffered a week earlier. It may now look exceedingly optimistic, given the enormous difference in size of the two opposing armies, but Captain Varela, who witnessed these events, judged it to be 'a sound plan'.[24]

There was work to do that Saturday in Corunna, with the same devastating racket as the previous day, although not as intense. The wall was inevitably losing height at the spot that had been chosen to breach it. At the same time, the English continued with their plan to keep digging the tunnel so as to arrive under the turret. However, as they went in and out of the tunnel, they risked being shot at by the harquebusiers on the wall, for the explosion the previous day had exposed some of the tunnel. 'The enemy repaired the tunnel and finished digging it, although they were in more danger than before because they were exposed as they went in and out and some of them were killed, and from time to time they bombarded us with cannon fire to hamper the repairs to the wall and to batter it.'[25] Amid such anxiety-inducing preparations, night fell. According to the plan, the galleys would bring five-hundred heavily armed men to the city under cover of darkness. They could not have set out at a better time, since everything seemed to suggest that the following day the English would begin their final assault.

[22] *Papeles Tocantes a Felipe II*. Vol. II. BN mss 1750, fol. 246.
[23] *Diario del capitán Juan Varela*. BN mss 3790, p. 193.
[24] Ibid.
[25] *Relación Anónima*. BN mss 3790, p. 219.

Chapter 12

The Mined Turret

With the first red streaks of dawn on Sunday 14 May 1589, the tense and difficult calm that had reigned during the night was shattered by the invaders' resumption of their terrifying pounding of the breach in the wall. Something had gone wrong, for there was no sign of the galleys the defenders had been hoping for. The hopes of the besieged were dashed, while every new roar of artillery fire made them wonder what had happened to their reinforcements. The age of the wall, made of masonry and time-hardened clay, meant there was little hope that it would last for much longer.[1] The army of women who were embanking and shoring up the turret under which the English were finishing their tunnel, were also preparing wooden parapets, fascines and sacks of earth.

The English were firing their cannons from close range and with great accuracy and effectiveness, while the besieged could only watch helplessly the frightening spectacle of the breach in the wall growing from the top downwards. Stone fragments, cannonballs that bounced unpredictably before falling inside the city, coping stones that after centuries in place were dislodged from the wall, all of these left the besieged in a state of growing anxiety. Despite this, they manned the wall opposite the battery at all times and fired back with cannon, harquebuses and muskets in order to obstruct the constant pounding of the breach as much as they could. Meanwhile that morning from El Burgo, headquarters of the reinforcements, Andrade sent a large detachment in search of looters. The expedition was led by Don Lope de Andrade and Sergeant Major Bartolomé Pardo de Cela and consisted mainly of Galician nobles. In Vilaboa, two kilometres inland from the El Burgo base, they came across an English detachment. A major skirmish followed in which 'coming across a group of them they killed twenty-nine or thirty and took a captain prisoner; he was so badly wounded that he died on the way'.[2] This

---

[1]   In a note on the margin of Cerralbo's letter to the King on 11 May, he expresses his concern: 'The walls of this city are made of stone and clay. What has been added to them is stone and earth, and so Your Majesty may judge how impossible it will be to resist any battery, or defend ourselves without walls. For this as well as for other impossibilities, it is a wonder it has lasted this long.' The Marquis of Cerralbo to the King, Corunna, 11 May 1589. AGS. Guerra Antigua, File 248, fol. 81.

[2]   BN mss 1750, fol. 246. *Papeles Tocantes a Felipe II*. Vol. II. We know, thanks to a peculiar court case in 1593, of the important part played by the nobles of Ortigueira and Vivero in this skirmish, including the names of the two captains of the northern army (Gabriel Freire and Pedro Ares de Galdo), and of some of the nobles who took part (Juan Fernández de Aguiar, Rodrigo Alonso Alfeirán and Antonio López de Almendras). In 1593, Bartolomé Pardo de Cela denounced these noblemen for not helping to defend Corunna. The accused argued in their defence that 'the said Bartolomé Pardo cannot deny that on every occasion and every surprise attack, including the siege of the city of Corunna, and every other time there has been a call to arms, we have always been among the first to be there on such occasions with our presence and our arms, and he well knows

Figure 12.1 Medieval wall and turret of Corunna.

new attack, when added to the preceding ones ('in recent days more than three-hundred were killed'[3]) made Norris decide to fix his sights on Andrade. Back in Corunna on that distressing morning, the breach in the wall kept growing 'until 5 or 6 o'clock in the afternoon, by which time it was quite low, although not very wide'.[4]

There was then a silence that turned out to be even more terrifying than the roar of the cannons and the English troops began to assemble en masse in Santo Domingo. Meanwhile, Andrade probably still thought – mistakenly – that the galleys had fulfilled their mission. But now time had run out for sending reinforcements. The crucial moment had arrived, for the English were about to attempt the final assault. Precise orders were given without delay and they were carried out to the letter. With regard to the defence of the breach opened up by the persistent pounding by the cannons, 'the men were ordered to withdraw' and soldiers were positioned 'as sentries with orders to keep quiet and hold fire until the enemy was two-thirds of the way towards attacking the wall'.[5]

This tactic was adopted for several reasons. By letting the attacking troops come so close to the wall before any fighting began, the combination of harquebuses, muskets and the four

that in the skirmish we had with the enemy at Vilaboa, when our headquarters were in El Burgo, we were his friends and acted bravely, and since the truth speaks for itself, and we have been neither rebellious nor cowards, he should not be accusing us'. To make it clear that they have played their part as noblemen, they added: 'As for the other matter of our not being there, it was because we knew that only day labourers and workmen were needed to move stones and earth, and other materials for making forts, and he should not bring up the matter with us, since our Lord the King does not wish, nor does the law allow, that noblemen serve in such tasks nor attend them.' Carlos Breixo et al., *Historia de Ortigueira* (Corunna, 1999), pp. 241–2.

[3]   *Papeles Tocantes a Felipe II*. Vol. II. BN mss 1750, fol. 246.
[4]   *Relación Anónima*. BN mss 3750, p. 219.
[5]   Ibid.

cannon of the turrets near Puerta de Aires would be more effective when directed point-blank against a crowd of men who could get boxed in because of their sheer number. Also, since the breach was 'not very wide', it was likely that a bottleneck would form and the English troops could be hit hard from the wall and the turrets that could fire through the breach.

The only problem with this plan for the defence of the battery was the terrible risk that came from putting everything into resisting to the death for those who were in the breach facing the intense attack based on vastly superior numbers. To this end, Captain Pedro Ponce and Ensign Antonio Herrera were ordered to take twenty hand-picked soldiers and when the alarm was given they were to defend the breach with their lives. At the same time, the rest of the company were to station themselves in the turret nearest to the breach and open fire on the attackers as well as protect the nearby wall with pikes and stones.

With regard to the defence of the mined turret, it was agreed that Troncoso's company would crouch down as close as possible to it, 'such that when it was blown up they would not be harmed'.[6]

Their mission, following any anticipated collapse, was to take immediate charge of anything that was left standing, in order not to allow the attackers to enter via a second breach that would likely be opened up by the explosion. For his part, once an explosion had occurred, Captain Diego de Bazán, son of the Marquis of Santa Cruz, would climb up to the top of Puerta de Aires, with a number of harquebusiers to protect the artillery that had been set up there and fire across the area where the English would launch their assault on the mined turret. In addition, there were about a hundred men to be used as reinforcements from Captain Pedro Manrique's company and another forty not yet assigned 'and that was all the men there were'.[7] Following the alarm call, they were all to be placed under the orders of the Marquis in the small square of the Puerta de Aires 'so that they could get to either of the two batteries as quickly as possible'.[8]

Once everyone was in the best place to get to wherever they were needed after the explosion or the alarm call, a deathly silence came over both armies. Time stood still and the seconds seemed like hours. The English were waiting for the explosion in order to start the attack on both breaches at once. The only activity was taking place under the wall, where the English experts lit the fuse in the tunnel and ran quickly back to the orchard of the Santo Domingo monastery. This time no one shot at them, for on the wall there were only the sentries whose sole orders were to give warning when the English troops had advanced a good way towards the breach that had already been opened up by the artillery. Once the explosives experts had left the tunnel, everyone knew that the short time it would take before the start of the battle – in which many would be killed – depended only on the length of the fuse that was burning away underneath the wall.

'With everyone clear about the damage the mine could do, they were not surprised when it exploded and destroyed a large part of the turret.'[9] The English unleashed a

---

[6] *Relación Anónima.* BN mss 3750, p. 219.
[7] Ibid., p. 221.
[8] Ibid.
[9] Ibid., p. 220.

furious barrage of artillery and harquebus fire from the monastery of Santo Domingo and, as expected, attacked both breaches at once. The explosion of the mined turret proved providential for the defenders of Corunna with their meagre forces. The English attacked this turret 'through an opening that they created in the monastery orchard some 15 paces from the blown up part of the turret'.[10] This meant that the wall of the monastery orchard was very close to the city wall. Such negligence can only be partially explained because the monastery had been built before the introduction of artillery, but as luck would have it, the proximity was about to benefit the defenders in this instance.

The besiegers aimed their assault to coincide with the explosion under the turret. They were certain that, given the location of the charge and (or so they thought) the weak condition of the wall without any embankment, it would collapse inwards. They would then reach the top of the rubble before the defenders, and thus not only would the city fall, but their losses in the assault would also be minimal. But they had not counted on the Herculean job the women had done working against the clock to embank and prop up the turret in a matter of days.

The powerful explosion took place underground only a few metres away from where Troncoso's company were waiting, and made the earth and the wall shake so much that some of the men thought they would be buried alive. It was as if the turret had taken off for a moment and had fallen right back into the same place. There were strict orders that no one was to move until they heard Troncoso's voice above the din. Troncoso wanted to wait until the ground beneath his feet stopped reverberating with the impact of the huge stones that had been violently brought down from where they had been placed centuries earlier by distant ancestors.

The blood-curdling cries of the English, which could be heard immediately after the explosion, turned into pitiable moans when a terrible explosion followed by a shower of rocks and rubble drove back the invaders. 'It pleased God that the embankment placed at the turret forced the mine to explode outwards and killed over 300 of the enemy.'[11] Work on the embankment had started days before, when work also began in the orchard of the Santo Domingo monastery. It functioned properly on 12 May, when the first mine failed, but from 12 May to 14 May, it was strengthened and extended until it reached the top of the turret and filled it to the brim. It was ten metres wide, and its base reached as far as the nearest houses inside the wall. Considering the limited height of the medieval wall, the mined turret and the adjacent wall were, by 14 May, quite a bit larger in width than in height. The angle of the embankment was probably closer to thirty degrees than to forty-five degrees and the turret and this section of the wall had become like a dam holding back not water but stones and earth. The size of the buttress was such that it turned the old wall

---

[10] *Relación Anónima*. BN mss 3750. Santiago Daviña writes '*a el obalado del cubo*' (the oval part of the turret) rather than '*a lo bolado del cubo*' (the blown-up part). Daviña Sainz, *La Coruña*, p. 171.

[11] *Papeles Tocantes a Felipe II*. Vol. II. BN mss 1750, fol. 243–4. Fenner agrees with the figure of three hundred English dead due to the explosion of the mine. William Fenner to Anthony Bacon, 1589. Wernham, *Expedition*, p. 237.

from narrow and hollow to broad and solid.[12] Worse still for the English, the gases from the explosion, in spite of the calculations of the explosives experts, had no way out either towards the inside of the wall or upwards, owing to the weight of the embankment. The force of the explosion, intensified by having no escape route, was unleashed with such violence that it took the path of least resistance: towards the English line. All Norris had succeeded in doing was to create the most extraordinary cannon ever made and to literally fire the stones of the wall, like deadly shrapnel, right into his own face. It is logical to assume that, had he known the size and nature of the embankment, he would not have tried to blow up the turret as he did, but, all the same, it is surprising that he did not foresee this. However, it must be said that at that time there was a chasm between England and Spain in the technical knowledge of siege warfare. The words of Roger Williams in 1590, an experienced military man, and, as we shall see, one of the latecomers to the English Armada, are revealing: 'The Spaniards have such technical superiority in the systems and methods of fortification, that this advantage makes them capable of defending and attacking walled cities with half the number of men used by other armies.'[13]

The English had fallen into their own trap, which was a severe initial setback in the battle of the mined turret, for the invaders who had been buried in the rubble or injured were the best men they had in this attack as well as the most experienced soldiers, and this had an effect on the morale of the second wave. Moreover, the Spanish were free to take up positions in the rubble and by the adjacent wall that was still intact.

Troncoso raised his arm to give the agreed signal and the Spaniards roared their battle cry. 'Captain Troncoso was the first to take his place at this critical moment, for as soon as part of the turret had fallen, he attacked the enemy, charging at them with determination and courage, accompanied by his ensign.'[14] The soldiers who had climbed up on the ruins of the part of the turret that had been blown up were met with the macabre sight of a large number of men lying lifeless on the ground, many of them buried beneath the rocks on which the Spanish were now perched. Others were dying of their injuries. Weapons, helmets and corpses were lying scattered everywhere. The solid heavy rocks had dented armour and crushed bodies as if they were made of butter. The sight made the Spaniards as familiar with death as Charon, the ferryman, who carried souls to Hades across the Styx. The red of the blood, the smell of gunpowder and the pitiful moans of the wounded merged into a single substance in their minds, but Troncoso scarcely had time to gaze upon that hellish landscape, as a new phalanx of infantry came forward against his men.

Fierce fighting followed amid the rubble and the corpses of the attackers. Following Troncoso's orders, Bazán reached the top of the wall. In addition to their initial losses

---

[12] Ensign Pedro Rodríguez Muñiz, superintendent of fortifications, advised the Marquis on the technical aspects of embankments and defence. Five months later he accompanied Tiburzio Spannocchi, royal engineer, when the latter visited Corunna to design its new fortifications. González Garcés, *María Pita*, p. 184.

[13] Roger Williams, *A Brief Discourse of War*, London 1590. Quoted in González-Arnao, *Derrota y muerte*, p. 47.

[14] *Relación Anónima*. BN mss 3750, p. 221.

from the explosion and in combat, the English were now receiving heavy punishment from the harquebusiers on the wall and the turret. They put up a struggle but were forced to flee in terror back to their trenches at the monastery wall. 'Diego Bazán with part of his company and most of the local men there gave them such a welcome that they thought it best to run, leaving their banners in the orchard.'[15]

The invaders now angrily began a heavy bombardment of the breach where the mined turret had been, and this hail of fire exposed the northern end of the walled enclosure near Puerta de Aires, endangering some of the houses in Calle de la Herrería. A squadron of the besieged, which included many women, skilfully put in their fascine parapets without regard to the risk of being shot at through the gaping hole in the mined turret. Thanks to the fact that the English had been repulsed, 'it was possible to make a parapet to provide some kind of cover for the defenders from the harquebuses and muskets in Santo Domingo'.[16]

And so ended the attack on the mined turret, the first great Spanish victory of the campaign of 1589. It would be no pyrrhic victory, such as those achieved in the English Channel by the Spanish Armada ten months earlier.

English losses amounted to approximately four hundred of their best men. Five precious days (and we must not forget the size and the mission of the English army) of hard work had been spent on the complex task of digging and planting mines that turned out to be nothing more than a huge English grave. Even more disheartening was the fact that they had to abandon their dead and wounded, who they could do nothing to help, at the foot of the turret, as Luis de León recognized.[17] As for the Spanish, the ending of the attack on the turret allowed the Marquis to go wherever he was needed with his reinforcement troops.

At the other breach, however, opened after several days of continuous bombardment, things were looking very different. It seemed unlikely that the miracle of the mined turret would be repeated, and the exhaustion of the defending forces who were facing far larger numbers suggested that military logic would inevitably win the day.

[15]   *Relación Anónima.* BN mss 3750, p. 221.
[16]   Ibid., pp. 221–2.
[17]   Ibid., p. 224.

Chapter 13

María Pita

The helmets of the sentries crouching among the masonry from the wall were barely visible. They were responsible for giving a warning when the attacking troops had advanced two-thirds of the way towards the breach that had been opened up by their artillery battery. Suddenly their fluttering banners appeared behind the monastery of Santo Domingo, and with a deafening shout 'they came towards the battery along the street beside the monastery and their trenches'.[1]

The two sentries held their breath as the huge, heavily armed infantry column ran towards the open breach. Moments later they both turned round towards the troops awaiting the order at their feet and shouted as loud as they could. In a flash, Captain Pedro Ponce, Ensign Antonio Herrera and twenty of their men placed themselves in the opening and 'being the first to get there they fought hand-to-hand with their pikes, and kept up the fight'.[2] Meanwhile, the rest of their company climbed the turret next to the breach and the neighbouring wall and set about peppering the English forces at will, firing with their harquebuses at close range. Thus began the struggle for the breach in the wall from the artillery, which was simultaneous with and close to that of the mined turret.

The bulk of the English infantry, which was positioned behind the monastery of Santo Domingo, came along the adjoining street and in successive waves headed for an opening that gave them easy access: 'The enemy found no difficulty coming up through the breach they had made with their artillery.'[3] The invaders' advance was protected by *mantas* (metal-plated boards), armour and shields. At the same time, from their bulwark of Santo Domingo, from the monastery itself and the nearby trenches, their rearguard continued to rake the breach and the men defending it from the wall with a barrage of fire from their artillery, harquebuses and muskets. Losses on the English side were high for, from the top of the walls 'with the harquebuses at the traverses and the artillery from the two turrets they were permanently under fire'.[4] The four guns on the two turrets guarding Puerta de Aires roared constantly at the bulwark and the enemy, but given the size of their army, it hardly made any difference and the English casualties were quickly evacuated and replaced by reinforcements.

On the Spanish side, the numbers of dead and wounded gradually increased although, as one fell, another took his place. However, their limited numbers made their

[1] *Relación Anónima*. BN mss 3750, p. 221.
[2] Ibid., p. 222.
[3] Ibid.
[4] Ibid.

situation increasingly tense. Exhaustion and casualties began to weaken their resistance. Muskets or harquebuses cannot be compared to modern firearms and the same applies to sixteenth-century cannons and their modern equivalent: their firepower was considerably lower. Hence everything about this attack seemed laborious, almost craftsman-like, and carried out not only on the basis of courage and strategic advantage but of the most elementary of limitations, that is, sheer physical endurance. Loading muskets, harquebuses and cannons was a slow process. Eighteen years earlier at the great battle of Lepanto, the Ottoman Admiral Ali Pasha had poured scorn on the harquebuses of the Christian forces in the belief that the Muslims' arrows were much more effective: five could be shot in the time it took to load a harquebus and they were nearly as successful. Inside the wall near the breach, the number of wounded was mounting and, with their stamina spent, they fell back motionless. Meanwhile, from the top of the wall, Diego de Bazán continued to urge on his harquebusiers as they kept on firing. The Marquis could not leave other sections of the wall unprotected, knowing that the enemy might suddenly attack anywhere at any moment. Even so, some troops came to Puerta de Aires to hold the position.

All the while, a number of the women were looking for anything that could be used as ammunition for the guns. With the dwindling number of defenders on guard in other sections, there was a good deal of horse-trading all over the high town to find supplies. Slowly the role of the women was becoming more and more decisive. They would stand by the harquebusiers on the wall helping to reload their weapons, remove the wounded or bring gunpowder, ammunition and, above all, huge quantities of stones to throw at the attackers. Indeed, 'during the whole time this stubborn assault lasted, the women did not stop bringing stones to the soldiers and throwing them themselves from the same battery. Some loaded harquebuses and muskets behind the soldiers and swapped them over so they did not have to stop shooting.'[5] However, this situation could not go on indefinitely.

The English were utterly determined to take the city and stubbornly persisted even though they were suffering a high rate of losses. The greater the resistance they encountered, the more necessary it became to take the city in the name of the men already sacrificed towards that end. In light of what they had found in Pescadería, they believed that in the high town they would find a large quantity of supplies and money that was intended to finance a new expedition against England. The increasingly acrimonious struggle was sufficient proof for them that they were right. Besides, having invested so much time and effort – not to mention so many supplies and men – on the task, they were not about to give up. For what was at stake was not only the desire to damage Spanish pride but also to find the perfect excuse for the delay and the failure to carry out their mission in the eyes of the Queen.[6]

---

[5]   *Relación Anónima*. BN mss 3750, pp. 222–3.

[6]   'The demolition (of Corunna) would have been a great honour and service to Her Majesty.' A communiqué to the Right Honourable the Lord High Treasurer of England, 25 February 1591. Wernham, *Expedition*, p. 297.

Above all, however, the fight was a continuation of the naval operations of the previous year, in which most of the ships and men had taken part. To that end, a huge propaganda campaign had been set up in which the whole of England was fully involved. There was no way that England could fail against those reckless but unyielding defenders of the breach. Morale was too high for that, especially after the ease with which they had landed and taken the prosperous quarter of Pescadería. The army that had been brought together for the occasion was designed for much grander plans and was of a size that called for a decisive end to the siege. Fresh companies formed behind the monastery of Santo Domingo and attacked the breach time and again. The hospitals, monasteries and houses of Pescadería were soon filled with the wounded.

The sight on the Spanish side of the breach was horrific, with countless dead and wounded everywhere, and those that were still fighting looked to be in a pitiful condition. Many of them were wounded. The men, with their armour and clothing broken and torn; the women, enraged and bloodied, looking like wild animals. It was hardly possible to walk on the top of the wall because of so many lifeless bodies. The sight of piles of banners, weapons and corpses on the English side was even more dreadful. Only utter stubbornness on Norris's part could explain why he persisted with such a cruel assault when 'all the time he had four banners on the ground'.[7]

With the firing from the Spanish harquebuses flagging, the English companies began an attack that looked as if it might be decisive. They began to clamber to the top of the breach while their own firing intensified. Hundreds of men braced themselves to go in. An English ensign got to the top and only had to climb down to be inside the city. 'The enemy ensign atop the breach stood there rallying and shouting to his men, until a woman called María Fernández de la Cámara y Pita managed to kill him. This unsettled the men coming up who were fighting the tiring defenders, but the latter were encouraged by what had happened and recovered sufficiently to fight off the enemy.'[8]

It is not surprising that the role of women should be mentioned at this point, towards the end of the attack and when the professional soldiers and militiamen had reached the limit of their endurance. But what is remarkable is the mention of one person by name, particularly in the case of an ordinary non-military figure who is not even of the nobility and, furthermore, is a woman. The reason for the mention is most likely the fact that what she did could in no way go unnoticed for several reasons. The first was that it happened at the top of the breach, where everyone could see and indeed where everyone was looking, for this was where the final outcome of the attack was at stake. The second is that María Pita succeeded in toppling the only banner-bearing ensign who got to the top of the breach.[9] The main mission of an ensign who carried a banner was not to fight in the front line, for the banner would be a major encumbrance. His job was to set an

[7]   *Relación Anónima.* BN mss 3750, p. 222.
[8]   Ibid., p. 223.
[9]   Apart from the previous mention, in the singular, this ensign is mentioned again: 'On was carrying it and got atop the breach was dead.' Ibid., p. 222.

example and his banner was a device to inspire courage in the men who were fighting under it. For this reason, the bearer of the banner on the one side and, on the other, the act of toppling him, both had a collective significance that had an effect on morale. A third possible reason, in spite of what was usual at the time, was that being a woman, which was clear merely from her appearance, actually favoured her being mentioned by name. For a woman to kill an ensign, in other words a professional soldier, was much more 'newsworthy' than if the bearer had been struck down by a regular soldier. One way or the other, the fact is that the *Relación Anónima* (Anonymous Account), the most detailed document on the matter, mentions María Pita by name.

Beyond the undoubted personal merits of this woman from Corunna, this mention of her tells us that during this closing act of the assault on the artillery breach, the women took on roles that were usually reserved for men, out of necessity:

Women and youths went enthusiastically to the most dangerous places, carrying a lot of stones which they hurled at the enemy. They wounded and did a lot of damage to many, and some of the women wore morions (helmets) and held pikes and showed great courage in helping their husbands and the rest of the men at the wall. In this way they did much to help defend the city, and on the day of the main attack which took place at the battery when the mine exploded, much was owed to the women, for many fought like men, encouraging their husbands and other soldiers, and some of them died while they were embanking the turrets and defending the wall ... Those who survived helped take away and bury the soldiers and others who died at the wall. Even though some of them were killed, the others did not lose heart, but rather conducted themselves with ever greater courage and put even more effort into the defence of the city.[10]

Against all the odds, the relatively small number of exhausted defenders managed to hold out until the end. They had harquebuses, muskets, pikes, swords and cannons, but especially large quantities of stones. Thus 'the English were forced to withdraw after going all out in attack for more than two hours with great determination and resolve. They left behind many weapons, all of which, together with the banner, came into our hands.'[11]

The Marquis of Cerralbo gave the first orders to maintain the defence of the entire walled enclosure. The elderly brought more fascines, made out of anything they could find, to build a parapet with which to close the breach, and the wounded were accommodated as best they could in the hospital of the Collegiate Church of Santa María and in the beds of private homes in the high town.

---

[10] Archivo General de Galicia (P. sig. 16-nº Iº), quoted in Martínez Salazar, *El cerco*, pp. 54, 61–2. English sources also mention the terrible damage caused by stones: 'There was divers assaults given by our captains and brave English gentlemen, which were slain with musket shot and bruised so sore with stones from the walls that it was impossible to endure it.' William Fenner to Anthony Bacon, 1589. Wernham, *Expedition*, p. 237. It could be said that to a degree the English were driven back by women armed with stones.

[11] *Relación Anónima*. BN mss 3750, p. 222.

Figure 13.1 María Pita, by Árturo Fernández Cersa, Corunna Council Offices.

Several depictions of María Pita have appeared over the years. They all bring us closer to what took place in May 1589, for when the women fought side by side with the militia, they gave rise to countless other battle scenes. María Fernández de la Cámara Pita distinguished herself in battle and was amply rewarded for it, but above all she symbolizes the resistance of the people, especially the strong and well-armed women who had been roused to save the city.

Apart from the civilian losses, 'in this attack on the city the enemy killed 150 of our best soldiers who had fought their best that day'.[12] However, English losses were considerable.[13]

---

[12] *Relación Anónima.* BN mss 3750, p. 224.

[13] Data relating to the English are few and fragmentary. We know that captains, knights, lieutenants and soldiers died in these attacks, but we know only a few names: Captain Spencer, artillery lieutenant, and

In order to provide a full account of what happened in Corunna on 14 May, it should be acknowledged that the besieged had the benefit of three groups of defenders. First and foremost was that of the professional soldiers, the regulars. It must be said that the famous Tercio regiment system of organizing the Spanish army worked well within the walls, converting the besieged population into something like a Tercio themselves. The second group was the militia and the male population in general, who fought spiritedly alongside the military, thereby doubling the number of troops with men who did their duty. Third came the female population, and the fact that this group was not originally taken into account is, no doubt, one of the main reasons why the city survived, for the women took on a huge, unending task that no one else could have done without leaving the walls undefended. From the outset, they constantly provided supplies for the defenders.[14] They were the ones who pulled down the walls of houses to provide the endless and vital supply of stones that were one of the main weapons used by the besieged to fend off the attack at the foot of the wall. Under military supervision, not only did they gather the stones and earth to make the embankments for the mined turret, but they also actually built the embankments themselves.[15] Furthermore, after each attack they made fascines and built parapets by using all the wood they could find in their homes, including crosspieces from beds and wardrobes. The women also gathered all the pewter[16] available in town to be used to make ammunition. Thanks to the women, the besieged were never short of stones to hurl down on the attackers below during the several assaults endured by the city. Indeed, they were the ones responsible for a good deal of the deadly bombardments of stones. Towards the end, when it became necessary, many of them took up the weapons of their dead, wounded, captured or missing husbands and fought to the death. They killed and they died. And their womanhood is relevant to the boundless courage they showed, based on two constants of human nature. First,

Captain Sydenham, but we have no names of dead knights. As for the wounded, we know about Colonel John Sampson, Captains Cook, William Poole, John Winall, Seagar, Boyer and Thomas Jonson and Lieutenants Klifford and Somers, who died shortly afterwards. William Fenner, in his letter to Anthony Bacon, mentions 290 dead soldiers from the ranks, in addition to the three hundred killed by the explosion of the mine. William Fenner to Anthony Bacon, 1589. Wernham, *Expedition*, p. 237. What is clear is that this army insisted on taking the city and did not succeed, but – as was shown two days later in El Burgo – it did not easily let go of its prey, however hard the punishment. In any event, over six hundred men died that day at Corunna and the number of wounded was even higher. The English Armada's star was beginning to fade.

[14] 'And these women, however distinguished many of them were, carried jugs full of water from the wells up to the wall, and others full of wine, and biscuits and supplies so that all the soldiers and other men defending it did not have to leave to fetch these things.' Archivo General de Galicia, (P. sig. 16-nº Iº). Quoted in Martínez Salazar, *El cerco*, p. 61.

[15] 'To embank the turrets and the wall ... everyone, young and old, took part and were helped by the women and their children, carrying huge amounts of stones, barrels of earth, wooden pontoons and other essentials every day.' Ibid.

[16] Pewter is a zinc, lead, and tin alloy, much used at the time for household items. 'When the Marquis knew that they were running short of ammunition, he ordered everyone to gather all the pewter, be it plates, bowls or jars, from the townsfolk. A large amount was collected and all of it used to make ammunition.' *Memorial de la ciudad de La Coruña a Felipe II*. Corunna, 26 July 1589. AGS. Guerra Antigua 250, fol. 132. Quoted in Martínez Salazar, *El cerco*, pp. 79–86 and González Garcés, *María Pita*, pp. 353–5.

they must have felt an intense hatred for those who had killed their husbands, destroyed their city and their homes – in short, ruined their lives. Even more than that, though, the women embodied one of the most fundamental elements of humanity. With little regard for their own lives, as any mother would do, they fought to the death for their children.

However, while all of this was taking place, another tough battle was being fought which was no less crucial. Control of the castle of San Antón was essential for the survival of Corunna and the castle was being put to the sternest test it had had to face in all of its remarkable history.

Chapter 14

San Antón and El Burgo

From the day they arrived, the English were aware of the special strategic importance of the castle of San Antón. Not only did it prevent any approach to the high town by sea, but it also commanded the port and the bay of Corunna. In addition, with the old dock of Parrote under its protection, it made a naval blockade of the city impossible. The city had its own 'Sea of San Antón' where galleys bringing reinforcements could dock safely. Consequently, the English had launched two major attacks already, at dusk on Friday, 5 May with four ships, and on Wednesday, 10 May with launches equipped with artillery. On 14 May 1589, the most celebrated day in the history of Corunna, the English launched their major assault on the castle, in keeping with their tactic of simultaneous offensives.

The defence of San Antón had been entrusted to the companies of Captain Jerónimo de Monroy and militia Captain Francisco de Meiranes. They were joined by Martín de Bertendona and his men after they had abandoned the galleon *San Juan*, but not without first preparing a few powder kegs that turned out to be a deathtrap for the Englishmen who attempted to retrieve the ship's banners. As in the city, regular soldiers and townsmen came together to form a troop that combined the experience of the former and the resolve of the latter, who were fighting for their families and their property. The Spanish were expecting the assault and prepared to resist as best they could. Thus, 'in anticipation of the assault, those in the castle had shut themselves inside and surrounded the piers with trees and masts, making it very difficult to reach the castle or even cause much damage to it with artillery'.[1]

The sounds of the battle being fought at the foot of Puerta de Aires could clearly be heard from the bulwark that was being built. The Spanish kept themselves occupied that day by blocking any places where the enemy could land. They awaited news from Corunna, which resisted the attack valiantly and against all the odds. The survival of the fortress was essential for the city, for if it were taken by the attackers the besieged would be hopelessly lost. But its defenders were also aware that their resistance could be in vain if the city fell into English hands.

The English launches then set out on their final attempt against the islet, for 'while the city was being attacked, up to forty large launches with men and artillery and smaller ones with men only departed from Pescadería and rowed hard towards the fortress of San Antón'.[2] Violent barrages of artillery fire then came from the castle's guns but,

---

[1] *Relación Anónima*. BN mss 3750, pp. 223–4.
[2] Ibid., p. 223.

unfortunately for the English, they were joined by those of the fortress, as in previous attacks. For, 'together with the four cannons on the wall of the city, which face the port, they were sent such a barrage that with two of their boats destroyed and many of their men killed, they all fled wherever they could without waiting for orders'.[3] The defence of the castle of San Antón was no less bloody than that of the city. The defenders left their cover and some of them were killed, but the English attempt was aborted thanks to the invaluable help of the fortress' artillery. The attackers returned to their base in Pescadería after suffering a number of casualties.

Evening came on that unforgettable day of 14 May 1589. The town's defences had taken a lot of punishment and the Marquis of Cerralbo himself did not believe they could possibly withstand another day like it:

> The following night a sergeant major went out through the battery to inspect it and see from the outside what state it was in, and came back in through the same battery. He found that both [the breaches] where the enemy had attacked were easy to break through, and in the blown up part of the mine found some wounded enemy soldiers who were still alive and others dead among the rubble. Since they were shooting at us through the ruins of the mines from the Santo Domingo monastery, all that night was spent working to raise the embankment.[4]

So the besieged could not even rest that night, but slaved away, propping up improvised parapets in the places left unprotected by the attacks of the English battery and the mine. All the defenders had in their favour was the exhaustion the attackers were already suffering.

There is no way of knowing what the English would have done had they taken Corunna that Sunday, but given their obsession with making their invasions profitable by looting, it is not impossible that they would have decided to march on Santiago de Compostela. The fear in the hearts of the Galicians stemmed from the certainty that Corunna would fall. When it did not do so, the position of the English forces in the city's peninsula and the bay where their fleet lay at anchor was far from secure, so they could not move very far. Besides, they had been weakened by the loss of troops, they were exhausted after the battle and the euphoria following the taking and sacking of Pescadería had given way to a new awareness of their situation, which did not look as promising as on the morning of 8 May. In fact, on Monday, 15 May, 'the two enemies did not fight, while in the city all that was done was quickly to repair what had been damaged'.[5]

That made it possible to do some repairs to the defences of Puerta de Aires and there was also the hope that the English attack would be limited to Corunna and its surrounding area. It was also a day of mourning for the invaders, for from the battle of the previous day one of the most important men in the expedition, Mr. Spencer, an artillery

[3]   *Relación Anónima.* BN mss 3750, p. 223.
[4]   Ibid., p. 224.
[5]   Ibid.

lieutenant in the English Armada, was among their many casualties. The English took some time to give him the last honours and to bury their other dead.

That Monday there was someone who had a frustrating problem, for

> seeing that the galley captains had not brought in help during the last two nights, the Count of Andrade went in person to speak to them. Using both inducements and threats, he promised freedom for the galley slaves and having left there with them Don Pedro de Sotomayor and Don Juan de Otalora, judge of the Audiencia Real, to urge them on and make them deliver the help that night, he returned to his lodgings.[6]

Andrade's inability to impose his authority on Captains Pantoja and Palomino is surprising, especially considering that he had been appointed first in command by Cerralbo himself from the beginning of the siege. If this was not enough, 'His Majesty sent his letters patent to the Count of Andrade so that all would obey him, and wrote to the prelates, lords and cities of the kingdom to ensure that they did so.'[7] It is here that the minor role played by the galleys emerges as one of the major mysteries of the siege. They could have brought in reinforcements the night before the main assault, but did not do so. Sailing from the point of Seixo Branco to the castle of San Antón within sight of the enemy fleet was not as risky as it might seem, for it was only four kilometres and the last third of the trip would have had the protection of guns from the castle. Besides, since the galleys are rowing ships they would have had an unbeatable advantage, provided that they waited for the wind to blow from the north, for no sailing ship would have been able to approach them. Furthermore, if any English launches had tried to intercept them, they would have been no match for the two galleys armed with artillery, harquebusiers and musketeers. Even without counting the cannon, a musket can hit a target a hundred metres away and its full range was even greater.

The galleys could have managed it and the various commentaries on their role are all in agreement. There are three main accusations against them: first, on 5 May they allowed the English cannon that destroyed the *San Juan*, the *San Bartolomé* and the *Sansón* to be transported by sea. Second, they fled to Ferrol and left the bay of Corunna undefended. Third, they did not bring in reinforcements when they could have done so. Martín de Bertendona called for the captains of the galleys to be given exemplary punishment and we already know what Varela had to say. No one has written in their defence, but there is a strange mystery surrounding it all, including the warm reception given to them by Cerralbo once the siege was over.

On Tuesday, 16 May, with the breaches in the Puerta de Aires section repaired as best they could be, the English changed their strategy in view of the damage they had suffered when attacking in that area. They decided to attack from the east. Although the land here was narrow between the wall and the sea, it offered a new opportunity given

---

[6]   *Papeles Tocantes a Felipe II*. Vol. II. BN mss 1750, fol. 246.
[7]   Ibid.

that the wall was weak at that spot. So 'some banners were seen leaving Santo Domingo monastery and heading for that of San Francisco, which is on the other coast and outside the wall, for this monastery was very close to the city on that side and it was where the wall was weakest'.[8]

The Spanish reacted in time and before the English could establish a new bridgehead at the San Francisco monastery, 'the Marquis immediately decided to set the monastery and its churches on fire. Because they did not have much time, only a small part of it burned, but it was enough to deter the enemy from going in'.[9]

However, on this day, Tuesday, 16 May, the English turned some of their attention towards the Count of Andrade's troops – who had been harrying them for days – and attacked in force towards the bridge of El Burgo. The present-day bridge of Pasaje might cause us to forget the strategic importance of the El Burgo bridge, which was the only means of access by land to the municipality of Oleiros on the other side of the estuary. The Count of Andrade had established his headquarters in that bottleneck, which would have to be crossed by the English if they wanted to extend their pillaging beyond Culleredo.

The Count's strategy was to send patrols from the bridge to attack the more or less uncontrolled bands of English troops who, due to the expedition's lack of provisions, roamed the area in search of booty. The English had lost quite a few men as a result of this and so, with any greater undertakings ruled out, they decided to try and take the bridge, this time in battle order and led by their captains.

Andrade had been given very strict orders regarding his mission. He was supposed to assist Corunna as much as he could, certainly, but that was not his main task; his main task was to prevent the destruction of Santiago de Compostela, so he could not risk the few troops he had in an encounter of uncertain outcome that would put this mission in jeopardy.[10] Wisely, Andrade held a strong position at the bridge of El Burgo and from there he sent detachments to wear down the enemy without risking his position. Holding this enclave was indeed part of his mission, since the bridge was on the only route to Compostela. In one of the ironies of history, even today the bridge is on what is known as the *Camino Inglés* or English Way (of St James), which British pilgrims take following their arrival at the port of Corunna. Andrade's strategy bore fruit every day, but especially two days earlier, in the bitter skirmish of Vilaboa.

It was in the battle of El Burgo that Andrade fought to the death for Santiago and, in so doing, did Corunna a huge favour. He was not the first Andrade to defend the place

---

[8] *Relación Anónima.* BN mss 3750, p. 225.

[9] Ibid.

[10] 'Aiding that city should be undertaken with such caution that the enemy should not be attacked unless there is the certainty of accomplishing what is intended without suffering any harm. If by taking risks the rescue force were defeated, the enemy would be free to destroy the hinterland, and particularly the city of Santiago, which would be much worse than failing to aid Corunna, considering the antiquity of the holy veneration of the relics therein.' The King to the Count of Andrade, San Lorenzo del Escorial, May 1589. AGS. Guerra Antigua. File 257, fol. 255.

against the English, for Fernán Pérez de Andrade had shut himself inside the walls with his troops generations earlier, in the summer of 1386, when the Duke of Lancaster landed with 12,000 men to enforce his dynastic right to the crown of Castile. The people of Corunna, supported by Don Fernán, closed the city gates and vowed to open them only if Santiago did the same. Lancaster headed for Santiago de Compostela, where he established himself briefly, and then moved on to the Castilian tableland in an expedition that would also end badly.

Returning again to the sixteenth century, the war was not going well for the English. Among many consequences the defeat on 14 May had one very clear one: the English Armada unexpectedly found itself without control of the port of Corunna, a port sufficiently safe from storms and protected from land-based attacks to enable re-embarkation to be undertaken safely. Thus, the last men to abandon the city would leave behind a centre of resistance and have to skirt the estuary for more than two kilometres, during which time they were vulnerable to attack by Andrade from inland. In fact, Andrade did not have enough troops to mount a significant operation but, at the same time, Norris could not be entirely sure of that.[11] Norris may even have been informed of the imminent arrival of reinforcements for Andrade. In any event, among other objectives the English march on El Burgo was to ensure the safe boarding of their troops.[12] Whatever its aim, it would ultimately provide the Galicians with the opportunity to fight:

When the enemy saw what little effect they were having in the city, and with the intention of embarking, as we later learned from a Portuguese who deserted to the Count's camp, and with the news that three companies of regular soldiers plus two light cavalry ones would join the Count the following day, sent from Porto by *Maestre de Campo*[13] Pedro Bermúdez, they decided to dislodge the Count, and so they set out on the Tuesday with 4,000 hand-picked men for the bridge of El Burgo. When the Count heard of this, he made his men ready, however inexperienced and ill-armed, and encouraging them as best he could, he sent one hundred harquebusiers and musketeers to the other side of the bridge and waited for the enemy.[14]

Andrade was aware of the movements of the English from the outset and used every trick he knew to take maximum advantage of his position. His first order was to send a hundred harquebusiers to lie in ambush and shoot at the long English columns from

---

[11]   Several English sources point to Norris's belief that Andrade's detachment was substantial. For example, Fenner in his letter mentions the figure of 4,000 Spaniards billeted in El Burgo. William Fenner to Anthony Bacon, 1589. Wernham, *Expedition*, p. 237. John Evesham put the number of Spanish at 8,500. John Evesham's account of the voyage. Ibid., p. 230. Norris and Drake, in a letter to the Queen's Privy Council written on 17 May, refer to 15,000. Norris and Drake to the Privy Council, 17 May 1589. Ibid., p. 147.

[12]   As Wingfield would state in his famous discourse. Discourse by Anthony Wingfield, 9 September 1589. Ibid., p. 265.

[13]   A rank created by Emperor Charles V (Charles I of Spain), only subordinate to captain general and given to the commander of a Tercio regiment [translator's note].

[14]   *Papeles Tocantes a Felipe II*. Vol. II. BN mss 1750, fol. 246.

a distance. They were to use the fortified bridge on the other side of the river as their rearguard for withdrawal. To judge by the way in which this was reflected in English sources, the harquebusiers were as effective as usual.[15] After this, the harquebusiers returned to their positions, that is, to the trenches flanking the bridge on the other side of the river, in order to catch in the crossfire anyone attempting to cross it.[16] Norris's decision provided the Count with the unique opportunity to face as many thousands of men as Norris cared to send against him and his tiny professional force plus a handful of Galician knights. The numerical superiority of the English was overwhelming, but so too was the strategic advantage of defending a 130-metre long Romanesque bridge, which, as can still be seen today, is barely three metres wide. In any event, however advantageous his position, Andrade had only a small core of veteran soldiers and most of them had embarked on the galleys with the aim of reinforcing Corunna by sea, as per the Marquis of Cerralbo's orders. In this respect, the words of the Archbishop of Santiago, informing Philip II of what had happened in El Burgo in a letter dated 18 May, are significant:

> The news is that yesterday, Tuesday the 16th, the enemy, having learned that two companies of good soldiers of Your Majesty's army, one of Portuguese noble-men and another formed from the two Asturian ones, had been dispatched to aid Corunna by sea, and that the remaining men were not experienced soldiers, they sent eleven banners from Pescadería, where they are quartered, and attacked our camp.[17]

Sadly for the Spanish, while Andrade fought desperately with a small number of men to defend the narrow bridge, his five hundred best men, all well-armed, sat idly in Sada, waiting for Captains Pantoja and Palomino to show enough courage to take them to El Parrote. The wait turned out to be in vain.

The English got to the bridge and launched their first attack: 'As the enemy started to cross the bridge, the Count of Andrade ordered the harquebusiers to fire on them from the trenches, and he charged towards the bridge armed with sword and buckler, followed by the Count of Altamira and a few knights. The enemy withdrew.'[18] It was certainly rash to attack the stone bridge under an 'incredible hail of bullets',[19] and they became

---

[15]   The Earl of Sussex, in a letter to Walsingham, puts the number of harquebusiers at 'seven or eight hundred', skirmishing along an entire mile. The Earl of Sussex to Walsingham, 26 May 1589. Wernham, *Expedition*, pp. 158–9. For their part, Norris and Drake describe the situation as follows: 'And encountering with them, they continued to fight the space of three-quarters of an hour and then we forced them to retire to the foot of a bridge.' Norris and Drake to the Privy Council, 17 May 1589. Ibid., p. 147.

[16]   'And after a skirmish which kept the harquebusiers busy for almost half an hour, they withdrew to this other side of the bridge where the Count was, ordering and encouraging the men with the Count of Altamira.' *Papeles Tocantes a Felipe II*. Vol. II. BN mss 1750, fol. 246.

[17]   The Archbishop of Santiago to the King, Santiago, 18 May 1589. AGS. Guerra Antigua. File 248, fol. 96. Quoted in Martínez Salazar, *El cerco*, pp. 77–9 and in González Garcés, *María Pita*, pp. 331–2.

[18]   *Papeles Tocantes a Felipe II*. Vol. II. BN mss 1750, fol. 247.

[19]   Discourse by Anthony Wingfield, 9 September 1589. Wernham, *Expedition*, p. 264.

an easy target, especially when they were near the foot of the bridge, where men heavily armed with pikes and swords were waiting for them, defending a three-metre-wide passage. The English began to suffer casualties without causing any in return, and so they turned back. There was nothing there that was worth so many lives. The only thing that could justify the effort of taking such an easily defended position was the common good of the army as a whole, or else that it cleared the way to wealthy Compostela, the destruction of which would have been a milestone in the history of Protestant iconoclasm, for it would have been more difficult to justify such an ill-advised operation in the name of honour. Norris, however, prepared a more ambitious attempt and sent his men forward once again. This second, stronger wave resulted in a bloody skirmish in which they managed to reach the bank where the Spanish were, but in the end the defenders were able to regain the bridge through some fierce fighting. By the end of the battle, 150 English soldiers had died and many more were wounded.[20] With his reinforcement troops, Andrade was certainly supporting Corunna, where the sounds of the battle could be heard, albeit muffled by the distance.

It was then that, given the difficult and heroic nature of the attempt to take the bridge, the English knights claimed their glory. They would certainly have had the toughest armour possible. For them, a sense of honour and rivalry, a determination not to be outdone, were of the essence. A new wave of attack was prepared and this time the brave knights advanced together three by three, shoulder to shoulder, with armour and pikes, towards death or victory. The flower of the army was then seen on the bridge together with the English nobility: Sir Edward Norris, Colonel Thomas Sidney, Captain Cooper and several other captains.[21]

> And Don Martín de Ayala went to the Count, and seeing him with no more arms than those mentioned, told him to ride to the trenches to stop the inexperienced men should they start to run away. The Count and his cousin of Altamira did so, and then a large number of the enemy marched on the bridge, which had been fought over for an hour and a half. The Count's men began to withdraw, and the Count, his cousin and a few knights and noblemen stayed to face the enemy in the rearguard.[22]

It then became clear that if the nobles and veteran soldiers gave in to the determined English, the bulk of the Spanish troops, consisting largely of peasants, could well be cruelly annihilated. Weighing up the situation, the Count, who was 'unconvinced that he would be able to resist the enemy, had given the men permission to go to their homes and villages and to defend them'.[23] Andrade ordered the disbandment of his improvised

---

[20] 'Coming to the river's side, he entered upon the bridge and was beaten back, and so the second time, with the loss of about 150 men.' William Fenner to Anthony Bacon, 1589. Wernham, *Expedition*, p. 237.

[21] As described in several English documents. Ibid., pp. 159, 237, 264.

[22] *Papeles Tocantes a Felipe II*. Vol. II. BN mss 1750, fol. 247.

[23] Francisco Arias Maldonado to the King, Puentedeume, 17 May 1589. AGS. Guerra Antigua. File 248, fol. 101. Quoted in González Garcés, *María Pita*, p. 331.

army in good time and his men returned to their homes to avoid being killed. The final attempt on the bridge was therefore successful and the English came across it. Their triumph was made complete by the fact that in addition to victory it resulted in the dissolution of Andrade's improvised army of peasants.

It was a very costly victory, however. We know the names of three captains who were killed: Cooper, Edward Pew and Spigott.[24] We also know of knights who died,[25] and that Edward Norris, Colonel Sydney, Captains Herdan, Barton and Fulford were wounded[26] (the latter later died from illness).[27] As for the number of dead soldiers, we know of the 150 who died in the second wave and at least that number died in the third, so there were probably no less than three hundred. It is reasonable to assume that the number of wounded was greater. It was therefore a pyrrhic victory, and although the figures were falsified in triumphalist accounts (Wingfield later wrote that only Cooper and one soldier died,[28] and other accounts put the number of Spanish dead as high as 1,500),[29] it did generate some internal criticism, such as that of Lord Talbot: 'We won a very narrow bridge. But, as I hear privately, not without the loss of as many of our men as of theirs, if not more, and without the gain of anything unless it were honour and the acquainting of our men with the use of their weapons.'[30] It can therefore be said that the Spanish reinforcement troops who fought at El Burgo amply accomplished their mission and were able to take advantage of exactly the right moment to carry out their task of wearing the enemy down. There is no denying the courage and resolve shown by the English in completing such a difficult action, but it is rather more difficult to justify the attack. They could have marched to Oza in combat formation, protected by their ships' artillery. As for the other possible reason, clearing the way towards Compostela, despite the anxiety felt by the Galicians about this, the English did not even try.

'Seeing that with the men he had he could not hold the enemy, [Andrade] slowly withdrew towards Betanzos. Some thirty-six of his men died and there were some wounded. Many more of the enemy were killed.'[31] The English troops collected a lot of weapons and supplies following the departure of the Spanish, for the Count's army 'was forced to withdraw, leaving behind almost all its baggage and even the food it had ready to eat'.[32] After the defeat, Andrade 'arrived in Betanzos' with his regular soldiers, 'and ordered Sergeant Major Bartolomé Pardo and other captains to get their men together and keep them there for when he returned from Santiago, where the Count spent that night'.[33]

---

[24] William Fenner to Anthony Bacon, 1589. Wernham, *Expedition*, p. 238.
[25] John Evesham's account, probably July 1589. Ibid., p. 230.
[26] Discourse by Anthony Wingfield, 9 September 1589. Ibid., p. 264.
[27] List of Captains Killed, 1589. Ibid., p. 213.
[28] Discourse by Anthony Wingfield, 9 September 1589. Ibid., p. 264.
[29] Ibid., p. xli.
[30] Lord Talbot to the Earl of Shrewsbury, 5 June 1589. Ibid., p. 168.
[31] *Papeles Tocantes a Felipe II*. Vol. II. BN mss 1750, fol. 247.
[32] The Archbishop of Santiago to the King, Santiago, 18 May 1589. AGS. Guerra Antigua. File 248, fol. 96.
[33] *Papeles Tocantes a Felipe II*. Vol. II. BN mss 1750, fol. 246.

Once the English had taken the bridge of El Burgo, Andrade's main concern, as well as that of Philip II, was that they would attack the most venerated and symbolic resting place of the Apostle St James. This would have been an unprecedented outrage against everything Spain's Catholic Monarchy represented.[34] This was also Andrade's reason for riding at once to Santiago, now the most prized jewel for which he was responsible. Night fell as he and his men approached the holy city.

---

[34] In a letter dated 27 May, after the attack on Corunna had failed, Philip II wrote to his nephew the Archduke Alberto, Viceroy of Portugal: 'What hurt the most was knowing that they were so close to the body of the Apostle St James, and I further away than I would have wished in order to be able to help'. Quoted in González-Arnao, *Derrota y muerte*, p. 81.

Chapter 15

Full Sail to Lisbon

On the night of Tuesday, 16 May, the Count of Andrade was not the only one with an urgent mission. In Pescadería the English, who were reluctant to put their army at risk again in another bloody attempt on the wall, took to the notorious incendiary skills they had developed while specializing in the sacking and burning of cities. This activity had become highly profitable, for they had set up the 'right to burn', whereby the inhabitants of the cities under attack had to pay in order to avoid being put to the torch. And so after the sun had set,

> during the first part of the night when the tide was low, the enemy tried to burn the city by putting tarred sticks under the corbels of the houses that projected over the wall in the part guarded by Lorenzo Montoto. He defended it well enough to cause the English to run off, unable to withstand the musket fire and the stones that were hurled at them and leaving behind the sticks and incendiary material they had brought, which were gathered and taken into the city the next morning.[1]

While Andrade rode to Santiago and with the incendiary attack thwarted, the Marquis of Cerralbo became increasingly concerned about the unaccountable lack of reinforcements he had ordered to be sent via the galleys. It was not only that these reinforcements were urgently needed by the city's garrison, but supplies of both food and ammunition were also becoming scarce. He therefore insisted once more on having such aid delivered, for it was essential if resistance was to be continued.

> That same night during the second watch, the Marquis ordered Francisco Arias Maldonado, judge of the Real Audiencia, to go out to sea in a small boat and land before dawn in the part of the town they call Mera on the other side of the bay to make sure that Corunna's desperate situation was known everywhere and to ask for help without delay, for none had arrived during the battles fought by its defenders and townsfolk for two weeks, in spite of it having been requested on the first day the enemy arrived.[2]

After an uneasy night, on Wednesday, 17 May, the English radically changed their approach: apparently wishing to put an end to the siege, 'they sent a captain to offer an exchange of prisoners'.[3] This was probably a sign that, following the rout of the

[1] *Relación Anónima.* BN mss 3750, p. 225.
[2] Ibid., pp. 225–6.
[3] Ibid., p. 226.

Count's army at El Burgo and the sacking of the area surrounding the bridge, they had finally given up any intention of taking Corunna or marching on vulnerable but wealthy Santiago de Compostela. However, the arrogance of the Marquis of Cerralbo remained undimmed throughout the entire siege, and 'they [the English] were told to finish what they had started, and that [the exchange of prisoners] could be discussed later'.[4] The English then began to withdraw their artillery and started a systematic act of destruction in which they set fire to windmills 'just for the sake of causing damage'.[5]

Meanwhile, Andrade, who had arrived in Santiago the night before, tried to calm the anxieties of the people, who did not yet know that the apparent intention of the English was to leave Galicia shortly. The fear prevalent in Santiago was clearly expressed in the following letter from the Archbishop of Santiago to the King:

> Today marks the arrival of the Count of Andrade, Count of Altamira, and Don Martín de Ayala (for Pedro de Sotomayor remained with the two galleys in Betanzos, in order to have aid sent to the Marquis in Corunna), and after meeting them, it seems that the Count has decided, in his capacity as Your Majesty's General, to rally the men who dispersed yesterday, and with the five companies, three infantry and two cavalry, that are five leagues from here in Poulo, to prepare themselves and return to face the enemy, at least to prevent them from doing so much damage about the land, burning churches, houses and everything they encounter. Believing that Your Majesty has the ports of Portugal well fortified, given the intentions of Dom António Prior of Crato, there is fear that the enemy proposes to reach Portugal through Galicia with 6,000 men, crossing the Miño wherever they can, and to desecrate this Holy Church, steal from it and sack the city, which, after such a long period of peace, is so unprepared for war that if God and the patronage of the Holy Apostle do not protect it, I can see no way that it can be defended. I therefore beg Your Majesty to send men of arms, so that this holy body of the Apostle, for our sins, will not be desecrated by these heretic barbarians.[6]

The Count took urgent measures to organize the desperate defence of a city devoid of any military structure. One of his main orders was 'to send three companies of regular soldiers and 500 militiamen to be brought by Don Fernando de Andrade and Don Rodrigo de Mendoza, and two of light cavalry, to be positioned at the bridges of Sigüeiro, for he had received word that the enemy would be heading for Santiago'.[7] Andrade was aware that, rather than provide a defence of the city, the English had to be stopped at a point they would have to pass through on their way there. That was why he placed them in Sigüeiro: he would try to prevent them from crossing the River Tambre.

---

4   *Relación Anónima*. BN mss 3750, p. 226.
5   Ibid.
6   The Archbishop of Santiago to the King, Santiago, 18 May 1589. AGS. Guerra Antigua. File 248, fol. 96.
7   *Papeles Tocantes a Felipe II*. Vol. II. BN mss 1750, fol. 247.

However, far from marching on Compostela, the English were still intent on destroying Corunna and carefully prepared another major incendiary attack, for

> at nightfall, in the same place and at the same time as the night before, they tried once more to burn down the city. They came in large numbers, with the support of the infantry; but it was only forty or fifty of them who attempted it with real determination, although those defending the wall drove them back with muskets, harquebuses and stones, but they came back four times protected and covered by their infantry, until many of them, some of them officers, were killed from the wall, at which point they called a halt and left four tarred sticks leaning on the wall as well as many bloodied weapons that our soldiers collected.[8]

By Thursday, 18 May, the English had been in Corunna for two weeks. They had to try and complete their mission, however, and their growing frustration at being unable to take the city caused them 'in desperation to set fire to the monastery of Santo Domingo from all sides, but not before they had desecrated its church and fired at the images of its saints. Then they put the whole quarter of Pescadería to the torch, but luckily most of it did not burn.'[9]

Then they got on board, 'without even a dog to bark at them' in the words of Bertendona. This was reprehensible from the defenders' point of view, since this is a time when an army is at its most vulnerable as they cannot all board at the same time and the last to do so are dangerously exposed to attack. Following the English victory in El Burgo, however, those who might have attacked them had been dispersed. So, with no one to trouble them, 'they got their artillery and other cargo on board followed by their men, without parley about their prisoners nor expecting any about ours, and remained very peacefully on board until the next day'.[10]

Meanwhile, after putting the Archbishop's mind at ease as best he could – yet unaware that the English were getting ready to leave – the Count of Andrade returned from Santiago on Thursday, and 'along the way assembled the companies and other men he had released, and returned to Corunna'.[11] With this small army, which included some new men, he returned to the theatre of operations with the aim of becoming the scourge of the English once more. He must have wondered several times whether Pantoja and Palomino had finally brought in reinforcements to the city in the galleys.

However, the Count's worries were nearly over, for 'at dawn on Friday, from Peto Burdelo, which is four leagues from Corunna, he saw the enemy fleet sailing away'.[12] Straight away

> he sent the infantry and cavalry back to Pedro Bermúdez in Porto with a message, and to Captain Antonio de Puebla who was in Bayona, informing them

---

[8] *Relación Anónima*. BN mss 3750, pp. 226–7.
[9] Ibid., p. 227.
[10] Ibid.
[11] *Papeles Tocantes a Felipe II*. Vol. II. BN mss 1750, fol. 247.
[12] Ibid.

of the fleet's departure; he also sent Don Pedro de Sotomayor and Don Diego de las Mariñas to their localities in case the enemy tried to do any harm there along the way.[13]

In view of the departure of the English fleet, Andrade redrew his plans and sent the men where they were most needed under the new circumstances. He also sent orders to the infantry and cavalry who were on their way to Corunna from Oporto – and were already quite close – to head back to the border. Next, he went to Betanzos 'and collected the money and ammunition sent by His Majesty'.[14] The following day, Cerralbo got ready to head for Bayona to take personal charge of the defence of Galicia's southern coast.[15]

Leaving aside the significant blemish of not imposing his authority on the galley captains to get reinforcements into Corunna, the Count of Andrade played a satisfactory role. It is unfair to criticize him for the defeat at the bridge of El Burgo. He did what he could with the few regular soldiers he had and managed to avoid the catastrophe of an open battle between his 'raw recruits' and an English army that was meant to conquer Portugal. In any event, he put up stiff resistance at El Burgo and forced the English to despatch their bravest soldiers and captains, those who wanted the honour of being the first to cross that narrow bridge. The attackers then found out what they could expect to encounter en route to Compostela. Resistance was considerable and, according to witnesses, lasted for over two hours.[16]

If the English ever seriously considered marching on Santiago, what really saved the city was the resilience of Corunna, for the English generals could not stray too far from their fleet nor leave Pescadería undefended. What is certain is that at dawn on 19 May, two weeks after their arrival, having lost over 1,500 men and taking with them an even greater number of wounded in appallingly unsanitary conditions, 'they set sail out to sea, which they completed at 6 in the morning and disappeared from view at 8'.[17]

The English failure in Corunna would have serious repercussions for an expedition that was heading for total disaster. Pescadería, however, the largest and richest part of the city, was in ruins and at least two hundred fishermen, fifty women and twenty children had been lost. The six hundred houses of the neighbourhood had been destroyed; so, too, the hospital of San Andrés and its church, perhaps the town's emblematic building

---

[13] *Papeles Tocantes a Felipe II*. Vol. II. BN mss 1750, fol. 247.
[14] Ibid.
[15] The Marquis of Cerralbo to the King, Corunna, 19 May 1589. AGS. Guerra Antigua, File 248, fol. 84.
[16] Emilio González López has described the small army put together by the Count of Andrade as specifically Galician and still feudal in nature. He is critical of the fact that experienced Spanish troops did not come quickly to defend Corunna and the reinforcements were restricted to just the nobles and their vassals. However, he does see the role of these men in a positive light: 'That army forced the English to withdraw troops from the siege of the city, to interrupt the attacks on the wall, to lose hundreds of men in battle near Corunna, and made the besiegers appreciate that they could easily become the besieged.' González López, *La Galicia*, I, p. 328.
[17] *Relación Anónima*. BN mss 3750, p. 228.

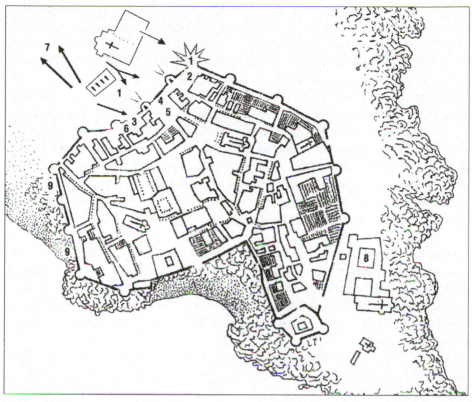

Figure 15.1 Map 5, 14–19 May, Corunna.

1. At 6.00 pm on 14 May, the English blew up the turret and began their attack on the wall which, thanks to the embanking by the women, exploded outwards and buried three hundred men of the English vanguard.
2. Captain Troncoso fought off those attacking the mined turret.
3. Captain Pedro Ponce and Ensign Antonio Herrera resisted the first waves sent against the breach opened by the artillery.
4. Diego de Bazán defended from the top of the wall with artillery and harquebuses.
5. The Marquis of Cerralbo and Pedro Manrique stayed in the placeta (small square) of Puerta de Aires with the reserve forces.
6. As the resistance of the fighting men grew weaker, the women took on an increasingly important role. When the attackers were about to break through, María Pita, leading an army of women, joined the fight in the front line.
7. After two hours of fierce fighting, the English were forced to withdraw. The attempt proved so costly that they would not try again.
8. The monastery of San Francisco was partially burned down on 16 May to prevent it from being used as a bridgehead like Santo Domingo.
9. At low tide on the nights of 16 and 17 May, there were several attempts to set the city on fire, which were bitterly resisted. These would be the last attacks against the high town, for on 19 May Drake sailed out to sea.

and symbol of the power of the fishermen's guild. The six sardine-fishing 'galleons' and over one hundred vessels, large and small, belonging to the guild, were also destroyed by fire, with no more than four surviving.[18] The hardy, prosperous seamen lost everything: furniture, clothes and precious objects, plus their nets, fishing gear, the treasures of their churches as well as their archives, books and documents.

Corunna saved its honour by retaining the high town and by calling a halt to an incursion that could have had devastating and irreversible effects on Santiago. It also delayed and weakened the invading army, which made it possible to defend Lisbon and caused the failure of the mighty English expedition, and all this should be properly recognized. The fame of María Pita, however, as a symbol of that vital episode, has been confined to the historical memory of Corunna. If Spain had looked after its own history in the same way that England has, one of the main squares in Madrid would be named after her, just as London has its Trafalgar Square or Portobello Road.

Several factors are helpful for an understanding of Corunna's surprising capacity to survive. The basic feature was the defence preparations mentioned in Chapter 6, particularly the stationing of experienced Spanish infantry, the construction of fortification works – especially San Antón – the abundance of war supplies and an effective, wide-ranging and single military command. The experienced infantry soldiers may not have been many in number, but as we have seen their effectiveness was notably superior to that of other nations.

Another inescapable factor is that, following the loss of Pescadería, the largest and most populated part of Corunna, its inhabitants took refuge in the small walled enclosure of the old high town, with a total perimeter of about 1,100 metres and a land frontage of no more than 350 metres. There, after suffering directly the horrors of war on the night of 5 May, the six hundred fishermen's families vowed to fight to the death defending Corunna. They knew what they could expect if the English managed to break through the walls.[19] This attitude was a reflection of the culture of freedom and shared responsibility typical of a city that owes obedience directly to the King and is free from the submissiveness that is imposed by the feudal yoke. Such a city was not subject to the protection of a feudal lord, but had to defend itself by its own means, often against such lords and their vassals. In this respect, the ability to organize their own defence and the formulation of a strong sense of belonging into a well-organized and armed citizens' militia, the very essence of which is to stand up to outside interference, explain why the Corunna militia were so effective. In February 1477, 112 years before the siege by the English, the Catholic Monarchs had tried to transfer the city from the crown and hand it to Don Rodrigo Alonso Pimentel, Count of Benavente. The noble from León came with his men to take possession of his new estate. He was met with such strong resistance that, after a three-month siege, he was forced to give up his plan. Corunna was also supported on that occasion in its spirit of freedom by an Andrade, Don Diego, who

---

[18] Martínez Salazar, *El cerco*, Chapter II.
[19] Ibid., p. 53.

Figure 15.2 Engraving of Fernando Ruiz de Castro, Count of Andrade, by Filippo de Grado, 1692, University of Seville.

Fernando Ruiz de Castro, sixth Count of Lemos and third Count of Andrade, was at the top of the feudal hierarchy of Galicia. As such, he was commissioned by the Marquis of Cerralbo to lead the reinforcement troops. He did a good job, getting the most out of his Galician troops which consisted of noblemen with their vassals. He did so much damage to the English that it resulted in the battle of El Burgo bridge, where he wore down the best of the English army. His principal shortcoming was not having forced the galley captains to obey their orders and take reinforcements into Corunna. Philip II, and later Philip III, held him in high regard, and he was appointed Viceroy of Naples, where he died in 1601.

was unwilling to tolerate an attempt to impose a feudal arrangement so close to his own possessions.

There are other important factors that account for the resistance of Corunna in 1589, such as the tactical and topographic nature of the defensive feature of the high town in the shape of San Antón, and the very capacity for survival of San Antón itself. But perhaps what best explains its success is the combination of the resolve by the Marquis to resist at all costs, together with a growing stubbornness that reached its natural high point – once the military forces were about to be overcome on 14 May – with an act of steadfast collective heroism in which women made their presence felt in the front line. Unlike the men, they were not committed to staying at their posts along the wall, so they became a surprise strategic reserve corps that appeared wherever it was necessary. Their involvement was decisive, not only because of the large number of women who took part, but also because of their attitude, which was no different from that of the regular soldiers.

Chapter 16

Heading South

On the morning of 19 May 1589, the English Armada was able to leave the estuary of Corunna thanks to a southwest wind, which was favourable if heading out to the open sea but not for steering a course past Cape Finisterre en route to Lisbon. Consequently, that night Drake was still within sight of the coast of Corunna.[1] With the wind unchanged, 'he skirted the coast until eight in the evening, staying as close to land as he could'.[2] Drake did not want the wind to take him eastward, away from the coast, while waiting for it to turn to a northerly. On 20 May, Gómez de Carvajal arrived in Bayona on a secret mission for the King,[3] which was to sail to England with two heavily armed light caravels to reconnoitre and gather information on the state of the English navy and its defences.[4] With his ships almost repaired, Philip II was eager to be on the offensive again against Queen Elizabeth. It would take Carvajal 'three days to prepare the ships, fitting them with new foremasts and bowsprits and getting them shipshape for the journey'.[5] At the same time, news arrived from Lisbon that the work to strengthen the artillery of the castles and bulwarks of São Julião, Oeiras, Trafaría and Caparica, which defended the entry to the Tagus estuary, had been successfully completed.[6]

[1]   'I wrote yesterday to inform Your Majesty that the enemy had embarked and today at dawn they set sail with the southwesterly. This has freshened to the extent that I believe they will not be able to get past the Cape, so they will have to skirt the coast, as they have done. At night they were still within sight, two or three leagues off shore.' The Marquis of Cerralbo to the King, Corunna, 19 May 1589. AGS. Guerra Antigua. File 248, fol. 84.
[2]   The Marquis of Cerralbo to the King, Corunna, 24 May 1589. AGS. Secretaría de Estado. File 166, fol. 45. Quoted in González Garcés, *María Pita*, p. 336.
[3]   The Count of Fuentes to the King, Lisbon, 25 May 1589. AGS. Guerra Antigua. File 248, fol. 141.
[4]   The Marquis of Cerralbo to the King, Corunna, 26 July 1589. AGS. Guerra Antigua. Quoted in González Garcés, *María Pita*, p. 358.
[5]   Captain Antonio de Puebla to the King, Bayona, 30 May 1589. AGS. Guerra Antigua. File 248, fol. 105.
[6]   'By the agreement of the Count of Fuentes and the order of His Highness I have taken the surplus artillery to both Oeiras and Trafaría. To Oeiras, two 40-pound battery cannon, two 20-pound half cannon and a 16-pound culverin, plus two falconets and their accessories, and I have reconnoitred the route in case it has to be withdrawn to the Castle of São Julião. In a wooden building only powder and other ammunition has been stored for these guns, with a keeper to distribute them under the orders of the officer in charge. To Trafaría, four iron guns, three chamber falconets and a 7-pound half culverin, plus a 12-pound quarter cannon belonging to Don Juan de Manrique, with all its accessories, powder and a man to guard them. In Torrevieja de Caparica, apart from the guns already there, we have taken a 14-pound small swivel cannon and another 16 pounder, with their support carriages and other accessories, with all necessary repairs completed. In the Castle of São Julião the remaining platforms have been glued on the under and sea sides, and the artillery there is mounted and placed to the best effect. It has been supplied with ramrods and *lanadas*, wooden blocks, poles and all necessities.' (A *lanada* is a tool for cleaning artillery pieces after they have been fired. It consists of a pole with a cylindrical wooden block on one end covered in sheepskin with the fleece intact.) 'Gente de guerra y artillería de este reino. Provisiones en los castillos cercanos a Lisboa: Oeiras, Trafaría, Torrevieja de

However, Alonso de Bazán, brother of the deceased Álvaro and general of the galleys that would defend this front, was aware of its vulnerability. Even with all the defensive improvements commissioned by Philip II in recent years to protect the estuary, it would be exposed if attacked by a large fleet. For this reason, also on 20 May, he sent an interesting report with his conclusions.[7] First he pointed out the unusual location of the castle of São Julião, on the open sea and outside the strait that leads to the estuary: 'The Castle of São Julião can do little to prevent the entry of the enemy fleet, given the great distance from it to Cabeça Seca, which it [the fleet] can get close to.' Once past São Julião, with the fleet in the strait, 'although some damage may be inflicted on it from the fort built in Paço de Arcos and from the galleys, since there are so few of these and the fleet is so large it can sail upriver between Belém Tower and Torre Velha'. At the narrowest part of the mouth, the English would have to sail between Belém tower and the Torre Velha de Caparica, but 'will defer whatever damage may be inflicted on them, for with favourable wind and tide, they will pass so quickly that there would not be enough time for the artillery to fire on them more than once. Even if it were twice, the number of vessels is such that the damage done to them would not stop them.' Once they had got past the coastal defences, overwhelmed the few galleys and crossed the strait, Bazán believed Lisbon was as good as lost if attacked from the sea, 'since there are so many places along its coast where they can land soldiers and we do not have enough people to defend ourselves'. The solution proposed by Bazán was to 'build a chain made of fifty tree trunks from one tower to the other, each as long as necessary for the job, with iron links as thick as an arm, and on the ends of the trunks large rings nailed to them'. Thus, Drake would be physically blocked by a floating obstacle that all his weapons could do nothing about.

The idea of stopping a huge fleet at full sail and with a favourable tide using a chain of trees may seem futile today. Not so then. It was practicable and was actually applied successfully on several occasions, such as the great attack against Corunna by the French in 1639, when a chain of tree trunks stretched across the 1,100 metres that separated the castles of San Antón and San Diego. Even today, if you visit the abandoned bulwarks of the narrowest part of the Ferrol estuary, you can see the thick bollards where, if required, the chain was hooked. For Lisbon, it had to be especially strong and so it would have to be reinforced with 'anchors underneath'. In this way, Bazán goes on, 'once in place, the chain will be so strong that there will be no way that it could be broken or sailed over'. However, on its own and unprotected, the obstacle was not enough: nothing would prevent the English in a boat simply sawing through a tree trunk. The chain was just the place to oppose the advance of the enemy fleet: 'Near the chain,

Caparica, Cascaes, Lisboa.' ('Soldiers and artillerymen of Spain. Provisions in the castles near Lisbon. Oeiras, Trafaría, Torrevieja de Caparica, Cascaes, Lisbon'.) Illegible signature. Lisbon, 20 May 1589. AGS. Guerra Antigua File 248, fol. 135.

[7] 'Proyecto de cadena de cincuenta árboles eslabonada con eslabones de hierro para cortar el paso al enemigo.' ('Plan to chain together fifty tree-trunks with iron links to cut off the passage of the enemy'.) Alonso de Bazán, Lisboa, 20 May 1589. AGS. Guerra Antigua. File 248, fol. 114.

on the inside the twenty ships will be anchored prow and stern, with their prows towards the north wind and against the tide with one side facing the entrance, and they would mount all their artillery on that side, the better to attack the enemy.' Thus the available ships would form a line close to the chain and firmly drop anchor. With the chain and with all their artillery on the port side of the ships, they would constitute a formidable line of fire that, combined with the artillery on land, would make the taking of Lisbon a very costly proposition indeed. Bazán, true to his family tradition, had thought of every eventuality: 'In case they should anchor in Santa Catalina for fear of the chain, fireships will be ready to launch against them from the chain with the falling tide and from São Julião with the rising tide.' In fact, if Drake had taken the castle at São Julião and had then been stopped by the chain and forced to drop anchor in the strait, his fleet would have been at the mercy of the strong currents generated by the tidal rise and fall, as the water ebbed and flowed through the bottleneck of the estuary. With fireships carried on the tide, the English Armada could be heavily beaten. Alonso de Bazán presented his meticulous plan on 20 May, when it was already known that Drake had set sail for Lisbon, and it did not look as though there were sufficient resources to put it into practice at such short notice. Sure enough, the plan was rejected. But Bazán's ideas made two things clear. The first was how vulnerable Lisbon was to a frontal attack by sea by the English Armada; the second, what a great ally an English attack would have in the tides, which would allow them to go in on the rise and to leave on the fall.

While the Spaniards worked against the clock to strengthen Lisbon's defences before Drake's imminent arrival, he continued to struggle against the wind. On the next day, 21 May, with the same south-westerly, part of the fleet drifted towards Estaca de Bares and the coast of Lugo, leaving it somewhat dispersed.[8] Two merchant ships were captured there – one French, the other Scottish.[9] It was only on 24 May that the bulk of the fleet was able to pass Finisterre and, now with a favourable wind, head for Lisbon. They then came upon the *Swiftsure* of Roger Williams and Robert Devereux, second Earl of Essex.[10] What was one of England's most powerful vessels doing, with the cream of English nobility on board, skirting the coast of Galicia and Portugal while their countrymen were fighting in Corunna?

To explain such unusual behaviour, we have to go back to the beginning of April, when Plymouth was swarming with men arriving from all over the country to join the great expedition. At the time the young, handsome Earl of Essex, heir to one of the most powerful noble English families, was not expected to take part. The fact was that Robert Devereux had become Elizabeth's new favourite and so he had taken the easiest and

---

[8]   The scattering of English ships along the Galician coast, separated from the core of the English Armada, lasted a surprisingly long time. Even on 31 May, Cerralbo wrote to the King: 'There are still some English vessels scattered along the coast. One of them freed a Portuguese at the port of Burela, near Ribadeo and then it freed another two on the Isle of Ons. All three are prisoners, and in Pontevedra there are two who came from the same ship.' AGS. Guerra Antigua. File 248, fol. 88.

[9]   John Evesham's Account. Wernham, *Expedition*, p. 231.

[10]   Ibid.

Figure 16.1 Map of the Lisbon Estuary, Office of Lisbon Studies (Gabinete de Estudos Olisiponenses).

In this map one can appreciate the strategic importance of the fort of São Julião, the first major obstacle the English Armada would have encountered while at anchor off the monastery of

Figure 16.1 (*cont.*)

São Antonio, where the fort of the same name stands today. It is also clear that São Julião defended access to Lisbon on one side only, and as Alonso de Bazán warned, it could be outflanked, especially since the fort on the Island of Bugio, which Philip II immediately ordered to be built, did not yet exist. After entering the estuary, the next obstacle was Belém tower, but with the ships carried along not only by the wind but also the strong current of the strait, there would be little time to fire on the invading fleet. This was why Bazán came up with the idea of a chain of tree trunks to block off the strait from the tower. For a frontal attack on Lisbon, Drake would have had the invaluable advantage of there being no wall there any longer. The worst threat to his ships, however, would have been the powerful artillery of the castle of São Jorge.

quickest way to the top of Elizabethan society. The Queen was not in the least willing to allow war to take him from her side, but the idea of staying in London under the ageing Elizabeth's wing was too much for the impetuous twenty-one-year-old Earl. Thus Essex, against the very clear orders of his possessive royal mistress, chose to ride away from London on his fastest horse and arrived in Plymouth on 13 April. By then the all-powerful wind had foiled the first attempt of the huge fleet to set sail, so Essex was glad to see that the large vessels were still there. Like a youth escaping from his rich and capricious lover, he wasted no time and hid aboard one of them, the *Swiftsure* of Roger Williams, second in command of the army. He got caught up in the fugitive lover's story, which sounded like an episode in a picaresque novel, and the powerful galleon set sail at once. By the time the Queen's courtier, Francis Knollys, reached Plymouth with the task of finding the young lover and returning him to the desperate lady's arms, it was too late. When questioned by Knollys, Drake and Norris whistled and looked the other way. This was not surprising, for what was otherwise just an affair of the heart could (considering the eminence of the owner of the heart in question) have turned into a serious matter of state and more than one person could have lost their heads. But Drake, Norris and Roger Williams all showed solidarity with Essex and Knollys's enquiries were met with a wall of silence. Conscious of how the matter was looking, the courtier set sail in a pinnace on the trail of the *Swiftsure*. The minor matter of the love and the possessiveness of the Queen for her Earl ran in parallel with the major story of the English Armada itself. Elizabeth was furious when she received the bad news from Plymouth and sent the Earl of Huntington with clear instructions for Drake and Norris, in which she ordered that 'if Roger Williams and the Earl of Essex, both accused of serious misconduct, had not been captured, they should be detained and held in the local prison'.[11]

But by then no one knew where the *Swiftsure* was, for it had been forced by the wind to take refuge in the nearby port of Falmouth. Consequently, having incurred the Queen's wrath, the English Armada had to set sail on the 28 April without the galleon, while two days later the *Swiftsure* set sail incognito from Falmouth. Following his flight from England, Essex sent a letter to the Queen to explain himself. However, the

[11] González-Arnao, *Derrota y muerte*, p. 63.

Switfsure did not head for Santander but went straight for the coasts of Portugal, where it patiently awaited the arrival of the English Armada and even had time to capture a coastal vessel or two. Did Roger Williams know that Drake and Norris were about to disobey the Queen by avoiding the Cantabrian Sea? Was there a secret agreement already in place for such disobedience? There can be little doubt about it.

After the fiasco at Corunna, meeting up with the *Switfsure* brought some good cheer for the leaders of the expedition. Drake thought this reinforcement could make an important contribution to the invasion's success. Essex was more eager than ever to be credited with having performed some memorable action, not only for the sake of riches and glory but also to mollify the Queen. As we shall see, his presence would give a boost to morale after the humbling experience in Corunna. Meanwhile, from the two caravels, Carvajal, who had left from Bayona on 23 May, got sight of the main body of the English Armada on 24 May and sent an urgent warning back to the town about the fleet's imminent arrival so that it could prepare its defences.[12]

After meeting up with the *Switfsure*, however, and with a northerly wind blowing, the English fleet carried on sailing towards Lisbon. On the following day, 25 May, level with the Islas Berlengas (Burling Islands), they sighted Cape Roca, the seafarer's land-mark showing that the Tagus estuary is not far off. The day's run came to an end and the English Armada dropped anchor in the Bay of Peniche, where a war council was held. The differences that arose in Corunna between Admiral Drake and Norris, com-mander of the land army, took a serious turn for the worse. Basically there were two possible plans: the first, to attack Lisbon directly by breaking through the Tagus estu-ary – the plan Bazán most feared; the other, to give credit to the promises of Dom António, Prior of Crato, and land at an easier and safer place, with the aim of calling for an Antonian uprising against the Spanish and forming an Anglo-Portuguese army on the way to Lisbon. But Crato's promises and phantasies amounted to very bad advice for the English Armada, just as the Spanish Armada's vain and ingenuous hopes of gathering and escorting Farnese's troops in Dunkirk had been damaging to the Spanish Armada a year earlier.

Drake and Norris had a heated argument. Their views were irreconcilable and their respective powers were crucial. One had the command of over two hundred ships, the other controlled the army they were transporting. The fleet was nothing without the infantry to achieve the set objectives and, from that point of view, Norris won out over Drake. But the infantry was nothing without the fleet, as would soon become apparent. Drake knew the Spanish weak spots better than Norris and had much more experience than the General in fighting them. In addition, the Admiral had successfully attacked his adversaries and occupied and looted several places in the vast Spanish Empire. The job in hand, after all, was to take a coastal city, Drake's speciality no less. True, the size of the challenge was greater than anything he had attempted before, but the means at his

---

[12] Letter to the King. Illegible signature. Bayona, 30 May 1589. AGS. Guerra Antigua. File 248, fol. 103. Captain Antonio de Puebla to the King, Bayona, 30 May 1589. Ibid., fol. 105.

disposal were also greater than ever. Norris, for his part, had known nothing but defeat in land battles against Spanish infantry and this had the potential to be the worst of his career.

Drake ranted and raved but in vain, repeatedly insisting that the army did not have the transport for such a long march, had insufficient supplies to cope with such an adventure in enemy territory, with hardly any cavalry to protect the infantry, no field artillery and, above all, once the land invasion had begun, the army would lose the protection and support of the fleet.[13] All Drake was advocating was to keep to the original plan, so he found Norris's new proposal all the more unacceptable. He did not have the power to insist, however, since the army leaders were not under his command. Certainly a frontal attack against Lisbon had its risks in the very short term, and it would mean a decisive battle leading to nothing other than total victory or defeat. Thus, Norris's plan, which was enthusiastically supported by Dom António, seemed less risky and more sensible. After all, they were there to help the Portuguese, led by Crato, in their struggle for independence. For that reason, they expected a massive response from the people and the local nobility. It was right that the Portuguese should take part and fight for their would-be king; if Dom António was right, and the country was eager for him to return, the march on Lisbon would be triumphant and the English army would be no more than the core of a huge offensive. However, the actual standing of Dom António in Portugal was quite different from what he led his temporary allies to believe. As we have seen, he had been repudiated by Henry, the elderly King and cardinal, before Henry's death, his theoretical dynastic rights were highly questionable and most of the Portuguese authorities rejected him.

In the end, the fleet opted for the land plan and abandoned the more logical naval option defended by Drake. Had they chosen a combined land and sea attack on the stronghold of São Julião and the Lisbon estuary, it is likely that the history and present reality of Europe, and, above all, the Americas, would be very different. But after its failure against the small city of Corunna, the English expedition was stunned and weakened, despite the enormous power that came from its size. The most serious problem was psychological in nature, for very low morale and mistrust had left their mark on both the men and their officers. Who was going to risk a direct attack on Lisbon after having their fingers burnt and losing many of their best men in Corunna?[14] The English were also aware of the important fact that because of their unforeseen delays, the Spanish were already waiting for them in the Portuguese capital.[15] This explains how incredibly overcautious the English were in Portugal. In any event, with Drake totally opposed, it was decided to begin the landing in Peniche, seventy kilometres north of Lisbon, and attack the city by land while Drake did the same from the sea. A lack of

---

[13]   Hume, *The Year After*, p. 46.

[14]   'It may be that they dared not, having been beaten and having lost men,' Philip II wrote to the Viceroy of Portugal. Quoted in González-Arnao, *Derrota y muerte*, p. 81.

[15]   Ralph Lane later complained: 'The useless and unnecessary siege of Corunna gave 20 days to the Spanish to prepare their resistance to the invasion of Portugal.' Quoted in ibid.

coordination and improvisation began to figure heavily in the expedition, but perhaps another important element was Drake's resentment towards Norris, for Drake and the fleet had found themselves playing a secondary role. Norris could do as he wished with *his* men, sure enough, but then nothing could stop Drake from doing what he thought best with *his* ships.

While such weighty matters were being settled near Lisbon, a French vessel loaded with barley and wheat arrived in Bayona, which was on maximum alert. It was none other than the ship captured a few days earlier by the English Armada, but was suspected of being an enemy ship in disguise, so 'we had its sails and masts removed and took away its boat, for we had seen two enemy vessels sailing close to it'.[16] Thus the French vessel, perhaps Huguenot, perhaps Catholic but controlled by English soldiers hiding inside, was not only immobilized in the port but also incommunicado without its boat. At the same time, Gómez de Carvajal was trying to round Cape Finisterre with his two caravels in order to complete his royal mission. The north wind was too much even for such tough vessels, so again and again, their efforts thwarted, they had to take refuge in the inlets of the Rías Bajas, for 'they tried to round the Cape two or three times, but the weather did not allow it'.[17] However, that was not the worst danger that was closing in on him, since hospitable Galicia, as if in a recurrence of the earth-shaking assault of a few days earlier, was still being attacked by the English.

---

[16]   Letter to the King. Illegible signature. Bayona, 30 May 1589. AGS. Guerra Antigua. File 248, fol. 103.
[17]   Captain Antonio de Puebla to the King, Bayona, 30 May 1589. AGS. Guerra Antigua. File 248, fol. 105.

Chapter 17

Landing in Peniche

On 26 May, the English Armada was sighted from Peniche. Juan González de Ataide, Squire of the House of Atouguia, had been expecting it for days. The mission he had been given by the Archduke Alberto, Viceroy of Portugal, by order of King Philip II of Spain and I of Portugal, was 'to reside in that port with the vassals that he could bring together from his lands and face the enemy with them'.[1] The men Juan de Ataide had been able to recruit were inexperienced locals and so he felt greatly relieved when the Archduke ordered Pedro de Guzmán, Count of Fuentes,[2] commander of the Spanish forces outside the walls of Lisbon, 'to send a few companies of Castilians to provide more effective resistance to the enemy there and prevent them from entering'.[3]

Ataide's garrison was strengthened by two good companies of harquebusiers commanded by Don Pedro de Guzmán. But four hundred men were not enough. The reinforcements provided by Captain Gaspar de Alarcón and his cavalry company who arrived from nearby Torres Vedras did not make much difference. Nor did the few men of Dom Martinho Soares, Mayor of Peniche, or Dinis de Lancastro, from Obidos. Ataide raised the alarm in Peniche, however, and sent a swift patache (tender) to Lisbon with the news that 'a few leagues from the Berlengas Islands a large number of sails' had been sighted.

Although the preventative measures in Peniche were taken 'more out of caution than need, for no-one believed the enemy would choose such a long route to reach Lisbon',[4] they would soon be considered timely, since 'the enemy, who in their haste to land could do so with ease, and did so with such diligence that two hours after noon ... they began to spill straight onto the beach of Consolação and sent out many men to land, despite the view of the sailors that it was the most difficult place to disembark'.[5]

Ataide and his men, who knew the coast well, were deployed in the areas where the landing was easiest. Antonio de Araujo, 'a veteran soldier of India with some local men',[6] remained in the fortress. Forty Castilian soldiers were positioned at Porto da Arca, a small but convenient cove, and Ataide, with most of his troops – some 250

---

[1]   *Memoria da Vinda dos Ingleses a Portugal em 1589*, p. 255. This report was quoted by Durval Pires De Lima on pages 245–85 of the book *O ataque dos ingleses a Lisboa em 1589 contado por uma testemunha*, Lisbon 1948. The references to it come from this book. The *Memoria* was also known to and used by Hume in his book *The Year after the Armada*, first published in 1896.

[2]   Pedro Enríquez de Guzmán, or de Acevedo, Count of Fuentes, was one of the major Spanish military men of his day. For a study of him, see Cesáreo Fernández Duro, *Bosquejo Encomiástico*, published as Vol. 10 of the *Colección de Memorias de la Real Academia de la Historia*, Madrid 1884.

[3]   *Memoria da Vinda dos Ingleses a Portugal em 1589*, p. 255, quoted in Pires De Lima, *O ataque*.

[4]   Ibid.

[5]   Ibid., p. 256.

[6]   Ibid.

Spaniards and 150 Portuguese – headed for the part of the bay where it was assumed the landing would take place.

The English, however, spurred on by Essex's impetuousness and the experience of Roger Williams, and lured by the desire to emulate them and the thirst for glory of their noblemen, took thirty-two barges straight to where neither harquebuses nor the two cannon that were there were expecting them. No one imagined they would attempt a reckless landing at the most dangerous point of Consolação beach, open to the sea and the furious crashing of the waves in deep water. The expedition paid a high price for such daring, for fourteen barges foundered because of the waves and others smashed against the reefs.[7] Over eighty men drowned, but the invaders had established a beach-head and it was there that the first important skirmish took place. The bold initiative of the English had caught the Spanish by surprise and they were 'half a league away'. Captain Benavides rushed to the spot with a hundred men and after him came Ataide and Captain Blas de Jerez with another eighty, while Pedro de Guzmán stayed in the rearguard looking out for other possible landing spots.

The clash took place at Consolação beach, at a time when the English were still at the precarious stages of a landing. Ralph Lane, in his letter of 12 June, described the episode as follows:

> The Earl of Essex and the Colonel-General – Roger Williams – there took their first landing with some 2,000 with them and made fight with the enemy almost two hours before the General – Norris – could take land by reason of the huge billows and most dangerous rocks that splitted divers of our boats and many of our men cast away in landing.

That was how the English ended up fighting the Spanish infantry: 'Very brave charges the enemy gave and made two retreats and in the third were clean repulsed and quitted the field to the Earl and the colonel-general before the General – Norris – or any of our regiment could come to the seconding of the fury.'[8]

Benavides, Ataide, Blas de Jerez and others who arrived later led charges against the men who had disembarked. The first two charges caused the enemy losses and after the third they withdrew. It was a bloody encounter in which Captain Castillo's ensign and fifteen Spaniards were killed. Among the English dead were Captain Robert Pewe, run through by a pike, Captain Jackson and a good number of men.[9] Although inferior in number, the Spanish were able to exploit the weakness inherent in the first stages of a landing, and as Ralph Lane admits in his letter, 'the Spaniard truly did abide it even to the very pike'.[10] The audacity of the English had broken the Iberian defences and, with other places left exposed, the landing spread out. Thus

[7] González-Arnao, *Derrota y muerte*, p. 84.
[8] Letter from Ralph Lane, 12 June 1589. Wernham, *Expedition*, p. 185.
[9] Ibid. and González-Arnao, *Derrota y muerte*, p. 84.
[10] Letter from Ralph Lane, 12 June 1589. Wernham, *Expedition*, p. 185.

Don Pedro de Guzmán, on the alert and protected from the enemy when the barges reached the shore, came out and charged as swiftly as he could, wounding and killing men as they disembarked. While in the skirmish, he saw a number of the enemy land at another spot not far away, and having no support nearby and to avoid being caught in the middle with needless loss of life, he withdrew in very good order.[11]

The landing was carried out so quickly that the troops stationed at Porto da Arca had to leave the cove, which had already been taken by seven companies, while Ataide and Guzmán hurriedly assembled their men and left at the double. They headed for the fortress of Peniche where the plan was to hold the line after obstructing the landing, but they soon discovered that they were too late because the fortress was already surrounded by the English. Their only way out was to withdraw inland towards the village of Atouguia da Baleia. Guzmán thought it too risky to try to break the siege in order to enter the fortress and that even if they managed to do so, given the disproportion in numbers, the fortress was easily assailable.[12] As it was, the English had swept in like a hurricane and had 12,000 men on the ground. The reserve troops plus the knights aboard the *Swiftsure* had played no small part. With the presence of the old Queen's wayward favourite, the English Armada was now complete, and although the memory of Corunna weighed on their minds, the fleet was where it was intended to be: preparing to conquer Lisbon and, with it, the Portuguese Empire.

At midnight, once the vulnerable Spanish headquarters had been established in Atouguia, Ataide and Guzmán, who were still feeling stunned by the dauntingly huge landing, saw Captain Alarcón arrive with forty horses. The same number would be added later. Dom Martinho Soares joined them with a hundred soldiers from Torres Vedras, and Dinis de Lancastro came with his men from Obidos. However, some of the latter, 'in awe of the huge fleet', ran away that night.[13] Most of them had obeyed the call, since 'it was urgent to prepare the men they had, so that they could keep the enemy busy for another day and obstruct them and prevent their men from making forays'.[14]

During the first night of the campaign in Atouguia, the Spanish had their doubts about their Portuguese allies. After all, the English army had landed to support a Portuguese pretender to the throne of Portugal which was held by Philip II, thus undermining the trust between supposed Spanish–Portuguese allies. And so, 'since according to Juan González de Ataide it was not safe to stay at the castle, nor could they rely on its people or those of Atouguia, they chose a comfortable place in the fields, where they spent the night keeping watch, with one eye on the locals and the other on the enemy'.[15]

---

[11] *Relación de lo subçedido del armada enemiga del reyno de Inglaterra a este de Portugal con la retirada a su tierra este año de 89*. BN mss 18579, p. 34. This important report was used by Hume in *The Year after the Armada*, where it is referred to as a 'Spanish diary'.

[12] *Memoria da Vinda dos Ingleses a Portugal em 1589*, p. 257, quoted in Pires De Lima, *O ataque*.

[13] Ibid.

[14] *Relación de lo subçedido del armada enemiga*. BN mss 18579, p. 34.

[15] Ibid.

In short, once the English landing was complete, the men recruited by Ataide in Peniche abandoned the Spanish camp.[16] In general terms, the presence of the Prior of Crato – fresh from the promising reception in Peniche – and above all the enormous size of the invading army meant that the ordinary Portuguese people did not join ranks with the army of Dom António but nor were they willing to be part of the Spanish resistance.

Meanwhile that day, with the news of the arrival of the English fleet in Peniche, the Archduke ordered Alonso de Bazán – once he had embarked another two infantry companies in Lisbon – to take his twelve galleys to strengthen the line of fire at the castle of São Julião, 'and he sent these galleys to the place where the artillery of the castle and his own could best inflict damage on the enemy should they attempt to enter with the fleet, and since the currents were so strong, the galleys were placed with the prow towards the sea entry'.[17] The garrisons were also reinforced and supplies were stored in the castles of Cascais and São Julião.[18]

On the morning of 27 May, the Spanish cavalry – their trump card – under Captain Alarcón carried out a surprise attack on a flank of the English army. Their mission was essentially to reconnoitre the enemy and take prisoners to obtain information. Five or six soldiers were killed[19] before a Spanish-speaking Frenchman was captured and he reported that the fleet included 20,000 men and six hundred horses[20] (the information concerning the cavalry was later shown to be false).[21] Accordingly, Guzmán withdrew to Torres Vedras and sent Ataide to Lisbon to report to the Archduke.

The defections of the Portuguese that had occurred the day before in Peniche happened again that day in Lourinhã. Gaspar de Alarcón and Guzmán sent word to the militia that the knight commander in the town had joined forces in order to face up to the enemy. The plan was to organize detachments to harass the enemy, including Spanish veterans and Portuguese militia, but the Portuguese did not follow their leaders. Nothing could be done to allay the collective fear of the locals, for

> what changed their minds was that word had spread about the size of the Armada and the many fighting men the ships had brought, plus tall stories of 900 Irish

---

[16] *Relación de lo subçedido del armada enemiga*. BN mss 18579, p. 34.

[17] Letter from Francisco de Coloma. AGS. Guerra Antigua. File 249, fol. 129.

[18] 'On receiving the news that the castle of Cascais had no more than 30 men and was short of supplies, another 30 men and the provisions requested by the castellan were sent from the galleys. 600 quintals of biscuit were moved from the galleys to the castle of São Julião and two vessels came in from Lisbon loaded with biscuit and wheat. Also, the galley slaves were used to help put the artillery of São Julião in place and to undertake all necessary repairs in the castle.' Ibid.

[19] *Memoria da Vinda dos Ingleses a Portugal em 1589*, p. 257, quoted in Pires De Lima, *O ataque*.

[20] Ibid.

[21] Once in Lisbon, this prisoner would maintain that he had said sixty horses, not six hundred. Letter from Falçao de Resende, quoted in Ruela Pombo, *Portugal 1580–1595*, 3rd part, col. 16. The same figure of sixty was given by some who counted them later. Letter from Falçao de Resende, quoted in Ruela Pombo, 3rd part, col. 31. González-Arnao, *Derrota y muerte*, p. 85, gives the figure as forty-four. The actual number of horses was small, around fifty, as stated by Roger Williams in *A Brief Discourse of War*, quoted in Wernham, *Expedition*, p. 224.

fighting dogs, as large as lions and even more ferocious, that would take over the world, and other fables of the same kind that put great fear into country folk.[22]

In contrast to the ambiguous attitude of the ordinary population, João González de Ataide, the knight commander of Lourinhã, and later other Portuguese nobles and officers, remained loyal to the terms agreed at the Cortes of Tomar. But the trust between Spanish and Portuguese, or rather between supporters of Philip and António, was undermined by the formidable power of the English Armada. No one could be sure whether, beneath an apparent acceptance of the established order, some Portuguese were not at heart Antonians who welcomed the splendid opportunity presented by the English of installing a king who to all appearances was exclusively Portuguese.

Meanwhile with the news of the arrival of the fleet, defensive preparations were stepped up in Lisbon as panic (as well, perhaps, as the prospect of independence) spread among the ordinary population. But the English army was still far away and the Archduke's first decision was to send, to the Torres Vedras front,

> Don Sancho Bravo, Knight of the Order of Alcántara and native of Seville, with his company of mounted harquebusiers, together with Captain Antonio de Jones' company of light cavalry, and three hundred harquebusiers of the Tercio regiment of Don Francisco de Toledo, with Captains Pliego and Francisco Malo going to Torres Vedras in search of Don Pedro de Guzmán, so that everyone together would harass the enemy, hinder their progress, take prisoners and attack from various parts, in the order and as time and the lie of the land allowed.[23]

However, not everything in Portugal that day was under the jurisdiction of the capital, for after landing and setting up camp in Peniche the previous day, the English offered terms of surrender to the city fortress. Captain Araujo, with his small garrison, announced that he would only surrender the fortress to the pretender Dom António, which he did as soon as Crato appeared shortly afterwards. Araujo was unaware that he had just signed his own death warrant. Dom António took possession of Peniche and, escorted by a hundred men of his personal guard, was proclaimed King of Portugal. But the Portuguese chronicler of the anonymous diary held no sympathy towards him for his actions:

> After Dom António landed in Peniche, he took lodgings in the houses of Juan González de Ataide, where he found his silverware and other valuables he had for his comfort, and that of Don Pedro de Guzmán, whereby he acted out the role of king. By treating the locals with kind words and flattery and taking nothing that was theirs, but rather giving a good deal, he began to sow the seed of his deception by saying that everyone's property would be fully protected and that harm would

---

[22] *Relación de lo subçedido del armada enemiga.* BN mss 18579, p. 35.
[23] Ibid.

come to no-one. With such feet of clay he stayed in Atouguia on 26 and 27 May, and with the same lies preceding him, took lodgings in Lourinha on the 28th.[24]

The Spanish manuscript was no less critical of the attitude of Philip's bastard cousin:

They say that as soon as Dom António set foot on land, he was very friendly to all those who came to kiss his hand, treating them with kind and affectionate words, making them lengthy offers of favours of every sort and putting his arm around the wretched women there. Whenever a half well-spoken peasant came to him, he would tell the English gentlemen there with him in attendance that this was Don So-and-So, a prominent personage close to the King and that he was in disguise so that the Castilians would not recognise him.[25]

The antipathy felt towards Crato was understandable. He had not only squandered the Portuguese crown jewels – which he had taken when he fled the country – to meet the cost of expeditions and of buying allegiances, but he had also pledged to Queen Elizabeth the most abject submission and a permanent financial sum, as well as a free hand in gaining access to the Portuguese Empire.

While the army settled and rested in the newly conquered land, with very strict orders not to upset the inhabitants,[26] Drake remained idle and at anchor off Peniche on 26, 27 and 28 May. The famous erstwhile privateer, made admiral at the age of forty-eight, had lost his private rivalry with General Norris.

Back in the north, we find that on 27 May the Rías Bajas of Galicia were still under threat, and a strange incident took place there which, even though it provided little information, shows at first hand the nature of the Anglo-Dutch challenge: 'Between the [Cíes] Islands and this town [Bayona], a large vessel resembling a Flemish *charrúa*[27] appeared, and fired a shot to signal its need of a pilot to enter into port.'[28] It was most odd that such a ship should ask for assistance in Bayona, but the sea is, has been and always will be the common enemy that inspires solidarity among fishermen, and so,

two men setting out on a small fishing-boat from the parish of Panjón happened to be nearby, and they were called from the ship and went aboard. One of the crew who seemed Flemish and spoke good Spanish and Galician told them they were carrying wheat and asked them if they would guide them into Bayona. They agreed and were invited to drink some beer.

---

[24] *Memoria da Vinda dos Ingleses a Portugal em 1589*, p. 258, quoted in Pires De Lima, *O ataque*.
[25] *Relación de lo subçedido del armada enemiga*. BN mss 18579, p. 35.
[26] Captain Crisp was publicly hanged for looting a house, with a piece of board attached to his chest stating the reasons for his execution. This was intended to keep the undisciplined troops under control and mollify the terrified population. Discourse by Anthony Wingfield, 9 September 1589. Wernham, *Expedition*, p. 267. González-Arnao, *Derrota y muerte*, p. 84.
[27] An old Spanish word for a type of ship, the *urca*.
[28] Letter to the King. Illegible signature. Bayona 30 May 1589. AGS Guerra Antigua. File 248, fol. 103.

The fishermen thought they were being rewarded for their humanitarian gesture, but soon the warm welcome turned sour as the foreigners revealed their cunning intentions: 'Then they were pressed to tell them what had happened to a French ship that had arrived in Bayona with wheat on the Thursday, whether they had taken any prisoners, and they were to tell them the truth or they would be hanged from the topsail.' The Galicians must have choked on their beers. 'They answered that they had not seen the ship and knew nothing.' They were not done with their questioning: 'They asked them how many soldiers there were in the town, what artillery there was and what the Begoña was doing there close to the shore.'[29] To save their necks the fishermen had no choice but to tell them everything they knew, that is, that 'there were many Castilians defending the town and a lot of artillery, which the said ship had brought, and that it was so close to land on account of the enemy'. Encouraged by the information they had obtained, 'they told them to go below decks where they would be given some food'. The true nature of the ship was then revealed, for 'as they went down more than thirty Englishmen came out of a hatch, all of them young, with harquebuses and their matchlocks lit, with much shot hanging from their belts and under their arms, and asked if there were any galleys and also about some caravels'. As we can see, while most of the English Armada was pursuing its destiny of a great naval offensive to change the geopolitical map of the world, two odd ships, both of them captured and used for the benefit of camouflage, remained true to the English way of doing things at that time. After a second but unsuccessful interrogation, 'they let them return to their boat', wrote the military commander of Bayona to the King,

> and later they came to tell me what had happened, and I took their testimonies. I suspect that the French vessel is a spy ship, and that since it was unable to return on the night it arrived, nor on any other, nor send word, since its sails and yardarms and skiff had been taken away, the ship that signalled for a pilot did so to receive news of the said French vessel and find out about the situation in the town.[30]

He was not far off the mark. What remains unclear is whether, in prowling near Bayona with their camouflaged ships instead of heading for Portugal, they were obeying the orders of the English Armada or were acting on their own initiative.

Back in Portugal, dawn arrived on 28 May over the beautiful bay of Peniche. Sir Francis Drake surveyed the imposing forest of thousands of pikes and harquebuses advancing in orderly columns, with their few wagons, some fifty horses and their

---

[29] The *Santa María de Begoña* (750 tonnes, 24 cannon) was one of the ships of the Spanish Armada that returned to Galicia, more precisely Cangas, opposite Vigo, on 14 October 1588. On 8 August that year, in Calais, it had been surrounded by English ships and rescued by Medina Sidonia's *San Martín*. After a stop on the coast of Ireland it managed to return to Spain, and months later its infantry and artillery were crucial for the protection of Bayona. The Marquis of Cerralbo to the King, Bayona, 10 May 1589. AGS Guerra Antigua. File 249, fol. 106. Also Urgorri Casado, 'Hombres y navíos'.

[30] Letter to the King. Illegible signature. Bayona, 30 May 1589. AGS. Guerra Antigua. File 248, fol. 103.

colourful standards. They were heading inland through unknown territory. He saw the resplendent halberdiers, the personal guard of Dom António who the English now treated like a colourful puppet. He saw also the attractive figure of Essex, accompanied by 2,000 confident, eager knights. In Corunna, however, Drake had also seen the magnificently repaired *San Juan* before its destruction. He knew that perhaps almost a hundred ships could be being given their finishing touches before setting sail again against England. He must have felt guilty for not having gone to Santander. The taking of Pescadería and the large amount of supplies and wine obtained had not put an end to the danger of a new expedition against England. Roger Williams was right: on the contrary, it was a sign that Spain was preparing to strike again. Failure was not an option. Taking Lisbon would remove the danger to London once and for all and open up a whole new bright world of riches and opportunities.

However, Drake did not seem to believe this. It was as if he had lost faith after Corunna. He knew the Spanish were vulnerable to surprise attacks on unprepared coastal towns, but he was also well aware of the superiority of their infantry in battle. He surveyed the army for the last time and headed for the port. With a fleet with reduced numbers of troops, it seemed unwise to go any further than Cascais. After bidding farewell to the five hundred men – three companies and the cannon and crew of four ships[31] – that Norris had stationed in Peniche, he weighed anchor. Although leaving those men there was not a good omen, he did not realize that he would never see them again.

[31] González-Arnao, *Derrota y muerte*, p. 85.

Chapter 18

The March Begins

On 28 May 1589, the long march of the *Invincible* army began. The English columns, which had now become the armed forces of the new King, set out on their campaign. Meanwhile, the Spanish troops in Portugal that spring were caught unprepared for a major military encounter. The wear and tear of the previous year had hit them hard and, to make matters worse, they were dispersed across several different fronts.

That spring was one of crucial military significance. Henry III of Navarre, soon to become Henry IV of France, planned to cross the Pyrenees in collusion with Queen Elizabeth. For this reason, Philip had no choice but to mobilize forces towards the French border. The Tercios regiments of Flanders, in a bloody and costly defence of their King's inheritance, were holding their position. In addition, Philip's spies knew about England's contacts with the Berbers, with Morocco and with Ottoman Sultan Murad III. Messages and agents increased considerably during those months. The outcome of it all was that England, France, the Dutch Republic and the Islamic powers had formed a formidable coalition ready to attack Philip simultaneously on several fronts. Of all those threats, one in particular had now become real, for on the same day that Norris began the land march from Peniche to Lisbon, the vast English Armada, its sails too numerous to be counted, stretched out majestically along the Portuguese coast.

Nevertheless, the Spanish infantry set about doing its job on the Atlantic front. And its job was very clear: to protect Lisbon and, with it, Portugal. There would be no point in taking on the English in a pitched battle if, in so doing, they left the capital undefended. Such a situation could have allowed António's supporters to take control of the city.[1] While the English began the first of their exhausting marches, the Spanish were organizing themselves in order to neutralize such a dangerous threat. Their challenge was to stop the invading army without leaving Lisbon defenceless. Their tactics were to be an exact copy on land of those used by the English in the channel a few months earlier. Their aim was not to fight the enemy but to harass them into abandoning their mission. The Count of Fuentes got the various fronts organized in a war council. He called upon Don Alonso de Bazán, the general in charge of the galleys defending the Lisbon estuary; Don Gabriel Niño, of the Order of Calatrava and *Maestre de campo* of the infantry; Don Bernardino de Velasco, of the Order of Santiago, *Cabo de las compañías*

---

[1] 'And since it is in no way expedient to put at risk your person, who I so much care for, I have decided to send this message to order you in writing not to leave this place (Lisbon) in any circumstance, for the peace should be kept there, and from there you may help the Count of Fuentes with the people of the land together with the soldiers.' The King to Archduke Alberto, 27 May 1589. Quoted in Luis Cabrera De Córdoba, *Historia de Felipe II Rey de España* (Salamanca: Junta de Castilla y León, 1998), III, p. 1253.

de armas of the cavalry; Francisco Duarte, general supplier; Esteban de Ibarra; Pedro Venegas de Córdoba, governor of São Julião castle plus others. They were all instructed to submit regular reports in order to coordinate and organize the various operations under the direct authority of the Archduke.

That day, while Drake was sailing for Cascais, Archduke Alberto instructed the Count of Fuentes, along with the troops led by Don Bernardino de Velasco, 'to spend the night at Orlas (Oeiras), three leagues from Lisbon in the direction of Cascais'.[2] This troop movement was the Spanish response to the threatening pincer movement advancing upon Lisbon. Alberto's intention was to strengthen the first line of defence of Lisbon's maritime front, namely the formidable castle of São Julião, and so at nearby Oeiras he deployed infantry capable of frustrating a land attack against the strategically important castle. He also ordered three of the so-called old companies from the castle of São Jorge to embark on the galleys. Together with Claudio de Beamonde's companies, they were to land at the castle of São Julião before moving on to Oeiras in order to join the troops of Don Francisco de Toledo. The Portuguese troops of Don Fernando de Castro and Rui Peres de Távora also headed there. And so that afternoon of 28 May the Count, Bernardino de Velasco and Esteban de Ibarra set off, 'and some other men of high rank above the captains and dependants obliged to accompany him'.[3] While Alberto made his move in that game of strategy, the troops remaining in Lisbon were left under the command of Don Gabriel Niño, assisted by Francisco de Duarte, who was familiar with the city and who would remain in close contact with the Archduke. In addition,

> since we find there is much to be done in the little time we have and the Portuguese are reluctant to be led by Castilians, and with almost all of the regular officials and ministers of justice having left the city, it has been necessary for his Highness to appoint other Portuguese in order to fill those positions and to provide for them, and thus they were sent by Francisco de Duarte all over the land in order to bring carts, saddles and packsaddle horses, and sappers for the service of the army; others were sent to the main storehouse to have all kinds of sustenance sent to the city and the army.[4]

The Archduke thus prepared a corps of Portuguese agents who were loyal to Philip, the legitimate heir of Isabella of Portugal and the Emperor Charles, and responsible for collecting everything that the city and the army needed.

And so 'they gathered a large quantity of equipment from the storehouses of Portugal in order to entrench the army and fortify the city wherever necessary'.[5] At the same time, Don Gabriel Niño 'had inspected the walls of Lisbon and understood very well the condition they were in and the work to be done, and was able to inform His Highness

---

[2]   *Relación de lo subçedido del armada enemiga*. BN mss 18579, p. 38.
[3]   Ibid., p. 37.
[4]   Ibid., p. 39.
[5]   Ibid.

of the gates, wickets and other entrances to be sealed'.[6] Furthermore, as a preventative measure and to improve the performance of the Spanish headquarters, 'the King's maids and servants' clothes were taken to the castle (of São Jorge) for their convenience so as to be able to serve at the palace near to His Highness's person'.[7] Also, the inhabitants who lived on the route to be taken by the English army began to head for Lisbon. Many chose to cross the Mar da Palha southwards, thus putting both land and sea between them and the English, while others sought refuge under the walls of Lisbon. The churches and monasteries inside the capital began to fill with refugees.[8]

While these and other precautionary measures were taken in Lisbon, Don Sancho Bravo arrived at Torres Vedras

> with the cavalry and infantry under his command, where he found Don Pedro de Guzmán. They discussed the town's readiness, whether it could be fortified and defended with the men they had, given the size of the enemy, and considering morale to be low among their men,[9] and since it was open country where horses could not be used to great effect, they decided to leave that night at ten o'clock before the enemy arrived from Louriñán, two leagues away, and trapped them[10] … making forays into the country and always staying in places where they could see the enemy, sending out scouts in every direction to establish their intentions, and undertaking attacks day and night, whenever they could, to kill, wound, and take prisoners.[11]

It is clear that the Spanish held a huge logistical advantage, since unlike the slow and cumbersome English army whose infantry was weighed down by baggage and munitions, it had complete freedom of movement. The invading army slowly made its way to Torres Vedras. At the same time, Guzmán and Sancho Bravo, who had withdrawn from the town because of its vulnerability, settled 'two leagues further on in Enxara dos Cavaleiros', and with them 'came a judge from Torres Vedras who did not wish to wait there for the enemy and who threw a number of powder kegs that could not be salvaged into a well, so that they did not end up in enemy hands and do us harm'.[12] Meanwhile, Gaspar de Alarcón 'stayed near the enemy with his two companies of horsemen in order to head off their absconders and send an account of their plans'.[13]

However, while Lisbon was busy with preparations for war on 28 May, Galicia, still shocked by the size of the fleet that had mercilessly assaulted its coasts, continued on a war footing. The Marquis of Cerralbo, who had moved on to Bayona, supervised the

---

6 *Relación de lo subçedido del armada enemiga.* BN mss 18579, p. 40.
7 Ibid.
8 Ibid., p. 37.
9 Checking the morale of the troops before battle was a practice recommended by treatises on infantry.
10 *Relación de lo subçedido del armada enemiga.* BN mss 18579, p. 40.
11 Ibid., p. 37.
12 Ibid., pp. 40–1.
13 Ibid., p. 41.

defence of the lengthy Galician coastline, while Captain Gómez de Carvajal persevered in his private endeavour to sail past Finisterre and head towards the England coast. During the evening of 28 May, having failed to do so after numerous attempts, Don Gómez took refuge in the port of Corrubedo. His manoeuvres, however, did not go unnoticed by two English ships lurking around the Rías Bajas, and they lowered two large launches. Thus,

> at midnight on 28 May, two enemy launches with over a hundred Englishmen on board violently attacked us. They both managed to charge the caravel *Concepción* where Don Gómez de Carvajal was on board, and since the other caravel was a bit too far away it was unable to come to its aid in time, and so we both fought the best we could. It was God's will that Don Gómez died from the shot of an *esmeril*,[14] and there were another four dead and ten wounded. They killed one of our two Scottish pilots and our Portuguese pilot was killed as well. We could still go on, however, since we still had our best pilot, and together with another Portuguese or Castilian one, we were able to continue.[15]

The attack focused on the caravel *Concepción*, and although they managed neither to capture nor sink it, the brave captain whose company played such an important role in the defence of the Galician capital died in the exchange of harquebus, musket and small-calibre artillery fire. Both the Spanish and the English were surprised by the outcome of this skirmish: the latter because they were unaware of the enemy's secret mission and were not expecting them to be so well armed and manned that they could repel an attack. They thus suffered unexpected losses: 'It is not known how many of the enemy died … (but) as they withdrew only three men were seen rowing, and in the other (launch) very few were standing, and hence we suppose that there were very few who were not dead or wounded.'[16] The skirmish, however, prevented or at least delayed the Spanish reconnaissance mission.[17] We know that 'there were two ships that the launches came from, each of them between fifty and eighty tons',[18] in other words they were two of those small, manoeuvrable vessels so common among the English fleet. We also know that these two ships were the same ones that had controlled the two captured and camouflaged boats, one of which had already been returned to Spanish hands, leaving the Frenchmen as prisoners.[19] A certain dispersal thus became apparent in the massive dispatch of warships from England that spring, since all this took place on the 28 May, when Drake, having set ashore most of the army at Peniche, was already on his way to Cascais. Perhaps those small ships were

---

[14] A small calibre light cannon, somewhat smaller than a falconet.
[15] Ensign Mérida to the King, Bayona, 30 May 1589. AGS File 248, fol. 106.
[16] Letter to the Marquis of Cerralbo. Signature illegible. Corrubedo, 29 May 1589. AGS. File 248, fol. 89.
[17] This mission would be continued by Ensign Mérida. Ensign Mérida to the King. Bayona, 30 May 1589. AGS. File 248, fol. 106.
[18] Letter to the Marquis of Cerralbo. Signature illegible. Corrubedo, 29 May 1589. AGS. File 248, fol. 89.
[19] Letter to the King. Signature illegible. Bayona, 30 May 1589. AGS. File 248, fol. 103.

behaving like corsairs and were taking advantage of the favourable circumstances to ply their trade.

The night of 28 May wore on and with it came the cool air which was so welcome to the people from the more northern latitudes who had been trapped in the discomfort of the oppressive heat of the day. In such a pleasant atmosphere, Norris and his men rested in anticipation of the moment when, to cheers and applause, the gates of ancient Lisbon would be opened to them. Once inside, they would be welcomed into the great airy salons of the palaces and offered banquets, cloth from India, musk and silk ... a whole new world would be at their disposal when they entered Lisbon. They had not had to face any army in battle and there was no way back for the English Armada, nor any reason not to be hopeful. All they had to do was await the general Portuguese uprising in support of Crato and the desperate resistance or flight of the clearly inferior Spanish forces.

On 29 May, the English army, together with Dom António and his entourage, all finally came together at Torres Vedras and it was then that the Prior of Crato presented himself as King. With great pomp, a solemn triumphal procession headed by Crato under a canopy wound its way through the streets of Torres Vedras.[20] In all their finery, Norris, the Earl of Essex, Roger Williams, the colonels and the main men of noble rank all flanked poor Dom António in order to show enthusiastic support for his power and encourage the people to feel a sense of calm, confidence, optimism ... and a determination to join the expedition. Except for the pressing problems of provisioning, everything appeared to be going well for the English. Yet appearances can be deceptive and something did not quite fit. It could not have gone unnoticed by the leaders of the march, the elite of Elizabethan England, gathered that day in the Portuguese countryside. Strong suspicions were soon being voiced privately among the English command. For all the cheering of the people, for all the fifes and drums, pennants, banners and flowers, for all the bowing and the smiles ... Torres Vedras was empty. Most of the nobility and the powerful were absent[21] and those were precisely the individuals, along with their men, who were supposed to act as an example to the people for the Antonian uprising to take place. Essex, Williams, Norris and the others then took a fresh look at Dom António and could hardly conceal their deep contempt. His promises of a military parade to Lisbon were evaporating and out of the long list of grand celebrities who were supposedly his supporters, none of them was there. Why not? Who really was Dom António? That afternoon, Norris reluctantly remembered the council held within sight of Peniche and wondered if he had landed the best England could offer in order for a fantasist to pursue his dreams of power. It then occurred to him that those exhausted men, without carts, horses, artillery or provisions, had been led up the garden path.

The 29 May was, however, no easy day in Lisbon, either. Quite unpredictably, there was a sudden feeling of great anxiety which indicated the degree to which the news of

---

[20] *Relación de lo subçedido del armada enemiga*. BN mss 18579, p. 44.
[21] *Memoria da Vinda dos Ingleses a Portugal em 1589*, p. 258, quoted in Pires De Lima, *O ataque*.

the English landing had affected morale in the Portuguese capital. It so happened that while men from Alarcón were taking some English prisoners, captured the day before, to the Archduke's palace,

> they came within sight of some women selling food, and when they heard that they were English, they began to shout that the English were coming into town, and then others began to shout the same without knowing what it was all about, and everyone there ran through the streets spreading the same rumour and this went on all over the city causing great upset and dismay.[22]

Nothing could illustrate better than this anecdote the fears and the unwillingness of the people of Lisbon to come to the aid of the Spanish in the defence of their city. Thus, 'all kinds of people lost all hope that the city could survive without being sacked ... and so they almost totally abandoned it, including many ministers and worthy dignitaries and nobles'.[23] Lisbon was therefore a very different case from Corunna: there was no prospect of the besieged population rising up in arms to defend their city. However, to try and mitigate this state of affairs, the Archduke ordered 'four nobles from amongst the most prominent in the kingdom and who held great authority, who were at His Majesty's service on this occasion, to look after everything necessary in the different quarters of the town, their walls and gates, and remain at all times in their streets, so as to give hope of a favourable outcome'.[24] These noblemen loyal to the King were Alderman Fernando da Silva, his nephew Diego da Silva, Diego de Sousa, from the Council of State, and Manuel de Melo, Master of the Hunt of the realm. The situation among the population of Lisbon was thus improved.

Meanwhile in Torres Vedras, there was a dogged struggle between the preventative measures of the Archduke, who was intent on clearing the countryside through which the English would have to pass, and Dom António's desperate attempt to obtain provisions. To this end, Crato, who was 'aware that a legal professional called Gaspar Campello, a criminal law judge in Lisbon, was near Torres Vedras in one of his properties, twice sent soldiers to fetch him and he was put in charge of supplies'.[25] Reluctantly and under duress, Campello was thereafter in charge of provisioning the army, but he had to overcome a difficult problem. Many of the locals were leaving the area with their possessions, either for fear of the inevitable looting by a hungry army or of being plundered by Campello, plus a natural aversion towards the English invasion. As a consequence, 'the land was suffering from a lack of all kinds of essentials, because as most of the people from the places Dom António went through and the surrounding area had left with most of the contents of their homes ... the English starved and died'.[26] However much they tried to disguise themselves in sheep's clothing, the English could not counteract the

---

[22] *Relación de lo subçedido del armada enemiga.* BN mss 18579, p. 42.
[23] Ibid., p. 43.
[24] *Memoria da Vinda dos Ingleses a Portugal em 1589*, p. 258, quoted in Pires De Lima, *O ataque.*
[25] Ibid.
[26] Ibid., p. 259.

reputation that went before them. We find an example of the Portuguese attitude in Don Juan da Rocha, 'an old servant of the Kings of Portugal, over seventy years of age, who when he heard that Dom António was approaching, abandoned his house and possessions to the enemy and was taken as far as he could on a handbarrow'.[27] Consequently, Campello had to resort to violence, and 'forced the people to provide the invaders with provisions'.[28] But it was not enough. Due to a combination of factors – the mistrust of the local population, the Archduke's precautions aimed at depriving the English of provisions en route and the Antonian-inspired strategy of the English which forbade looting – the invaders were dying of sickness, weakness and hunger. To make matters worse, they made the same mistake as in Corunna: they drank to excess, but this time on empty stomachs.[29]

Meanwhile, in the Spanish camp, the rumour spread that the English army – one of whose objectives in landing so far from Lisbon was to recruit a Portuguese army loyal to Dom António on the way– intended to head for Santarém. This meant a great detour on the route to Lisbon, but 'it became known that the army would march to Santarém, since it was powerful and fertile, populated by wealthy supporters of Dom António and the first place where he had been sworn in as king. The example of Santarém would attract the rest of the kingdom, and make it possible to raise a very large army.'[30] This news was soon disregarded, though it does tell us a little of the correlation between the two armies, not only in strength, but also in fears, longings and expectations. It also shows how well the Spanish camp was informed of the intentions of the English. There were indeed persuasive arguments that supported the notion of a stopover in Santarém, but the notion was soon dispelled. It was clearly a false rumour 'aimed at concealing the route they would actually take and at distracting our men and our purpose. It was soon seen to be false and it became clear how mistaken it would be for them to delay their arrival in Lisbon'.[31] Norris, for whom a delay could lead to catastrophe given the scarcity of provisions, decided to proceed directly to the capital and take no further risks by giving credence to Crato's optimistic expectations. Furthermore, marching to Santarém meant moving too far away from Cascais and possible rescue by the fleet to which they could withdraw in case of failure. In any case, the close linguistic similarity between Castilian and Portuguese formed an insurmountable barrier for speakers of a language that was far different from the Romance languages spoken in those parts. The mere consideration of possibly going to the Santarém region would have turned the English

---

[27] *Memoria da Vinda dos Inglises a Portugal em 1589*, p. 258.
[28] Letter from Falçao de Resende. Quoted in Ruela Pombo, *Portugal*, Part III, col. 21.
[29] Ibid., col. 18. Resende describes the English stay at Torres Vedras as follows: 'The English came without any sustenance and were so hungry that, once quartered, they ate all manner of rubbish, being unable to steal almost anything of value except provisions when they could find them. Many of them got drunk, since there was much wine to be had in the town and no one stopped them from doing so, and they became ill or died. Had our fighting men attacked them there and then, I believe they would have finished them off.'
[30] *Relación de lo subçedido del armada enemiga*. BN mss 18579, p. 44.
[31] Ibid.

army into nothing more than a mercenary force, paid for by Dom António and leading an army of his to the conquest of Lisbon.

> Meanwhile in the Portuguese capital the population was extremely agitated, for given everyone's dread of the enemy's army there were neither men nor beasts available to be put into service, and those animals that there were had to be taken for the field officers, who did not have any, from the private homes where they could be found, and many did not take their animals with them. Given the scarcity of carts and baggage for supplies, ammunition, tools and tents, all of the mules from His Highness's stables had to be used, leaving only those used to carry water to his kitchen, and apart from the noblemen of his chamber, all of his servants had to carry their weapons at the ready.[32]

Many Lisboans were leaving the city. As the Spanish searched house by house for pack animals and carts to transport troops and equipment that would harass the English army as it approached, they understood quite clearly that the defence of the city was now down to them.

---

[32] *Relación de lo subçedido del armada enemiga.* BN mss 18579, p. 45.

Chapter 19

In Loures

At dawn on the 30 May 1589, the English infantrymen loaded their weapons, munitions and baggage on their backs once more and set out again on their march. This was the longest and most exhausting stretch on their journey towards Lisbon, since with a halt at Enxara they had to cover more than thirty kilometres between Torres Vedras and Loures.[1] The Spanish continued with their strategy of harassing the army without facing it in open battle and continually monitoring the route it was taking in order to prevent it from obtaining supplies. Gaspar de Alarcón's cavalry had orders to keep within sight of the enemy in order to track its route and 'report on anything of interest'.[2] On this Tuesday, while Alarcón kept watch, the small Spanish force held a military parade at Nossa Senhora da Luz, some ten kilometres along the route that it was assumed the English would follow and

> His Highness (Archduke Alberto) arrived in the afternoon with many Portuguese noblemen and was pleased to see everyone so elegant and smart. And their morale was strengthened by the sight of their leader, and after the Count gave the appropriate order, he returned to the city with fewer men, since many stayed with the army, the better to serve him.[3]

The purpose of the Archduke's excursion was ceremonial and its aim was to strengthen Iberian morale in the face of the English advance. It was certainly not his intention to disobey Philip's orders not to abandon Lisbon, since this Habsburg monarch was aware that the key to success that spring lay in holding on to the capital. There was no doubt that only six years after the end of the struggle for succession in Portugal there were groups in Lisbon who would take advantage of the power vacuum that would have been left by the absence of Alberto and the best part of the Spanish garrison. These groups may have attempted to seize power in the name of Dom António, who had a less legitimate dynastic claim to the throne than Philip II, but who presented himself – fraudulently– as champion of Portuguese independence.

Norris, however, was commanding an army beset by hardship that 'moved with all haste and speed, driven by the pangs of hunger and overjoyed at the thought that it would soon be home to enjoy the milk and honey promised by Dom António'.[4] Having rested at Enxara, the Spanish set off again for Lisbon, but feeling dissatisfied with their

---

[1]   *Relación de lo subçedido del armada enemiga.* BN mss 18579, p. 46.
[2]   Ibid., p. 45.
[3]   Ibid.
[4]   *Memoria da Vinda dos Ingleses a Portugal em 1589*, p. 262, quoted in Pires De Lima, *O ataque.*

role of constant harassment and skirmishing, they were looking for a convenient pass where, with only a few troops, they could halt the advance of the English army. But they could not find one and the Count of Fuentes was unable to fight the enemy:

> The Count of Fuentes, who had ordered Captains Sancho Bravo and Gaspar de Alarcón to constantly trouble the enemy and see how strong they were, went in person to the pass of Montasique, in the belief that it was somewhere where a few might be able to take on many. However, whether because going around it was easy for the enemy, or because the cavalry had not sufficiently reconnoitred the area, their progress was not detained even for a single day. Perhaps there was some other unknown reason that made them realise that it was unwise to face the enemy in the open, and he decided not to await the enemy at the pass ... he nevertheless continued with the army in the field.

Thus, the English army 'suffered some damage from the Spanish cavalry, which never ceased in its prodding and harassing'.[5] The English colonel, Ralph Lane, wrote in this respect: 'The enemy, both horse and foot, every day made head before us, but every night we lodged in his quarter.'[6]

While the army advanced with great difficulty towards its goal, Drake managed to reach the port of Cascais 'and his fleet could take shelter in it while remaining out of range from the tower artillery because the port entrance was so wide'.[7] The fear aroused in the Lisbon area by the English Armada's arrival in Cascais was in direct proportion to its size. The sheer magnitude of the amphibious operation meant that it was a real exercise in bravery to believe that Lisbon was not already lost. Those who saw the English Armada mooring in Cascais could not help thinking of another enormous fleet of a similar size: the Spanish Armada. But there was also a strange coincidence, if such things exist, that highlighted the similarity of those two great expeditions, since 'when the fleet entered it was a year to the day since ours left from the same port'.[8] We shall deal later with the extraordinary set of similarities between the two armadas although, for those who witnessed them, their imposing appearance was the first similarity. The second – a curious fact for the superstitious or for those given to looking for hidden signs in historical events – was, as has been mentioned, that the English Armada reached Cascais exactly one year after its Spanish–Portuguese counterpart's departure. What could this mean? Was it a symbol of revenge? The continuation of the disaster of the Spanish Armada, one year later? Or was it perhaps a sign that the same curse that had caused the Spanish Armada to fail would bedevil the English Armada too? The terrible uncertainty regarding the future during those anxious days made it pressing to find answers where there were none, since

---

[5]   *Memoria da Vinda dos Ingleses a Portugal em 1589*, p. 262, quoted in Pires De Lima, *O ataque*.
[6]   Letter from Ralph Lane, 12 June 1589. Wernham, *Expedition*, p.186.
[7]   *Relación de lo subçedido del armada enemiga*. BN mss 18579, p. 46.
[8]   Ibid., p. 47.

the arrival of the enemy fleet in the city at the same time as they were approaching by land gave no small cause for concern. It was clear that we would be attacked by land and sea and that the reason why the army had not brought siege artillery must be that they were to land it from their ships close to the city.[9]

While from the land anxious men pondered on the significance of what they were witnessing, the Admiral deployed the tactical defensive manoeuvre of his fleet for the duration of its stay in Cascais, or, to be more precise, between Cascais and São Julião castle. To this end, he ordered 'that anchor be cast in the cove of San Antonio, where on a spit of land there is a Franciscan monastery, half a league further towards the estuary than Cascais, and a full league from São Julião'.[10] He was thus protected from the northerly wind, as well as from the artillery of the castles of Cascais and São Julião. He then made his move, 'ordering all of the larger and best armed ships to adopt a crescent formation, setting the flagship amid the two horns, anchoring as close to land as he could'.[11] Thus Drake formed a protective arch with his most powerful vessels, placing himself in the middle of this English armour-plated sea, right up next to the coast, together with his smaller ships and his many tenders. The ships remained, at all times, 'with their masts raised and ready to set sail in the event of any surprise attack'.[12] Not content with this defensive formation, however, 'every day they sent out squadrons to sail along the coasts north and south and out to the Berlengas Islands, in order to capture as many vessels as they could find and plunder them, and to mount guard in case they came across any galleys or other warships and quickly report back'.[13] Thus, with his lighter ships, Drake hunted down every merchant vessel in sight and brought them into his protective arc.

During the long afternoon of that Tuesday, 30 May, while Drake was settling in the fleet, the English army reached Loures, barely ten kilometres from the walls of Lisbon. For that reason,

> when His Highness realised that the enemy was not taking the detour through Santarém and was heading for Lisbon, he ordered everyone from all the monasteries outside the city walls and in the surroundings of Lisbon to come with their clothing to the city, where they would be given decent lodging for as long as there was any danger that the enemy might do them harm, since it was their custom to defile the images and relics of saints and mistreat men and women of the cloth.[14]

---

[9] *Relación de lo subçedido del armada enemiga.* BN mss 18579, p. 47. There could be another reason for the absence of siege artillery in the English Armada: Queen Elizabeth did not supply them with any so that the fleet would not be distracted from its main objective, which was to destroy the Spanish fleet in Santander. Wernham, *Expedition*, p. xxxi.

[10] Ibid., p. 46.

[11] Ibid.

[12] Ibid., p. 47.

[13] Ibid.

[14] Ibid., p. 47–8.

It should be remembered that Lisbon was at that time one of the largest cities in Europe and the capital of a great empire that had grown continuously since the days of Henry the Navigator. For that reason, the great Portuguese metropolis had spilled over beyond its huge walled perimeter with many monasteries and villas.

It was an unprecedented affront that members of the large community dedicated to a spiritual and contemplative life – the highest calling, according to ancient philosophers – should be forced to abandon their sacred places, leaving empty their private and sunlit cloisters. It was well known, however, that since the days of the atrocities of the Vikings, the brutal northerners, who were savage and primitive in their violence, had no respect for anything. Six hundred years earlier, the ruthless Almanzor (al-Mansur, 'the Victorious') had shown more respect for religious symbols than those so-called reformers who enjoyed debasing sacred images, and desecrating sacred places. The terrified English Catholics – a third of the population – were suffering at first hand from brutal persecution due to the wave of religious intolerance that was bleeding England to the core.[15] Thus the peace of the peacable was broken and many monks and nuns got ready to leave their monasteries and convents and take refuge behind the city walls.

Night fell on that Tuesday with the English army quartered in Loures. The positive side of this was that they had now completed an exhausting and perilous journey through a torrid and hostile land, made harder by attacks from the Spanish. Another positive was that they were now on the verge of fulfilling the great strategic mission for which the fleet and the army had been assembled. But there was also a number of negatives, not least the fact that they were now so close to the main body of the Spanish troops. Thus,

> so that the enemy should not enjoy too much rest, the Count ordered Don Pedro and Don Sancho to attack those who had arrived, as near as possible to the enemy camp but keeping their own men safe, and these set off for Santo Adrião, about half a league from the enemy, and posted guards all around their camp so as to

[15] Religious intolerance in England reached harrowing levels during the sixteenth and seventeenth centuries. Henry VIII's decision to become the head of the Christian Church in England and the refusal to swear an oath of allegiance to him being treated as a crime of high treason ended with the execution of the most eminent Englishmen of the day, among them Thomas More and John Fisher. Then came torture for Catholics and Protestants, and to add insult to injury they were often tied together back to back and burnt in the same bonfire. The persecution got worse during Elizabeth's reign and became ever more cruel, including the disembowelling and quartering of live victims. Then the *Commission*, an equivalent of the Inquisition, was introduced, but it operated under cover of darkness, with Catholic households being attacked at night, and the commitment of all manner of atrocities. In the seventeenth century, Cromwell continued with the barbarity, having 3,000 Irish Catholics knifed to death in the attack on Drogheda. The issue of religious intolerance being specific to Spain thus acts as a smokescreen. On this subject, see Julián Juderías, *La Leyenda Negra* (Salamanca, 2003) (1st edition 1917), pp. 368–75. It includes a bibliography.

reconnoitre it better and cut off their supplies, all of which were brought by the people of the land. Hence, the army brought neither carts nor baggage with them. At dawn they began to attack them from several sides at once, wounding and killing some of their men and taking others prisoner.[16]

After so many months of preparation, having being rejected by the local population and the pitiful number of soldiers defending Galicia, and after the arduous march to Lisbon, the English Armada had finally reached its objective.

---

[16] *Relación de lo subçedido del armada enemiga.* BN mss 18579, p. 48.

Chapter 20

On the Outskirts of Lisbon

Wednesday, 31 May, dawned with the promise, the suspicion, or the terrible certainty that the awful monotony that was beginning to take hold of the English expedition in the spring of 1589 was about to be broken. The attackers were actually at the gates of Lisbon. If they attempted another day's march they would reach the city walls before they had completed half of it. The English were about to lay their cards on the table and make clear their true intentions, objectives and strategy. Was it to be a combined, simultaneous attack, with Drake by sea and Norris by land? Were the suspicions of the Spanish, therefore, about to be proven correct? Would they attack with siege ladders? How committed was the Portuguese faction supporting the Prior of Crato? Was there some collusion within Lisbon? Was there a Trojan horse within the city ready to open the gates when the moment came?

The Spanish had taken every possible precaution. Philip's orders were unequivocal; the objectives were clear-cut; the forces were limited. Philip's strategy was based on achieving a balance between the two extremes of remaining entrenched in Lisbon and going beyond the city walls. The Spanish could not afford to concentrate on the English without also keeping an eye on possible conspirators against the King. The people of Lisbon were still abandoning the city, while the price of a passage to the opposite side of the estuary continued to increase several times over.[1]

The Archduke's primary mission was to prepare the defence of Lisbon's long perimeter wall. The Spanish forces inside the walls were to deal – as we have seen – with two possible incidents, the internal and the external. However – and this was also known to the Viceroy of Portugal – siege warfare, as well as tactics, honour and the careful management of morale all demanded a show of fighting strength against a hungry English army. Captain Juan de Torres received the order to confront the enemy. Like all professional military men, he was aware that time was a sword that

---

[1] 'The boatmen, cartmen and *almocreves* (handlers of beasts of burden) took advantage of the situation and raised the prices for their horses, carts and hiring. A cart from Aldeia Galega to Elvas rose to over 60,000 reales and renting a pack horse or mule went up to 10,000; it cost 12,000 to go to Estremoz, Évora, and most parts of that area ... the excesses and overcharging reached such a level that the damage and tyranny done to their own countrymen was greater than that of the enemy heretics. But these outrages were later punished by His Highness, who ordered the competent judges to investigate those responsible for these excesses, arrest those guilty of them and have them return the money in excess of what was commonly charged before this incident. This action was deemed necessary and was very well received by the people.' *Memoria da Vinda dos Ingleses a Portugal em 1589*, p. 267, quoted in Pires De Lima, *O ataque*.

was slowly sinking into the breast of the invading army. He also knew, however, that a cornered bull, already wounded by such a sword, can be a very dangerous animal. The order was clear:

> Having been informed that the enemy had stopped over the night before in Loures, and fearing they would attack the following day in the area of Santa Clara and the coal docks, the Count ordered Don Juan de Torres to take 200 harquebusiers and musketeers to try to keep the enemy occupied, even if it were to cost them some of their own men. He also told him, in case he needed any further help, to ask Don Sancho who was in the vicinity. He thus chose a path between Loures and São Adrião, with captains Don Sancho Bravo and Antonio de Torres protecting them from the sides and from above, and taking on the front with some of the musketeers on some of the walls.[2]

Torres thus prepared a passage where he could face the advancing English army, as well as a rearguard to be used in case of any need to retreat. All that was left now was to drive the English towards the place where, even if the defenders lost a number of men, they could inflict some damage on the invaders. To that end, with some of the remaining harquebusiers 'he entered the enemy field about a quarter of a league and sounded the horn in an attempt to get them to come out of their trenches'. But Don Juan de Torres achieved nothing on that occasion for, having dug in, the English did not leave their trenches all day and were determined to recuperate after the exhausting marches of the preceding days: 'From two in the afternoon until ten at night nothing could be done, since the enemy were unwilling to come out.'[3]

At least the Spanish soldiers had the consolation of knowing that the passive attitude of the English denied them a surprise booty. Indeed, had the English marched straight to the outskirts of Lisbon that 31 May, fighting their way past Torres's forces – however much heroism the Spanish had shown and however much they would have suffered – they would have hit upon an vast stock of supplies outside the city walls:

> Great care was taken that day to make sure that all the storerooms of wheat and biscuit, flour, rye and barley, and the houses of bakers outside the city walls, should provide for the people of the city and castle, since much greater harm would come from their falling into enemy hands, for if they were to find such a great provision of supplies that they could use for their army and fleet it would have meant the complete destruction and loss of the entire city and kingdom.[4]

It was ironical that after such a long march that had been blighted by hunger, the English stopped just when a great feast was within their grasp. Although the attackers were probably unaware of the extent of the opportunity they had missed to revive their

---

[2]   *Relación de lo subçedido del armada enemiga.* BN mss 18579, p. 49.
[3]   Ibid.
[4]   Ibid., p. 50.

army, it was comparable to the Spanish lack of foresight in not getting the supplies inside the city walls sooner. Such bad judgment is reminiscent of the same sad mistake made a month earlier in Corunna. However, transporting the huge quantity of supplies stored in one of the largest and most active ports in Europe was a task as demanding as it was complex, and it is therefore understandable that it was left until the very last moment. Besides, it is also possible that both Cerralbo and the Archduke had weighed up the negative effect such a measure would have had for the morale of the towns and cities they were to defend. But then the size of the problem became clear: 'Having decided to have it all taken into the city, there was neither the time nor the men to do it, nor boatmen who were willing to work for any amount of money. The solution was to allow the poor to take whatever supplies they could in exchange for moving them.'[5] In that way, all the supplies that it was possible to move in the time were taken into the city. This also pleased the city poor who, for a few hours, were free to enjoy the pleasure of fetching all the food they could carry over several journeys. In spite of all of this, after several hours of work it became apparent that such a quantity of supplies could not all be moved from the many storerooms that supplied greater Lisbon. It was then that, as a last resort,

> seeing how little the enemy was being deprived of and the great risk involved in letting them have it, it was decided to set fire to all the warehouses where there were any supplies left so that it could be of no use to the enemy. So that is what they did, and it gave great hope to those in charge of conducting the war.[6]

The storehouses of Lisbon burned, just as those of Moscow 223 years later would burn, a portent of the inescapable fate of Napoleon's ambitious *Grande Armée*. And this rather smaller sixteenth-century *Grande Armée* – at a time when England's population was less than four million inhabitants – also watched while the solution to their problems of hunger went up in smoke within their very grasp.

The soldiers enjoyed the fire. They knew that logistics had to come before tactics, even if the spectacle of so much human effort sacrificed and so much food wasted was a perfect example of the miseries of war. Drake saw the brightly coloured flames from Cascais, the columns of smoke rising into the Lisbon sky. He was very familiar with the smell of fires burning, but for once he was not responsible for them. Drake's situation was distressing: he was excluded from the military operations and daunted by having to cross the straits that separated him from Lisbon, with a fleet so large that rarely had such a concentration of English ships ever been seen – not even in Plymouth – and yet he was unable to take any action. He did not have many troops[7] but he did not need them to get to Lisbon. All he needed was a favourable wind and tide. It is difficult to tell whether it was cowardice that pushed him into that situation or whether it was the situation that

---

[5]   *Relación de lo subçedido del armada enemiga*. BN mss 18579, p. 50.
[6]   Ibid.
[7]   About 3,400 men. González-Arnao, *Derrota y muerte*, p. 85.

turned him into a coward. His reputation for bravery had been based on the element of surprise, on his unexpected audacity, on nimble vessels that always made escape easy. This time things were different. They were waiting for him with loaded cannons. He had many more cannon and he had two hundred ships, but entering the estuary meant either the victory of a lifetime or laying himself open to defeat, prison or death. Besides, Drake had no communication with Norris and knew nothing of the army that had landed.[8] And so, while he remained stuck in Cascais, one cargo ship after another, filled to the gunnels with grain to trade in Lisbon, fell into his hands. Beyond the resentment for the way in which Norris had demoted him, his habits as a pirate ran counter to leading into full combat the largest English fleet that had ever set sail from England.

However, while the storehouses of Lisbon were burning, an even sadder spectacle unfolded outside the walls of the great capital. It was the abandonment of so many convents and monasteries and the solemn processional retreat of their devout residents taking refuge behind Lisbon's walls. In those distant, spiritual times such a move created a vivid impression: 'On this day the monks and nuns from outside the walls entered in procession and their feelings were so strong that it broke the hearts of all those who saw it and encouraged them to avenge the wrong done to the servants of God who spent their lives doing harm to no-one.'[9] The nuns who arrived were from 'the convents of Nossa Senhora da Quietação das Flamengas, of Esperança, Santa Clara and Santa Ana, all of them Franciscans, as well as from Odivelas and the Bernardas, and A Anunciada and the Carmelites'. No one trusted the behaviour of the heretic reformers, but some did trust in their own ability to resist them or else were in more easily defensible locations, and so stayed where they were. These included the members of 'the convent of the Madre de Deus of Sóbregas, as Arrepentidas, in the right-hand street of Santa Catalina, and the Hieronymite monks of Belém'.[10] It was not only the nuns living outside the city walls who sought safety, however, but 'also most of the women left in the town itself went to the monasteries and were so afraid that, not content with being in the churches, they took refuge in the closed quarters, and even in the cells of the monks themselves, which caused no small amount of rumour and scandal'.[11]

While all these precautions were being taken, the English continued to feel under time pressure since 'that day Francisco Ángel came with 500 men in two companies ascribed to the Duke of Feria which made a timely arrival'.[12] The enormity of the error the English had made in stopping at Corunna and not heading straight for Lisbon was now becoming apparent.

A couple of leagues from Lisbon, the Count of Fuentes was haunted by suspicion and mistrust and decided to move his main camp. He was aware that a great pincer

---

[8] Kelsey, *Sir Francis Drake*, p. 357.
[9] *Relación de lo subçedido del armada enemiga*. BN mss 18579, p. 49.
[10] Ibid.
[11] *Relación de la venida de Don Antonio de Portugal prior de ocrato con la Armada de la Reyna de Inglaterra en el año de 1589*. BN mss 1749, fol. 228.
[12] *Relación de lo subçedido del armada enemiga*. BN mss 18579, p. 49.

movement was threatening Lisbon: from the north, barely two hours' march away, Norris's army awaited its orders; from the west, Drake presumably intended to force his way into the estuary and attack Lisbon from the sea. Fuentes could not neglect either flank and his head was filled with questions: Why had the English army entrenched itself at Loures, without even coming out once to confront Juan de Torres's men and their harquebuses? Was this for fear of the notorious Spanish harquebusiers?[13] Why had he brought no carts carrying supplies, entrusting everything to the unreliable assistance of António's supporters? Above all, why had he not brought any artillery in order to breach the walls? What ominous mystery was hidden here? What was Drake waiting for in Cascais? Fuentes could find only one plausible explanation for the strange conduct of the English army:

> The Count considered that he was away from the city, while the enemy was so close that it could reach the walls as quickly as his own army, and he thought it a bad sign that they were avoiding combat to such an extreme, and that they had brought neither carts nor baggage with supplies and artillery to breach the walls. Furthermore, their position could not be held without considerable help from the people of the land, nor would they choose to come up so close to a walled city without trying to breach it if they did not have an agreement with those who lived within the walls.[14]

The Count believed that there was a third, Antonian front inside the city, but such a front was the responsibility of the Archduke and, given the slow arrival of reinforcements, it could be neutralized by degrees. In order to fulfil his mission, he decided to occupy a strategic position from where he could assist Lisbon on either of the two flanks:

> He decided to approach the city, entering Alcántara itself where Dom António's army was when the Duke of Alba entered,[15] because of its strong natural defences, and with the aim of being on hand so that if the navy attacked from the sea in an attempt to support the army, he [the Count] could better obstruct the enemy, and he did so that very day.[16]

While these tactical manoeuvres took place on the eve of Corpus Christi, the day (according to widespread rumour) that Crato had promised to enter Lisbon, the Viceroy 'went out that afternoon to inspect the field accompanied by many Portuguese horsemen, and

---

[13] Spanish harquebusiers were renowned throughout Europe for their effectiveness. William Garrard, a famous English military man, attributed this to 'iron discipline, strict obedience and the perfect orderliness of the Spanish soldiers'. Quoted in González-Arnao, *Derrota y muerte*, p. 47.

[14] *Relación de lo subçedido del armada enemiga.* BN mss 18579, p. 50.

[15] This led to the Battle of Alcántara in 1580 and resulted in Philip II of Spain becoming King of Portugal the following year [translator's note].

[16] *Relación de lo subçedido del armada enemiga.* BN mss 18579, p. 51.

the Count informed him of what was happening and of his understanding'. Fuentes also disclosed to him a most disturbing fact:

> The Portuguese colonels had found many soldiers missing the previous night, who had been found staying at their homes, and that come the time of the attack they doubted very much that their men would fight, since they were all inexperienced and had never known any similar occasion; they were moved by the sight of their families and they were not used to combat.[17]

The Archduke decided that by dawn of the following day, the day of Corpus Christi, the army outside the walls should enter the city, since 'if the army on the outside met with any misfortune when encountering the enemy, there would be a great risk of losing the kingdom'.[18] However, once the army was behind the walls, 'it could remain for many days and wait for help before coming out and removing the enemy when the time was right'.[19]

Having made these arrangements, the Archduke returned to his palace.[20] Night fell upon Lisbon. There was an obvious reason for Crato to let it be known to all and sundry that Corpus Christi, traditionally the most important ceremonial and processional day in the city, was to be D-Day for seizing the capital. In that complex war, the Anglo-Spanish political struggle and the Protestant–Catholic religious rivalry had the extra dimension of the struggle for Portuguese succession. Crato, a Catholic, had chosen the symbolic day of Corpus Christi for his entry into Lisbon in order to cancel out the obvious irony arising from his fighting alongside a powerful Protestant army against Catholic Philip II. The message was that under Crato Portugal would continue to be a Catholic country. The challenge was clear and candid: the illegitimate pretender would be acclaimed at the Praça do Rossio the following day. All the restless Spanish had to do was to decide exactly when they should start fighting in order to prevent it from happening.

---

[17] *Relación de lo subçedido del armada enemiga.* BN mss 18579, p. 51.

[18] Ibid.

[19] Ibid., p. 52.

[20] The determining factor in the decision to bring the army within Lisbon's walls was the expert opinion of the Portuguese commanders. Here is how the issue was described in the Portuguese journal: 'Once His Highness had returned to the city, there were some discussions among the Portuguese colonels on the matter, during which Don Fernando de Castro was for many reasons of the opinion that the camp should withdraw into the city, since it was most expedient to delay the encounter with the enemy, for the help expected from many parts had not arrived and any delay was of great benefit to us, as we were awaiting fresh troops who were starting to arrive. It was known that others were on their way and would most likely not be long in coming. The enemy, on the other hand, was suffering from hunger and sickness and in the skirmishes with us they were losing men they could not replace. Hence delaying all-out combat was a good solution for us in order to obtain some advantage and for the enemy to lose it. So the safest course was to bring the camp into the city and strengthen the main buildings, since given the size of the city it could not be besieged on land by less than forty thousand men, and so that there were men enough to protect the walls in the places where they could be attacked, the advice was to withdraw inside.' *Memoria da Vinda dos Ingleses a Portugal em 1589*, p. 262, quoted in Pires De Lima, *O ataque*.

Chapter 21

Encamisada

Captains Juan de Torres, Sancho Bravo, Gaspar de Alarcón and Francisco Malo were planning the action that had been ordered by the Archduke that they had not been able to carry out the previous day. In order to do so, they had been 'reconnoitring the places and sites suitable for an attack'.[1] The location was chosen and the unit selected by the Viceroy – two hundred harquebusiers supported by some cavalry – awaited the approach of dawn. The orders were clear: 'To attack the enemy, even if it meant losing some of their own men.'[2] Since the English had not wanted to come out, the fight had to be taken to them. The Spanish approached the camp as stealthily as they could. When they got close by, they shouted 'Long live Dom António!'[3] making the guards think that the long-awaited Portuguese reinforcements were arriving. The guards had their throats slit without a sound and the Spanish went for the flank chosen for the attack, between Loures and Lamarinha, which turned out to be the camp of Lieutenant Colonel John Sampson.[4]

At that time the Spanish army was very well known for its surprise commando attacks. So much so that there was a specific Spanish word for them, just as later the words *guerrilla* and *guerrillero* would appear, to the consternation of the Corsican General Napoleon.[5] The word was *encamisada*, from *camisa* meaning 'shirt', since the Spanish soldiers wore white shirts over their breastplates in order to identify themselves and avoid killing each other in any furious skirmish. In English, the word was shortened to *camisado*,[6] although these operations were also referred to by the word *bravado*.[7] However, in the Spanish journal, this guerrilla tactic is referred to as *dar Santiago* ('to give Santiago, or St James') in memory of Santiago 'the Moorslayer'.[8]

---

[1] *Relación de lo subçedido del armada enemiga*. BN mss 18579, p. 52.

[2] Ibid., p. 48.

[3] Edward Norris to Thomas Heneage, June 1589. Wernham, *Expedition*, p. 184.

[4] Letter from Ralph Lane, 12 June 1589. Ibid., p. 186.

[5] The Peninsular War (1807–14) saw the emergence of groups of Spaniards rising up against Napoleonic troops by using *guerilla* (literally, 'little war') tactics [translator's note].

[6] Letter from Ralph Lane, 12 June 1589. Wernham, *Expedition*, p. 186.

[7] Another account of the journey, after 16 July 1589. Ibid., p. 244.

[8] The expression '*dar Santiago*' or '*dar un Santiago*' meant any sudden and direct attack or assault leading to hand-to-hand combat and was not restricted to nocturnal or guerrilla attacks. They were defined rather by the battle cries '*Santiago y a ellos!*' ('Up and at 'em') or '*Santiago y cierra España!*' (where the verb '*cerrar*' means 'attack' and '*España*' is the subject of the verb, not the direct object, as it may appear). '*Santiago!*', with nothing added to it, was a way of invoking the help of the apostle as patron saint and protector of the nation, and in memory of his legendary participation in the famous Battle of Clavijo, which gave rise to the iconography of St James on horseback or '*Santiago Matamoros*' ('the Moorslayer').

Whatever it was called, this commando tactic is widely referred to in English sources and, apart from several minor skirmishes, it was the main military engagement since the ferocious resistance offered six days earlier during the landing. This is how it was described in the Spanish diary:

> Before dawn on Thursday, the day of Corpus, they 'gave Santiago' on a hill where there must have been some thousand enemy soldiers, between Loures and Lamarinha, with the 200 harquebusiers and horsemen, where they slit the throats of over 200 men, and if no greater damage was done it was because the terrain was very uneven and they were very well entrenched. Twelve of our men were injured, among them Juan de Torres, sent by the Count on this foray, who was shot in the arm by a harquebus. At first it was treated as a light wound, since it had not broken any bones nor hit any of his joints, but he died from it twenty days later. His death was much mourned, since he had conducted himself and fought as a great knight.[9]

Thus Don Juan de Torres met his fate as a soldier, as a pawn in a game of strategy, ready to be sacrificed and to die with his men for the sake of the common good. This brave captain had already tried to carry out his orders the previous night and, in the face of English passivity, was forced to take the offensive himself a few hours later. He did not sleep, therefore, until he had fulfilled his mission of 'keeping the enemy occupied', or perhaps he did, availing himself of the early hours to recover and unleash his *encamisada* with even greater energy. Ralph Lane[10] reports that since the detachment was slightly set apart from the rest of the army – and due to the rapid, surprise nature of the Spanish attack – by the time they tried to react, the Spanish had already left. Another anonymous account[11] also maintains that the sudden attack occurred at great speed. The Spanish, some of them on horseback, did indeed enter the camp quickly and stealthily, ripping open the tents and killing the sleeping soldiers. Loud shouts were soon heard and the English, half naked in the warm night, rushed out of their tents. Scattered around the camp, the Spanish did their job quickly and silently, but the daggers were soon replaced by the thunder of the harquebuses. At the furthest point from the Spanish attack, the stunned English invaders established a makeshift line of resistance armed with swords, pikes and harquebuses. Many of the English soldiers died in hand-to-hand fighting and others withdrew to the place where Sampson was setting up the

---

[9] *Relación de lo subçedido del armada enemiga.* BN mss 18579, p. 52.
[10] Letter from Ralph Lane, 12 June 1589. Wernham, *Expedition,* p. 186.
[11] This account describes the episode thus: 'And the next day being Thursday, very early in the morning by the break of day the Spaniards gave us a bravado, both with footmen and horsemen, to the number of 1508 [*sic*] as we were credibly informed. They charged our watch so fast with their musket shot that that they caused us to retire to our court of guard. And so our court of guard did put themselves in arms, and some of other companies with ours, so we went forth to charge the enemy. But before we came forth the enemy had very near entered our barricades. So we played with our shot for the space of an hour and there came no man to relieve us. Our shot did retire and 20 pikes did stand in the face of the enemy for a time. But in the end we were driven to retire some two rods, until our shot came on with a fresh charge and we went out with them and gave the enemy such a retreat twice so far as they retreated us.' Another account of the journey. Ibid., pp. 244–5.

defence, while the din had already alerted the entire English army. Thunderous harquebus volleys were exchanged and Torres was wounded. The Spanish withdrew as quickly as they had come. A moment later, the only sound was that of horses' hooves, then silence and the cries of the many wounded. As the day slowly dawned, the place attacked by the Spanish was a pitiful sight. The corpses called out for revenge, but in logistical terms a much greater problem was posed by the many wounded who needed to be evacuated, fed and taken care of. On the English Armada's D-Day, the Spanish had acted first. The invading army was thrown into confusion by the news coming from the hill of Lamarinha. If it actually was the day chosen for the attack on Lisbon, the Spanish had got them started early and had let them know that this land was not theirs. The only land they had was where their army was situated. So now they knew where things stood.

A little later, once it was daylight, the Spanish detachments outside the wall got ready to enter the powerful Fernandine perimeter in formation.[12] Their fluttering flags entered the city, to the great joy of the people of Lisbon.[13] Fernando de Castro was right. The defence of the enormous walled perimeter of Lisbon would require all available Spanish forces. It was then that the defence of Lisbon was prepared. By the end of the sixteenth century, the old Fernandine wall was no longer complete. Indeed, the lively activity of the port of Lisbon during the fifteenth and sixteenth centuries had been responsible for the demolition of the maritime stretch of the historic wall that separated the city from the port. There were new buildings in its place, and although these followed the old line of the wall and were adjoining – thereby providing a new walled perimeter with houses for walls and street entrances for gates and wickets – the waterfront was the weakest structural link in the whole wall. To this had to be added the buildings and squares outside the walled perimeter and next to the sea, such as A Ribeira das Naos Square, the Paço (Palace) da Ribeira, Terreiro do Paço Square, the Alfándega (customs), O Terreiro do Trigo or the Chafariz waterfront up to the coal dock. In short, Lisbon's weak spot was its waterfront, but on the other hand it had developed new and powerful defence mechanisms to completely seal off the Tagus Estuary. These included São Julião castle, the castle of Caparica, or the beautiful Manueline Belém tower. There was, of course, another powerful weapon that could bombard any navy daring to approach, let alone set anchor opposite the city. This was the imposing castle of São Jorge, at the heart and origin of Lisbon, perched on its highest peak. Given the land-based nature of the challenge, however, Lisbon had to be defended inch by inch from the wall, or even, on the waterfront, from outside the walls and at street level. Let us consider how the various detachments were deployed on the morning of Corpus Christi, 1 June.

Under the command of Lope Suárez and pointing out to sea beyond the walls, six pieces of field artillery had been installed opposite the entrance to the Paço da Ribeira (which was a bit further west than the present-day western façade of the Praça do

[12] The Fernandine wall, the solid Lisbon wall built by King Dom Fernando in 1373–75, had thirty-six gates, seventy-seven high turrets and a perimeter of 5,350 metres. Chistovam Rodrigues de Oliveira, *Summario e que brevemente se contem alguas cousas (assi ecclesiasticas como seculares) que ha na cidade de Lisboa*, (Lisbon, 1554). 1755 edition, pp. 121–2.

[13] *Memoria da Vinda dos Ingleses a Portugal em 1589*, p. 263, quoted in Pires De Lima, *O ataque*.

Comércio). Companies from the Tercio regiment of Don Manuel Castelblanco covered from Arco dos Cregos (present-day Arco da Rua Augusta) to the Alfándega (present-day Ministerio das Finanzas) and Terreiro do Trigo Square. At the Alfándega, an artillery platform with a parapet was installed, with four cannon pointing towards the sea and another pointing inland in order to bombard those assaulting the wall. This cannon was pointed towards the Porta do Mar, located at present-day Rua dos Bacalhoeiros. From there up to the coal docks (present-day Museu Militar), several other artillery pieces were set up at intervals. At the Porta da Cruz four Spanish companies were posted. The small gate of São Vicente and nearby walls were in the charge of the Tercio regiment of Rui Peres de Távora. The Nossa Senhora da Graça Square was defended by Captains Álvaro de Mendoza and Pedro de Salazar with another four Spanish companies. In the area of Terreiro do Paço (present-day Praça do Comércio), which presented a difficult challenge, the real owners of Lisbon and masters of half the world – the men of Portugal – were about to show their worth. These were not, however, the only precautions taken in order to make Lisbon impregnable to both the army and the fleet, for with suspicions about the enemy within, 'Portuguese horsemen were ordered to watch the streets in groups day and night, ready for battle, in order to keep the city safe from any popular disturbances.'[14]

While Lisbon prepared itself for the assault, Francisco Coloma reported from the reinforced waterfront of São Julião that there was no news, and put forward the idea that Drake's plans did not include forcing his way into the estuary: 'I cannot be persuaded that they will come in so close, for since they have been alongside Cascais they could have done so before now, with the winds and the tides having both been very much in their favour.' He also reported on the English fleet's strategy of keeping a number of vessels permanently on alert and patrolling on the open sea to prevent any surprises, for 'some of their ships are always sailing out at sea on the watch, for they must be fearful of a fleet appearing'. He also mentioned artillery activity at the castle of Cascais ('Today the enemy has fired a few artillery rounds against Cascais,') and said that he does not know if the English will unload artillery in order to storm it. He also referred to the final preparations in the castle: 'We have been working with the men from the galleys to finish embanking the moat of the Castle of São Julião.'[15]

Back in Lisbon, we find that 'while His Highness was in the chapel, there was a throng of people at the storeroom opposite the palace gate, where they were handing out harquebuses, matchlocks, powder and pikes to the Portuguese infantry'. Indeed, it had been decided to arm the Portuguese infantry since they had shown their loyalty to the son of Queen Isabella of Portugal, who acted as regent of Spain in the absence of Emperor Charles.[16] There was no time to lose, and it was essential to combine the

---

[14] *Relación de lo subçedido del armada enemiga.* BN mss 18579, p. 55.

[15] Francisco de Coloma to the King, São Julião castle, 1 June 1589. AGS. *Guerra Antigua.* File 249, fol. 118.

[16] Isabella (1503–39), daughter of King Manuel I of Portugal and María of Aragón, married the Emperor Charles in 1526 and gave birth to Philip the following year. She served as regent during Charles's absences in the 1530s fighting the Ottomans and Francis I of France [translator's note].

efforts of the Spanish and the Portuguese if Lisbon was to be saved from the sacking that Crato had promised the Queen of England. With such an urgent need to distribute the weapons, 'the officers proceeded so quickly that many arms were handed out without any order, and a spark managed to fall into the powder left in the bottom of a keg. The flames got to a number of men and a horse,'[17] and the thunderous noise was such that 'it brought the halberdiers out of the chapel, and His Highness comported himself with the dignity required by the place and by his own person'.

This was all evidence of the city's thorough preparations: Portugal's capital was ready for the challenge. But on the English side, the promised date of Corpus Christi was out of the question, however opportune for its Catholic symbolism and Crato's obsession. The English did not even have control of the battlefield, since 'that day Ruy Lorenzo de Taide stayed outside the city with his cavalry company, and Antonio Pereira cut off land connections, supplies and forays of some of the enemy, which he kept working at without returning to the city until he withdrew to Cascais with a great number of valuable men'.[18]

Meanwhile, the Count of Fuentes, with his horsemen and infantry, carried out his orders and waited for the arrival of the English. By the afternoon, however, with no sign of the enemy and making the assumption that the invading army would come from Loures to Lisbon via Alvalade, he decided that it was necessary to prepare the defence of that route, since 'it is all well-entrenched and with good walls, there being few places by which to enter, and it would be of the utmost importance to occupy it before the arrival of the enemy'.[19] The plan was conveyed to the Count of Villadorta so that 'on this day, at sundown, he went to the field with all the Portuguese cavalry and infantry that he could muster and manned the entrances'.[20] Fuentes, however, misjudged the timing of the English approach to Lisbon: they did not attack that day of Corpus Christi of 1589, nor did they remain stationed in Loures. It so happened that 'when the spies that the Count had sent forth arrived, the enemy musketry was already inside and had begun to form the squadron of pikemen who were making their entry. Thus, the Count could advance no further and had to return to the city.'[21]

The Count de Villadorta returned to Lisbon with the alarming news that the enemy was in Alvalade. This meant that at any moment there could be a surprise attack under cover of darkness. Up to a point, the threat of Crato's vow was not over, as it was still the night of Corpus Christi. Many torches were lit at intervals along the wall and the number of guards outside was heavily reinforced. The care taken by the Archduke that night to protect Lisbon was truly worthy of the thoroughness of King Philip. Moreover, Fuentes was growing increasingly suspicious regarding the secret inside help on which the

---

[17] *Relación de lo subçedido del armada enemiga.* BN mss 18579, p. 56.
[18] Ibid.
[19] Ibid.
[20] Ibid.
[21] Ibid. p. 57.

English army, under Crato's guidance, might have been counting. As previously mentioned, the Count found it very strange that Norris had brought no siege cannons. Thus,

> with the enemy stationed that Thursday night in the fields of Alvalade, less than a league from the city and able to reach the walls so quickly, that night there was as much vigilance as was necessary concerning matters outside the wall as well as for anything that might arise within. Outside the walls a few guards were placed here and there, while soldiers went out to spy in the field and see if there was any movement, but that night all was quiet.[22]

---

[22] *Relación de lo subçedido del armada enemiga.* BN mss 18579, p 57.

Chapter 22

The Awakening of Saint George

The day dawned on the 2 June and, without any consideration for human exertion, it promised to be very hot. Every league covered by the English army in a southerly direction meant an increase in the heat and even worse; every day the attack on Lisbon was delayed their enemy gained more reinforcements. Philip II's strategy, endorsed and put into practice by Fernando Castro, was slowly proving to be decisively effective. Meanwhile, as if preoccupied, Drake continued looking out to sea instead of towards the land. His fleet was like a gigantic butterfly net, or rather an *urca* net. Conditioned by the habit of a lifetime, he made sure to capture every boat coming into Lisbon. In this way he filled the centre of his crescent formation with prey – almost exclusively Hanseatic *urcas* – while anchored in the Bay of Cascais. This had been Drake's life: not one of discovery, exploration or foundation but instead a life of raiding, in a sea already charted with both his would-be and his widely scattered victims. However, apart from Drake and his wearisome *urca*-catching game in the Bay of Cascais – an exercise that did not even block the entry to the estuary – the fragrant and delightful freshness of that morning heralded a day of sound and fury.

The English army spent the morning reconnoitring 'the site they would use as quarters from the entire area of the city, and decided upon the part going from the windmills of São Roque and the gate of Santa Catalina up to La Esperanza, as it is a high part of town and has good houses for lodging'.[1] Norris set himself up in some comfort in the splendour of the outskirts of Lisbon. He was aware of the tactical superiority of his army in the face of a Spanish contingent that was smaller and could not come out to confront him. His chosen place had additional advantages, as it was 'as close as it could be to receiving help from the navy if it came in, and anywhere they might be attacked, by day or night, they were in a better position than our people and would be able to find them'.[2]

The defenders had a number of difficult physical tasks to perform. In addition to examining the city wall closely to discover any possible weak spots, they had to do what had been done in Corunna very conscientiously by the women of that city, which was to shore up the inside of the gates, even though the gates temporarily lost their function as throughways and became just another part of the wall. Thus, 'on that day the order was given to shore up the gates of the city, which was done by the infantry on guard at each one of them'.[3] Transporting earth, stones, wood and performing heavy construction work proved most arduous,

---

[1] *Relación de lo subçedido del armada enemiga.* BN mss 18579, p. 57.
[2] Ibid.
[3] Ibid., p. 59.

and since a lot of work was expected during the siege, and the weather was very hot and the land very dry, and at the time there was a lack of supplies of every kind, with a lot to defend and few soldiers available to take turns and relieve each other, His Highness ordered Don Francisco Duarte to satisfy their needs as required in each case, and sent a lot of biscuit and cheese to all the guards with casks of wine and half-casks of water.[4]

Clearly the defenders faced a difficult predicament, but if the Spanish complained about the heat, what must the English have been going through? If Philip's soldiers had to make do on that day of guard duty and uninterrupted work on the walls with bread and cheese, wine and water, frugal but abundant fare, what did the attackers have to sustain them?

That Friday the invading army's situation was becoming critical. Campello's determined efforts to obtain supplies had had to deal not only with Ataíde's attempts to frustrate him but also with the attitude of the Portuguese people. But over and above that conflict, there was something irresponsible in keeping the army in such pitiful conditions. They were even worse than – but to a large extent similar to – those the Spanish had had to endure nine months earlier on the return voyage of the Spanish Armada. Where the Spanish had suffered from cold, thirst and hunger, the English were burnt by the sun and made even thirstier and so took to drinking stagnant pond water. This resulted in mass poisoning and gastroenteritis that was added to the already long list of afflictions that members of the expedition had had to endure. Hunger, not as lethal as thirst but still damaging when taken to extremes, took its toll too, since the only food thousands of men could find to eat that day was honey. They ate honey on its own without water and this also contributed to the start of the dramatic rise in the mortality rate.[5]

That same day a tireless captain from Seville continued with his systematic task of harrying and wearing down the enemy: 'On this day Don Sancho Bravo set out with his infantry and mounted companies to take on the enemy camp from behind, cutting off their path back to the quarters they had left behind and also to Cascais where they could communicate with their fleet.'[6] The idea, as we know, was to give the English army the permanent impression of being surrounded, and an essential part of that strategy was to attack the lines of communication between the two prongs of the English pincer movement. To that end, Bravo climbed to a strategic place 'to rest and feed barley to the horses on the hill of Santo Amaro, where there is a chapel overlooking sea and land from where part of the enemy camp could be seen'.[7]

While the English were dying of hunger and thirst and also from the heat and exhaustion due to a lack of carts carrying supplies, that Friday in Lisbon food and ammunition

---

[4]   *Relación de lo subçedido del armada enemiga.* BN mss 18579, p. 59.

[5]   González-Arnao, *Derrota y muerte*, p. 87. Also Hume, *The Year After*, p. 56.

[6]   *Relación de lo subçedido del armada enemiga.* BN mss 18579, p. 61. This was the reason for the lack of communication between Drake and Norris.

[7]   Ibid.

were distributed to the Spanish troops who could not leave their posts around the walled perimeter. Thus, 'without the means to carry it all, as well as ammunition for the soldiers, on the first few days His Highness' mules did so, until some workers and ox carts started to appear'.[8] For the first time, on that 2 June, the future King of the Spanish Netherlands had to keep an eye on hundreds of gates large and small, as well as sections of the wall, bulwarks and the city's weak points. It was certainly to his advantage that for this he could rely on Spanish specialists, the best soldiers at that time in the art of defending and attacking strongholds.[9]

Given the location of the attacking army and fleet, it was anticipated that the possible combined attack would focus on the south-western sector of the Lisbon perimeter, next to the sea and between the two ends of the English pincer. This was also the weakest part from a structural perspective. Thus,

> having been told that from Corpo Santo danger could be expected, the Count called upon Captain Almonacir, who was in charge of that gate, and told him to visit in person the area between the gate and the sea both inside and outside the wall, and that as a veteran and practical soldier he entrusted him with his honour and with the city, warning him that the enemy's intention was to attack there, and telling him, given the little time available and the weakness that he found, to prepare everything necessary without delay, given the danger they faced.[10]

There was no time to lose and all the defenders knew that in a matter of hours, or in a day at most, large areas outside the wall of Lisbon would be crawling with enemy troops. It was time to prepare the terrain so that the English would not find any places where it was easy for them to dig trenches and prepare their attack. Lisbon had to be made ready for a siege, or at least for a regular attack. A number of factors had made an attack on the capital unlikely: the long period of peace; the coastal defences that guarded the entry to the estuary; Portugal's hegemonic standing and the geographical location of the country and the city themselves. For pirates on the high seas, the capture of a single one of those imposing carracks from the Indies was the highlight of their dreams. Besides, there was no nation on earth that was sufficiently interested and strong enough to conquer Lisbon; none, to the north or to the south, could threaten a city defended by the row of castles formed by São Julião, the tower of Belém, the castle of São Jorge and others. Only their Iberian neighbours could pose a real threat, but the peace treaties and understanding between Spain and Portugal during the sixteenth century – and even the fifteenth – meant there was no threat to Lisbon. It was true that the rivalry between Spain and Portugal had generated the sharpest contest in the history of exploration and the opening up of trade routes. There had never been a race like the one between Spain and Portugal to be the first to reach the Spice Islands, requiring such

---

[8] *Relación de lo subçedido del armada enemiga.* BN mss 18579, p. 59.
[9] This is what Roger Williams said (see Chapter 14).
[10] *Relación de lo subçedido del armada enemiga.* BN mss 18579, pp. 59–60.

technical knowledge, skill, bravery, initiative and good judgement. Having overcome the challenge of Cape Bojador, the daring Portuguese had finally managed to round the Cape of Good Hope,[11] thereby emulating the Phoenicians, the great explorers of antiquity. After that, with no limitations other than those set by the winds and the seas and able to lay claim to a unique triumph, they wrote bright new pages in the history of the world. The Portuguese went beyond Africa and on into the Indian Ocean, reaching the place where neither Alexander the Great nor Marco Polo had dared to go: the Moluccas, the dreamed-of Spice Islands.

At the same time, and showing as much initiative as Portugal, Spain boldly set sail westward. If it be true that fortune favours the brave, then great rewards were granted to Columbus's three caravels, which would have come to a tragic end on a planet larger than the mariner had calculated without the Caribbean islands coming to their rescue. However, the frenzied race for spices had only just begun, since in this context America was nothing but a major obstacle. Magellan and Elcano overcame it, and Spain also found a source of many spices: ginger, pepper, clove, cinnamon, nutmeg ... It was then, in the third decade of the sixteenth century, when only the Iberian nations in Europe could even dream of reaching the other side of the world, that war broke out in the Pacific between the Spanish and Portuguese. This was a minor skirmish that barely had any resonance in Madrid or Lisbon, and even after Charles I put an end to it by selling the Moluccas to Portugal for 350,000 ducats, it continued until this news reached the battle site.

But let us leave such rivalries aside and return to the situation of the great city of Lisbon, the new besieged Tyre of the Portuguese half of the world. Although protected by several powerful defensive measures, by the beginning of that torrid month of June of 1589 Portugal had been removed for so long from the prospect of war that many buildings and indeed entire neighbourhoods had been built outside the walls. In addition, the once strong walls, now dilapidated from a lack of upkeep, had lost a great deal of their solidity, and thus

> the aforementioned Captain [Almonacir] found that in the houses of the royal court built next to the wall that from the gate referred to face the sea in that square, there were more than twenty gates open, large and small. These could easily be knocked down or burnt down, and he informed the Count of the bad state they were in and how much work was necessary to repair them.[12]

---

[11] It was not until the 1430s that Portuguese mariners first sailed past the Cape Bojador on the west coast of Africa in what is now the disputed territory of Western Sahara. Although trading posts were established further south, it was not until 1488 that the Portuguese explorer Bartolomeu Dias rounded the southern tip of Africa. Dias called it the 'Cabo das Tormentas' (the Cape of Storms) but it was renamed the 'Cabo da Boa Esperança' (Cape of Good Hope) by King John II of Portugal, as it led to a route to India. See A. J. R. Russell-Wood, *The Portuguese Empire 1415–1808: A World on the Move* (Johns Hopkins University Press, 1998) [translator's note].

[12] *Relación de lo subçedido del armada enemiga.* BN mss 18579, p. 60.

Work had to begin straight away, especially as the task was both demanding and urgent, since 'apart from the sad business of closing the gates, the stone steps on the outside had to be knocked down'.[13] Furthermore, since the houses had been built adjoined to the wall, they could not be abandoned but, as Captain Almonacir suggested, it was necessary to 'warn all the houses on the outside, for if the enemy attacked from there, they would place marksmen to prevent the damage our people could do to the attackers from the royal court houses, and thus they could enter under the protection of those occupying that row of houses'.[14] Captain Almonacir, in charge of that crucial flank, 'needed many more people than those assigned there, and so another three companies were sent along with the authority to carry out the work, and he knocked down the steps and with the stone and everything he could gather he strengthened all of that row inside, burning the houses opposite and a few others'.[15] Therefore, in the row of houses built adjacent to the wall, he prepared a first line of defence, and burnt the row of houses opposite that might have been used as possible bridgeheads for an attack on the wall. Architectural and urban fate led to the houses built outside the wall and attached to it on the south-western flank being used as bulwarks, with the pavement and the burnt houses acting as a moat. On this dangerous front, the assault on the wall would essentially be an attack on the barricades defending the houses built next to it. Such was the solution for the defence of a wall weakened by the constructions built onto it.

The decisive encounter between the Spanish and the English appeared to be approaching inexorably. Facing the imminent arrival of the army, 'the twelve galleys were ordered to come up to the city so that if the enemy attempted entry by sea, the men could be slaughtered by artillery'.[16] In fact, given Drake's inactivity, the estuary was under Iberian control. The galleys of Alonso de Bazán abandoned São Julião castle and prepared their artillery and musketry in order to sweep Lisbon's estuary and the sections of the wall next to the sea in case Norris dared to approach. While these defensive preparations took place late into the afternoon, the heavy English military machine, having rested at Alvalade, began the last, brief stage towards their objective. The English infantry looked forward in expectation, but experienced mixed emotions when from a distance they caught sight of the imposing and threatening mound on which the castle of São Jorge was built. This sight represented both their target and the end of their days of tough marching, but it was also the embodiment of the difficulties that were yet to be overcome.

The high, steep hill of the castle of São Jorge commanded an extraordinary panoramic view of Lisbon. At its feet lay huddled together the squares, palaces, avenues and churches of the fine city, girded by the sharp contour of the Fernandine wall. Beyond that were the outskirts of Lisbon, which had spilled out into extensive areas westwards,

---

[13] *Relación de lo subçedido del armada enemiga.* BN mss 18579, p. 60.
[14] Ibid.
[15] Ibid.
[16] *Relación de lo subçedido del armada enemiga.* BN mss 18579, p. 61.

into what is now Bairro Alto, A Bica and Santa Catalina. Further away still, crowning the many small hillocks that were dotted around, were monasteries, villas and farms at the meeting points of the hilly tracks that separated well–laid out olive groves. Under the radiant sun of that spring afternoon there could be few more harmonious combinations of the human and natural worlds.

From the north wall battery of São Jorge, Antonio Fernández de Córdoba and Diego de Quesada enjoyed such views. They could see newly made reinforced culverins pointing towards the English camp, threatening but still silent. The gunners had to test their range. The elongated bronze cannon, which were enormously thick for their calibre, required large amounts of gunpowder for the cast iron cannonballs to gain sufficient height from their eagles' nest. The Portuguese claimed that they could sweep the field to a radius of half a league. They would soon have the opportunity to prove it. When the English rearguard had barely left Alvalade and the vanguard of the huge column had reached as far as Saldanha, the countless flags and the cloud of dust raised in the hot Lisbon afternoon were clearly visible.

A roar shook the air all around the city. On the one hand it announced to all and sundry that the invaders had finally arrived, causing 100,000 souls to feel a shudder of unease. On the other hand, however, it loudly proclaimed the awakening of that titan of stone, gunpowder and bronze, the powerful father and protector of Lisbon, ready to show its power. While the echo ran through the air, the cannonball began a high parabola until it disappeared into the sky. The roar reached the hill of Saldanha, and thousands of English eyes looked up in anguish. A heavy iron ball bounced at the feet of the troops, who had suddenly become the bowling pins in a macabre game. And so, 'in the afternoon the enemy came out from the camp of Alvalade, moving away everywhere they could from being visible from the castle so as to protect themselves from its artillery'.[17]

São Jorge's artillery tested their parabolic shots while the most expert Portuguese and Spanish gunners fine-tuned their aim. The fact that the distance to the target was at least 2,000 metres was made up for by the sheer size of what they were aiming at. São Jorge's cannonballs, with their lethal power and unpredictable bounce, would thereafter be the constant companions of the intruders as long as they stayed within range. The closer the English came to the city, the more they would feel the deadly force of the cannon.

The columns then had to turn towards Lisbon. On the advice of Dom António, who knew his native city inside out, they looked for a westerly route that would be less favourable for the expert marksmen. In fact, 'they were still troubled by a few cannon shot that killed some of their men and made them take a route with better cover until after dark when they were safer, and it took them until after midnight to quarter with the ninety-seven flags that were counted, and they dug trenches in all the street entrances that they occupied'.[18] Ninety-seven flags indicated the size of the English army, even though it was somewhat depleted. In a show of strength, 'they formed a squadron with

[17] *Relación de lo subçedido del armada enemiga.* BN mss 18579, p. 61.
[18] Ibid.

many flags hoisted atop the mills from where they could see a large part of the city and could be seen from the castle'.[19] The meagre Galician reinforcements had similarly announced their presence on a much smaller scale two weeks earlier at the Monte das Arcas, but the people of Lisbon did not have a sense of joy that they were soon to be liberated – rather the opposite. Once Norris's army had announced its presence, 'in a most orderly fashion they moved on towards the property of Andrés Soares, near Os Cardais, before advancing towards the town of São Roque and Santa Catalina'.[20]

Meanwhile, Sancho Bravo and his men had recovered after their rest on Santo Amaro hill. From that high point facing the sea between Lisbon and Belém, there was a good view all round. Bazán's twelve galleys closed the flank of Corte Real, the tower of Belém, which was ready to open a thunderous volley of fire at any ships that attempted to enter the narrow channel connecting the Mar da Palha to the ocean. On the other side of the strait, the guns at Caparica castle were waiting to catch them in any crossfire. The Captain knew it was possible that Drake would head for Lisbon when Norris was ready to attack and he also knew that the English plan was a high-risk strategy. What no one could have foreseen was the extreme lack of coordination between the two men in charge of the English Armada, just like the situation with Medina Sidonia and Alexander Farnese months earlier. Sancho Bravo had seen from close quarters the conditions of Norris's army and the English prisoners he captured kept him fully informed about the alarming scarcity of supplies. He knew of their worrying situation and had come across many hastily dug graves. He knew, in short, that something momentous was taking place that spring. The English had not given them much time to weep for those who had died in the Spanish Armada; however, he understood that this was no time to weep, but rather to avenge so much pain and so much cruelty: the testimonies of those who had been shipwrecked but managed to return were hair-raising. He looked at the orderly English columns entering the district of São Roque, divided his cavalry into three groups and prepared a new assault. He knew exactly the job he had to do: 'He very often attacked the enemy in three or four different places at the same time in such a way as to always be in control, and he would slit their throats and capture and kill guards, along with other things very much to his advantage.'[21]

The invaders kept themselves away from the artillery of São Jorge as much as they could, but nothing could prevent them from occupying 'the stretch from the windmills of São Roque and the gate of Santa Catalina up to A Esperança, since it is a high part of town with a lot of good houses for lodging'.[22] In any case, they did not attempt to approach the walls near the sea, since 'with the burning of the houses and the arrival of the galleys the enemy must have realized that the fire had been seen and how little they had to gain by attacking from the sea, and so they did not attempt it'.[23] Thus, the burning

---

[19] *Relación de lo subçedido del armada enemiga.* BN mss 18579, p. 61.
[20] Ibid.
[21] Ibid., p. 62.
[22] Ibid., p. 57.
[23] Ibid., p. 61.

of the houses close to the walls and the proximity of the galleys and their firepower, as well as their practical effectiveness, had the appropriate deterrent effect.

The English found the best place to set up their new quarters – it was suitably protected from the castle artillery and the galleys and as close as possible to their fleet. They knew they were in a new situation since, for the first time after setting sail from Plymouth, they were inferior in numbers. However, after carefully digging themselves in, they were at last able to sleep with a roof over their heads. Not everyone slept, however, for it was on that night of the 2 June that Dom António was planning to get his Trojan horses into Lisbon.

Chapter 23

The Trojan Horses

After the English army had entered the outskirts of the city on the night of 2 June, anticipation and vigilance were at their peak. The attack on the city could begin at any moment and in addition they may be expecting inside help: 'On Friday night there was much anxiety and fear at how still the enemy was, and everyone was on full alert as to what might happen.'[1] But the real reasons for settling in São Roque and Santa Catalina and for billeting in the outskirts without preparing an assault or threatening a siege or pincer movement went beyond those given. Fuentes was right. Crato had laboriously prepared his Trojan horses for his entry into Lisbon, as his letters that were found later would show. Some noblemen, who were understandably tempted by Antonio's promises or even sincerely but naively inspired by the desire to make Portugal independent once again, were persuaded to help him. One wonders if those nobles would have come to the aid of the illegitimate pretender if they had known of the outrageous agreements that Crato had signed with Elizabeth. In the absence of any explicit and documented response, it is likely that those who were motivated by a genuine desire for independence – rather than any personal advantages in the new puppet government that would be set up – would have rejected the shameful contract between Elizabeth and Crato and would have sided with the Iberian cause. In fact, the majority of the Portuguese nobility did exactly that. In any event, one of those who collaborated in favour of the entry of the starving army and enabled the sacking of the city was Rui Dias Lobo, 'noble by birth but not by habit'.[2] He was the first of the Trojan horses.

While thousands of men anxiously awaited the results of his inquiries so that they could go straight into the great city of Lisbon and finally get to eat, Dias Lobo was on a secret mission. Under cover of darkness, he took a message to the abbot and friars of the monastery of the Trinity, built next to the wall. Dom António's message was that 'since the section of the wall where their monastery was built was very weak, he asked them for permission to enter the city through there, keeping the break-in secret until it had been carried out'.[3] In other words, the English would discreetly enter the monastery, breaching the wall as Alexandre Dumas's hero the Count of Montecristo did with the walls of his cell in Marseille, and once they had completed the entry they would pour silently into Lisbon. This terrifying scheme would have led to the downfall of Camões's immortal city, bringing grief, poverty and dishonour to thousands of

[1] *Relación de lo subçedido del armada enemiga.* BN mss 18579, p. 62.
[2] Ibid., p. 57.
[3] Ibid., p. 58.

Portuguese families.[4] The abbot 'replied with many signs of goodwill and treated him and others who had accompanied him very well'.[5]

It is often true that the most significant historic events may depend on the most insignificant of circumstances or on a single man. Columbus discovered America just as the deadline promised to the Pinzón brothers expired, after which he would have had to return.[6] Only thirteen men crossed the line drawn in the sand by Pizarro when he set out to conquer what became the Andean countries and the fate of Europe and America then hung in the balance.[7] While Rui Dias Lobo and his company rested peacefully after being treated to a fine dinner at the monastery of the Trinity, some hooded friars had a quiet talk with the guards at the gate of Santa Catalina. Immediately, two men of the cloth walked the cobbled streets in the Lisbon night heading for the ducal palace, escorted by two soldiers. Once the Archduke had been informed, 'a captain was sent with a number of men to arrest them, which was done by the said officer quietly and discreetly, to the extent that they were not even aware of it in the house itself, and with the imprisonment of Dias Lobo any disturbance there may have been was contained and the wall was reinforced'.[8]

Thus was foiled a means of entry into Lisbon that was more frightening than any artillery battery. The fact is that the behaviour of the English pirates had become infamous throughout the Catholic world. It would have been hard to find a monk who was ready to open the door to the Protestants, however sweet the words that Dom António had put into the mouth of Dias Lobo.

However, that failed attempt did not spell the end of the secret manoeuvrings of the Antonians to gain entry into the city. Another attempt was being planned, closer to the traditional siege methods of the time. This meant carrying out several diversionary attacks at low tide while launching the real one elsewhere in a particularly weak place close to the sea and involving the collaboration of the guard at one of the gates. The action would begin by 'attacking when the tide was low, first at the gates of Santa Catalina and San Antón de la Morería'.[9] This diversionary action would require 1,000 men 'so as to bring all the defenders to these gates'.[10] Once the defending forces

---

[4]   Luis de Camões (1524–1580) is considered to be one of Portugal's best poets [translator's note].

[5]   *Relación de lo subçedido del armada enemiga.* BN mss 18579, p. 58.

[6]   The three Pinzón brothers who sailed with Columbus on several voyages had to intervene on more than one occasion between Columbus and his mutinous crew. On the night of 9 October 1492, the brothers proposed a compromise that if no land was sighted during the next three days, the expedition would return to Spain. On the morning of 12 October, land was in fact sighted. See José Manuel Azcona Pastor, *Possible Paradises: Basque Emigration to Latin America*, (Reno: University of Nevada Press, 2004), p. 14 [translator's note].

[7]   In 1527 on his second expedition to conquer Peru, Francisco Pizarro, following two years of setbacks and at a critical moment in his ventures, drew a line in the sand with his sword, with Panama on one side and Peru on the other. He invited his men either to return to Panama and poverty, or to join him, either in death or in glory and riches in Peru. History records that thirteen men decided to go with him. See J. Hemming, *The Conquest of the Incas*, (New York: Harcourt Brace Jovanovich, 1970) [translator's note].

[8]   *Relación de lo subçedido del armada enemiga.* BN mss 18579, p. 58.

[9]   Ibid.

[10] Ibid.

had come to protect those flanks, all that would be needed would be 'to send 3,000 men silently to enter by the Corpo Santo and the coal docks at the same time, finding it undefended, even if they had to wade up to their knees'.[11] Such attacks upon besieged strongholds in which the infantry had to go into the water are reminiscent of several Spanish operations during the wars in Flanders.[12] It was frequently the case that in coastal strongholds there was a certain structural weakness in the walled sections where man-made defences combined with the added difficulty of the sea. When the tide was low, however, in becalmed waters and at night, the sea was rather more friendly, as had been the case in the incendiary attempts upon Corunna two weeks earlier. Thus, once the 3,000 men set to attack 'were between the water and the wall', they had to 'attempt the assault via the easiest of the many gates there and very easily hold enough of them to be able to enter the city. To do so, it is said they had an understanding with one of Matías de Alburquerque's captains, the one in charge of the last gate before the Corpo Santo.'[13]

Again it is clear that the Spanish strategy of waiting in Lisbon was the right one, since even for this defensive purpose the number of defenders was only just sufficient. Even with all the precautions taken, the structural weakness of Lisbon's defences was self-evident. A single Antonian captain would have been enough to set off the catastrophe, for the English were clearly superior in numbers and the reaction of the Portuguese troops – and especially of the Lisbon population – was unpredictable.

According to the account of one of the prisoners, Crato had a third possible scheme to get into Lisbon:

> According to a prisoner who was questioned, Dom António was coming without artillery, having agreed with the people of the land that, when he reached the walls, they would rebel against the Spaniards and would make certain signals with fire atop the walls at the gates of Santa María and São Roque, so that the English would know it was time to come. The Spaniards would be busy with the fighting inside the walls, and the walls and the gates would have little or no defence, so that the English would be able to enter without difficulty.[14]

However, the author of the Spanish account gave no credence to that prisoner's confession, since the English troops 'brought no siege ladders to scale the walls, nor was there

---

[11] *Relación de lo subçedido del armada enemiga*. BN mss 18579, p. 58.
[12] For example, the so-called Miracle of Empel (referred to as 'Het Wonder van Empel' by the Dutch Catholics). On 8 December 1585, the Tercio Regiment of the *Maestre de Campo* Francisco de Bobadilla found itself trapped by the waters from the dykes that had been opened up by Admiral Holak. Under fire and in a critical situation, they waited until dawn, crossed the frozen River Maas and destroyed the Dutch fleet. See 'The Miracle of Empel: An Astounding End to a Decisive Battle for the Spanish', *Ancient Origins*, 16 December 2015. (http://www.ancient-origins.net/history-important-events/miracle-empel-astounding-end-decisive-battle-spanish-004943?nopaging=1).
[13] *Relación de lo subçedido del armada enemiga*. BN mss 18579, p. 58.
[14] Ibid., pp. 58–9.

any assault either inside or out'.[15] Nevertheless, this would have been the most 'Trojan' plan of the three.

The sound of birds finally filled the Lisbon air. Such joyfulness seemed excessive for such an imperceptible change of colours, since the faintest bluish tinge was barely starting to replace the darkness. The crowing of cocks joined the celebration as night silently made way for a new day. Such an everyday occurrence brought immense relief to the thousands of men who had just been through the most perilous darkness Lisbon had had to face at that time. The arrival of the day did not promise respite, but it did at least bring an end to the uncertainty arising from the thousands of nocturnal noises of a great city under threat.

At dawn on Saturday, 3 June, the attackers came out of their trenches and aimed to show their strength on the weak western front. This flank, however, was being given special protection by the defenders, for, as we know, both sides were aware that possession of the streets and buildings next to the wall could make the slender difference between success and failure. In order to prevent this possibility, their top marksmen, São Roque and Loreto, had been placed on the rooftops of the churches outside the walls of the north-western sector to reinforce and flank the marksmen on the wall. The churches were thus converted into bulwarks or ravelins. Their use as bridgeheads, as had happened with the monastery of Santo Domingo at Corunna, had to be avoided. Thus 'the day arrived and they began to appear on the streets, and our men who were atop the wall and the churches of Nossa Senhora do Loreto and São Roque shot at them in the open, wounding and killing them without any danger to our men. Thus they were able to avoid going where harm could come to them.'[16] Apart from protecting that flank, they were able to protect these two churches that would otherwise, as in the case of Santo Domingo, have met their end if the English had occupied them. But the Santa Catalina sector, which had been so bravely defended, had to be reinforced by clearing the area next to the wall: 'After dawn, the houses outside the gate of Santa Catalina were set on fire, for as they were the enemy could very easily have used them to scale the wall in safety, and some of the houses that were on the inside were also set alight.'[17] The usefulness of burning houses becomes clear when considering the fact that most of the houses outside the wall – and many of those inside – were still made of wood at that time.

The defensive tactics bore fruit and the attackers were bloodily fought off from the north-western sector of Santa Catalina. However, although taken aback by their difficult situation and perhaps the more so on account of the ease with which the Spanish allowed them to move through areas that were not crucial, the English headed south towards the sea. 'In the morning word was sent from the gate of Santa Catalina that the enemy was moving down to the sea on that side, where it was feared they might attempt

---

[15]   *Relación de lo subçedido del armada enemiga.* BN mss 18579, p. 59.
[16]   Ibid., p. 62.
[17]   Ibid.

entry through the royal court houses, while also taking advantage of the low tide.'[18] That sector had not been left unattended either, however, but had been carefully prepared the day before under the directions of Captain Almonacir. Thus,

> they found the houses in front of the wall had been burnt, with the galleys at the ready, from which, together with a *nao* of Sebastián de Chacarreta back from last year's expedition, they began to fire at those who could be seen, so that the attackers decided not to continue, seeing that the defenders were ready for them and that they [the attackers] would be the losers.[19]

It was at that time on Saturday, 3 June, after the attackers had been driven back from the vicinity of the walls and after a month of English military operations, that the situation was transformed. Until then the English army had held the initiative and the Spanish had done nothing but monitor their movements. Now, each had to face his own destiny. The vast outskirts of Lisbon and the sheer size of the city as seen from the mills of São Roque had made a deep impression on the English:

> Enrique Nores [sic] was so much in awe at the prospect of besieging the wall and at the size of the outskirts of the city that he thought it could not be besieged even with a much larger number of men, nor entered with those that he had … and thus, having surveyed the place, the walls, the size of the city and its outskirts, they say he asked if all their people had taken refuge in the city. They told him they had, and looking from the height of Os Moinhos do Vento at the parade ground set in O Rossio, in front of the Hospital de Todos os Santos, he thought all was lost.[20]

Lisbon was about the same size as London at the time. However, no defensive measures on the banks of the Thames could compare to the walls and castles of Lisbon. Norris knew that his army was larger than the Spanish, but also that that superiority, displayed weeks earlier in the north-western corner of Spain, was being weakened little by little. The English went on the defensive and withdrew to their trenches, and that was the turning point of their Spanish adventure. The besiegers were to become the besieged and vice versa, 'since as they reached only two parts of the city walls, it was they who were truly the besieged, not daring to leave their trenches but rather being attacked in them by our men'.[21]

In fact, the Iberians took up the offensive and did so swiftly and decisively like an animal chased by another into a cul-de-sac, which then turns back on its pursuer and drives it away. Perhaps a better comparison would be that of a predator waiting patiently for its prey to walk straight into its mouth. All it then had to do was to close its jaws. Once the Spanish counteroffensive had been decided upon, it was not a time

---

[18] *Relación de lo subçedido del armada enemiga.* BN mss 18579, p. 62.
[19] Ibid.
[20] *Memoria da Vinda dos Ingleses a Portugal em 1589*, p. 271, quoted in Pires De Lima, *O ataque.*
[21] Ibid., p. 272.

to risk troops in a useless assault on a large and well-entrenched camp. It was not easy to decide where to start, but the strategy itself was clear. Norris had not set up his camp at a prudent distance from Lisbon, as had been the case in 1147, when, as defenders of the Christian faith, the English joined in the effort to regain the city from Islam.[22] The present situation was very different: the English, in alliance with the Muslims, proposed to attack the heart and southern flank of the Christian world.

Why did Norris set up camp at the foot of the walls when it was so risky? On the one hand, the houses and streets protected them from the artillery of São Jorge that would otherwise have destroyed them and it seemed a good place to entrench. On the other hand, their numerical superiority gave them a false sense of confidence. Besides, the army expected Dom António's schemes to work out, whereby someone from the inside would let them in, or that Drake would show up at last to synchronize the attack with the fleet. One way or another, out of a sense of overconfidence, the English army stayed too close to Lisbon. The Spanish were about to turn that to their advantage.

---

[22]   The Siege of Lisbon from July to October 1147 was part of the Portuguese 'Reconquest' and the Second Crusade. It was carried out by a combined army from northern Europe and Portugal [translator's note].

Chapter 24

Counteroffensive

The monasteries of Nossa Senhora do Loreto and São Roque were magnificent bastions that were well protected with marksmen and gave Philip's forces the advantage over the short stretch between the walls and the English army. The Spanish attack was due to start there. It was from this position that they could strike most quickly and – given the impossibility of taking the camp – it was a position to which they could also withdraw most speedily once their objectives had been achieved. In addition to this attack from short range, another attack on a larger scale would be launched simultaneously against the rearguard of the camp. Opening two opposing fronts in this way would add to the confusion and fear and make it more difficult for the English to organize their defences. Added to this, the harassment of the land attack would distract them from the constant 'rain of death' from the castle of São Jorge.

The three simultaneous attacks would prove so effective and bold that they would utterly confound an army that was about to realize how dire its situation was. 'One detachment attacked near the estate of Andrés Soares, at Moinhos do Vento, others took the road from the Anunciada area to São Roque, and some attacked the barbican of the wall next to the monastery itself.'[1] The first of these attacks could not have been more daring. It was directed at the rearguard, where the headquarters of the Antonian troops were, at the furthest point from the walls.

And so,

> given that the enemy stayed in their trenches and neither attacked the wall nor gave any other sign of being willing to fight, and lest they should think the withdrawal of our army on the Thursday had been due to weakness or fear of the enemy, some five hundred harquebusiers and a number of pikemen came out through the gate of Santo Antón to scare them into sounding the call to arms and coming out to skirmish.[2]

This was no *encamisada*, nor a lightning strike aimed at wearing the enemy down. The intention was to get the English out of their trenches and start a battle on a larger scale. And this time it was the Spanish who were advancing, commanded by 'Captains Don Claudio de Veamonte and Francisco Martínez Malo, Felipe Sumiel of the Order of de San Juan, Bernardino de Velasco, Jerónimo de Guevara, Francisco de Pedraza,

---

[1] *Memoria da Vinda dos Ingleses a Portugal em 1589*, p. 274, quoted in Pires De Lima, *O ataque.*
[2] *Relación de lo sübçedido del armada enemiga.* BN mss 18579, p. 63.

and Blas de Jerez.' After this contingent, there were three more companies on horseback: 'And after them three companies of Men-at-Arms went forth to where the harquebusiers and musketeers were making the enemy come out and fight or breaking up their trenches, so the cavalry could go in and slay them and throw them into disarray.'[3] The cavalry's task was to broaden the fight after the infantry had managed to break up the trenches with their harquebuses and pikes and force the English out of their hideout. The world had turned upside down: the English were no longer on the march to conquer and sack Lisbon. It was the Spanish who were now marching on the invaders' camp.

The crossbeams were taken down from the thick hooks and the heavy hinges of the Santo Antón gate began to creak. It was the city's main gate that connected Rossio Square with the outside world, a double gate that was protected beneath a solid square tower. First the captains appeared, followed by the formation of musketeers and harquebusiers with sloped arms. Spanish flags were soon waving aloft. From the top of the walls and the nearby towers of Inquisiçao and Sinos, a number of harquebusiers watched out for the slightest movement, their weapons at the ready. Some four hundred metres to the west were the nearest entrenched streets of the camp where some 11,000 English soldiers were quartered. Between the Spanish contingent and the attackers stood the great monastery of São Roque, now a deadly bulwark protecting the wall.

Flags, pikes, harquebuses and then the cavalry, in the perfect order so admired by the authors of military treatises of the time, 'marched shortly after midday up the slope from the Anunciada, among olive groves, to the mills of São Roque'.[4] The contingent, made up of about 500 experienced infantrymen and 150 on horseback, left the walls of Lisbon behind with the English army to its left. The brazenness with which the seven captains led their troops close by the enemy camp could be seen as a provocation aimed at bringing out one or more English regiments in pursuit. However, the condition of that formidable army, a month after the start of its violent actions on the sands of Nuestra Señora de Oza, had gradually been changing. Norris knew this was not Corunna, the town sarcastically called 'fishmarket' by Hume.[5] He was familiar, as was Roger Williams and all who had seen the Spanish in combat, that when it came to the harquebusiers that 'perfect order' became a rapid succession of surgical volleys capable of cutting off any part of the enemy formation. He was equally familiar with the use of pikes in close formation, which enabled them to continue their advance in adverse circumstances, as well as the passion of their cavalry charges that was taken up by others. In short, he knew that the respective sizes of the opposing forces was not always a deciding factor in encounters with experienced Spanish soldiers.

The soldiers marching towards Moinhos do Vento – the place where the previous afternoon Norris's army had made a show of its presence – were the very soldiers upon whose shoulders rested the security and expansion of the West. They had been the backbone of the armies of Charles V who, with the Tercio regiments, had lifted the siege of a

[3]   *Relación de lo subçedido del armada enemiga.* BN mss 18579, p. 63.
[4]   Ibid.
[5]   Hume, *The Year After*, p. 40.

moribund Vienna sixty years earlier.[6] They had been at the forefront of the greatest naval battle of all time, the battle that had saved the western Mediterranean for Europe only seventeen years before.[7] An essential part of their purpose was to maintain the political, territorial and religious unity that would act as a counterweight to the colossal power of the *Sublime Porte*.[8] Those soldiers of Lepanto formed part of the structure of a state of huge dimensions and upheld the dream of glory and honour, the glory of men who create, build, open new paths and spread the Gospel.

By contrast, the men gazing at their fluttering banners, entrenched in the streets outside the wall, were not burdened by any such important mission. Freed from the challenge of defending western civilization thanks to the effort of the Catholics, their only task was to sail in fast ships capable of fleeing from the mighty, imposing, bronzed galleons that plied the sea routes of the world, patiently awaiting opportunities for robbery and booty. The aura of amorality, criminality and the daring ventures of pirates had turned the illegality that had led to the war into the national norm. The lack of moral scruples and the impunity afforded by the English Channel was reflected in the way in which the Queen boldly sought alliances with Morocco – and even with the Ottoman Empire itself – in order to make common cause against the bastion of Europe. The Ottoman galleys would never reach the Thames, and the ruins of the Spanish Empire would bring fabulous riches and power to England. These were the only things that mattered to them.

The small Spanish regiment reached Moinhos with a certain amount of ceremony but also in battle order. Between there and the walls of Lisbon lay the English camp. The captains sent spies to reconnoitre the terrain and confirmed that 'the enemy camp was very well-entrenched all around and all they had to defend was a very narrow entry'.[9] That entry was closed and the only way to attack the trenches and barricades was by launching a furious frontal battering with pikes, supported by muskets and harquebuses firing at will. As the marksmen got ready, the risks of attacking an entrenched urban camp of such a size became clear. The situation that Portugal itself was in was even more fragile, however. The country had fallen into a state of extreme frailty as the emerging nations were acquiring power. Over a century since the start of its global expansion, Iberian fortitude was being put to the test. The time had come either to hand over and divide up its territories or to support them.

---

[6] In 1529, the forces of the Ottoman Empire led by Suleiman laid siege to Vienna. Eventually, Charles V assembled a force of 80,000 men to compel the Ottoman army to withdraw. The siege 'brought to a standstill the tide of Ottoman conquest which had been flooding up the Danube Valley for a century past'. Arnold Toynbee, *A Study of History* (Oxford University Press, 1960), Vol. 1, p. 119 [translator's note].

[7] The Battle of Lepanto (1571) was fought between a fleet of the Holy League, a coalition of European Catholic maritime states, and the fleet of the Ottoman Empire on the northern edge of the Gulf of Corinth, off western Greece [translator's note].

[8] The term being used as a metaphor to denote the central government of the Ottoman Empire [translator's note].

[9] *Relación de lo subçedido del armada enemiga*. BN mss 18579, p. 63.

While the castle artillery fired with considerable accuracy on the English positions and the other detachment left the walls of Lisbon, the captains, ensigns and sergeants led their men against the trenches:

> Those coming in from the estate of Andrés Soares had a much harder time, since there they attacked the enemy in very narrow and entrenched streets, where they could do little damage but be in danger themselves, but in truth they were so spirited that they had no fear of ambushes, nor of finding the enemy in their trenches, and they broke in and engaged in a violent skirmish for a good while and with much effort. The enemy fought back just as bravely and must have been experienced men. Our own men broke down six of their trenches and swept through them, killing and wounding with such fury that the racket was heard all over the area. So many charged back against them with muskets and harquebuses that a very bitter fight ensued.[10]

The daring bare-chested attack by the Spaniards at midday on 3 June against the trenches in the northern part of the camp caught the defenders by surprise. When the Spanish infantry set about them, they had to pull back from their positions in disbelief.

At the same time, the other two assaults were unleashed against the eastern sector of the camp, the one closest to the walls:

> At the same time Don Fernando de Ágreda advanced with about two hundred marksmen who had guarded the gate of Santa Catalina, and since this was closed, they came out over the wall and from inside the church of Loreto, covered by the musketeers who were on the church of San Roque. They all attacked the enemy very bravely, destroying their trenches without the enemy coming out of the streets.[11]

The English were no longer fighting for Dom António, for booty or for their Queen, but for their very lives. It was no longer a large number of ordinary soldiers who were engaged in combat but the ever-smaller number of veterans. Colonel Brett's regiment of some 1,000 men was unable to withstand the Spanish onslaught and suffered severe casualties. The veterans mentioned in the Spanish diary were probably Brett himself and his best troops. Their bold attack went to the heart of the northern flank like an arrow and came perilously close to the English headquarters. Brett himself, his captains, Kearsey and Carre, plus over two hundred of their men lost their lives in the attack. Captain Chichester was wounded and died shortly afterwards, but the Spanish captains and their elite troops did not emerge unscathed:

> And the cavalry rode into the streets, and were at a disadvantage for they were narrow and there were snipers in the doorways and windows, and they were

---

[10] *Memoria da Vinda dos Ingleses a Portugal em 1589*, p. 274, quoted in Pires De Lima, *O ataque*.
[11] *Relación de lo subçedido del armada enemiga*. BN mss 18579, pp. 63–4.

wounded without being able to hit the enemy. After four or five riders had fallen, the cavalry had to withdraw and rode over our own infantry, knocking the men down for lack of room, and thwarting much of the effect that the infantry had started to have on its own. Even so, over two hundred of the enemy were killed, including three captains.[12]

On the northern flank of the English camp, a ferocious skirmish started up in the streets with muskets and harquebuses fighting it out with pikes, swords and daggers. After the attack, the retreat was covered with more men, for 'Captain Pedro de Yepes and Juan Ruiz went out to assist in the retreat with two hundred harquebusiers and fifty pikers.'[13] The fighting on the estate of Andrés Soares had the most devastating effect on the damaged morale of the English army. Also on 3 June there was fighting in the São Roque sector: 'Also near São Roque our men wrested two trenches from the enemy, who they fought most spiritedly with swords and fists.'[14] In the skirmishes of São Roque, on the north-western corner of the Lisbon wall and at the place where the wall came close to the 'English' area, given the narrowness of the battlefield, there was hand-to-hand combat.

Meanwhile, the northern flank of the English encampment was being bombarded by large cannonball fire from the fortress of São Jorge, with its powerful cannon and elevated position. Gathering speed as they descended in an arc, this artillery fire did severe damage to the invading army. Both of the leading diaries offer detailed information of this: according to the Portuguese journal, 'three flags with their ensigns were hit, and others who were on high ground (at Os Moinhos), the cannonballs from the nearby castle falling thick and fast among them and greatly terrifying the enemy'.[15] The Spanish diary also highlights the role of São Jorge: 'The artillery of the castle was very effective that day against the enemy camp and did much damage. A single cannonball blew away four flags at the same time, although later they were put back on poles and flew again.'[16]

Apart from the losses suffered by English troops on 3 June, these attacks changed the military scenario in which the English Armada had operated until then. Norris was informed of the casualties that had occurred, of course, but what no one could have guessed was the Archduke's next move. The expeditionary force knew that reinforcements were rapidly flocking to Lisbon from several parts of Spain and Portugal. If the English had had such trouble with the Spanish offensive on 3 June, what would happen with fresh troops arriving? How would the next confrontation turn out? Not only was time working against an English army for whom conditions were getting worse every day; it was also working to the advantage of Philip's troops. The sum of such variables was turning the English presence in Lisbon into a most dubious venture and the

---

[12] *Relación de lo subçedido del armada enemiga.* BN mss 18579, p. 64.
[13] Ibid.
[14] *Memoria da Vinda dos Ingleses a Portugal em 1589*, p. 275, quoted in Pires De Lima, *O ataque.*
[15] Ibid.
[16] *Relación de lo subçedido del armada enemiga.* BN mss 18579, pp. 65–6.

weight of this uncertainty would become intolerable in only a matter of hours. Thus, the operations of 3 June would have a devastating effect on the subsequent development of military activity. The defenders whose lives were sacrificed did not die in vain. Their fate, so admirable had it been simply to witness the impotence and disintegration of the enemy from the safety of Lisbon's solid walls, became heroic as soon as they came out to fight. They did not emerge only to ambush or harass the enemy but also to attack the trenches of a camp so vast that taking it was out of the question. It is they who in those days achieved the greatest glory, and among them some casualties should be remembered: 'Of our men twenty-five died, among them Captain Pedraza from Baeza, and Ensign Torres, and about forty were wounded, including Captain Francisco Martínez Malo by a musket shot from which he died after twenty days. Captain Don Claudio de Veamonte was wounded by a lance, as was Sergeant Castillo.'[17]

---

[17] *Relación de lo subçedido del armada enemiga.* BN mss 18579, p. 64.

Chapter 25

Turning Point

There were obvious similarities between 3 June in Lisbon and 14 May in Corunna. On both dates the English lost hundreds of men in combat, and both were turning points that resulted in a change of strategy in the respective sieges. There were, however, also crucial differences. On 14 May, the English launched an attack and were driven back at the walls, whereas on 3 June it was the other way round, with the Spanish taking the initiative and going on the offensive. If on 14 May it was the people of Corunna, men and women, who desperately defended their city, now it was the English who were fighting for their lives. After the first date, the attackers were still masters of the land they were standing on; after the second, the ground started to shake beneath their feet.

The common factor in the two most significant episodes in the war was the crushing numerical superiority of the English. In the case of Corunna we already know the reason, while in Lisbon, although the superiority was around a ratio of two to one (some 10,000 or 11,000 survivors compared to 5,000 Spaniards, without counting Drake's men in Cascais), such superiority was also overwhelming given that the Spanish were spread right throughout the city in an attempt to protect it. That day, around 1,100 men took part in combat, some of them reinforcements who had recently arrived from the north of Portugal.[1] In addition to this contingent, there were the regular corps of Sancho Bravo and Alarcón and some cavalry under Bernardino de Velasco.

After a bitter day of loud, deadly gunfire, lethal hand-to-hand combat, blood and death, after a day of courage and bravery from the Spanish veterans and the second defeat of the English Armada, the exhausted sun went down over Lisbon. Although that same sun had shone down on the great land and sea battles of history, here it had played a different role: there was no decisive battle, either in the English Channel a year earlier or now in Spain and Portugal. The two great amphibious operations of the war had not brought scarce resources into play. The fact is that neither the English in '88 nor the Spanish in '89 had sufficient forces to crush the enemy offensive, but it was enough for them to foil the great strategic objectives of the enemy, to repel the great fleets and send them back out to sea.

On the night of 3 June, there was a frenzy of activity at the hospital of Todos os Santos in the Praça de Rossio.[2] The breastplates, backplates, helmets and then clothing of the injured Spanish and Portuguese were carefully removed to reveal their bloody wounds. Some had been inflicted by pike, sword and dagger, but the most common were

---

[1] *Memoria da Vinda dos Ingleses a Portugal em 1589*, p. 274, quoted in Pires De Lima, *O ataque*.
[2] Ibid.

the gaping flesh wounds from musket and harquebus shot. The surgeons tried very hard to remove the shot whenever possible, using a type of punch, pincers and other tools used in medicine at the time and also into preparing bandages and dressings. Forty men with wounds of varying severity were lined up in the large rooms of the hospital, among them brave Captain Francisco Malo, hit by a musket shot that went right through him. Such a wound would be simple to treat for modern medicine, but it became infected. After twenty cruel days of agony, he died in Lisbon on 23 June while the remains of the routed English Armada struggled to get back to England and, in doing so, littered the bottom of the ocean with ships and corpses.

Next to Malo lay Don Claudio de Veamonte and Sergeant Castillo, both of whom managed to recover from lance wounds. The man who had been the most heroic of all, Captain Pedraza, could only be washed, anointed and dressed for his journey to the next life. The same fate befell the no-less-brave Ensign Torres. There were twenty five dead from among the most experienced veterans, and in addition to these there were forty wounded, many of whom would die days later, especially those hit by firearms: 'From there those wounded by harquebuses and other weapons were taken to the Hospital of Todos os Santos, but of these few recovered, so it was supposed that the enemy shot was infected with some kind of poison, or in the view of others, so many died because there were no surgeons experienced in treating wounds from shot.'[3]

It may have been a time of mourning in the Iberian camp, but for the men from the north it became a gruesome night of moving corpses by the chilling light of torches. Apart from the hundreds of dead there were the many wounded, who had to be tended without the most basic of medical facilities. The situation of the invading army was by now critical. Military ambition had been replaced by the desire to get out alive from that hell of exhaustion, hunger, thirst, skirmishes, artillery fire, illness and death.

> A large number of English dead were left in the streets, but very few of our own, for at least in that part of São Roque we had the great advantage of the cannon at the castle, which never stopped firing to good effect, and our musketeers firing from the balconies and parts of São Roque. Between them it seemed like the world was upon the enemy.[4]

Sunday, 4 June, dawned with the invading army still stationed in the Barrio Alto. The defenders, 'Portuguese and Castilians alike, were keenly awaiting assistance to arrive from Castile, and their hope carried them through from one day to the next.'[5] They knew that various reinforcements were on their way on a forced march. It was a sad day in Lisbon, for after the frenzied activity of the previous day, when the victims were accepted in the heat of battle, now in the quiet of the morning the awareness of the losses became

[3]   *Memoria da Vinda dos Ingleses a Portugal em 1589*, p. 275, quoted in Pires De Lima, *O ataque*.
[4]   Ibid.
[5]   *Relación de lo subçedido del armada enemiga*. BN mss 18579, p. 66.

even more painful. Thus during the funeral preparations 'there was much sorrow among our men for those who were killed and wounded in the skirmish of the day before'.[6]

The presence of the English so close to the walls, so well entrenched and protected by the streets and buildings of the Lisbon outskirts, caused great indignation among the Iberian troops: 'It angered them to see the enemy so settled in the town, so entrenched that they could not often be attacked, and were less at risk than they had been in Cascais.'[7] That morning the English were totally inactive. However, in the eyes of the defenders such inactivity at the foot of the walls was full of ill omens. Armies do not act at random and the behaviour of the English, with their huge fleet in Cascais and their army in the outskirts of Lisbon, meant that they had to have some secret plan. Therefore, 'the fact that the enemy did not attack made everyone suspect some trick, as well as remaining watchful so as not to be taken by surprise'.[8]

Amid this state of unease, fear and uncertainty, a strange anecdote was put about and recounted in the Spanish journal. An important Portuguese dignitary, loyal to the legitimate King of Portugal, went to the palace of Archduke Alberto and there 'was so bold as to plead with His Highness with great persistence to protect his person, for within two days he would be unable to escape prison or death'.[9] Such was the fear that Lisbon would fall and reprisals would be meted out by the English, or by Dom António against those Portuguese who, true to the agreements of the *Cortes* of Tomar,[10] had decided to oppose him. The Archduke's answer showed his determination and confidence in his own forces: 'In reply His Highness told him not to worry and that he was not in as much danger as he thought, for whoever feared this was unaware that there were five thousand armed Spaniards within the walls, and that as long as a single one was left to die by his side he would not change his view.'[11] However, the confidence of the Archduke was in contrast to the fear prevalent among the population of the city, among whom the rumour inexorably spread that 'His Highness had given the city up for lost and had fled.'[12]

The military then became fully aware of the need to improve morale, so 'Gabriel Niño ordered all the infantrymen and cavalry to be inspected in their quarters once they had eaten and to form in squadrons in all the parade grounds of the city.'[13] Morale is fundamentally important to all human activity, especially in war, and is the driving force in personal lives as well as in building empires. It was therefore essential that under firm authority Lisbon regained confidence in its ability to resist such a powerful challenge. The Archduke himself had to be seen in full dress and in festive mood, with his entire

---

[6] *Relación de lo subçedido del armada enemiga.* BN mss 18579, p. 66.
[7] Ibid.
[8] Ibid.
[9] Ibid.
[10] The town of Tomar was the seat of the Portuguese *Cortes* or Parliament in 1581, which acclaimed King Philip II of Spain as Filipe I of Portugal, following his victory at the Battle of Alcântara the previous year [translator's note].
[11] *Relación de lo subçedido del armada enemiga.* BN mss 18579, p. 66.
[12] Ibid., p. 67.
[13] Ibid.

army, in order to make a show of power and confidence. And so 'His Highness rode with the Count of Fuentes and the other Portuguese courtiers and Castilian servants, with the officers at their gates, with orders that none should be absent from their post. The city looked so fine and the men so gallant that any reasonable man would feel fully assured that the business at hand would be successfully concluded.'[14]

Thus Lisbon became one enormous, colourful military parade, with the sound of the Spanish and Portuguese horses echoing on the flagstones. The order and discipline of the Spanish infantry, with their doublets, breeches, helmets and plumes, their dashing bearing and their smiling and relaxed demeanour, made the appropriate impression on the town. However, this was not the only aim of the parade: 'The day was cool and clear and the sun glinted on bayonets and helmets for the enemy to see.'[15] Three parade grounds were used: the one at the castle of São Jorge, Lisbon's main defensive bastion; another at Nossa Senhora da Graça which was also high up and clearly visible to both sides, where 'behind the armed men many others went to watch',[16] so that the impression of unity between the armed forces and the civilian population reinforced the deterrent effect of the display of power. The third and most important parade ground was 'Praça do Rossio, a very large quarter where the companies of armed men were most visible.'[17]

The English could therefore see for themselves that, far from being daunted, Lisbon was thoroughly relaxed and confident. Throughout the parade, the detachments on the wall remained on full alert, but also let themselves be seen and added to the military and civilian festivities. The parade along the external sea wall was particularly impressive. This was very close to the English position and well protected, not by the walls this time but by the brave Portuguese companies,

> and although it could not be seen from the beach or beaches that lie between the sea and the wall, it was no less crowded, for it was full of squadrons in formation with their guns at intervals aiming toward the sea, with barrels full of earth for gabions, as the Count of Villadorta went along the palace terrace, from the way station to the meat market, with his men on horseback in rows of seven. And it was all a remarkable sight, for the men were all looking splendidly smart and in such high spirits that many wondered at the little regard they seemed to have for the enemy.[18]

And what of the English while Lisbon was celebrating and strengthening its defences? Were they preparing an attack, as the defenders suspected? Nothing could be further from the truth. As we have seen, the previous day (3 June) was the second turning point for the English Armada. This was the day that buried forever the grandiose and

---

[14] *Relación de lo subçedido del armada enemiga.* BN mss 18579, p. 67.
[15] Ibid.
[16] Ibid.
[17] Ibid.
[18] Ibid., pp. 67–68.

carefully planned objectives of that great expedition. Just as they had done on 15 May in Corunna, the English set about burying their dead. There had been stately funeral rites for Mr Spencer and the hundreds of dead in the attacks of 14 May and the same was done in Lisbon for the men who had fallen on the previous day, especially for Colonel Brett, 'who had a Christian burial in Santa Catalina, with all the pomp and ceremony of war, with muffled drums, pikes and standards dipped and harquebuses inverted'.[19]

Following the burial of Brett and his men, plus those who had died in other attacks or fallen victim to the artillery, and fearing even more deadly attacks, they made preparations for a secret flight. This was to be completed hours later under the cover of darkness. Norris's excursion was looking forlorn and even pathetic. They had marched for seven long days from Peniche to Lisbon, but not long after their arrival they were scared away by Iberian attacks and fled again to Cascais where they could re-embark. It is striking how this ignominious flight on the night of 4 June would be omitted from the reports written later in London, in order to mislead both the Queen and public opinion about the real outcome of this great expedition. The prime example is the memorable exculpatory report produced by Captain A. Wingfield. It is notable for its length, prolixity, literary nature and, above all, the remarkable inventiveness Wingfield employed to create a fictitious journal of military operations to replace what had actually occurred.

This invented account would be one of the main sources used by historians in later periods to reconstruct what happened that spring. In a domino effect that has lasted for over four centuries, everyone who wished to know the historical truth about the English Armada was totally misled by Wingfield. The brave English captain quite simply and with considerable nerve invented the acts of war that, according to his account, happened to the English army in Lisbon on June 5–9. Such events have been retold by every text written on the subject ... but on those dates the English army had already left Lisbon!

This is how the anonymous Portuguese account described the withdrawal:

> They decided to withdraw from the outskirts of town and take advantage of the protection of their fleet, which was in a cove next to the monastery of Santo Antonio, near Cascais. Thus, the following Monday, from midnight onwards on the 5 June, quite fearful of being attacked and without any call to arms or making the slightest noise, they moved camp, staying away from the sea to keep away from the galleys. They avoided the roads and made their way across difficult terrain so they could not be followed by the cavalry. Thus, they fled as quickly as they could, but many could not escape from the pursuing Spanish cavalry, who killed all the tired and sick who were unable to keep up with the pace of the others, numbering over four hundred men.[20]

---

[19] *Relación de lo subçedido del armada enemiga*. BN mss 18579, p. 64.
[20] *Memoria da Vinda dos Ingleses a Portugal em 1589*, pp. 277–8, quoted in Pires De Lima, *O ataque*.

According to the Spanish account, 'after two o'clock in the morning, they began to withdraw without playing the drums or any other instrument, but very quietly, and they say the first to leave was Dom António, who had taken up lodgings in the last house of the Docongro road'.[21] According to Falçao de Resende, 'from midnight onwards they lit many bonfires to make our men believe they were still camped and fled in an orderly fashion and as silently as they could without sounding a drum'.[22]

In the dead of night, the orders to leave were passed through the regiments in whispers. The Iberians had to be made to think that the soldiers were still in their trenches. To that end, a number or fires were lit and kept burning in order to give the impression that men were still there. With strict orders not to make a sound or carry any lights that could give away the fact that they were running away, that great army set off on tiptoe. In the vanguard, heading for Cascais, was Dom António, who had already provided proof in El-Ksar el Kebir, where King Sebastião had died with thousands of Christians,[23] of a marked dislike for danger. At the rear, the most dangerous position in a retreat, was his son Dom Manuel and the cavalry.

The orderly retreat did not last long and soon ended up in disarray. By chance on that same night, the Archduke, who was unaware of the actions of Norris's army, had decided that after the bloody attack on 3June, he would give the invaders another fright in order to encourage them to leave Lisbon. The attack would take place at night and by sea, and so he ordered Bazán to feign an assault with the galleys on the coastal flank of the part of the city occupied by the English. He had no intention of sending the galley infantry on an actual offensive against this area, but instead wanted to terrorize the invaders by reminding them of the attack of thirty hours earlier. And so,

> at night, before the enemy withdrew, His Highness ordered that at midnight the men of the galleys should attack from the monastery of the Discalced Carmelites, and so they lit over two thousand matchlocks aboard the galleys, sending all the skiffs to land and putting out the rest of the matchlocks remaining on the galleys so that it seemed that the men were headed for land.

The lighted matchlocks of the harquebuses could be seen in the night. Taking advantage of this, which in another situation could have given away a surprise attack, the Spanish made the English believe that two thousand harquebusiers were about to land. 'The attack was very timely, for the enemy was just beginning to withdraw and thought they had been discovered and for that reason our men were after them on land, and so they headed very quickly for Cascais.'[24] However, an army of such size cannot sneak away like a petty thief, especially when it has to keep away from the coast and also the wider, more accessible roads. As dawn began to break and with the bonfires still burning, the last of the men were leaving the outskirts of Lisbon.

---

[21] *Relación de lo subçedido del armada enemiga.* BN mss 18579, p. 68.
[22] Letter from Falçao de Resende in Ruela Pombo, *Portugal 1580–1595*, 3rd part, col. 25.
[23] See above, Chapter 5.
[24] Letter from Francisco de Coloma. AGS. Guerra Antigua. File 249, fol. 129.

Chapter 26

Two Banners

It was growing light on 5 June. The darkness that had protected the furtive withdrawal was lifting as Norris frantically urged his demoralized men westwards, away from the rising sun. Bazán's galleys then spotted their movements and from the nearby coast began to rain fire down upon the fugitives:

> The rearguard left as day was dawning, and with it Dom Manuel, son of Dom António, and the cavalry. They were unable to leave sufficiently quietly so as not to be heard from the galleys, which fired on them at will at least to the height of Alcántara. Some of the men were killed, and realising how much more harm would come to them by coming out of the streets to where they could be seen from the sea, they decided to keep their distance and go above Alcántara to the old windmills, where they were safe from attacks from the sea.[1]

Lisbon was awakened by the sound of gunfire from the galleys and soon learned of the flight of the English in the night. 'The alarm was sounded and word spread that the enemy had been routed and they were leaving as quietly as they could.'[2] The Count of Fuentes adopted a cautious attitude. In the first place, instead of pursuing the enemy from the walls of Lisbon, 'he sent Don Pedro de Guzmán out to reconnoitre the entire quarter, and he went carefully from the city into the country in case it was a ruse to bring his men out and keep most of them busy in an ambush so the English could attack the city or try to trap them in a pincer movement'.[3] Only when it had been confirmed that the withdrawal was complete and that there was no trick involved did they prepare an expedition to Cascais in pursuit of the enemy. The abandoned English camp and nearby hills were searched, 'and having returned before midday, the men were prepared to set out after lunch'.[4]

---

[1]   *Relación de lo subçedido del armada enemiga*. BN mss 18579, pp. 68–9. This is Francisco Coloma's account of this first phase of the withdrawal: 'And at dawn the galleys from Alcántara discovered a large number of banners, and their artillery fired upon them at the back of the estate of Luis César four or five times, and they were very good shots, for there were so many men withdrawing, and so very quickly they fled and moved from the seafront to above the mills of Alcántara. It is clear that the artillery did them much harm.' Letter from Francisco de Coloma. AGS. Guerra Antigua. File 249, fol. 129. Alonso de Bazán describes it as follows: 'We fired upon them with many guns, for a large number of men were within range of all the artillery on the galleys, so they left the seafront and climbed up to the mills above Alcántara. As far as could be judged, although they were spread out there seemed to be more than eight thousand men.' Alonso de Bazán to the King, Lisbon, 5 June 1589. Ibid., fol. 127.

[2]   *Relación de lo subçedido del armada enemiga*. BN mss 18579, p. 69.

[3]   Ibid., pp. 69–70.

[4]   Ibid., p. 69.

Meanwhile, after the galleys had fired upon the enemy and forced them away from the coast, 'they returned to Lisbon to receive their orders from His Highness. From there they went to take up their position at São Julião and on the way spotted many of the enemy in disarray and these were also hit by the artillery'.[5] Thus on the return journey to São Julião and in full daylight, the galleys had another opportunity to fire on an enemy which in its haste and under attack was marching in disarray.

The troops stationed in Lisbon were not about to abandon their mission of protecting the capital, but there was nothing to stop the Spanish detachments that controlled and guarded Cascais and the outskirts of Lisbon from joining the fray. Thus, 'on hearing the sounds of men passing, the guards positioned by Don Sancho reported to him and then prepared to reconnoitre'.[6] Shortly afterwards, Alarcón and Sancho Bravo with their riders and mounted harquebusiers set out to attack the English column to the battle cry of '*Santiago and at 'em*'. 'Seeing the enemy flee, they went at them with their men and those of Gaspar de Alarcón and killed over two hundred of their men.'[7] It was on this occasion that Don Sancho Bravo, of the noble house of Arce, seized two banners that he would take as trophies and place in the Cathedral of Sigüenza where, thanks to the dry conditions in that Castilian town, they have been preserved to this day.[8]

After this, 'he returned to Alcántara to allow his men to rest'.[9] While he had been seizing banners, in Lisbon they were getting ready to go after the retreating English, for 'Don Pedro de Guzmán had returned from his reconnaissance of town and country without finding any sign of an ambush, so it was decided to set off in pursuit.'[10] A large detachment was prepared for the march to Cascais, and 'the Count set out with Masters at Arms Don Gabriel Niño, Don Francisco de Toledo, Don Pedro de Guzmán and Esteban de Ibarra, with the captains, young gentlemen and a few men other than the professionals'. Also with the expedition were

> Don Bernardino de Velasco with the men-at-arms, four field guns brought by Captain of Artillery Orejón, a thousand infantrymen with selected pikemen (*coseletes*) under Captain Don Álvaro de Mendoza, the musketeers under Captain Don Álvaro de Carvajal from Seville, the harquebusiers under Captains Don Bernardino de Zúñiga, Diego de Quesada and Juan Pacheco, Ensign of Master at Arms Don Gabriel Niño and other captains of the Tercio regiment of Don Francisco de Toledo.[11]

---

[5] Letter from Francisco de Coloma. AGS. Guerra Antigua. File 249, fol. 129.
[6] *Relación de lo subçedido del armada enemiga*. BN mss 18579, p. 70.
[7] Ibid.
[8] Fernández Duro. *Armada Española*, III, p. 51. For a study of these banners, see Antonio Manzano Lahoz and Luis Sorando Muzás. 'Las banderas de la capilla del Doncel de la catedral de Sigüenza'. *Banderas* (Boletín de la Sociedad Española de Vexilología), No. 44, 1992.
[9] *Relación de lo subçedido del armada enemiga*. BN mss 18579, p. 70.
[10] Ibid., p. 71.
[11] Ibid.

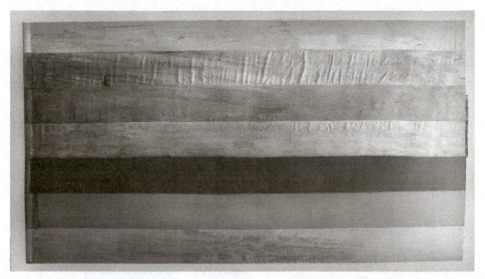

Figure 26.1 The English banner captured by Sancho Bravo on 5 June 1589 during Norris's withdrawal from Lisbon to Cascais. Photo by Kronos Art Restoration Service.

The banner was placed in Sigüenza Cathedral and for centuries was on display in the chapel of Martín Vázquez de Arce, the "Doncel" (Young Man) of Sigüenza. It measures 168 cms in height and 330 cms in length. It consists of seven horizontal taffeta strips, coloured (from the top) white, red, turquoise, yellow, maroon or purple, light green and white. The first strip was in tatters, the next three (red, turquoise and yellow) were intact and the remainder were in fragments until the banner was restored in 2016, as seen here.

On its way to Cascais from Lisbon, this small pursuit army 'went past Alcántara and near Santo Amaro met up with Don Sancho with his mounted harquebusiers and Gaspar de Alarcón with his riders, who reported what had happened and who had arrived in great need of rest'.[12] After the encounter with Sancho and Alarcón, the Count of Fuentes felt unsure about what to do. On the one hand, he ought not to waste the opportunity to attack an army in disarray, for he could inflict severe damage on them without too much risk to his own men. Besides, the infantry 'was very keen to attack the enemy, knowing they were marching as quickly as they could, and that the horses could only catch them up with difficulty'.[13] On the other hand, there were the orders given by the Archduke, whose mission it was to keep Lisbon safe and not take any action that could threaten that crucial task. He did not forget for an instant the presence in Cascais of an enormous fleet that was powerful enough to force its way through the estuary and attack the city. Besides, the army in retreat was still several times more numerous than his detachment, so

[12] *Relación de lo subçedido del armada enemiga.* BN mss 18579, p. 71.
[13] Ibid., p. 72.

Figure 26.2 The second banner captured by Sancho Bravo on 5 June. Photo by Kronos Art Restoration Service.

Like the other one, this one too was displayed in the chapel of the "Doncel" of Sigüenza, whose famous prone statue was described by Ortega y Gasset, not without some justification, as 'the most beautiful in the world'. If the banner was displayed in such a perfect spot, it is because Sancho Bravo was from the same warrior stock as Martín Vázquez de Arce, his great-uncle. The banner, which is made of strong taffeta or canvas, is 147 cms in height and 165 cms in length. The gyronny shield that it represents suggests that the banner is Portuguese. This is how it looks following restoration carried out in 2016.

since the Count was in doubt about the causes of the withdrawal, with many reasons to keep what little Spanish infantry he had, and suspecting that the withdrawal was part of a ruse aimed at luring his men out of the city, and returning with the fleet using both its men and artillery to find some of our men outside the walls, this was an opportunity for any double dealing that the townsfolk might have agreed with the invaders.[14]

---

[14] *Relación de lo subçedido del armada enemiga.* BN mss 18579, p. 72.

The Count's precaution was justified considering the two risks that he had to face: the first, missing a great opportunity to deal a crushing blow to the invading army; the second, falling victim to a deadly trap and being caught off guard by an attack on Lisbon by sea. He chose to take the first risk, especially because 'the wall was too old and weak to be relied on and had almost thirty gates and entrances that had been sealed so recently that the mortar was still fresh. Without much noise and few tools they could be broken into almost anywhere, especially near the water where they could suddenly land.'[15]

In short, neither Spanish nor English were in their own territory, and neither of them could ignore the fact that victory could fall to whichever cousin, Dom António or Philip II, managed to get the support of the Portuguese people and nobility. Therefore,

> the Count of Fuentes decided that Don Bernardino de Velasco with the three companies under his command should go out in pursuit, and that with him should go Don Sancho Bravo for his experience in the campaign, leaving his men at Santo Amaro, for after the efforts of the last few days his horses were in no condition to keep up with the fresh ones, and so Don Sancho led them in pursuit of the enemy, and the Count returned with all his men and artillery to the city.[16]

So while the mounted harquebusiers of Sancho Bravo rested at the strategic hill of Santo Amaro, the man himself – after his memorable morning and the capture of the two banners now stored in the Cathedral of Sigüenza – was once again in the vanguard of Iberian resistance.

Fuentes not only returned to Lisbon without seeking to fight but also did not allow the Count of Villadorta's cavalry to go after the fugitives. If he had done so, he would have had about 2,000 men with which to attack the withdrawing English infantry. However, Fuentes ordered the Portuguese nobleman to remain in Lisbon and had even completed his own departure from the gate of Santa Catalina, meeting beforehand at Terreiro do Paço without telling the Portuguese cavalry. Did Fuentes not trust Villadorta? Was he afraid that Dom António could persuade him to defect to his side? Was it one more precaution to ensure the defence of the city and to retain complete control at a moment full of uncertainties? Did he fear a ruse by Norris to force him to fight at a disadvantage?

The anonymous Portuguese account offers some clarification regarding the role of the Count of Fuentes on that 5 June:

> On the morning the enemy were retreating, the Count of Villa Dorta wished to pursue them with the Portuguese cavalry and repeatedly asked the Count of Fuentes. The Count was in no hurry to follow the enemy nor did he see fit for the Count of Villa Dorta to do so in spite of the latter's insistence. For as the enemy's powerful reputation was so great and in three days their retreat was so disorderly, with no hope of it improving, he had reason to suspect that there was a snake in

---

[15] *Relación de lo subçedido del armada enemiga.* BN mss 18579, p. 72.
[16] Ibid.

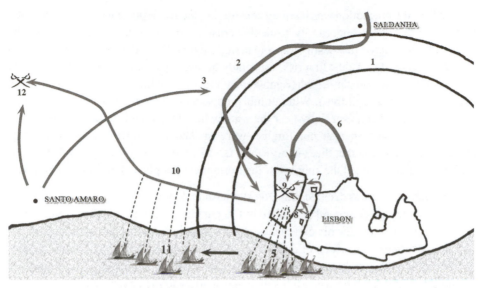

Figure 26.3 Map 6, 2–5 June, Lisbon.

1. Maximum range of the castle of São Jorge artillery.
2. On 2 June, the English army advances towards Lisbon, but detours because of the São Jorge artillery and waits until nightfall to occupy the outskirts of the city between San Roque, Santa Catalina and A Esperança. Ninety-seven banners were counted.
3. On 2 June, Sancho Bravo's cavalry harasses the army from its base up in Santo Amaro.
4. On the night between 2 and 3 June, attempt by Antonian Rui Dias Lobo to sneak the army in through the monastery of A Trindade, adjoining the wall. The attempt fails.
5. On the morning of 3 June, Alonso de Bazán's galleys bombard the English quarters. The English were heading towards the sea but were forced away from the coast.
6. On 3 June at midday, a detachment of some seven hundred veteran pikers, harquebusiers and cavalry led by Captains Claudio Veamonte, Francisco Martínez Malo, Felipe Sumiel, Bernardino de Velasco, Jerónimo de Guevara, Francisco de Pedraza and Blas de Jerez attack the northern flank of the English quarters and break up six trenches.
7. On 3 June another detachment attacks from the monastery of São Roque, with elite marksmen posted on its roof.
8. On 3 June another detachment, led by Captain Fernando de Ágreda with two hundred marksmen attacks from the monastery of Loreto, also garrisoned with marksmen.
9. On 3 June, Colonel Brett's regiment, some 1,000 men, suffers severe casualties. Brett himself is killed along with his captains.
10. On 4–5 June, the English army flees at night towards Cascais, leaving many bonfires lit to conceal their departure and leaving the wounded and the sick behind.
11. On 4–5 June, the galleys pursue and bombard them, forcing them away from the coast.
12. On 5 June, Sancho Bravo and Gaspar de Alarcón's cavalry attack. Two flags are captured and remain to this day in the Cathedral of Sigüenza. The English lose over five hundred men as they withdraw to Cascais.

the grass, a secret poisonous ruse of war in which the men within their grasp lured them away from the city into the country until they were unable to retreat without risking their chances in open battle. We were bound to come to harm, since the reinforcements that were on their way had not yet arrived and it would have been the enemy's only remedy, as they were unable to seek an alternative. To avoid this, and since the enemy had lifted the siege, they should be offered a 'silver bridge', as the Spanish proverb says, for without their honour, their reputation, with losses and disrepute their only option was to embark. Above all, the main thing for the service of His Majesty was to keep the enemy out of the city and defend its walls, prevent the sacking of the riches belonging to the King and the property of the suffering people, and prevent the church silver from being stolen. First and foremost was the duty to protect the worship of the images, relics and bodies of the saints of the city, and prevent the abominations, theft, death and fires that are the whole aim and intention of that Lutheran and heretical horde. Finally, their departure provided not only the preservation of and solution to so much, but also the certainty of the best service to His Majesty, and any other option meant risking what had been won without losses, but rather with much praise and glory.[17]

As things turned out, the troops defending the walls of Lisbon did not go outside that day, although the detachment outside the walls did inflict some harm on the enemy and even Fuentes's reinforcements still had a further chance to go into action: 'The cavalry arrived in Cascais with half an hour of daylight left and the enemy was already there. So the cavalry could not achieve anything there, but a number of the enemy were killed in Quintal and some of those who could not keep up with pace of the army.'[18]

Reinforcements kept arriving that day: the second Marquis of Santa Cruz, the young Álvaro de Bazán, came with his cousin Don Pedro Ponce de León plus two more captains. Archduke Alberto, 'in memory of his brave father',[19] received him with great ceremony. As soon as the eighteen-year-old Álvaro de Bazán was informed that the army had been driven back and that the only remaining danger was the fleet,

> on stepping back from kissing the Archduke's hand and aware that with the enemy having abandoned its quarters the best chance of a battle was at sea, he embarked on a galley that happened to be in port and joined his uncle Don Alonso de Bazán, General of the galleys who was usually at São Julião to defend the entry to the estuary and seize any opportunity to do harm to the enemy.[20]

The night of the 5 June in Lisbon was a more peaceful one. The men were able to stand down and although a permanent watch was kept from the walls, the complex defensive system could finally be relaxed without the presence of the English. Attention

---

[17] *Memoria da Vinda dos Ingleses a Portugal em 1589*, p. 278, quoted in Pires De Lima, *O ataque*.
[18] *Relación de lo subçedido del armada enemiga*. BN mss 18579, p. 74.
[19] Ibid., p. 73.
[20] Ibid., p. 74.

could be entirely focused on the maritime front, for if the English were going to attack the city they could now only do so by sea. On the English side, the disagreements and reproaches between Drake and Norris sounded like a broken record, which took nothing away from the depressing catalogue of the dead and missing, for on the day of the frantic withdrawal it was every man for himself and at least five hundred men who had left Lisbon did not make it to Cascais. The English were completely exhausted and the total number of casualties was beginning to look like a disaster. The solemn funerary rites on 4 June had given way to a shameful disregard, not for corpses, but for the wounded, the exhausted, the slow and the sick. Along the twenty kilometres from Lisbon to Cascais, the English had a lost a man every forty metres, perhaps more, to attacks from land and sea. The number of casualties was at least four or five thousand men. The English Armada had not yet become the disastrous counterpart to the Spanish Armada, although the worst was yet to come. These were not the main concerns of the leaders of the grand English expedition, however, for following such setbacks they had not yet achieved a single one of their three objectives.

On the morning of 6 June, the Count of Fuentes's horse could be heard approaching under the arch of Santa Catalina gate. He was returning from Oeiras and announced that news from Bernardino de Velasco and Sancho Bravo would soon arrive from the front. On the basis of this news a war council was held later and it was decided that the Count 'would leave sufficient men in the city and would take the remaining Portuguese and Castilians plus all the riders and march to Cascais to try to disrupt the enemy or do them some harm before they embarked'.[21] The precautionary measures of the previous day regarding a possible diversionary tactic to get the troops out of Lisbon had been lifted, for people were told that 'there was no need to fear that the attack by sea would be so quick that the infantry could not return to the city before the enemy arrived, for while they sailed to their starting point and found a place to drop anchor, there would be plenty of time for them to get back'.[22]

An army was then prepared once more – and this time more thoroughly – to march on Cascais, and the Count again 'ordered Captain Orejón to set out with four field guns, which he thought would be sufficient, carried by his Highness's mules'. The carts carried 'bread, cheese and wine for the men'.[23] The Tercio regiment of Francisco de Toledo, reinforced by Portuguese companies, joined the march, 'with the remaining men distributed in the squares and at the gates'. After meeting up with the company of Rui Lourenço de Távora, 'who had also pursued the enemy', the Count of Fuentes soon reached Oeiras with the cavalry. There he decided that when the infantry arrived it should halt and rest, 'for the day had been hot and they had marched over sandy terrain'. From Oeiras he sent messages to Alonso de Bazán, general of the galleys, and Pedro Venegas de Córdoba, castellan of the castle of São Julião, and went to reconnoitre the

---

[21] *Relación de lo subçedido del armada enemiga.* BN mss 18579, p. 75.
[22] Ibid., pp. 75–6.
[23] Ibid., p. 76.

fleet, returning to Oeiras 'at some hour in the night, which was rainy and rather uncomfortable for those sleeping out in the open'.[24]

Meanwhile, on that 6 June, Lisbon started to return to normal, for 'some of those who had taken refuge in the churches began to emerge and there were some supplies again in the market squares'.[25] However, until the outskirts of the city were completely back to normal, Fuentes had issued strict orders to prevent and punish the looting of any abandoned dwellings.[26] Fortunately Portugal's beautiful capital had emerged unscathed from the terrible threat of unprecedented destruction that might have befallen it. Its people must have found it pleasant to enjoy that sense of calm, after the terrible days they had been through just a few years before, when Don Sebastião had left to meet his fate in Kasr el-Kebir, with the mourning and payment of ransoms that followed.

[24]   *Relación de lo subçedido del armada enemiga.* BN mss 18579, p. 76.

[25]   Ibid., p. 74.

[26]   'After the enemy retreated I took measures to prevent any disorder in the city, ordering that no soldiers or locals be allowed out of the gates. The locals who came to ask permission to recover property they had left in their homes outside the wall were rightly permitted to do so. On learning that same day that some took things not only from their homes but from others and brought it back saying it was theirs, I sent two court magistrates and two noblemen to put a stop to it and to keep order. They found that the locals brought clothes from houses other than their own, but it could not be proven since the owners were absent, and those present claimed the things were theirs. In the event of any indiscipline on the part of the soldiers, I sent the field captains and other officers to take care of it. Some houses and storehouses were guarded by trustworthy men. Having heard later that the boatmen from this shore and some men from the galleys and foreign ships were missing and came at night to loot, I have ordered that some inquiries and visits be made. There is so little information, since it has all been done so secretly, and however many enquiries we make I doubt we will find out much of use. Any soldiers found in the outskirts without orders from me or their officers have been hanged, so I believe that although the military are in part to blame, others are more so.' The Count of Fuentes to the King, Lisbon, 24 June 1589. AGS. Guerra Antigua. File 249, fol. 135.

Chapter 27

Essex, Cárdenas and the Windmills

It was cloudy at first light on Wednesday, 7 June and Alarcón and his riders, within sight of Drake's fleet, crossed the bay of Cascais and reached the English trenches. The fleet was quick to react, and 'a cannon was fired at them but the shot was too high'.[1] Soon the Count arrived and 'was able to get to appreciate the lie of the land and the size of the fleet and how close it was. He could see that the enemy was entrenched in Cascais and Santo Antonio and that the Spanish army had to pass within sight of the fleet and within range of the great harm its artillery could do.' Marching directly upon Cascais and the monastery of Santo Antonio was therefore ruled out. On the other hand, attacking it after a detour from the north would mean crossing the mountains of Sintra, 'and although a different route to Cascais would avoid the danger of the artillery, it would be along very difficult mountain roads, and as the men came down to attack, the enemy could place a few of their soldiers along the way and kill many men'.[2] An attack on the new English quarters in Cascais, which were protected by the fleet and the mountains of Sintra, was definitely discounted. As it was, the English could no longer march on Lisbon over land, nor could the Spanish force them out of Cascais. While the Iberian army returned to Lisbon, the Count of Fuentes stopped at the maritime flank to consult at the castle of São Julião 'with the Castellan and the General of the galleys'.[3]

During the morning of Thursday 8 June, with Norris's fruitless overland expedition from Peniche to Lisbon to Cascais and Fuentes's reconnaissance of the new English quarters both now over, and with both armies protected behind their respective positions, the anger and impatience of the Earl of Essex grew relentlessly by the hour. Robert Devereux had come to Portugal in search of glory and booty, with the boldness, vigour and nobility of youth. After the brilliant but costly landing in Peniche, he found the role he was being forced to play as a part of that slow, spineless army intolerable. He needed to fight for Queen and country, to achieve fame and glory through daring military adventures and return to England proud and heroic and be forgiven by his Queen, by his aggrieved mistress Elizabeth. For that reason he constantly demanded greater boldness from the English army. His harangues did not go unheeded and the English command decided on a new strategy. And so,

> with the English aware of how close to their camp the Count had come and that
> given the unfavourable conditions for an attack he had kept his army out of sight

[1] *Relación de lo subçedido del armada enemiga.* BN mss 18579, p. 77.
[2] Ibid.
[3] Ibid., p. 78.

and had returned to the city, and so as not to give the impression that they were lacking in spirit, in an act of bravado or arrogance they sent out an English trumpeter on horseback in the morning of Thursday the 8th of June, with a postilion who spoke French and a letter for the Count of Fuentes.[4]

Just as with the talks in Corunna, the English sent a new emissary, again seeking a meeting with the Spanish. This time the messenger did not bring threats urging the Spanish to surrender but the message at first had to remain a mystery: 'When they reached the gate of Santa Catalina, word was sent to the Count and he ordered that they be let in, whereupon they dismounted at the palace and they handed the letter to the Count.' Fuentes had no authority to open such a letter, so 'he took it and through the interpreter told them that he was unable to open it but had to send it to His Highness for him to do as he thought best'.[5] While the letter was taken to the Archduke, Fuentes saw to it personally that the English messenger was made welcome in accordance with the rules of hospitality, which were observed even in time of war. This made the Spanish garrison extremely curious, and knowing that the language of contact was French, several captains who spoke it were happy join the reception, for politeness should not be taken for weakness. And so the Count 'ordered that the trumpeter and his assistant be well fed, as if they were most distinguished men, as judging by their behaviour they seemed to be. A few captains who spoke French joined them and all enjoyed the most pleasant conversation.'[6]

So the English emissary, who had no doubt not had any decent food for some time, was able to enjoy a plentiful meal washed down with some good wine. According to the Spanish journal, the letter 'was returned to them just as they had brought it, apparently untouched'.[7] But it had in fact been opened very carefully and then closed again. It said:

We, the Generals Drake and Norris and Earls of such and such, having been informed that the Count of Fuentes, General of the Kingdom of Portugal, and others on his side, have said that we retreated and fled in secret from Lisbon, and not in the manner of an army intending to fight, hereby state that we have not fled. So that it may be known by our deeds that we are ready and willing, we are sending you this trumpeter with our challenge, and inform you that we await you on this field of Oeiras to offer battle until the end of the day.[8]

This desperate attempt to provoke an encounter recalls the action of Medina Sidonia ten months earlier at Gravelines, when he challenged the English to combat once more after the dispersed fleet had reformed, and in particular when he stopped the fleet three times over the next few days and got into combat formation.[9] The English did not dare

---

[4]   *Relación de lo subçedido del armada enemiga.* BN mss 18579, p. 78.
[5]   Ibid.
[6]   Ibid.
[7]   Ibid.
[8]   Ibid., p. 79.
[9]   See above, Chapter 5.

Figure 27.1 Don Pedro Enríquez de Acevedo, Count of Fuentes. Portrait by Dominicus Custos in 1595. Located in the Rijksmuseum, Amsterdam

He was one of the great Spanish soldiers of the sixteenth–seventeenth centuries. In 1589 he was at the head of the garrison in Lisbon under direct orders from the Archduke. His mission was to defend the city from three separate dangers: Norris's army marching from Peniche, Drake's fleet at anchor and at the ready right outside the entrance to Lisbon, and a possible Antonian faction willing to let the English in. He had weakened Norris through harassment, isolation and scorched earth tactics, and had avoided doing battle until he could do so in favourable conditions. Then he struck with just the right force to make Norris flee with heavy casualties but with minimal Spanish losses. He waited in vain for Drake at the Oeiras–São Julião defensive axis, with the galleys in support, while all the time keeping the bulk of the Spanish infantry within the city walls. The possible Antonian faction was also controlled in the same way, with masterful management of the nobility and the Portuguese population.

to accept the challenge, for they were in no condition to do so and it would not have been appropriate for them, considering that the Spanish were already heading for an uncertain fate. Howard had little to gain and much to lose from a dubious battle at short range against large and powerful galleons. England's great victory was to thwart the attempted invasion, and to take on actions that would jeopardize this success went against all military logic. The Archduke must have thought something similar. Nothing was more uncertain than to accept the English challenge and fight a larger army in the field. Nor was it the right time to organize a contest between the Spanish and the English on Portuguese territory that would bring no gain and would involve a lot of risk. So the letter went unanswered, and that very morning, as if to give some substance to their bravura, 'they sent out the few men they had in Santo Antonio, and in squadron formation set off for Oeiras. Having marched about half a league, they returned to their quarters.'[10] There is no better proof of the pointlessness of the English gesture than their lack of any attempt to attack the Oeiras–São Julião defensive line, which was what had been keeping Drake from entering Cascais. This defensive arrangement had been much strengthened on the day of the English Armada's arrival, but the Archduke did not find it necessary to send any more forces there.

While the English carried out the march in order to keep up the men's fragile morale, their emissaries 'requested permission to see the prisoners, since they were missing some distinguished men, and to discuss their ransom'.[11] But it was not the right time to talk about prisoners before the military operations had come to an end, so without allowing them to see the English prisoners or answering their letter, 'they saw them off between ten and eleven in the morning, with Captain Francisco Ángel and Captain Monzón taking them to the gate'.[12]

After the brief English visit and while part of Elizabeth's army rested in the area of Cascais, a grand, symbolic spectacle was about to begin in Lisbon. The most important aristocrat in Portugal by far, and the owner of a significant area of the country, was the great Duke of Bragança. His loyalty to the legitimate king was, above all others, crucial to the avoidance of a bitter war on Portuguese territory. Thus, his presence alongside the Archduke left Dom António looking like little more than a fugitive from justice. This was the day of Teodósio II of Bragança's arrival, which made the Portuguese forces, who were unflinchingly loyal to their king, Philip I of Portugal, the ultimate safeguard of the country's stability: 'Around midday the Duke of Bragança and his brother Don Duarte disembarked, bringing with them twenty noblemen, two hundred lancers and a thousand infantrymen, as well as the seventy halberdiers of his personal guard and his servants, plus hand-picked trumpeters and minstrels.'[13]

---

[10] *Relación de lo subçedido del armada enemiga.* BN mss 18579, p. 79.
[11] Ibid.
[12] Ibid.
[13] Ibid.

This impressive army disembarked to the sound of music and with great ceremony before solemnly beginning the climb to the fort of São Jorge. Conscious that he was dealing with his equals in terms of nobility of birth, Archduke Alberto, future King of the Spanish Netherlands, showed the highest respect for the Duke, himself the father of the future king of Portugal, and to his brother, and 'all three together showed themselves from a window standing apart from the rest of the gentlemen and knights. Then his Highness took them alone to the chamber where they spent some further time.'[14] The complete union of the neighbouring Catholic countries was there for all to see, leaving aside the Machiavellian whims of the Prior of Crato, who was capable of allying himself with heretics provided that he came away with the Portuguese crown,[15] and who was totally unconcerned that, given the balance of power at that particular time, such a venture could have unleashed an unforeseeable series of evils on his own country. After speaking privately and at length with the cream of Portuguese nobility, and without a thought for the ill feeling that the Spanish nobles may have experienced by being marginalized in this way, the Archduke 'accompanied them to the door of the chamber, where they were being waited for in order to be taken to the house of Luis César, for it was the nearest to the palace'.[16]

On Friday 9 June, with the English protected once again behind the walls of Cascais, the new logistics of the English Armada became apparent. They no longer went out on looting raids to seize provisions, nor could they expect any supplies from a population that was not on their side. They did have an inexhaustible source of supplies thanks to the several wheat-laden *urcas* captured by Drake in Cascais. Because of this,

> entrenched on land and protected at sea by its fleet, the enemy were able to survive for several days without going out to reconnoitre, using only the mills on the land they had nearby. The locals, as surreptitiously as they could, were providing them with flour and being paid handsomely in return,[17] since they had no other supplies but the wheat they confiscated from the French and German vessels arriving in the city. When our men discovered that they were secretly using the local mills, the Count sent Captain Francisco de Velasco with the companies of Blas de Jerez and one of the Duke's cavalry companies and they destroyed all the mills in Oeiras, Baqueraña and the surrounding country, which forced the enemy to boil their wheat. As a result, more and more of them became ill and died.[18]

While this source of supplies for the English Armada was cut off, new reinforcements arrived, and that day another three companies from the north of Portugal came 'and another of forty men in very good order sent by the Count of Oropesa, and very fine

---

[14] *Relación de lo subçedido del armada enemiga*. BN mss 18579, p. 80.
[15] Cabrera De Córdoba, *Historia de Felipe II Rey de España*, pp. 1258–9.
[16] *Relación de lo subçedido del armada enemiga*. BN mss 18579, p. 80.
[17] Namely through the *maquila*, the portion of grain or flour kept by the miller for his services.
[18] *Relación de lo subçedido del armada enemiga*. BN mss 18579, p. 80.

horses, ornate saddles and new clothes'.[19] The situation in the camp of Philip's forces was becoming ever more comfortable and secure, while that of the Antonians, now exclusively English, was becoming so desperate that eventually they would be forced to eat their own horses. The small amount of biscuit and other foodstuffs that the fleet might still have had was reserved for the seamen directly under Drake's command, while Norris's soldiers had to fend for themselves. Here was another example of the two-handed command, increasingly at variance and increasingly in disagreement, from which the English Armada was suffering.[20] The day came to an end with the huge and formidable fleet still at anchor off Cascais.

During the morning of the following day, one of Norris's old acquaintances, Don Alonso de Vargas of the War Council, arrived in Lisbon. He was one of the military leaders who were responsible for European analysts conferring the highest ranking on the Spanish infantry and recommending in their books that the only way to combat them was to imitate their structure and organisation. Don Alonso

> visited the whole of the city, inspecting every wall and gate and the castle, and ordered the whole beach to be entrenched near the water, from the palace fort to the coal wharf; the trenches which Matías de Alburquerque had ordered to be built with the wood from the ships on the shore to be rebuilt and covered with a large amount of earth, from the palace fort to the Corpo Santo; and more cannons to be placed at intervals in addition to those already there.[21]

Alonso de Vargas did not confine himself to reinforcing the walled perimeter and the maritime front – the only one now remaining for the attackers. He also strengthened the artillery of São Jorge, whose great effectiveness had been proven during the three days that the English had spent on the outskirts of Lisbon. With the arrival of Vargas and the resulting improvement of defensive measures, 'all Spaniards were generally well pleased'.[22]

---

[19] *Relación de lo subçedido del armada enemiga.* BN mss 18579, p. 80.

[20] 'And thus they came to need it [food] so badly that some locals in Cascais told us that they ate some of their horses and other animals, and boiled wheat, since the infantry did not receive any biscuits from the fleet or any other food, for what Francis Drake has is for the men on his ships.' The Count of Fuentes to the King, Lisbon, 26 June 1589. AGS. Guerra Antigua. File 249, fol. 136.

[21] *Relación de lo subçedido del armada enemiga.* BN mss 18579, p. 81.

[22] Ibid. The following day, the Count of Fuentes also described Vargas's new preparations: 'Don Alonso de Vargas arrived yesterday and was very well received, for at all times his judgment is sound, and now his presence is timely. He has seen part of the wall and the seafront and the Santa Catalina quarter. I believe he has found it less suited for the cavalry than might be necessary. Since there is always word that the enemy intends to attack again both by sea and land, and some say that this will happen on Tuesday, it has been decided to build a trench to protect the seafront so that our men may be covered while they defend it, and work has begun right away, distributing it barrack by barrack among the Portuguese and Castilian Tercio regiments. The available artillery will be installed along it, in addition to that mounted at the palace fort and the customs post, and I believe that if they come to put it to the test they will be met with the necessary resistance. The remaining men will be distributed where they are considered necessary according to where the enemy might attack, taking care that enough of them are left for where the need might be greater and to secure the land, which is

It is safe to say that with the arrival of the Duke of Bragança on 8 June and that of Alonso de Vargas on 10 June, the great historic opportunity that was open to the English at the end of the sixteenth century to break up and invade the Iberian empires had passed once and for all. Distractions and hesitations had caused them to miss out on an opportunity that would not be repeated during that period when the Iberians were still at the early stages of establishing and consolidating their position in the wider world. This is not the place to explore hypotheses or ask 'what would have happened if ...'. It is clear, however, that given the Antonian agreement,[23] Brazil was in serious danger of ending up in English hands. In the following century, when the long-established Anglo-Portuguese alliance was restored, Portuguese Brazil had successfully overcome the great threat that had nearly killed it in its infancy, namely the Dutch attempt to take it over.[24] An English victory in 1589 would have offered Portuguese America on a plate to Anglo-Dutch ambitions. However, history took a different course in the form of an Iberian recovery and preparations for an offensive with a new armada. From Galicia, Cerralbo reported that in the *nao Begoña*, 'they have found part of the rudder broken, but this can be repaired very quickly so that it will still be able to serve Your Majesty in the armada'. As for the supplies for the new fleet, 'wine from Ribadavia is being collected in Pontevedra, and local wine and bacon in Corunna, where I have been sending a few oxen for meat and have given orders for fish to be caught in the Ría de Arousa'.[25]

While Philip II ordered the new armada to be assembled quickly, Francisco Coloma kept a close watch on the English Armada. On the day he counted the ships, there were 147 according to his calculation. He also reported that 'there are many ships that they have captured recently, since they had no artillery and few men', and added that 'they still threaten, according to those taken prisoner, to attack the entrance to the estuary'. Coloma, however, having already seen Drake squander numerous days when the winds were favourable for an attack on Lisbon, did not believe that there would be an attack: 'I am quite confident they will dare not try, for in the last few days they had the best weather for it had they wished to do so.'[26] Alonso de Bazán also reported the lack of any movement on the part of the English fleet, as well as the routine he established for his ships: 'While the tide keeps the enemy from coming in, most days I go to Lisbon to see what the galleys can do to help.' Bazán kept watch on the entrance to the estuary, but always with an eye on Lisbon, as part of the delicate balance maintained by the army on land. Once again we see the importance of the tides that fill and empty the Mar da Palha. This rise and fall generates powerful currents in the strait that indicated which times were favourable and which were impossible for the feared English attack. Even

our main concern.' The Count of Fuentes to the King, Lisbon, 11 June 1589. AGS. Guerra Antigua. File 249, fol. 133.

[23] See above, Chapter 5.

[24] See Boxer, C. R., *The Dutch in Brazil, 1624–1654*, (Oxford: Clarendon Press, 1957). See also Hugo A. Cañete, *Los Tercios en América,* (Málaga: Ediciones Platea, 2017)

[25] The Marquis of Cerralbo to the King, Bayona, 10 June 1589. AGS. Guerra Antigua. File 249, fol. 107.

[26] Francisco Coloma to the King, entrance to Lisbon Estuary, 10 June 1589. Ibid., fol. 121.

in the absence of galleys and with a favourable wind, Drake could not attack against the current. Bazán also mentioned that it would be impossible to attack with the galleys during the hazardous time just before the English embarkation, for 'the cape protruding from the coastline near São Julião is much closer to the ships than the quay, and therefore the galleys will not be able to get past the cape to attack them as they board'.[27] And so the crescent formation of the English Armada not only protected the boats and men stationed on the coast, but also shielded the boarding zone.

The next day a strange event took place that later would make a deep impression on the Spanish military: 'On 11 June Captain Francisco de Cárdenas, a man of noble birth and calm temperament from whom, according to many, much better could have been expected, surrendered the castle of Cascais.'[28] The castle may well have been able to hold out a few more days, for 'he had forty or so soldiers, supplies and ammunition aplenty and was short only of harquebus and musket shot. The enemy did not bombard him from land, but two of his cannon were ruined and he had another fourteen left.'[29] Why had a respected captain like Cárdenas surrendered without a fight? There is little doubt as to the reason: he believed that Lisbon had already been taken. It was obvious that such rumours could become unstoppable, for there was no easy explanation for the highly strange behaviour of the English.

First, Cárdenas had sent two soldiers 'to request more men and ammunition'[30] and had never heard from them again. In addition he had received no news from Lisbon, either by sea or land. What prompted his surrender, however, was the arrival of 'two Franciscan monks from the monastery of Santo Antonio'. Whether through blackmail, bribery or conviction, the monks

> both certified with a solemn vow that Lisbon had surrendered to Dom António three days earlier, that he was at peace there, and that it was a mortal sin to keep fighting when all hope was lost. If he were defeated and killed he would be responsible for the souls of all the men who died there fighting for his cause.[31]

So the monks not only fooled him regarding the fall of Lisbon, but also threatened him with the everlasting tortures of hell for leading his men pointlessly to their deaths.

The Captain must have felt extremely saddened by such misfortune and great anxiety over the way in which such a major piece of news was conveyed to him. What had become of the defenders? Why had no captured high ranking officer contacted him? What horrors had befallen his countrymen? Cárdenas surrendered, 'trusting the piety of the friars and having faith in them, he was persuaded by what they said and obtained honourable terms by coming out with banner and weapons, as well as a vessel in which

---

[27] Alonso de Bazán to the King, Galley *Real*, Lisbon, 10 June 1589. AGS. Guerra Antigua, fol. 128.

[28] *Relación de lo subçedido del armada enemiga.* BN mss 18579, p. 81.

[29] Ibid. The Count of Fuentes puts the number of Cárdenas's men at sixty. The Count of Fuentes to the King, Lisbon, 11 June 1589. AGS. Guerra Antigua. File 249, fol. 133.

[30] *Relación de lo subçedido del armada enemiga.* BN mss 18579, p. 82.

[31] Ibid.

he and his men could take their clothing and sail to Setúbal, since they believed Lisbon was lost'.[32]

With their morale low, but with the honours of war, Cárdenas and his men arrived at nearby Setúbal. Their bewilderment on discovering that they had been tricked must have been indescribable. What sort of Catholic friars could be capable of such a thing? Cárdenas must have wished a thousand times over that he had died defending the castle, for his star had waned in the worst way imaginable. When the news of his surrender reached Lisbon, the bailiffs went to Setúbal to arrest him and as was to be expected 'they brought him prisoner to this city where, following his statement, he was beheaded, to the great sorrow of all those who knew him at seeing the tragedy of having lost both a fortress and an honest man on account of the deceit of two men of the cloth'.[33]

The Spanish journal is full of praise for Cárdenas and also recounts the impression Dom António made on those who saw him. He seemed more like a prisoner than a king, for 'he was never seen without the company of two English captains at either side of him on both sea and land, as if he were a prisoner'.[34] Sadness had already taken permanent hold in his soul and he was 'very upset when he spoke, as one who is utterly distressed and hopeless, and there are those who say he tried to remain in Portugal'.[35] These words contained an element of truth, for by then a short and miserable life was all the unfortunate gentleman had in store. After a wretched exile in France, he died six years later.

As for other matters, on this day, 11 June, the Count of Fuentes informed the King:

I have sent the message to make haste to all places where men are coming from and I have sent the prior along to ask the same of all. If Don Juan del Águila with his men and the Count of Santa Gadea with his galleys were here, I would not be waiting for the enemy to come and find me, but as it is I can do no more.[36]

---

[32] *Relación de lo subçedido del armada enemiga.* BN mss 18579, p. 82.
[33] Ibid.
[34] Ibid.
[35] Ibid.
[36] The Count of Fuentes to the King, Lisbon, 11 June 1589. AGS. Guerra Antigua. File 249, fol. 133.

Chapter 28

To the Sea

By 12 June there was very little the English army could do under siege in Cascais. In fact, their situation could have become extremely difficult, since the Portuguese army was gradually becoming strong enough to take the initiative at last and settle matters for good. Furthermore, in light of the facts, the Count of Fuentes and Archduke Alberto now had far fewer reservations regarding the loyalty of the Portuguese to the King. And so the most important men in Portugal planned to march on Cascais. The Count of Villadorta, general of the Portuguese cavalry,

> who insisted on leading his horsemen against the enemy – now with the consent of the Prince-Cardinal – told all his captains to get ready. On the Monday [12 June], having marshalled them at the Terreiro do Paço, he addressed them, telling them of his determination and urged them to go forth resolutely against the enemy who were quartered in Cascais. Seeing that they were all eager to do so, he decided to go on the following day, which was Saint Anthony's Day.[1]

This meant the end for Elizabeth's strategy regarding António de Crato. The close ties that bound the two Iberian nations – ties that were just as strong as the inherent dislike of neighbouring peoples everywhere – had prevailed. These bonds were personified in the figure of Philip, a king whose blood was as much Spanish as Portuguese, and who, it must be stressed, loved both countries equally. Ultimately it was a triumph for Iberian unity and the guarantee of Iberia's presence in the wider world which had been so seriously threatened by England or by Holland during that important century.

The current policy of the English of respecting – as far as possible – the lives, honour and property of the Portuguese had lost its raison d'être, as would finally become clear in Cascais. But Norris could no more get away from the fleet with Portugal as an enemy than he could when dealing with it as a subordinate partner. There was nothing left to hide – or to steal. There was no good news to report in the messages sent to England from the English Armada, although 'it was learned from prisoners on Monday 12th that four days earlier some had reached the Armada, with orders from the Queen to report on the state of the army and fleet'.[2] Everything had gone wrong for Elizabeth. The offensive had not been joined by either Berbers or the King of Fez or the Turks. Fear of her well-known temper on their return roused the spirit of the lumbering giant that was the English Armada, but its nervous system was no longer capable of moving its necrotic

---

[1] Letter from Falçao de Resende. Quoted in Ruela Pombo, *Portugal*, Part 3, cols 28–9.
[2] *Relación de lo subçedido del armada enemiga.* BN mss 18579, p. 83.

muscles. Its grand ambitions were sliding steadily into the realm of dreams – or night-mares. And yet over two hundred vessels, including those that had been captured, were real and clearly visible and, had they not been lifeless, were the very same that would have taken Lisbon and put Dom António on the throne.

It was for this reason that expectation in the face of the passive and mysterious con-duct of the English reached its height on Tuesday, 13 June, because 'it was thought certain that the enemy would invade by land and by sea, on account of the significant activity in their fleet'.[3] Resende explained the reasons for their alarm:

> As dawn broke on this solemn day the whole population was alive with rumours
> that the enemy was about to attack the city, even though it was Lisbon's own saint's
> day as observed by the Church, because they said that there was a full moon and a
> high tide and that with the turn of the tide the ships could come up river.[4]

The galleys and the entire defensive forces along the seafront, which had been heav-ily reinforced under Vargas's instructions, were put on maximum alert. The balance of power had been changing, however, and the Iberian cavalry was by now substantial. At last, after the frustrations on 5 June, the Count of Villadorta was authorized to take part in intercepting the expected simultaneous attack by land: 'In order to block the assault by land, the Count of Villadorta, General of the Portuguese cavalry, rode out with over six hundred horses, having asked His Highness to instruct Don Sancho Bravo to join him with his company of mounted harquebusiers.'[5] The Portuguese cavalry was rein-forced 'by many gentlemen and noble knights, almost a thousand lances strong',[6] so as to strike mercilessly at the small number of English cavalry and, above all, to inflict considerable damage on the slow-moving infantry. With that intention, they 'rode across the country until they got close to Cascais and Sintra'. But what would have been a reasonable and well-thought-out military operation by the English at the beginning of May, by mid-June was no more than a fantasy. The activity among the English Armada that day would be explained quite differently later: 'The cause must have been the news from some ship or other of the arrival of the *Adelantado* at the Cape [St Vincent].[7] The news – that a Spanish naval fleet was rounding the Cape and heading straight for them – could not have been any worse for the English Armada. The Spanish had been mistaken and the cavalry had prepared for battle to no avail, since not a single Englishman left the trenches in Cascais. The English no longer had designs on Lisbon; they merely wished to get out alive. If their previous ambitions had been thwarted, in the end this one would be, too. As 13 June drew to a close, Villadorta's strong detachment found itself stationed near Cascais 'that night, in the place called Juana.'[8]

3   *Relación de lo subçedido del armada enemiga.* BN mss 18579, p. 83.
4   Letter from Falçao de Resende. Quoted in Ruela Pombo, *Portugal*, Part 3, col. 29.
5   *Relación de lo subçedido del armada enemiga.* BN mss 18579, p. 83.
6   Letter from Falçao de Resende. Quoted in Ruela Pombo, *Portugal*, Part 3, col. 29.
7   *Relación de lo subçedido del armada enemiga.* BN mss 18579, p. 83.
8   Letter from Falçao de Resende. Quoted in Ruela Pombo, *Portugal*, Part 3, col. 29.

On 14 June, the Duke of Bragança's forces joined the Iberian troops and began to complete the siege of Cascais by land:

The following day they had lunch in Sintra and slept in Oeiras, where our cavalry were joined by the Duke of Bragança's men on horseback, who came with Cosme Nabo. They had been to the vantage points above Cascais and had taken three Englishmen for questioning, who told them they were getting ready to set sail for England. Once the Count of Vila de Orta was certain about this, he went back to the town, reassuring the people in the hamlets and settlements on the way who had been fearful of the enemy. When the English heard of the Count's excursion they made such great haste to embark that many fell into the sea and drowned, and some that dived in after them but were unable to get on board fled and were left stranded along the shore without being able to make a decision, for very few of these got away.[9]

It was on Thursday, 15 June, that the situation of the English Armada became particularly dangerous: 'The *Adelantado* of Castile arrived in São Julião on 15 June with fifteen galleys, which were very well armed and prepared, and having left eight ships there with the other galleys under Don Alonso de Bazán, he sailed on with his flagship to kiss the hand of His Highness and receive his orders.'[10] The arrival of these new reinforcements meant that the supposedly weak flank of Lisbon's defence, namely from the sea, was strengthened. The total number of galleys did not fall below twenty-eight, sufficient to reinforce São Julião and make an attack on Lisbon a rather reckless proposition. The galleys had not come alone, however, and the defence of the narrow passage between the ocean and the Mar da Palha was not the sole objective. Martín de Padilla had also carefully prepared six fireships, and was ready – as would be seen later – to attack the fleet at anchor when there was a favourable wind. Following his interview with the Archduke, the *Adelantado* 'ordered six ships to be left at San Felipe, which were prepared with all kinds of incendiary devices to be launched against the enemy when the weather permitted'.[11] As soon as the wind blew from the east towards the sea and the English Armada, they were to be 'set on fire and launched against the enemy fleet'.[12]

The English Armada finished embarking that very day:

With the news of its arrival, all the enemy's troops went aboard, after they had stolen everything from Cascais Castle, blown up part of it with a mine and sacked the entire town and the churches, unleashing the poisonous doctrine of their sect upon the images in the churches and in the convent of Santo Antonio, in particular a much revered image of Nossa Senhora da Guía.[13]

[9] Ruela Pombo, *Portugal*, Part 3, col. 29.
[10] *Relación de lo subçedido del armada enemiga.* BN mss 18579, p. 83.
[11] Ibid., p. 84.
[12] Ibid.
[13] Ibid., pp. 83–4. Cascais was left in such a dirty and dilapidated state that Fuentes had to order the garrison that was to be sent there 'to go and billet in Almada and Oeiras and in smaller places nearby while Cascais

It was quite clear that the English were leaving and of course they were doing so in their own fashion, burning, sacking and – their favourite passion – damaging and destroying churches and their images. By night-time on 15 June, there were no Englishmen left in ravaged Cascais.[14] The Elizabethan presence on Portuguese soil was reduced to the garrison at Peniche, where they were waiting impatiently for the ships that were to take them away.[15] In any event, everything now depended on the whim of the wind, which, mockingly and unsympathetically, was blowing strongly from the north at this time. This made it inadvisable to put out to sea, especially heading north, and it meant that the use of the fireships was out of the question.[16] But fear of the dark had now changed sides. In May it had harmed the stubborn defenders of the wall of Corunna. At the beginning of June, it was the people of Lisbon. Now it was the turn of the invaders from the sea to pray.

Dawn broke on Friday, 16 June. Martin Padilla was eager to inspect the English Armada in order to assure himself of the success of his incendiary operation, an exact replica of the plot used by Drake ten months earlier in Calais. And so

> the next day, Friday 16 June, he left São Julião with the cavalry and two hundred harquebusiers from his galleys, and when he caught sight of it he gave the order to halt. He took with him just Don Sancho Bravo and Don Pedro de Acuña and the galleys' principal pilot, and they went along the entire coastline, noting the composition, quantity and size of the ships, and when they had had a thorough inspection they returned to São Julião.[17]

Everything was now ready for the final offensive to be unleashed and the file to be closed on what had been a difficult year. The hour of the sea had arrived. Padilla was just waiting to give an order that was dependent on the unpredictable weather. Having organized the assault with the fireships,

> the *Adelantado* came to give his report towards nightfall and to take leave of His Highness in order to return to the pursuit of the enemy. He wished to take the eight galleys at his disposal in Portugal that were under the command of Captain Munguía but His Highness ordered that they should stay because of their important role in the river.[18]

---

was cleaned up'. The Count of Fuentes to the King, Lisbon, 26 June 1589. AGS. Guerra Antigua. File 249, fol. 136.

[14] Account by John Evesham. Wernham, *Expedition*, p. 234.

[15] According to Evesham, it was around this date that seven vessels were sent to evacuate the men at Peniche. For one reason or another, the ships did not arrive, as we shall see, until 23 June, by which time it was too late. Either Evesham's date was not accurate, or due to the strong north-north-westerly wind that was blowing on 16 and 17 June, these vessels were unable to get past Cape Roca to head north and so returned to Cascais. Account by John Evesham, ibid.

[16] Alonso de Bazán to the King, Galera *Real*, Belén, 18 June 1589. AGS Guerra Antigua. File 249, fol. 131. Account by John Evesham, ibid.

[17] *Relación de lo subçedido del armada enemiga*. BN mss 18579, p. 84.

[18] Ibid.

It is clear that the Archduke Alberto never for a moment lost sight of his objective to protect Lisbon. That is why for security he kept a number of galleys on guard but away from the possible theatre of naval operations. For the Archduke, the failure of the English invasion of Portugal was a greater prize than victory in the most glorious battle, and with good reason, for the geopolitical map of the world was at stake that spring: the preservation or the break-up of the empire; the survival or the decline of the Iberian powers. Everything else was just a secondary military consideration. For his part, Alonso de Bazán wrote to the King that day acknowledging receipt of major new orders and informing him that 'yesterday the Cardinal Archduke gave me the order from Your Majesty to serve you by joining the fleet that Your Majesty has ordered to be assembled in Santander'.[19] We can see that in the hectic succession of events during those months and before Drake left Cascais, Philip II was putting his fleet, largely based in Santander, on a new war footing. The fact is that the English Armada had failed to achieve Elizabeth's main objective: the destruction of Philip's fleet. Spain was now preparing to take the initiative once more, although in fact, as we shall see, Alonso de Bazán did not carry out this order until 24 June, by which time there was no trace of any English ships near Lisbon.

The commanders of the English Armada received a major surprise on 16 June, for two small vessels arrived in Cascais from England.[20] They announced the imminent arrival of a second supply squadron consisting of seventeen vessels that was sailing behind them.[21] That was certainly good news. But they also brought some correspondence from the Queen, and she was doubly furious. First, she had been tricked by Essex, not only on account of his strange departure from London and Plymouth, but also because the subsequent expectation that he would meet the English fleet when it was in Corunna was likewise disappointed.[22] So when the English Armada set sail on 19 May from the Galician city heading for Lisbon, William Knollys also left but in the direction of England, with bad news for his Queen.[23] After an easy crossing with favourable winds, his ship arrived on 26 May.[24] Having been fully informed about what had happened, on 30 May the Queen wrote a stern letter to Drake and Norris, which they received two weeks later in Cascais.

In addition to demanding the immediate return of her favourite, Elizabeth made some very harsh accusations and threats in her letter[25] against the already beleaguered

---

[19] Alonso de Bazán to the king, Galera *Real*, San Julián, 16 June 1589. AGS Guerra Antigua. File 249, fol. 130. Proof of the failure of the English Armada.

[20] Wernham, *Expedition*, p. liv.

[21] Ibid., and William Fenner to Anthony Bacon, 1589 in ibid., p. 240.

[22] Thomas Heneage, in a letter of 26 May to Walsingham, explains that from Corunna, and in pursuit of Essex, 'several boats and pinnaces were sent along the coast, and in their southward route some reached the coast off Lisbon'. Ibid., p. 160. But no one knew anything of Devereux's whereabouts.

[23] Account by John Evesham. Ibid., p. 230. The ship was carrying messages and letters back to England, but also important Spanish prisoners taken for ransom in Corunna. On their return they provided significant information about England and the return of the English Armada.

[24] Thomas Heneage to Walsingham, 26 May 1589. Ibid., p. 160.

[25] The Queen to Norris and Drake, 30 May 1589. Ibid., pp. 164–8.

commanders of the expedition. She told them that despite their repeated promises they had not done their duty, which was nothing less than the destruction of the Spanish fleet wherever they encountered it. Drake and Norris knew full well that this was their main task. They knew there was no possible excuse, and 'if ye did not ye affirmed that ye were content to be reputed as traitors', that was what they had to do. Moreover, the Queen bitterly criticised their stay in Corunna, where there were hardly any ships to destroy and yet a lot of resources were wasted on men, time and provisions.[26] In response to their desperate appeal for reinforcements and supplies, Elizabeth's rejoinder was heartless: their request made it perfectly plain that the preparation of such a badly provisioned fleet had suffered from serious negligence and disorganization. But although the Queen had already been informed that following Drake's stopover in Corunna his intention was to head directly for Lisbon, perhaps what was most devastating was the mention of her most cherished wish: 'We do not only hope but in a manner assure ourself that ye are before this time come to that place –Santander – and achieved the purpose.' To add insult to injury for Drake, Elizabeth's reference to her imperious wish was made after she had been informed that, following Drake's departure from Corunna, the wind blew strongly and persistently in the direction of Santander. In fact this was a problem, as we have seen, given the tortuous intentions of the English Armada. For if they had let themselves be taken by the wind after setting sail from Corunna, instead of heading westward they would have reached Santander much faster than it took to go round Cape Finisterre.

Drake read the letter and knew he was in a corner. He could not turn back the clock and he was in no position to head for Cantabria. Nor could he use the well-worked excuse of an unfavourable wind. Along with the resounding failure of the expedition, that letter marked the beginning of the end for Sir Francis Drake. That night many of the sick felt their lives ebbing away after painful suffering. Those who were wounded but left untended were rapidly deteriorating. But in one sense none of them had such a dark and troublesome night as Drake.

By Saturday, 17 June 1589, the terrible danger that hung over the wretched English Armada became even more evident. With the grain mills destroyed just days earlier, the lack of food supplies became a worrying factor. It was not exactly a question of a *lack* of food, with the seizure of several Hanseatic supply ships laden with wheat. In fact, a good number of them were captured that day near Cascais.[27] The problem was that wheat was the only provision that remained in abundance and there were no grain

---

[26] In a letter from Lord Talbot to the Earl of Shrewsbury on 5 June, it was reported that the Queen explicitly criticized the bloody but pointless attack on the High Town of the city. Wernham, *Expedition*, p. 168.

[27] As William Fenner reports in his letter to Anthony Bacon, in addition to wheat these supply ships were carrying copper, wax, hollands, sailcloth, Dutch cheese and rye. And Fenner adds: 'But one great ship which the King of Denmark sent with them for a wafter and eleven others richly laden escaped. Yet the goods we have in those we took, being sold to the uttermost had been worth in Spain 100,000 pound, and here will not yield 30,000 pound for the payment of men.' William Fenner to Anthony Bacon, 1589. Ibid., p. 239. Leaving aside the problems in England caused by the seizure of neutral merchant ships, the plunder of the cargo at the hands of the English soldiers and seamen, and Fenner's conservative valuation, this evident price disparity is another sign of the lethal inflation rate from which the Spanish economy was suffering.

mills to make flour to turn into bread or hardtack. And so the English, weak and sickly as they were, were obliged to eat boiled wheat, which aggravated the spread of disease to an unimaginable extent and continued to spread after so many days of squalor and overcrowding. This disease was the same one that had decimated the interception fleet the previous year until Elizabeth ordered its disbandment.[28]

But this was not the worst threat to the host of ships and barges that filled the Bay of Cascais. Worse lay in store for them at the castle of São Felipe in Setúbal, where six fireships were just waiting for a favourable wind before being sent towards the fleet's vulnerable sanctuary. The galleys, now considerable in number, could then sink or capture the ships that had been scattered. Even with all the precautions taken in Calais the year before, Howard's tactics with the fireships had been successful and allowed for the dispersal of the Spanish Armada and the artillery skirmish with some isolated ships at Gravelines. That put an end to any possible union – even though it was a remote one – between Alexander Farnese and Medina Sidonia. Drake could lose everything, including his prized capture, the supply ships. He had only one advantage: the wind that would propel the fire towards his fleet was the self-same wind that would allow him to move out to sea, which was precisely the safest place for the English Armada. But on 17 June, a strong northerly wind continued to blow, preventing him from setting sail but protecting him at the same time.

On 18 June, driven on by necessity and without waiting for a favourable wind for a return to England, Drake gave the order to set sail. It is not easy to establish the real intentions of the admiral of the fleet. William Fenner admits that 'we couldn't decide where to go, whether to England or to the Azores'.[29] Goaded by Elizabeth's reproaches and threats, Drake needed to give the Queen some victories so as to placate her imminent anger because he had not gone to Santander. A major triumph would have been to intercept the Indies fleet in the Azores, but after the failures of Corunna and Lisbon and the seriously weakened state of the expedition, it seemed a complex and risky notion. In addition, Drake had seized several dozen loaded merchant ships: that was what any pirate dreamt about – that, and to return home with his spoils or sell what he had stolen at a good price. Given the state of his fleet, was Drake deliberately going to risk his hard-won booty for something as uncertain as a trip to the Azores? It seems unlikely. But what is clear is that the experienced pirate Drake and the inexperienced admiral Drake were irreconcilable. The former looked at the supply ships, the latter re-read the letter from the Queen. However, there were factors that could not be ignored. One of these was that the fireships were waiting to set the fleet on fire, with the galleys ready to attack it. Another was that five hundred Englishmen were waiting impatiently at Peniche to be rescued. A third was that Essex, as well as a significant number of sick men, including many major figures, had to get home immediately. In addition, the Dutch ships seized for the expedition were no longer required for the transportation of troops

[28] Thomas Fenner to Walsingham. 24 July 1589. Wernham, *Expedition*, p. 194.
[29] William Fenner to Anthony Bacon, 1589. Ibid., p. 239.

(now drastically reduced in number), especially given that he had to put a captive crew into the supply vessels if he wished to hold on to them. A final factor was that Drake did not command the army – an army that was, moreover, now at the limit of its endurance.

For all these reasons, a number of clear actions were taken before departure. One of these was to discharge the Dutch so that they could take the northerly route at the same time as Essex and a good number of English ships and other vessels. Another was to distribute the remaining infantry among the captured supply ships, while a further measure was for the Dutch ships, Essex and the sick to set sail first heading north. After that the main body of the fleet would set off ... but where would they be heading?

With the wind coming from the north, it was impossible to head up past Cape Roca from the anchorage at Cascais, so Drake headed in a south-south-westerly direction.[30] It was better to head away from the coast with its fireships and galleys than to continue to tempt fate, so 'on the morning of 18 June the 210 vessels of the English Armada set sail'.[31] That was when the Dutch participation in the English Armada came to an end, for 'thirty of these, which were from the Isles of Holland and Zeeland, and some from La Rochelle, were discharged'.[32] Alonso de Bazán, from the Royal galley, also reported that when the English fleet set sail from Cascais, it was divided into two: 'This morning sixty ships from the Armada set sail together and went back out to sea. They appeared to be separate from the rest of the fleet because in the afternoon none of the sixty was to be seen and all the others have set sail.'[33] Bazán goes on:

> Both groups set out to sea with the northerly wind and it seems they were not heading for the Algarve or Andalusia because the wind had been favourable for many days and they did not do so until the wind was lighter. So when they went out to sea it was to return to England or to head to the Azores.

On 18 June, the Spanish galleys set out in pursuit, for 'the *Adelantado* set off that day with seventeen galleys under his command and Don Alonso de Bazán accompanied

---

[30] 'The following Sunday 18 June the Armada set sail from Cascais, heading south-south-west in a very orderly fashion and without firing their artillery, which was fully observed by Captain Álvaro Rodrígues de Távora under the orders of Matías de Alburquerque.' Letter from Falçao de Resende. Quoted in Ruela Pombo, *Portugal,* Part 3, col. 29. 'On 18 June ... there was a north-north-easterly wind and the weather was fine.' A further account of the journey. Wernham, *Expedition,* p. 245.

[31] *Relación de lo que ha sucedido a las galeras de España que están a cargo del Adelantado mayor de Castilla de que Draques sale.* MN Col. Navarrete, 5, p. 117. Evesham gives the number of ships as approximately 230. Account by John Evesham. Wernham, *Expedition,* p. 234.

[32] *Relación de lo que ha sucedido a las galeras de España* ... MN Col. Navarrete, 5, p. 117.

[33] Alonso de Bazán to the King Rey, Galera *Real,* Belén, 18 June 1589. AGS Guerra Antigua. File 249, fol. 131. Francisco Coloma gives a very similar account: 'The fleet set sail in two squadrons. One consisted of 60 vessels and set off in the morning with a northerly wind and the other with 160 left in the afternoon with the same wind, with the other squadron nowhere to be seen. They say that the smaller squadron was taking the sick to England and the larger one was heading to the Isles. I was not convinced of this, both because of the number of men they had lost in coming here and because they had had many days of good weather to sail to Andalusia or the Isles but without having taken the opportunity of doing so.' Francisco de Coloma to the King, Lisbon, 24 June. Ibid., fol. 125.

him with four of his galleys, with the intention of attacking some of the ships if the weather permitted but this did not happen because the Armada was always windward of them'.[34] The wind was not the best ally of boats with oars and with these northerlies the English fleet could raise anchor and permanently get away from the danger of the fire-ships. They were heading for the open sea, although they drifted southwards. They were unable to shake off the company of two Spanish caravels, which right from the start of this return voyage were under orders from the Count of Fuentes to position themselves 'right behind the Armada'. The caravels were small, very manoeuvrable ships and well suited to sailing close to the wind. Hence they were easily able to follow the English Armada at whatever distance suited them. Their task was to watch their movements and keep the Count permanently informed. In addition, each of them had a specific mission: 'One of them was to advise me of their route and the course they were taking and the other one was to stay with them until they knew for certain where they were heading and to try to work out their intentions.'[35] In this way, Fuentes was aware both of Drake's marauding off the Portuguese coast and his course if he were to go on the open sea. At least, following the removal of the spider's web with which the pirate-cum-admiral had amused himself for two weeks by hunting merchant ships, 'a French ship with a cargo of wheat turned to the galleys for help and they went over to meet it, so the enemy did not dare to pursue it'.[36] This was the first vessel captured by Drake that courageously got away from his grasp, encouraged by the presence of its Spanish rescuers. It is not clear that there were any English troops on board, from which it can be assumed that it had only recently been captured or that being a slow-moving fully laden merchant ship prevented it from escaping, plus its fear of being shot at or boarded if it tried. In any event, the presence of the galleys banished all their fear and none of the English ships tried to intercept it as it fled.

Meanwhile, the flotilla of supply ships, whose imminent appearance had been notified by the mail boats on 16 June, arrived that day or the following one.[37] It consisted of seventeen vessels[38] under the command of Captain Cross and although it did not bring the reinforcements asked for by Drake and Norris, it did bring some relief for the fleet.[39] It is interesting to note that this flotilla consisted, in large measure, of ships and men who, through desertion or necessity, had previously abandoned the English Armada.[40]

[34] *Relación de lo que ha sucedido a las galeras de España* ... MN Col. Navarrete, 5, p. 117.
[35] The Count of Fuentes to the King, Lisbon, 24 June 1589. AGS Guerra Antigua. File 249, fol. 134.
[36] *Relación de lo que ha sucedido a las galeras de España* ... MN Col. Navarrete, 5, p. 117. Bazán describes it thus: 'A French ship that they had taken sighted us, ran up its sails and came over to the galleys.' Alonso de Bazán to the King, Galera *Real*, Belén, 18 June 1589. AGS Guerra Antigua. File 249, fol. 131.
[37] Wernham, *Expedition*, p. liv.
[38] William Fenner to Anthony Bacon, 1589. Ibid., p. 240.
[39] Account by John Evesham. Ibid., p. 235.
[40] As was the case with the Spanish Armada, several ships abandoned the expedition. Hence six hundred men did not reach Corunna, a further four hundred headed from there to La Rochelle, one ship from Corunna went to Weymouth, and another six ships arrived at various ports in Cornwall. *Captains who Abandoned the Fleet, June 1589.* Ibid., p. 173. When the Queen's Council received this news, it immediately ordered an investigation about the purpose and the state of each ship, its speedy repair and return to service, together

So 18 June came to an end with the English having made their difficult departure and the galleys powerless to go after them. Meanwhile, Drake spent the night wishing for the wind to veer to a southerly – which would make the timbers of the Mediterranean galleys creak – and enable him to head north.

with its men, in order to make up the supply flotillas. Ibid., docs. 125, 127. Cross, who was put in charge of this matter, reported that these ships were appropriate for the task and could therefore carry out this mission. Captain Robert Cross to Burghley, 29 May 1589. Wernham, *Expedition*, p. 164.

Chapter 29

Battles at Sea

A gentle breeze was blowing as dawn broke on Monday, 19 June, and so the *Adelantado* of Castile 'set out that morning with nine ships in pursuit of the enemy fleet, which was coming round Cape Saint Vincent'.[1] As the ships sailed out, 'they encountered a French vessel that was fleeing from the Armada with seventy Englishmen on board; the French were allowed to take everything off them, which they did in such a way that they almost skinned them alive'.[2] That is how the tragic withdrawal of the English Armada began, and as we shall see, their losses were just as great as during the Spanish Armada. Stripped and with their bodies lacerated by their French captors, these Englishmen were the first of what was to become an almost unmanageable number of prisoners that soon gave the Spaniards some serious logistical problems.

Later that same day, 'a Flemish store ship appeared out at sea and the *Adelantado* sent across Don Francisco Coloma and Don Juan Puertocarrero with their galleys. They found about fifty Englishmen who were readily handed over by the Flemish without a struggle. Both this ship and the French vessel were allowed to sail for Lisbon.'[3] Not a great deal was gleaned from interrogating the Englishmen. 'It was understood from the English that the fleet was heading for Cádiz, and in view of that the *Adelantado* asked permission from the Cardinal Archduke to take all his galleys to stop the enemy. His Highness granted the request provided that he did not take more than nine of his galleys.'[4] And so as night fell on Monday, 19 June 1589, the fearless Padilla stayed on course with his nine galleys in pursuit of the English. At the same time, in Lisbon, fifteen caravels with extra men and munitions were being made ready in order to reinforce the strategically important Azores.[5] It is clear that day by day the Spanish recovery was taking shape at the same time that the defeat of the English was being planned, although, as will be seen, adverse winds prevented the reinforcement flotilla for the Azores from setting sail immediately.

The oars of the galley slaves followed the unvarying rhythm set by the overseer. Stroke after stroke the blades of the oars emerged from the water, were turned in the air and then thrust in the water once more. For its part, the gentle northerly breeze helped the galleys' oarsmen along as they blindly pursued their objective through the

[1]   *Relación de lo subçedido del armada enemiga.* BN mss 18579, pp. 84–5
[2]   *Relación de lo que ha sucedido a las galeras de España* ... MN Col. Navarrete, 5, p. 117. This incident was a consequence of the French slipping unnoticed onto the ship shortly before it set sail. Edmund Palmer to Walsingham, Saint-Jean-de-Luz, 25 July 1589. Wernham, *Expedition*, p. 218.
[3]   *Relación de lo que ha sucedido a las galeras de España* ... MN Col. Navarrete, 5, pp. 117–18.
[4]   Ibid., p. 118.
[5]   The Count of Fuentes to the King, Lisbon, 24 June 1589. AGS Guerra Antigua. File 249, fol. 134.

darkness of the night. There were only two cannons mounted at the prow and two at the stern on these ships, as there was no room at the sides because of the oars and the low clearance above the level of the sea. However, these cannons had been carefully chosen from among the reinforced culverins of the period. They were long-range cannons and, when fired from under five hundred metres, were very accurate, effective and had great destructive force. In addition, over short distances the power of the muskets and harquebuses could wipe out the decks, topsails, upper decks and embrasures of enemy ships. In this way,

> with these nine galleys he [Padilla] went in pursuit of the enemy but without any sight of him, and three hours before daybreak he found himself in the middle of the Armada. To confirm that was where he was, he sent an Englishman, Captain Eduardo Grecio, in a skiff to talk to the nearest ship, where they told him that they were not following the Admiral. From this conversation it was clear that this was the whole fleet and they had been among them without the enemy realizing it until dawn.[6]

So dawn on 20 June found the nine galleys in the middle of the scattered English Armada. It was time to intercept the stragglers, and so Padilla placed his ship like a wedge between them and the rest of the fleet. Sure enough, 'the *Adelantado* endeavoured to position himself on the right side of the wind and once he had done so he captured all the ships that were out of position. With his galley he attacked three large supply ships, a tender and a barge and other galleys came to his assistance, especially that of Don Juan Puertocarrero.'[7] For its part '*La Patrona*, with Don Andrés de Atienza on board, took a supply ship together with *La Peregrina*, *Serena*, *Leona*, *Palma*, and *Florida*, and these two stayed with it until it was set alight.'[8] And so, one by one, the ships that had become separated from the fleet fell into Padilla'a hands.

For his part, Alonso de Bazán 'attacked a ship from Plymouth which had fallen behind and in the boarding of the ship that followed its Captain Caverley was killed with most of his men. Two other straggling ships were attacked and sunk by the galleys. In one of them Captain Minshaw and his crew fought heroically until they disappeared engulfed in flames.'[9] There is a different report concerning the fate of Captain Caverley, which gives him as a prisoner, for 'having abandoned his ship, he escaped in a small boat and was then captured'.[10] Several documents record Bazán's attack. This is how John Evesham describes it:

---

[6]   *Relación de lo que ha sucedido a las galeras de España* ... MN Col. Navarrete, 5, p. 118.
[7]   Ibid. English sources also confirm that the attack by the galleys took place at dawn on 20 June. For another description of the voyage, see Wernham, *Expedition*, p. 245.
[8]   *Relación de lo que ha sucedido a las galeras de España* ... MN Col. Navarrete, 5, p. 118.
[9]   Quoted in González-Arnao, *Derrota y muerte*, p. 93.
[10]   William Fenner to Anthony Bacon, 1589. Wernham, *Expedition*, p. 240. Wingfield, however, states he was drowned. Speech by Anthony Wingfield, 9 September 1589. Ibid., p. 278. Yet another document reports him as 'having drowned while escaping from the galleys'. List of captains killed, 1589. Ibid., p. 213.

On the morning of the 20th and with the sea in a state of calm eight galleys headed in a windward direction towards us and attacked two of our small ships that were said not to have been able to defend themselves due to a lack of gunpowder and munitions. However, as far as I know and thanks to God's assistance these two escaped. Then the galleys attacked two other small ships head on and upwind and they were caught and set alight and the survivors taken prisoner. In addition, I was told that the *William*, commanded by Mr Hawkins of Plymouth, whose men, so I heard, sailed off in a small boat, was set fire to two or three times, although the fire went out. Then the Admiral arrived and with one cannon shot ensured that the galleys left him alone. But they pursued the small boat in order to capture the men and although they failed to do so they sank it and all the men drowned. And the (the word 'burnt' is struck out) boat was sunk by our own men because there were not enough men to sail it.[11]

Other documents and writers recorded these attacks by the galleys. For example, the Spanish press described it thus:

And so on the morning of the nineteenth of June [the *Adelantado*] sailed out with nine ships in pursuit of the enemy fleet, which was coming round Cape St. Vincent, and before any encounter they met up with a further six galleys that joined forces with them, and when they came across the enemy fleet they used their cannons against them on the twentieth and the twenty-fifth of June, for there was little wind and they were able to do a great deal of damage. They set fire to three ships, while others said five, they sank two others and took prisoners from them all, causing a lot of damage to the remainder but without the galleys incurring any serious damage in return.[12]

The Portuguese press referred to three sunk and two set on fire.[13] Cabrera de Córdoba wrote of four sunk and an unspecified number of ships burnt.[14] Juan de Arquellada mentions seven sunk or set ablaze,[15] while Duro had four sunk by the *Adelantado* and three set on fire by Alonso de Bazán.[16] Hume wrote of three sunk or captured and one burnt.[17] More recently, Kelsey wrote of five or six ships lost.[18] However, apart from

[11] Account by John Evesham. Wernham, *Expedition*, pp. 234–5. However, the *William* from Plymouth, which Wernham also acknowledges was abandoned by its crew, surprisingly appears in the payroll of the returnees. Ibid., pp. liv, 340.

[12] *Relación de lo subçedido del armada enemiga*. BN mss 18579, pp. 84–5.

[13] *Memoria da Vinda dos Ingleses a Portugal em 1589*, p. 285.

[14] Cabrera De Córdoba, *Historia de Felipe II*, p. 1257.

[15] Juan Arquellada. *Sumario de prohezas y casos de Guerra …* (Jaén, 1999), p. 420.

[16] Fernández Duro, *Armada española*, III, p. 48.

[17] Hume, *The Year After*, p. 70.

[18] He describes it thus: 'First they picked off three small vessels that were separated from the rest of the fleet. Then William Hawkins's ship William appeared, also isolated, and that was captured as well. After another ship or two were captured, a wind came up and allowed the remaining English ships to sail slowly away.' Kelsey, *Sir Francis Drake*, p. 358.

Figure 29.1 Engraving of the galley of the Adelantado of Castile, Royal Palace (Palacio Real), Madrid.

On 20 June 1589, the Spanish finally achieved what had been denied them ten months earlier: boarding English ships. The galleys, old-world Mediterranean vessels, had as their main weapon a sharp ram which punched into the hull of enemy ships and acted as a boarding bridge. Galleys were attack ships driven by the strength of the galley slaves or oarsmen and the courage of the soldiers on board. The galley slaves were prisoners of war, men sentenced by law or volunteers called *buenas bollas* ('good loaves') because they were better fed. Artillery was mounted on the bow and aimed by steering the whole ship. Propelled by oar and sail, they were more mobile than the heavy galleons, and if there was no wind they could get behind them and bombard them or board them, as happened at Cape Espichel.

González-Arnao,[19] no attention was paid to the fate of the ships captured earlier by the English Armada in Cascais, which had come to form part of the fleet. In summary, on 19 June, two of the merchant vessels seized by Drake and manned by captured crewmen were released. One of them, the French one, made its own way to join the galleys. On 20 June, another four supply ships, also with English crewmen, were captured, and in

---

[19] González-Arnao wrote of more than seven ships sunk or set on fire. González-Arnao, *Derrota y muerte*, p. 93.

addition most probably a tender and a barge from among the vessels seized by Drake. Between three and five English ships of low-tonnage – the most numerous by far in the English fleet – were also destroyed and others were damaged, a total of between nine and eleven ships and two smaller craft. About seven hundred Englishmen were taken out of action, of whom one hundred and thirty survived the attacks and were taken prisoner.[20]

While the rearguard was under attack, the rest of the fleet, far from coming to their aid, took advantage of the fact that the Spanish were distracted by their prey and they made their getaway. The English and the Spanish were unanimous in their contempt for Drake's extremely unhappy position at this time. In a letter on 20 July, the *Adelantado* explained:

> Even though there was little wind, it helped them to crowd together and take refuge, and the cowardice shown by the whole fleet was a sight to see. And it is clear that in this and in what the prisoners say about the hail of bullets that rained down upon them, this was the work of God to rid these heretics of their pride.[21]

Fenner would not have disagreed with this description by Padilla, for he called the resistance which they met as 'shameful'.[22]

Padilla treated the crew of the support ships well, as indicated in his letter: 'Some of the officers and sailors of the Flemish and German ships that were seized will be set free because they were taken by the enemy by force and brought to Spain. I do so without expecting anything in return and I will give them payment because it is desirable to have them willingly serve Your Majesty.'[23] Returning to the naval operations, 'the two largest supply ships were set on fire within range of Drake's cannons and the same action was taken with the other ships, but it wasn't as effective and one was sunk by the artillery of the flagship'.[24] Meanwhile,

> Drake's flagship and another large flagship carrying the infantry general, together with some other large ships, were trying to regroup their fleet, which they were all so eager to do that it required little effort. All five ships mentioned took part in the fighting, and the remaining vessels nearby assisted them with artillery, especially the flagship, which was being towed by two well-armed barges.[25]

Losses in the galleys were surprisingly few, for 'in all the galleys there were no more than two dead and up to seventy wounded, the best known of these a son of Juan Ruiz de Velasco'.[26] The explanation for the satisfactory part played by the galleys is explained

[20]   *Relación de lo que ha sucedido a las galeras de España* … MN Col. Navarrete, 5, p. 119.
[21]   The *Adelantado* to the King, Cádiz 20 June 1589. MN Col. Barutell, mss 390, no. 988.
[22]   Fernández Duro, *Armada Española*, III, p. 50.
[23]   The *Adelantado* to the King, Cádiz, 20 June 1589. MN Col. Barutell, mss 390, no. 988.
[24]   *Relación de lo que ha sucedido a las galeras de España* … MN Col. Navarrete, 5, p. 119.
[25]   Ibid.
[26]   Ibid.

as follows: 'The speed with which our harquebuses and artillery operated was of great importance and did not allow the enemy to get into the fight. The enemy's artillery caused no damage to the galleys, although some bullets did reach the flagship and other vessels.'[27] That campaign of attrition against the defeated English Armada ended in the early afternoon, for 'the fighting lasted from dawn until two hours after midday, when the galleys withdrew to rest a while in view of the fact that the enemy had regrouped'.[28]

It was fear of the galleys that led to the dispersal of the fleet. Evesham wrote of this fear in his account: 'So we two did bear in as near Bayona as we durst for fear of the galleys.'[29] Later the wind allowed the English to move away from the coast:

> At five in the afternoon the enemy sailed so far from the coast that scarcely a ship could be seen, and at this the *Adelantado* went round Cape St. Vincent to take on water because the galleys were in need of it, and there he waited until the enemy went past, as it would have to do if it was heading for Cádiz.[30]

It was impossible to discover the intentions of the English Armada from the nine prisoners taken during that morning. In fact,

> Captains, Sub-lieutenants, English gentlemen and an engineer were taken. They were asked many questions about the destination of the fleet and they all said different things and they all agreed that no-one knows but they suspect that it is heading for Cádiz. Others said that the Infantry General will be returning to England with the whole fleet, and Drake, with Dom António on board, is going with forty of the best ships to the Islands and the Indies. On the one hand they are on the right track to go to the Islands and for the fleet to go to England, and on the other hand it seems that if they had to go (to England) they should have gone from Cascais when the Dutch and Zealand and La Rochelle ships were allowed to go.[31]

In any event, Padilla was not far off the mark when he gave his opinion on the matter: 'I also believe that their lack of personnel, due to the number they have lost and those who have died and are dying from disease, means that it is quite likely that they have to return.'[32]

What was learned from these prisoners was the fleet's total lack of provisions:

> They said that if they hadn't seized the wheat-carrying ships that were heading for Lisbon, they would have left their men in Portugal without letting them on board, because they had nothing to give them. Now they have to manage with gruel made

[27] *Relación de lo que ha sucedido a las galeras de España . . .* MN Col. Navarrete, 5.
[28] Ibid., p. 120.
[29] Account by John Evesham. Wernham, *Expedition*, p. 236.
[30] *Relación de lo que ha sucedido a las galeras de España . . .* MN Col. Navarrete, 5, p. 120.
[31] The *Adelantado* to the King, Cádiz 20 June 1589. MN Col. Barutell, mss 390, no. 988.
[32] Ibid.

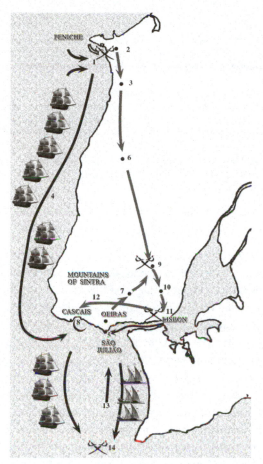

Figure 29.2 Map 7, 25 May–20 June, Lisbon.

1. 25 May. A council of war held off Peniche where it is decided to undertake an expedition on land, ruling out a naval attack on Lisbon on 26 May. Difficult disembarkation on Consolaçao beach; of the thirty-two landing craft, fourteen went under with over eighty men drowned. First skirmish on the beach: two hours and three charges with 250 Spanish and 150 Portuguese under Captain Alarcón and Juan González de Ateide. Death of Captains Robert Piew and Jackson plus other men. Death of a standard-bearer and fifteen Spaniards. 12,000 soldiers are landed.

2. 27 May. Contact with the Portuguese at Peniche and Atouguia. Preparations for the march. Attack by the cavalry of Captain Gaspar de Alarcón: five dead plus one French prisoner who speaks Spanish: he reports that the English Armada is bringing 20,000 men. Surrender of the fortress to Dom António.

3. 28 May. The English army reaches Lourinha, where it has proved impossible to raise a Spanish–Portuguese army. Start of the Spanish tactics to cut off supplies and communications. The army begins to starve.

4. 28 May. Drake sets sail from Peniche to Cascais with the whole fleet and 3,200 men. A further five hundred, left as a garrison in Peniche, will be killed or captured.

5. 28 May. Movement of Spanish troops transported in galleys from Lisbon to São Julião and Oeiras to strengthen the naval front.

6. 29 May. The English army reaches Torres Vedras. Nobles in the area take flight. Fear in Lisbon. Locals who live outside the walls take refuge in the city.

7. 30 May. Iberian military parade in Queluz, where the new headquarters has been set up.

Figure 29.2 (*cont.*)

8. 30 May. Drake drops anchor between Cascais and São Julião, adopting a crescent shape.
9. 30–31 May. The English enter Loures. Dom António announces that he will enter Lisbon on 1 June, the feast of Corpus Christi, but on the night of 31 May there is a surprise Spanish attack with more than two hundred dead.
10. 1 June. The English reach Alvalade. Arms are distributed to the Portuguese infantry.
11. 2–4 June. The English army reaches Lisbon. They are bombarded from the Saint George castle. Billeting in Lisbon. On 3 June there is a great attack of the besieged against the English barracks.
12. 5 June. Night-time withdrawal by the army to Cascais, pursued by Spanish detachments. More than five hundred dead.
13. 15 June. Arrival of the *Adelantado* of Castile with fifteen galleys and six fireships.
14. 19–20 June. The English Armada sails on a westerly wind, the galleys set off in pursuit and sink or capture nine ships, a tender and a barge. The fleet is dispersed.

from flour and boiled wheat, and more of them fall ill every day. But the ones who get this to eat are the soldiers; the sailors are much better fed.[33]

We do not know how much in these statements is accurate, but they are symptomatic of the malaise and demoralization that had passed through the fleet from one ship to the next. It has already been mentioned that the little food there was, was kept for Drake's sailors. This fact is significant. The proportion of sailors was already low when the English set sail, but now, after so many setbacks and so much time at sea, packed together without even basic conditions of hygiene and with disease rife on the ships' decks, the scarcity of sailors began to be a determining factor, as will later become quite clear.

Moreover the prisoners were also aware of the desperate attempts by Drake to secure assistance from the Muslims as promised: 'They said that Drake sent eight ships to Barbary with an ambassador of the Sharif who came while the fleet was in Cascais.' This information was corroborated in part, for 'the three galleys that had just arrived from Cádiz brought news that they went round Cape St. Vincent'. Padilla independently drew his own conclusions: 'The Sharif will deceive him, as he does with all those who have dealings with him.'[34] But what really moved the *Adelantado* of Castile was the sight of the state to which the monastery of Santo Antonio had been reduced after the English had passed through: 'Next to Cascais there is a monastery of discalced monks called Santo Antonio and its heartless neighbours broke up the altar and the choir and did some further minor damage, and it grieved me greatly to see it.' Padilla was so affected by the sight of it that in his letter to the King, he added:

And I vowed to God and to the Saint that if I am successful against those heretics, I would endeavour to persuade Your Majesty to restore it to its previous state, and if not, I would pay for it myself. May it please Your Majesty to perform this kind act, because I feel that it would be most pleasing to Our Lord.

However, the destruction of the monastery was but a prior warning of the state in which the Iberians would find Cascais.

---

[33] The *Adelantado* to the King, Cádiz 20 June 1589. MN Col. Barutell, mss 390, no. 988.
[34] Ibid.

The military operations on 20 June exacerbated a problem that would get even worse days later and that was the matter of the growing number of prisoners:

> Since I have been in charge of these galleys some prominent captains have been taken and held on board, in addition to some important French corsairs, and amongst the English that were taken on the 20th there are also, as I have indicated, some men of standing, so that all told there is a significant number of them and we have to keep a constant eye on them. I ask Your Majesty to command that we be given assurances that they will be placed somewhere where they are no longer our concern, and to determine the treatment that shall be given to the English. They will be given rations like the sailors, whether they are rowers or not. In my opinion this could be justified for those who have been captured since the war started and they can be given these rations for as long as they remain on the galleys, and unless Your Majesty orders otherwise, they will be given volunteer rations. They are dying off quite quickly, thereby leaving fewer of them for us to deal with.[35]

This terrible commentary indicates the virulence of the disease that took hold among the English expedition.

The action on the morning of 20 June brought about the dispersal of the English Armada with a good number of ships going off course.[36] Thereafter it became difficult to continue to follow the path taken by the fleet which was now largely broken up and dispersed. This situation has been attributed to Drake's inexperience or ineptitude in managing large fleets, for due to the way he acted he exacerbated the damage inflicted by the galleys on the English Armada, even though initially it was limited because the Spanish galleys were few in number. Drake did not give sufficient priority to ordering the fleet to divide into five squadrons, as had been agreed in Plymouth.[37] On the contrary, the pirate-cum-admiral, possibly unduly influenced by the laxity of piracy when commanding his ships, allowed the Spanish attack to create widespread chaos among the considerable number of English vessels because of his neglect. That is when he lost track of many of them and they were lost forever. One of these was the *Gregory* from London. On 20 June, this ship was fired on by the galleys and could no longer keep up with the fleet. Or the case of William Fenner, with his flagship of the recently arrived reinforcement squadron, which became detached from the fleet after the attack by the galleys and, in

---

[35] The *Adelantado* to the King, Cádiz, 26 June 1589. MN Col. Barutell, mss 390, no. 989.

[36] 'A wind sprang up, however, and the Spanish galleys were left behind; but soon the fleet got scattered.' Hume, *The Year After*, p. 70.

[37] 'Strangely enough, Drake made no attempt to draw his fleet into the divisions that had been organized before they left Plymouth. This was a perfect chance to employ the tactics that Howard had found so helpful in the Channel, but Drake made no effort to do so. Drake and his captains never practiced squadron manoeuvres, and Ralph Lane, the muster-master for the expedition, implied that Drake did not understand the need to do so. In Lane's opinion only divine intervention had saved the fleet from the attack by the galleys.' Kelsey, *Sir Francis Drake*, p. 432.

desperation, had to head to Madeira where it would later meet up with other ships.[38] In any event, the first squadron of the fleet to set sail, which included Essex, the Dutch and the sick among others, gained the open sea before the attack by the galleys and managed to head north. They were sighted a few days later off the coast of Galicia.

In spite of everything, following the attack by the galleys the majority of the fleet gradually managed to reassemble and so 'on Tuesday the 20th, at three in the afternoon, they reappeared above Cape Espichel and the town of Sesimbra, whereupon the Duke of Aveiro took up arms in Setúbal, where Your Highness had ordered him, and very bravely and diligently prepared to resist'.[39] All that Drake could do with the calm waters and the westerly breezes was to bring his ships together and wait for favourable winds. The English Armada could no longer undertake any action of significance and their situation grew worse by the day. Moreover, they could no longer land on that coast due to the maximum alert ordered by the Duke of Aveiro, 'with most captains having arms at the ready for any surprise attack'.[40]

But with the English fleet now at sea, the Iberians focused on Peniche, where five hundred men of the garrison that Norris had assigned on 28 May to provide cover if required were still waiting, with growing unease, for a rescue flotilla to enable them to get away.[41] But amid the chaos and dispersion caused by the galleys and the sea conditions, the rescue ships did not appear. Hence, 'so that they could attack the enemy in Peniche and take their artillery and prevent them from doing further damage ... Dom Martinho quickly wrote to His Highness and to the Counts Fuentes and Vila de Orta'.[42] In this way, 'that same day (20th) Don Pedro de Guzmán and Don Sancho Bravo set out with their mounted harquebusiers and horsemen under Gaspar de Alarcón, and four hundred harquebusiers with Captains Castillo and Ocampo, heading for Peniche where the enemy had left five hundred men'.[43] That march from Lisbon had to proceed at the pace of the infantry, so that it inevitably took them some time to reach Peniche.

As dawn broke on Wednesday, 21 June 1589, it was clear that the English Armada was still in sight of land. While the first detachment of the fleet continued its slow voyage northwards, Drake was to spend that day sailing into the light onshore wind and

---

[38] 'The galleys being gone, we put off into the sea, when there took us in the night a violent storm. I being separated from all company, wandered as a lost sheep in search of the Generals and chased day by day with the galleys, often times almost taken, was delivered when past hope of long life. I and my company, for want of water which was our drink, put for Porto Santo.' William Fenner to Anthony Bacon. Wernham, *Expedition*, p. 240.
[39] *Memoria da Vinda dos Ingleses a Portugal em 1589*, p. 285, Quoted in Pires De Lima, *O ataque*. The Count of Fuentes reported: 'The caravels to the rear of the fleet were not seen to leave the coast and therefore brought no news until during the afternoon of the 20th they reappeared off Cape Espichel and Sesimbra, remaining within our sights as they tacked to Cascais.' The Count of Fuentes to the King, Lisbon, 24 June 1589. AGS Guerra Antigua. File 249 fol. 134.
[40] Letter from Falção de Resende. Quoted in Ruela Pombo, *Portugal*, Part 3, col. 30.
[41] 'A warning in Torres Vedras by Dom Martinho Soares from the spies he had on the Peniche, that the English who were there were very perplexed and worried about the news of their fleet.' Ibid.
[42] Ibid.
[43] *Relación de lo subçedido del armada enemiga*. BN mss 18579, pp. 85–6

tacking off the coast before reaching Cascais.[44] For its part, the damaged *Gregory*, which was lost out at sea, struggled to sail northwards,[45] while Fenner, who was even more lost and who had to endure a storm in the night, headed off to the islands of Madeira, which were relatively close by.[46] These names make up for the anonymity of many other lost ships of which we know nothing further. Meanwhile, the fifteen caravels that had been made ready in Lisbon to come to the aid of the Azores were unable to set sail due to the calm seas and westerly winds.[47] While all this was happening at sea, with the Duke of Aveiro remaining on full alert on land, the detachment of Guzmán and Bravo reached Torres Vedras, where they learned of the situation at Peniche from Martinho Soares.[48]

Westerly winds continued to blow on 22 June, and nothing of significance changed at sea, although it did at Peniche. In fact, as Guzmán and Bravo's detachment reached Lourinhã on their way there, they received

> a report from a spy at Peniche that the enemy were trying to embark and take the artillery from the Tower. They all set off in haste towards Peniche, where they discovered some of the enemy already embarked on a small ship and a barge which were already in the water (and) about 40 of them got on board, while of those still on land they killed or captured almost 300.[49]

Although English sources do not appear to confirm that there were any survivors apart from Captain Barton, there must have been some, for 'although they were making haste, before they arrived they received news of the embarkation, and so spurring on their horses as much as they could they arrived with some two hundred yet to board and killed them or took them prisoner'.[50] About two hundred, therefore, remained on land, and they were killed or captured together with others who were already on board. It is not known how many others managed to escape, but if disease had not taken too great a toll in the English garrison at Peniche, it could have been a sizeable number.[51] What is clear is that, given the great urgency to prevent the men from getting on board, the only ones to arrive in time to prevent it were the cavalry. In any event, the haste to embark was such that 'a chest full of papers belonging to Dom António was found, and amongst some important

---

[44] 'Thursday 21 June, the enemy fleet returned off Cascais as the onshore wind was of no help to them, and this caused another alarm as it looked as though they were going to attack again, but as could be seen from the Portuguese coast they sailed past along the northern seaboard.' Letter from Falçao de Resende. Quoted in Ruela Pombo, *Portugal*, Part 3, col. 30.

[45] Account by John Evesham. Wernham, *Expedition*, p. 235.

[46] William Fenner to Anthony Bacon. Ibid., p. 240.

[47] The Count of Fuentes to the King, Lisbon, 24 June 1589. AGS Guerra Antigua. File 249, fol. 134.

[48] Letter from Falçao de Resende. Quoted in Ruela Pombo, *Portugal*, Part 3, cols. 30–1.

[49] Ibid., col. 31. Pires de Lima, *O ataque dos ingleses*, p. 320, puts the figure of English losses at forty drowned and three hundred killed or captured.

[50] *Relación de lo subçedido del armada enemiga*. BN mss 18579, p. 86.

[51] The Count of Fuentes, in a letter to the King on 24 June, reported: 'Don Pedro de Guzmán, who carefully made his way to Peniche, arrived at the moment when the six hundred men were starting to embark; he killed over two hundred of them and captured some of those who were already on board.' AGS Guerra Antigua. File 249, fol. 134.

ones there was one written in his own hand that described everything that had happened to him from the time he had declared himself king to the day he arrived in this kingdom'.[52] These papers would help to thwart Dom António's plans once and for all.

Following this bloody encounter, the Iberians reclaimed the castle and its artillery. 'In case any ships arrived, Pedro García's company of *Maestre de Campo* Francisco de Toledo's regiment, remained in the castle.'[53] With this new victory, 'Don Pedro de Guzmán and Don Sancho Bravo, with their infantry and cavalry, returned to Lisbon with about 60 prisoners.'[54] The failure of the English expedition and the subsequent feeling of relief on the Iberian side loomed larger by the day.

As he had on previous days, Drake continued to sail close to the Portuguese coast during the morning of Friday, 23 June in order to make progress northwards and that is how the English Armada found itself off the coast at Peniche. He then sent in the rescue boats but, as fate would have it, the men who had been looking for such a sign of deliverance from the battlements of Peniche were no longer there. The ships – there were nine or ten of them[55] – were kept at bay from Peniche by cannon fire and they returned to the fleet. Meanwhile, the English Armada was stretched out along the coast like the net of a fishing trawler or the Santa Compaña[56] that by night seizes anyone that looks at it. Yet another merchant ship – a Hanseatic supply ship from Lübeck – fell into their clutches that day. But the extraordinary thing was that its captain was held on Drake's *Revenge* until they reached Plymouth – perhaps because it was a ship captured at sea and to prevent any attempt to escape. Once he was back on the Peninsula, the captain, whose name was Juan Antonio Bigbaque, wrote a very interesting account of what happened.[57]

That day a north-east wind got up after all the calms and westerlies[58] and Drake set off for the open sea. That is when the fleet appeared to head for the Azores; as Hume put it: 'After sailing ostensibly for the Azores, Drake turned back.'[59] But given the state of the fleet and the diverse nature of its composition, to attempt such a voyage of conquest seemed like an act of recklessness. Bigbaque, who witnessed the events, reported: '(Drake's) principal objective was to end up in the Cíes Islands, but because the weather was so changeable from one day to the next, he decided to head for the island of Madeira. He sent barges to inform all the ships of the fleet, but later when the wind turned, he set course for Bayona and the Cíes Islands.'[60] With adverse winds for

---

52 *Relación de lo subçedido del armada enemiga*. BN mss 18579, p. 86.
53 The Count of Fuentes to the King, Lisbon, 24 June 1589. AGS Guerra Antigua. File 249, fol. 134.
54 *Relación de lo subçedido del armada enemiga*. BN mss 18579, p. 86.
55 Resende refers to nine. Letter from Falçao de Resende, quoted in Ruela Pombo, *Portugal*, Part 3, col. 31. The Count of Fuentes, in his letter to the King of 24 June, writes of ten. AGS Guerra Antigua. File 249, fol. 134.
56 The Santa Compaña is a deep-rooted mythical belief in rural Galicia, Asturias and Northern Portugal [translator's note].
57 Account by Juan Antonio Bigbaque, Lisbon, 12 August 1589. AGS Guerra Antigua. File 250, fol. 345.
58 The Count of Fuentes to the King, Lisbon, 26 June 1589. Ibid., fol. 136. Also other testimonies.
59 Hume, *The Year After*, p. 70.
60 Account by Juan Antonio Bigbaque, Lisbon, 12 August 1589. AGS Guerra Antigua. File 250, fol. 345.

the return to England, with the coast on a war footing and swarming with galleys, with the great prize of merchant ships, and above all with the state of the fleet worsening rapidly and making it increasingly necessary to stop in order to recuperate, the Madeira Islands could be seen as an appropriate place for a stopover after six perilous and point-less days at sea. In any event, 23 June was the last day that the fleet was sighted from the vicinity of Lisbon and Peniche.[61]

With the English Armada out to sea, the Spanish were suffering the same degree of uncertainty on Saturday, 24 June, as they had at the beginning of May: not knowing where a new landing by the English might take place. However, the situation was not the same, both on account of the drastic reduction in the power of the English fleet and the arrival of Philip's troops in Portugal, including Juan del Águila's infantry and Luis de Toledo's cavalry. Hence Fuentes ordered that

> as an attempt could be made between the Douro and Minho or in Galicia, it seemed advisable that the infantry and cavalry under Don Juan del Águila and Don Luis de Toledo should be accommodated in Coimbra and the surrounding area, for it is situated at the centre of the region and should the need arise they can reach any part of the area.[62]

The Count also ordered that 'in order for the billeting to be acceptable and conveni-ent for the locals,' everything should be done under the supervision of the Count of Portoalegre, and 'they should be given excellent treatment there'.

On the same day, Fuentes sent two more caravels with men and supplies to reinforce the two that were tailing the English Armada. In addition, he began the recruitment of sailors for the new Armada that was being prepared for the following year.[63] For his part, Alonso de Bazán, who had been called upon by the King for this new Armada, wrote to him on that day to say that with the invaders now definitely gone from Lisbon, he would travel to the Court immediately.[64]

As for the English, it was on the Saturday that Robert Devereux, Earl of Essex, more or less unwittingly rendered one last service to the expedition by providing Cerralbo with the same major headaches as he had suffered in May and in the process making the Vigo estuary more vulnerable. In fact, the first sighting of the first squadron of the English Armada occurred on that day in the Rías Altas, off the Costa de la Muerte. It included the favourite Devereux with many other nobles, a good number of English

---

[61] 'At four in the afternoon I received news from one of the caravels that (the fleet) was far out to sea heading westwards towards England, and although it is thought that they will keep to that course because they were in need of supplies and men and had problems of sickness, there is still reason to fear that they have taken that course to reach the islands because the weather had hitherto prevented them from doing so.' The Count of Fuentes to the King, Lisbon, 24 June 1589. AGS Guerra Antigua. File 249, fol.134. See also Alonso de Bazán to the King, Galera *Real*, Lisbon, 24 June 1589. Ibid., fol. 132.

[62] The Count of Fuentes to the King, Lisbon, 24 June 1589. Ibid. File 249, fol.134.

[63] Ibid., fol.135.

[64] Alonso de Bazán to the King, Galera *Real*, Lisbon, 24 June 1589. Ibid., fol. 132.

ships carrying the sick and the discharged Dutch vessels.[65] This sighting created a counterproductive movement of Galician troops, for when Cerralbo thought that the English Armada was going to attack Corunna again, he ordered the three companies that were stationed in Pontevedra as reinforcements for Vigo and the Rías Bajas to return at once to Corunna.[66] It would have been far better in this game of cat and mouse for these veteran soldiers to have remained in Pontevedra, for this would have spared them gruelling and futile marches across the Galician countryside that took them away from the place where the final attack by the English Armada would be unleashed shortly afterwards.

On Sunday, 25 June, the northerly winds and rough weather intensified.[67] As night fell, Drake, who had sailed out to sea on 23 June, was sighted off Oporto.[68] These facts suggest that Drake took advantage of the north-easterly wind on 23 June, sailed west-northwest at the start of what was to be a long tacking movement (that led some to think that he was heading for the Azores). At some point on 24 June, now at some distance from the coast and with the wind from the north, the tacking took them several miles out to sea. Following the change in direction and sailing into the wind as much as possible in order to get as far north as he could, he started a new tack, this time back towards the Portuguese coast. Finally, on 25 June, with the ships leaning hard to starboard, he completed the tack which took him to within five miles of Oporto. As far as the first squadron of the English Armada was concerned, it tacked using the northerly wind to reach Finisterre, while trying not to lose too much of the northern advance already made.

The northerly wind was still blowing on Monday, 26 June, and Drake was tacking gently off the north coast of Portugal between Vila do Conde and Esposende under the watchful eye of Pedro Bermúdez, commander of the military garrison in that sector.[69] The first squadron of the fleet was doing the same off the Galician coast and was seen again that day from Finisterre.[70] On the Spanish side, that was the day that the fifteen

[65] 'Today, Saint John the Baptist's Day, one hundred sails appeared at six o'clock in the evening off the Cape Touriñán on the way to Cape Nariga and the Sisargas Islands. I notified Corunna and I am also informing Your Majesty that they are sailing eight leagues out to sea.' Letter from Francisco Rig ... (illegible) to the King, Mugía, 24 June 1589. AGS Guerra Antigua. fol. 111. With the fleet sailing almost twenty-eight miles out to sea, the figure of 'one hundred ships' must be an approximation.

[66] Thus he stated: 'I have told the men to move quickly, so early tomorrow morning the three companies will arrive in Corunna.' The Marquis of Cerralbo to the King, Santiago, 27 June 1589. Ibid. File 249, fol. 110.

[67] The Count of Fuentes to the King, Lisbon, 8 July 1589. Ibid., File 250, fol. 150.

[68] 'Caravels were following him to keep us informed, and Pedro Bermúdez told me yesterday that very late on the 25th he had been sighted a league and a half away from Oporto.' The Count of Fuentes to the King, Lisbon, 26 June 1589. Ibid., File 249, fol. 136.

[69] 'I received word from Pedro Bermúdez that on Sunday 25th of last month to Wednesday 28th he was tacking within sight of Esposende and Vila do Conde, and sometimes close to the land.' The Count of Fuentes to the King, Lisbon, 8 July 1589. AGS Guerra Antigua. File 250, fol. 150. 'At midday on 26th I received word from Esposende, which is twenty-five miles from Oporto, that at dawn they were returning from Viana or Bayona close to land with more than 126 ships.' The Count of Fuentes to the King, Lisbon, 26 June 1589. Ibid., File 249, fol. 136.

[70] Bernardino Rodríguez to the Marquis of Cerralbo, Corcubión, 26 June 1589. Ibid., fol. 112.

caravels at last set sail to reinforce the Azores.[71] Meanwhile, the *Gregory* from London which, as mentioned earlier, had been hit by the guns from the galleys days before, 'was not sailing as well as the rest' and had got detached from the fleet, managed to join up with them again.[72] According to Evesham's account that was also the night when, in addition to the gradual dispersal of individual ships, the second squadron of the English Armada was in turn split in two. Evesham described how during the night Drake lit a beacon on the *Revenge*, which by daybreak had disappeared along with sixty ships.

On Tuesday, 27 June, the wind continued to blow,[73] resulting in the virtual standstill of the English ships, which were becoming more and more spread out as they tried to sail into the wind off the Portuguese and Galician coasts. Tragically, they were being held back, with the vessels beginning to look more like mortuaries owing to the relentless increase in hunger, thirst, sickness and death.[74]

By 28 June, most of the second squadron of the English Armada was close to the Portuguese–Galician border between Viana and Caminha. In fact, a number of ships showed signs of attempting to land on Ancora beach next to the river.[75] But the same day the wind veered to the south,[76] and so they were able to sail towards the estuaries which offered unparalleled respite for any ship exhausted from being at sea. However, they did not all anchor in Vigo as a number of them headed straight off to England. One of these was the *Gregory*, which headed north after abandoning a lost supply ship that it had come across and which decided to stay.[77] Shortly afterwards, the *Gregory* came across

---

[71] 'Fifteen caravels set off on the 26th for the islands, with two companies of infantry totalling 350 men, with Captain Rodrigo de Orozco, plus powder, rope, lead, swords and other things, and they would have set off earlier if the weather had not sent them back to Cascais.' The Count of Fuentes to the King, Lisbon, 26 June 1589. AGS Guerra Antigua. fol. 136.

[72] Account by John Evesham. Wernham, *Expedition*, p. 235.

[73] 'On the 27th he went round the Cape with the north-easterly wind far out to sea.' The Count of Fuentes to the King, Lisbon, 1 July 1589. AGS Guerra Antigua. File 250, fol. 149. The Count of Fuentes to the King, Lisbon, 8 July 1589. Ibid., fol. 150. Account by John Evesham in Wernham, *Expedition*, p. 236.

[74] 'The men died, and were thrown overboard by the hundred from scurvy, starvation, and wounds.' Hume, *The Year After*, p. 70.

[75] 'That day (28th) news came that between Caminha and Viana by the River Ancora some men began to disembark, and at the time of writing a thousand men had landed … and given that the rough weather over the last few days was coming from the north it was clear that there was no way they could have moved further up and they could take on water from the river … and on the 2nd of this month I received further news from Pedro Bermúdez who told me that although on the 28th they had appeared about to land they hadn't done so but renewed their voyage when a southerly wind picked up.' The Count of Fuentes to the King, Lisbon, 8 July 1589. AGS Guerra Antigua. File 250, fol. 150.

[76] The Count of Fuentes to the King, Lisbon, 8 July 1589. Ibid. Account by John Evesham, Wernham, *Expedition*, p. 236.

[77] 'And being becalmed all night, in the morning (28 June) came a gale of wind at south. So we considered with ourselves that victual grew scant and also that our sailors fell sick daily, for we had then but 8 sound men to trim our sails, which was a miserable case to lie beating up and down the sea. So with a general consent of all our company, we concluded to go for England. But the hulk did not consent to go with us, but would ply off and on 2 or 3 days to learn some news of the General.' Account by John Evesham, ibid.

another ship on its own, the *Bark Bonner* from Plymouth, and they decided to keep each other company on the tough voyage that awaited them on their homeward journey.[78]

But on 29 June Drake finally managed to drop anchor off Vigo and, throughout that day, a large number of ships came to join him there.[79] In conclusion, Drake had the wind in his favour to head for the Azores and against him to return to England. But what he wanted was to go home and, from setting sail from Cascais on 18 June until a southerly wind got up on 28 June, he had tacked against the wind in order to make some headway north. And during that time, disease and hunger began to seriously ravage the fleet.

---

[78] 'So that day about noon we met with a ship of Plymouth called the *Bark Bonner*, who likewise had lost the fleet and she through our persuasion determined to keep us company for England.' Wernham, *Expedition*, p. 236.

[79] 'And news came from the caravels on the 3rd that on the 29th a large part of the fleet was on the Cíes Islands and the rest were arriving.' The Count of Fuentes to the King, Lisbon, 8 July 1589. AGS Guerra Antigua. File 250, fol. 150.

Chapter 30

Port of Call in Vigo

After ten days of difficult sailing, Drake was forced to make an emergency stopover in the Vigo estuary (*ría*) owing to the state of the fleet, which was even worse than when it set sail from Cascais.[1] Ships began arriving in Vigo on the morning of 29 June and by nightfall the fleet had dropped anchor off Bouzas, Vigo and Teis, with twenty vessels left guarding the area around the Cíes Islands.[2] Dispatches with the bad news were sent from Bayona all over Galicia: Drake was about to attack the weakest and most vulnerable point on the coast. In a letter dated 16 February that year, the Marquis of Cerralbo had already warned of the difficulty of defending the extensive Galician coastline, 'for the invasions coming by sea are so sudden that there is no time to get all the men together, and this is even more true with those that are widely scattered, as in our case'. He also gave warning regarding the particular case of Vigo: 'I saw the Vigo estuary when visiting the ports and noted the impossibility of defending it with forts.'[3] It was no coincidence, then, that Drake should decide to attack Vigo, for he was very familiar with the weak spots of the Galician coast. Besides, not counting the heavily fortified estuary of Bayona, that of Vigo is the first to be encountered when sailing up from Portugal.

However, it was late to start a landing, so Drake's fleet waited at anchor until the morning. The Spanish would make use of these hours in two ways: first, accepting that it would be impossible to defend Vigo, its inhabitants would have time to complete a full evacuation in an orderly fashion; second, the messengers were given precious time to warn Cerralbo, as well as the towns and nobles that were able to come to the aid of the small fishing town with some 2,000 inhabitants and no wall.[4] While the people left the town with what they could carry, Jácome de Figueroa, lawyer of the town, guarded

---

[1]   The English prisoners themselves, who were later captured in Vigo, described the state and intentions of the fleet: 'They said they were so short of supplies that many were dying of hunger, and that they were just waiting for the weather to change [to a southerly wind]. As for their going to the open areas, it was for repairs, to find food and other things they much needed.' Told by Juan Rodríguez, captain of the ship called *La Trinidad*. AGS. Guerra Antigua. File 250, fol. 154.

[2]   'On Friday morning of 29 June, part of the Armada reached the Isles of Bayona and by afternoon the rest had arrived, 153 of them, and they made repairs that night in the Vigo estuary.' Ibid.

[3]   The Marquis of Cerralbo to the King, Corunna, 16 February 1589. Ibid., File 245, fol. 82. Quoted in González Garcés, *María Pita*, p. 313.

[4]   Cerralbo sent troops to Vigo immediately: 'I have at once sent Don Pedro de Sotomayor, who was here with me, to his district, which is Pontevedra and the Vigo Ría. I have also ordered the men of the kingdom to go to Santiago, where I shall go myself with some of the men here. I do not believe they will attack Bayona, but I much fear the damage they might do in this kingdom, which is poorly defended.' The Marquis of Cerralbo to the King, Corunna, 30 June 1589. AGS. Guerra Antigua. File 249, fol. 114.

the Franciscan monastery of Santa Marta with the most determined and best armed men available.[5]

Dawn came on Friday, 30 June, to the most southerly of the Galician *rías*. The morning chill did little to encourage Figueroa and his men to get up and out from under the warmth of their capes, but from their vantage point they watched the flagship launch a skiff with four or five men on board, which went between the hundred or so ships lined up off the coast, giving instructions. Soon afterwards the landing began at three points: Teis, Coya beach and the bank of the River Berbés. The small garrison, with its mayor and Captain, Fernán Pereira, withdrew a quarter of a league towards Beade. The Spanish strategy this time would be to ambush the English from the outlying areas of Vigo in an attempt to get the enemy, who felt thwarted by not finding anyone in the town,[6] to spread out across the nearby countryside. Ironically, this purely defensive and desperate tactic turned out to be quite successful that day.

The English who had survived Corunna and Lisbon and who were incensed by their past defeat showed no mercy towards Vigo.[7] They were not attacking a major port and they dared not approach nearby Bayona. This gave rise to the sarcastic accusation against Drake that 'he goes around like a kite but only dares to attack small lizards'.[8] The only aims the English now had were to find water and other supplies quickly and then cause destruction. The ease with which they took Vigo, however, and the lack of resistance gave them a dangerous feeling of confidence. This, combined with the widespread lack of discipline and the violent rapacity of the troops – who, unlike in Portugal, were now completely out of control – came back to bite the invaders. Their predatory greed caused them to disperse, in the hope that the fewer looters there were in the group, the more food, women, valuables and so on there would be for each one.

---

[5]   José Santiago y Gómez, *Historia de Vigo y su comarca*, (Madrid, 1919), p. 327.

[6]   According to the author of the anonymous English account: 'All were fled and all their barcademes standing, very strong, which when we saw, we wondered very much to see how strongly they had made themselves and yet ran away and durst not hold it.' Another account of the voyage. Wernham, *Expedition*, p. 246. From this we can see that the first intention was to defend the place. We do not know the reason for this change of strategy, but it should not be forgotten that the English Armada was still an imposing sight, and the fact that its ships were half empty of men in no way lessened its power to intimidate when seen through a telescope.

[7]   Santiago y Gómez described the episode as follows: 'The work of destruction begun by the Armada's artillery was continued by the English once they had taken control of the town, in order to reduce it to ashes and enjoy watching a great fire. They burned down the Collegiate Church, of which only the walls were left standing, tore down the saints from the altar, smashing all the sculptures to pieces on the ground, and in their iconoclastic fury knifed, scratched and ripped the paintings that adorned the walls and chapels, and cooked in the consecrated altars. Among the altarpieces they destroyed was the magnificent alabaster one in high relief containing the Resurrection of Our Lord Jesus Christ, much prized for its artistic merit and topped with the coat of arms of England, which was shown respect. Such was the desecration suffered by the Collegiate that they slaughtered pigs and other livestock there, leaving the remains with a lot of other rubbish in the church … Not even the hospital of La Magdalena in the Plaza Mayor was spared. After smashing the two images in the chapel, they set it and the adjoining hospital on fire and killed and burned a poor sick woman who had been unable to leave her bed when the English invaded the town. All the hermitages and wayside crosses in the surrounding area were knocked down and burned.' Santiago y Gómez, *Historia de Vigo*, pp. 328–9.

[8]   Fernández Duro, *Armada española*, III, p. 49.

Once again the English were on the rampage. The locals, hidden, armed and with their families safe elsewhere, were no longer afraid when they saw small, scattered bands of Englishmen. Consequently 'the townsmen, who had retreated, killed up to three hundred Lutherans[9] in Gandariña and the neighbouring countryside'.[10] Having burnt the church of San Salvador de Teis and taking the choir back to their ships, the English were driven back when they tried to do the same with San Fausto de Chapela. There was a much more violent skirmish at Santa Cristina de Lavadores, where an Anglo-Portuguese detachment led by a Knight Commander of the Order of Christ of Portugal lost many men, including their leader, when they tried to desecrate the church.[11] Aside from their vindictive, destructive anger, there was thirst to be dealt with and over the next two days the English went about their main task of filling their casks with fresh water. This was the only night that they slept on land.[12]

On Saturday, 1 July, the tables were turned. Don Luis Sarmiento, son of Don García Sarmiento, Squire of Salvatierra, arrived on a forced march with five hundred regular soldiers. This force became a sizeable detachment after it had been joined by others from nearby estates in Galicia and Portugal and it went on the offensive. Hundreds of the English were caught unawares and killed[13] and up to two hundred were taken prisoner, many of them with signs of sickness.[14] Sarmiento reclaimed the heap of ashes that had once been Vigo and Drake had to order the men to re-embark.[15] He sent a messenger with a dispatch promising to leave the estuary without causing further harm on condition that the prisoners were returned. When, to his horror, the Spanish commander saw the devastation, he had the prisoners hanged within sight of the fleet on the highest point of Mount Castro and challenged Drake to send more Englishmen so he could hang them all. More of the dispersed attackers were caught later, but instead of meeting the same fate as their comrades, Cerralbo had them sent to the Real Audiencia for trial. Among the men who were spared Sarmiento's wrath there were not only Englishmen, but also Portuguese and even Spaniards.[16] Also on that day, Fuentes wrote to the King informing

---

[9]   As there were virtually no Protestants in sixteenth-century Spain and Luther was the earliest and most prominent of the reformers in continental Europe, Spaniards at times used 'Lutheranism' to refer to all Protestants, including Anglicans [translator's note].

[10]   Letter by the Prior of Vigo Gregorio Servido. Parochial Books of Vigo. Quoted in Santiago y Gómez, *Historia de Vigo*, p. 330.

[11]   Ibid., pp. 330–1.

[12]   Another account of the voyage. Wernham, *Expedition*, p. 246.

[13]   'Captains Gregorio de Paços and Don Diego de Paços, Figueroa and Francisco and Fernán Pereira, with the men of the town to fight and expel them, which they did, killing four hundred Englishmen.' Juan Fernández Cid to the Marquis of Cerralbo, Vigo, 11 September 1589. AGS. Guerra Antigua. File 310. fol. 239.

[14]   'Many of the English who landed brought with them an epidemic of cancers, typhus and plague which they had contracted in the Portugal campaign.' Santiago y Gómez, *Historia de Vigo*, p. 332.

[15]   'Only those allotted the task of bringing water stayed on land.' Another account of the voyage. Wernham, *Expedition*, p. 246.

[16]   'The militia took some 18 prisoners, English, Portuguese and even Spanish, apart from those hanged on the Castro, but these they were not allowed to be killed, for the Judge of Vigo received a letter from the Marquis of Cerralbo ordering them to be sent immediately to the Audiencia Real for trial. Among the prisoners taken to Corunna was one called Juan de Regueras, who said he was from Almodóvar del Campo; another

Figure 30.1 Small English iron cannon. Photo by Yago Abilleira.
The cannon was probably from one of the ships that was dashed onto the rocks at Cangas and was set on fire by the locals. It measures 183 cms and has a 6 cms calibre. There are two groups of cannon, both with two cannon plus other fragments, fifty metres apart. They lie in shallow waters and are covered in concretions and vegetation.

him of the reassuring news received from Juan de Aranda, Commander on Terceira, the most important island of the Azores, that all was quiet and its defences were ready.[17]

At eight o'clock in the morning on 2 July,[18] the English Armada set sail from Vigo where they had unexpectedly lost several hundred men. Their exit from the estuary was made more difficult by strong winds, however, and Norris, with over thirty vessels that had anchored further up the *ría*, did not have time to make it into the open sea before the arrival of a storm which forced him to delay their departure. He had to drop anchor again, this time next to the Cíes Islands, and was left behind by the bulk of the fleet led by Drake, whose dispersion continued.[19] Marcos de Aramburu captured two of the

was a Galician called Cámara, with relatives in Vigo; a Burgundian cabin boy, the servant of a captain in Drake's Armada, was sent by Don Luis Sarmiento to his father, who lived in Madrid.' Santiago y Gómez, *Historia de Vigo*, p. 332.
[17] The Count of Fuentes to the King, Lisbon, 1 July 1589. AGS. Guerra Antigua. File 250, fol. 149.
[18] Pedro Bermúdez to the Count of Fuentes, 8 July 1589. Ibid., fol. 148.
[19] 'And the next day, being Sunday, we weighed and put forth of the harbour. The wind being against us, we were fain to turn it out of the harbour. The wind being great at south-south-east, some of the fleet could not

Figure 30.2 Second English small cannon preserved intact but badly eroded. Photo by Carlos Fernández-Cid.

Like the first one, this cannon too is made of iron and both are badly eroded and in danger. Given its historical value, it needs to be taken out of the water in order to be preserved.

vessels sailing with Drake, which he later took to Santander.[20] It was perhaps on this day that the English lost several other vessels. We know that one of them ran aground off the Cíes,[21] and that another two hit the rocks[22] and were burned by the people of Cangas.[23]

On Monday, 3 July, the bulk of the second contingent of the English Armada struggled against the north wind as they headed to Finisterre.[24] Drake then intercepted a Portuguese ship transporting sugar from Brazil, which he released two days later.[25] Meanwhile, Norris, still at anchor in the Cíes, had the artillery removed from the ship

fetch out. But General Drake got into the sea and all the fleet but my Lord General and about 30 other ships with him, which came to anchor in the mouth of the harbour and rid there until Tuesday morning.' Another account of the voyage. Wernham, *Expedition*, p. 246.

[20]   González-Arnao, *Derrota y muerte*, p. 94.

[21]   Pedro Bermúdez to the Count of Fuentes, 8 July 1589. AGS. Guerra Antigua. File 250, fol. 148.

[22]   'There were two ships of our fleet cast away upon the rocks, one a flyboat of Mr. Hawkins and the other Captain Francis Docwra's ship.' William Fenner to Anthony Bacon, 1589. Wernham, *Expedition*, p. 241.

[23]   'Two vessels hit the rocks and were burned by the locals, some of whom were wounded. There were a number of Spanish prisoners aboard.' *Relación de lo subçedido del armada enemiga*. BN mss 18579, p. 88.

[24]   Told by Juan Rodríguez, captain of the ship called *La Trinidad*. AGS. Guerra Antigua. File 250, fol. 154. The Count of Fuentes to the King, Lisbon, 8 July 1589. Ibid., fol. 150.

[25]   The Count of Fuentes to the King, Lisbon, 29 July 1589. Ibid., fol. 151.

that had run aground, an operation that lasted until the following morning. But by this stage, the situation aboard the English ships was starting to be ghostlike. The *Gregory* from London, for instance, set off for England on 28 June with only eight fit men. Now, on 3 July, in the company of the *Bark Bonner*, it had only two men and two boys fit for work. The situation had become drastically worse in only six days and it was therefore no exaggeration on Evesham's part when he stated that 'daily our men fell down sick.' The *Gregory* was in danger of becoming a ghost ship adrift and so help was requested from the *Bark Bonner*, which lent them two sailors and two soldiers and promised not to abandon it until they had both reached home. Then Evesham himself became sick.[26]

On the morning of Tuesday, 4 July, having salvaged what artillery he could, Norris set fire to the ship that was stranded on the Cíes.[27] With this done, and with the same northerly wind blowing, he set sail along with the thirty-five stragglers from the Vigo estuary.[28] Meanwhile, Drake could be seen by a ship from Dunkirk patiently tacking as he headed for Cape Finisterre.[29]

[26] John Evesham's Account. Wernham, *Expedition*, p. 236.
[27] 'And he left thirty-five vessels off the Isles, which spent until Tuesday salvaging the artillery of another ship that had run aground, and then set fire to it.' Pedro Bermúdez to the Count of Fuentes, 8 July 1589. AGS. Guerra Antigua. File 250, fol. 148.
[28] 'He left on Tuesday morning with the same fresh north wind, and it has continued to blow.' Ibid., fol. 154. Another account of the voyage. Wernham, *Expedition*, p. 246.
[29] 'And today two ships from Dunkirk have arrived. One of them brought the news that he had been seen rounding the Cape on Tuesday the 4th.' The Count of Fuentes to the King, Lisbon, 8 July 1589. AGS. Guerra Antigua. File 250, fol. 150.

Chapter 31

Return to England

The 5 July dawned with the Spanish coast finally liberated from the greatest attack it had suffered in its history. The main part of the second flotilla of ships of the English Armada was sighted by a ship that was also from Dunkirk, and it, too, would later inform the Count of Fuentes in Lisbon. Drake had reached level with Finisterre and was slowly progressing northward against the wind.[1] In addition, a *zabra* dispatched to Finisterre to report on the English confirmed that given 'the course the enemy was following and how they were sailing according to the wind, their only conceivable intention is to return home'.[2] On that day, the Portuguese vessel captured two days earlier was released and later reported that 'it left the armada fifty leagues offshore heading for Norway because the weather would not allow them to head for the Channel'.[3] This shows the difficulties of sailing towards England with north and north-easterly winds, a fact also mentioned in the English sources: 'And the wind at north-north-east, a great gale. And being bound for England, we turned to windward until Thursday.'[4] That day the Marquis of Cerralbo sent a report on the state of preparations for the new fleet. The presence of the English had slowed them down by a few days.[5] It was also probably on the same day that Essex, who as we know had set sail with the first group of vessels, arrived in England. His predicament was extremely delicate, and in order to sound out the Queen's disposition and ask her forgiveness, he sent his brother to the royal court.

From this point on it becomes difficult to follow the path of the English Armada. It is entirely possible, given the fleet's desperate condition, that there was another emergency stop in Galicia following the one in Vigo. We know that on 18 June, when it set sail from Cascais, the fleet was already in a highly compromised situation given the dreadful conditions and the lack of men. We know that the trip from Cascais to England would be the hardest part of the entire journey and that thousands of corpses would be thrown overboard. We also know that the second group of vessels would also lose more men in

---

[1] 'And the other that on Wednesday the 5th they were seen at the same Cape Finisterre, and that they seemed to be heading for England.' The Count of Fuentes to the King, Lisbon, 8 July 1589. AGS. Guerra Antigua. File 250, fol. 150.

[2] Juan de Cardona to the King, Santander, 11 July 1589. Ibid., fol. 5.

[3] The Count of Fuentes to the King, Lisbon, 29 July 1589. Ibid., fol. 151.

[4] Another report of the voyage. Wernham, *Expedition*, p. 246.

[5] 'We are collecting our supplies as quickly as possible and were it not for the bother the enemy has given us these days when bringing the wine from Pontevedra and when trying to fish, everything would be as ready as the pork fat and meat already are. We shall see to it that time is not lost because of this.' The Marquis of Cerralbo to the King, Santiago, 5 July 1589. AGS. Guerra Antigua. File 250, fol. 131.

Vigo, sailors included. Given these circumstances, with malnutrition and the consequent increases in cases of the plague, the fleet was literally left without men. It was almost as if a pathetic bargaining contest had begun among the ships of the English Armada to find the smallest number of men necessary to sail each one. We have seen the case of the *Gregory*, but things were not much better in other vessels. Generally speaking, given the small number of men who returned – which was less than five thousand, as we shall see – the problem can be generalized to the English Armada as a whole. A considerable number of smaller vessels, which were the most numerous kind of vessel in the fleet, had to be abandoned due to regrouping. One interesting account sheds some light on this:

> The enemy Armada landed men in Vigo, and although the people of the place had fled with clothes and supplies, they razed and burned it to the ground, and it is said they did the same in Redondela and Cangas, and not so safely that some of them were not killed … and the Armada then set sail again, but not covering much distance with their men being weak from illness and lack of supplies, it entered the port of Vivero, ten leagues past Corunna, where some 6,000 men landed to rest, and they say they had no more men left. They cleaned and checked the sides of the ships, and they say that for lack of men to sail them they abandoned and sank many vessels, which is quite different from what others say: that Francis Drake repaired forty sails and set off with them for the Islands of the Azores, which seemed hard to believe with so many dead and such a lack of provisions, unless they had received new ships and supplies from England.[6]

In any event, on Thursday, 6 July, the wind changed to west-south-west,[7] which allowed the English to set sail for home or for the Galician coast for those vessels who needed the port of call. The fleet was highly dispersed by then and an increasing number of vessels sailed alone or in small groups, as would be confirmed later by their staggered arrival on the English coasts. The aim at the time was quite simply to reach the green shores of England before the vessels ran out of men to sail them and were lost at sea. Information is available for only a small number of vessels, but what there is is quite shocking. For example, one of the Queen's ships – Thomas Fenner's five hundred–ton *Dreadnought*, which had been particularly carefully provisioned – had set off with almost three hundred sailors, but when it returned to Plymouth only eighteen were fit to work, while the rest had died or were sick.[8] Thomas Fenner himself, vice admiral of the English Armada and Drake's second in command, died on arrival in England. On the *Griffin* from Lübeck, the captain died and 'there were not five or six men on the ship who were well'. Fifty English soldiers had embarked upon that *urca*, and before they got to England '[they] hurled overboard 32 or 33'. Those who landed 'were very sick and two of them died so soon as they came a-land to Sandwich'.[9] Barely ten months

---

6   *Relación de lo subçedido del armada enemiga.* BN mss 18579, p. 89.
7   Another report of the voyage. Wernham, *Expedition*, p. 246.
8   Ibid., p. lxv.
9   Griffin of Lübeck, July 1589. Ibid., p. 211.

after the Spanish tragedy in Scottish and Irish waters, another even worse catastrophe was happening. In the Spanish case, the men lost their ships, which were smashed against the rocks. With the English, however, the ships were left without men, owing to malnutrition, hunger and the ensuing plague. This sickness was the same as that which had stricken Howard's fleet the previous year and had forced him to retreat, and was probably the same one that had delayed the Spanish Armada in Lisbon. It was a sickness often known as *enfermedad de cámaras* (diarrhoea), and it was so called by Guillermo Drellet, a freed prisoner who wrote a report.[10] In order to control and treat it a proper diet was essential, as the Marquis of Cerralbo had realized in Corunna. Inadequate food could turn it into an uncontrollable epidemic, as witnessed by Drake and Norris.[11] It is not easy to say exactly what the illness was,[12] but every English ship left a sad trail of corpses on the return journey, as illustrated by the bas-relief of the burial at sea of James Hales, treasurer of the English Armada.[13]

Towards the middle of July, what was left of the fleet began to arrive in separate groups. The arrival of the first group 'containing some people of note'[14] began to spread the terrible news,[15] but there was little need for words: the vessels arrived nearly empty or, even worse, full of sick and dying hungry men. When the survivors leapt off the boats, everyone was surprised by how few of them there were.[16] Drake, who had left Vigo before Norris, also arrived in Plymouth before him on 10 July, according to the report of 'David', the code name of Manuel de Andrade, Philip II's secret agent in Plymouth who passed himself off as a Portuguese supporter of Dom António.[17] The Admiral's predicament in Plymouth was highly awkward, since he had set sail in command of the largest fleet in English history, with so much expected of it, and yet Drake returned as the man responsible for a major disaster. Thus, 'as soon as he arrived, he was badly received by all'.[18] On 11 July, the *Gregory* completed its epic journey accompanied by the *Bark Bonner*.[19] The arrival of Norris in high dudgeon on Thursday, 13

[10] *Relación que hizo Guillermo Drellet*. AGS. Guerra Antigua. File 250, fol. 7.
[11] Ralph Lane to Walsingham, 6 August 1589. Wernham, *Expedition*, p. 221.
[12] Gracia Rivas, *La sanidad*, pp. 98–101.
[13] The memorial to the Hales family on the north wall of the nave in Canterbury Cathedral includes at the top the image of the body of Sir James Hales being lowered into the sea [translator's note].
[14] *Lo que refieren dos alféreces que fueron presos en La Coruña* (*What was reported by two ensigns held prisoner in Corunna*) AGS. Guerra Antigua. File 250, fol. 348.
[15] 'And later the bad news was put about and there was much weeping.' Ibid.
[16] 'When the ships came in everyone jumped onto land, healthy and ill alike, soldiers and sailors, and in total there were so few of them that they were not enough to sail the ships, with so many sailors having died.' Account by Juan Antonio Bigbaque, Lisbon, 12 August 1589. Ibid., fol. 345.
[17] Luiz Augusto Rebello Da Silva, *Quadro Elementar das relacoes políticas e diplomáticas de Portugal*. (Lisbon, 1858), Vol. 16, p. 220.
[18] *What Is Known about the English Who Arrived in Saint-Jean-de-Luz in Two Vessels*. AGS. Guerra Antigua. File 250, fol. 346.
[19] 'So, by the help of God, having fair weather, upon the first day of July [11 July according to the Gregorian calendar, not yet adopted in England] we came into Plymouth, where we found Sir Francis Drake with divers others of the fleet.' John Evesham's account of the voyage. Wernham, *Expedition*, p. 236.

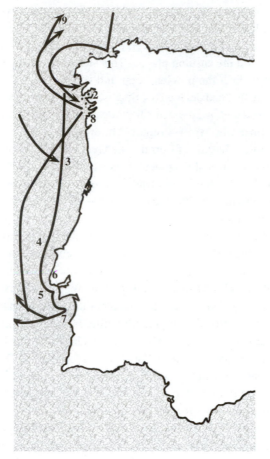

Figure 31.1 Map 8, sea route.

1. 4–19 May. The English Armada at Corunna, where it lost 1,500 men and most valuable time. Health conditions also deteriorated.
2. 22–28 May. Scattered vessels attacked the coast.
3. 24 May. Encounter with the galleon *Swiftsure*, on which the rebellious favourite of Elizabeth I, the Earl of Essex, had fled. Roger Williams and other noble and military men were also on board.
4. 25 May. War Council held off Peniche: Norris's plan to land and march prevailed over that of Drake, which was to attack in a single strike from the sea. Some 12,000 men were landed.
5. 28 May–18 June. The English Armada remained anchored at Cascais, without daring to attack Lisbon.
6. 5 June. The men who failed to conquer Lisbon arrived at Cascais having suffered severe losses. The plague began to spread.
7. 19–21 June. The English Armada set sail and was attacked by the galleys. Ships were lost and scattered.
8. 29 June–2 July. The English Armada in Vigo. Looting and Spanish counterattack.
9. 2–16 July. Ships lost and abandoned, crews redistributed, ships scattered and staggered return to England pursued by Marcos Aramburu as far as the English coast. Terrible death rate among the crews due to hunger and plague.

July,[20] only made things worse for Drake. As soon as he landed, he headed straight for the Admiral and had a serious argument with him in which they nearly came to blows. Several men, among them some Catholic prisoners such as Juan Antonio Bigbaque, a Walloon from Liège mentioned earlier, were witnesses to Drake's row with Norris, which 'even led to their putting their hands to their swords'. The same Bigbaque, once he got to Lisbon, was questioned on 12 August by the Count of Fuentes and

> asked if he knew why Drake and Norris had put their hands to their swords and the reasons each of them had given for doing so, he said that he had understood that Norris attributed their misadventure to Drake's failure to attempt to enter the river, but that he did not know what Drake had to say in his defence. [21]

Responsibility for the disaster was too much of a hot potato for the two aggrieved commanders not to blame each other, but Norris's reproaches may have been exacerbated by what happened in Vigo. That was probably the same day that the Earl of Essex, having sent his brother to placate the Queen's anger, as mentioned earlier, travelled to the court himself in order to take the bull by the horns. He was accompanied by Anthony Ashley, who significantly was carrying triumphalist but dishonest reports for the Queen, in a desperate attempt by Drake and Norris to buy time and get out of a difficult situation.[22] The importance of these reports would become clear later.

The following day, 14 July, however, John Norris wrote an interesting letter to Walsingham. In it, after admitting the failure of the expedition, he added:

> But for Her Majesty's honour and the reputation of our country, I trust there shall justly no fault be found in our actions. If the enemy had done so much upon us, his party would have made bonfires in most parts of Christendom. And if we shall disgrace our own doings, we are unworthy of good success. It will please your Honour to take upon you the protection of us and the cause.[23]

The General was making a national pronouncement, a call to patriotism which at that moment he was obliged to adopt as a sacred duty in order to cover up the disaster and conceal what had happened. Shrewdly, Norris made his genuine concern for England's reputation coincide with the protection of his own. In short, the soldier knew he would be unable to conceal the real outcome of the expedition from the Queen for very long.

Meanwhile in Spain, on 15 July, Alonso de Bazán arrived from the Court in Santander to take charge of the recently repaired fleet. He was very favourably impressed by the work that had been done:

> I arrived at the port on the 15th, where I found the ships there in such an advanced state of repair that within a week they will finally be ready and loaded with

---

[20] John Norris to Walsingham, Plymouth, 14 July 1589. Wernham, *Expedition*, p. 199.
[21] Account by Juan Antonio Bigbaque, Lisbon, 12 August 1589. AGS. Guerra Antigua. File 250, fol. 345.
[22] Wernham, *Expedition*, p. lvi.
[23] John Norris to Walsingham, Plymouth, 14 July 1589. Ibid., p. 200.

Sir John Norris.

Figure 31.2 Sir John Norris (also spelt Norreys). Artist unknown. Portrait from National Trust Collections.

Norris was one of the greatest English soldiers of his day. He had to fight the Spanish on land and often came off worse. In 1589 he committed his greatest error by allowing himself to be seduced by the fantasies of Dom António and landed at Peniche instead of heading straight for Lisbon. Moreover, his army was seriously short of armaments and lacking in logistics and preparation, for which he was responsible. The complete absence of coordination with Drake, for which they were both to blame, made it impossible to carry out an amphibious operation with any guarantee of success. On his return, Norris very nearly came to blows with Drake. Norris then sounded a timely call to patriotism in order to cover up what had happened.

supplies and water. And because the largest ships will only be able to leave with the spring tides to pass the reef of St. Martin, they will have to wait until the 25th, 26th and 27th, when they will all be able to leave.[24]

Meanwhile, vessels continued to arrive on the English coast singly or in small groups.[25] Information is patchy: we know, for example, that on Sunday, 16 July, a vessel arrived in Portsmouth, because one of its men wrote an account of the journey,[26] or that eighteen supply ships reached Torbay around this time.[27] But if these were hard times for the English, they were not much better for Dom António and his supporters. Manuel de Andrade, the secret agent mentioned earlier, reported that 'Dom António and all of his men had reached Plymouth in a pitiful state, and that the Portuguese were looked down upon by the English much more than the Spanish were. They had no regard for Dom António and were highly insulting to his supporters, even in the presence of the Prior, and went unpunished for it.'[28] This attitude of the English was due, according to Bigbaque, to 'the hatred towards him prompted by the death of so many noblemen'.[29] This intense hostility even put the life of the Portuguese aristocrat in danger.[30]

On Monday, 17 July, Elizabeth's reply to the reports conveyed by the skilful Ashley arrived in Plymouth. Although – for reasons that have nothing to do with the generals – not all of the expedition's objectives had been accomplished, the Queen was delighted by the "happy success" in Spain and Portugal. The council, in a letter of the same date, also declared its satisfaction and thanks for the great achievement. In another letter, also written on that Monday, the council requested information regarding the number of soldiers and sailors who had returned and an estimate of how many ships and men would be necessary to finish the task as soon as possible. This task, of course, was to destroy the ships that remained in Santander, and to intercept the Indies' fleet – at last. Rarely in the history of England had the government, or the crown, been so badly informed.[31]

We are therefore faced with a most peculiar situation: whereas in Plymouth and throughout England there was a growing awareness of the disaster, Elizabeth and her council in London remained deluded. It was then that Norris's national proclamation caught on with startling intensity. Thus, while the men responsible for the expedition waited in Plymouth, in London a formidable race against time began, by means of the pen, to transform defeat into victory. Although such activity was not, strictly

---

[24] Alonso de Bazán to the King, Santander, 18 July 1589. AGS. Guerra Antigua. File 250, fol. 23.

[25] 'And daily came in more and more of them. Where we continued without pay or anything else.' John Evesham's account of the voyage. Wernham, *Expedition*, p. 236.

[26] Another report of the voyage. Ibid., p. 246.

[27] The Privy Council to Norris and Drake, 17 July 1589. Ibid., p. 201.

[28] Rebello Da Silva, *Quadro Elementar* , p. 221.

[29] Account by Juan Antonio Bigbaque, Lisbon, 12 August 1589. AGS. Guerra Antigua. File 250, fol. 345.

[30] 'Dom António was removed a quarter of a league from Plemua (Plymouth), living very poorly and always with a pistol in his hand. The day these two ensigns left (21 July), an English captain threatened him with a dagger and demanded to know why he did not pay the soldiers, and the Portuguese, of whom there must have been up to 50, took up their arms.' As told by two ensigns held prisoner in Corunna. Ibid., fol. 348.

[31] Wernham, *Expedition*, p. lvi.

f the military operations that year, in a sense it was, since propaganda
art of war, as England understood so well at that time. Thus, a series
pamphlets were to appear, inspired by Norris's call. With hardly any
⸻ y the truth, they put together a fictitious account of the military operations in place of the harsh reality of the facts. The writings we are referring to were not
in any way crude, but were instead magnificent examples of the Renaissance episto-
lary genre still in vogue. One of the prime examples is *A True Discourse* by Anthony
Wingfield. It is hard to describe the great service that Wingfield rendered to his country.
The epistle, which offered a brilliant and detailed alternative account of the military
operations, completely buried an historical truth that it was not in England's interest to
reveal. Although this was no minor matter, Wingfield went even further. His is a document that irrefutably defines the English 'bulldog spirit'. It is the ultimate example
of the spirit of a nation that, in the face of adversity, fiercely closes ranks and asserts
the national dogma that 'dirty linen should not be washed in public'. In the process, it
shows an unlimited disdain for everyone else alongside unlimited acclaim for all that
is English. Wingfield's account, essentially an appeal to the deepest recesses of the
heart, is also an appeal to the intelligence. Written in English, and therefore aimed at
domestic consumption, it also became the main source for another elegant Renaissance
epistle, written shortly afterwards in Latin and aimed at establishing the clichés about
the expedition within European opinion.[32] This memorable response to Norris's call
appeared very quickly, within a matter of weeks, while Norris and Drake waited in
Plymouth for their friends and compatriots to smooth the way for when they inevitably had to go to London to give their account. This agile, rapid reaction, much more
than the unpredictable outcome of the war, offers us a picture of the real nature of the
English spirit.

However, leaving aside the ephemeral realm of matters spiritual, while the generals waited in Plymouth, England faced a pressing problem: as the sick of the English
Armada had landed without being checked out and headed for their respective homes,
the plague spread relentlessly on land. It was then that Lord Burleigh made a public announcement in which access to London by all participants in the expedition was
strictly prohibited.[33] The devastation was unremitting, however, and in Plymouth alone

---

[32] This epistle is titled *Ephemeris expeditionis Norreysius et Drakus in Lusitaniam* (Journal of the Expedition
of Norris and Drake to Portugal). Beneath the title it states *LONDINI, Impensis Thomae Woodcokce, apud
signum Ursi nigri. 1589.* (In London, financed by Thomas Woodcocke, next to the sign of the Black Bear.
1589). The *Black Bear* was the mark (the logo) of Woodcocke's printing press, which also published *A True
Discourse. Ephemeris expeditionis Norreysius et Drakus in Lusitaniam* (London: Thomas Woodcocke's
Printing Press, 1589). The epistles of the Renaissance were intended to emulate Virgil or Cicero, and their
contrived syntax is full of baroque elements. As part of their attempt to go back to Roman times, the protagonists of the expedition become Praetors, Consuls or Centurions. In addition, distortion and embellishment
regarding events often gets the better of Wingfield himself. This pamphlet was known and used by Victorian
authors such as John Barrow, in his *Life, Voyages and Exploits of Sir Francis Drake*, published in London by
John Murray in 1861.
[33] Rebello Da Silva, *Quadro Elementar*, p. 218.

four hundred of the local population died in the first few weeks after the return of the ships, a number which continued to grow.[34]

This was the main problem for the English, but not the only one: the survivors of the expedition had to be demobilized and paid. The problem was insoluble, since Elizabeth had used up all her funds in the expectation of a rich booty to be brought back from Spain and Portugal, or of Moroccan help. Without that booty, and following the vast expense of the previous two years, the crown was simply unable to manage such payments. On 14 July, Norris had already asked for the men to be paid with the money obtained from the sale of the cargo from the seized merchant ships, but this hope was also frustrated: those ships had been seized at sea and most of them belonged to neutral cities that were part of the Hanseatic League.[35] These cities demanded the return of what had been seized, which was somewhat problematic since the ships had largely been sacked on arrival in port, or even beforehand.[36] Thus, pay for the members of the expedition was settled at five pitiful shillings per head, that is, a pound to be divided between four of them. Some disobeyed the ban on going to London and angrily protested before the court. The disturbances were mercilessly suppressed and seven rebels were hanged, seven more men to add to the long list of losses from the expedition. One of them, before the rope silenced him, shouted out: 'The gallows is our reward for going to war.'[37]

The size of the tragedy of the English Armada was devastating. According to the pay list of 15 September, 102 ships and 3,722 men returned to England.[38] Other participants, such as knights and their servants, should be added to these. Hume states that there was a maximum of 5,000 survivors.[39] Bearing in mind that the number who left Plymouth was 27,667, this would mean losses of over 20,000 men. In fact, Philip's spies in England reported losses exceeding 18,000 men,[40] and Wingfield, in his *Discourse*, had to deny the widely circulated report that 16,000 men had been lost.[41] French and Italian reports never put the number lower than 15,000 dead.[42]

---

[34] 'There is dead in the town of Plymouth since our coming here of the townspeople 400 and at this hour divers lies sick.' William Fenner to Anthony Bacon, 1589. Wernham, *Expedition*, p. 241.

[35] The Hanseatic League was an alliance of trading guilds that established and maintained a trade monopoly along the coast of Northern Europe, from the Baltic to the North Sea, from the thirteenth to the seventeenth centuries [translator's note].

[36] 'Two-third parts of all the lading were spoiled and embezzled by the men of war and mariners at the sea before they were brought into Plymouth and that one-half of that third remaining was purloined and scattered since the arrival of the ships in that haven, so that nothing was left aboard the ships but that which was too cumbersome or heavy to carry away.' Dr Aubrey and Dr Caesar to the Privy Council, 16 February 1594. Wernham, *Expedition*, pp. liv and 315.

[37] González-Arnao, *Derrota y muerte*, p. 96.

[38] A list of ships and payments, 15 September 1589. Wernham, *Expedition*, pp. 338–41. These figures were accepted by Julian S. Corbett in his book *Drake and the Tudor Navy*, II, (London: Longmans, Green, 1917), p. 331.

[39] Hume, *The Year After*, p. 71.

[40] Wernham, *Expedition*, p. lxiv.

[41] *Discourse*, Anthony Wingfield, 9 September 1589. Wernham, *Expedition*, pp. 254–5.

[42] Fernández Duro, *Armada Española*, III, pp. 50–1.

However, British historians have always been most reluctant to accept these figures. For centuries their casualty lists have been inordinately brief. As Mariano González-Arnao reminds us,[43] the article on Drake in the modern *Dictionary of National Biography* begins to offer us a clue: 'Strenuous efforts were made to conceal this [the loss of life] by mis-stating the numbers which originally started, and possibly exaggerating the numbers which had deserted. But if it is true that about six thousand only returned it would seem that the Spanish estimate of sixteen thousand dead was not so egregiously wrong as the chronicler of the voyage wished it to appear.'[44]

The figures given by the Spanish who had access to first-hand information are different. We have already seen what the spies – not propagandists – had to say, and we also have interesting information from prisoners who were there. Two ensigns who were taken prisoner at Corunna next to the Pescadería wall on the night of 5 May, and who were taken back to England, were in Plymouth as the English Armada returned and for days thereafter. Once back in Spain, they reported on 'the fleet in which 3,000 men returned out of 25,000 who had embarked, and of those 3,000 many died after arrival'.[45] It is difficult to determine the actual scale of the tragedy, but it cannot have involved fewer than 20,000 casualties. To these would have to be added those casualties caused by the virulent plague brought back by the defeated participants that devastated Plymouth and other English ports. The documents collected in Wernham's book offer revealing data that have not yet been fully studied or accepted. They also make clear the contradictions and weaknesses of English sources, which are far less numerous and structured than the Spanish ones. In any event, over four-fifths of the participants in the expedition never saw the rustic hues of an English autumn again. This defeat, because of its sheer size, represents the worst naval catastrophe in the history of England. It is once again impossible to avoid comparison with the disaster of the Spanish Armada. The number of men lost in that great expedition was no greater than 11,000[46] and therefore, in merely quantitative terms, the English Armada was a much greater disaster. However, Spain lost a substantial number of experienced soldiers from the best infantry of its day, while among the English casualties there was a large proportion of inexperienced men from a nation whose army did not bear comparison with the Spanish military at that time. Quality thus compensates for quantity, so from that perspective it can be said without fear of contradiction that Spain lost more than England.

To ascertain the number of ships lost is a complex question. Let us take 180 as our starting point, plus the vessels that sailed individually, that is, a total number of probably not less than two hundred ships.[47] We find that only 102 appear on the pay list of 15 September 1589. It was possible to identify all of the Spanish ships lost in the Spanish Armada, but in the case of the English Armada things are not so straightforward. To

---

[43] González-Arnao, *Derrota y muerte*, p. 98.
[44] *Dictionary of National Biography*, 1888, Vol. 15, p. 439 [translator's note].
[45] *As Told by Two Ensigns Held Prisoner in Corunna*. AGS. Guerra Antigua. File 250, fol. 348.
[46] Gracia Rivas, *La sanidad*, p. 320.
[47] See the end of Chapter 5 above.

begin with, we only have the names of eighty-four ships that set sail from Plymouth, the eighty-four on the list of 19 April which were, generally speaking, the largest vessels. Of these, only sixty-nine appear on the 15 September pay list and thus, according to Wernham, we must assume that fifteen ships were lost. Four from Plymouth: the *Thomas*, the *Fortune*, the *Nightingale*, the *Minion*; three from Dartmouth: the *Emmanuel*, the *Phoenix*, the *Crescent*; two from Hampton: the *Godspeed*, the *Gift*; from Exmouth, the *Bartholomew*; from Portsmouth, the *Relief*; from Aldeburgh, the *Greyhound*; from Foley, the *Francis*; from Dover, the *Gift* and the *Golden Hind*. It is striking that the only ship specifically mentioned as lost in English sources, the *William* from Plymouth, nevertheless appears among those that returned. Another vessel worth discussing is the *Golden Hind*.

There were two ships with that name in England at that time, one of them being one of the most famous ships in English history. It was an English copy of the *nao Victoria* with which Juan Sebastián Elcano completed the first circumnavigation of the globe. Drake was the first Englishman to do so in the *Golden Hind*,[48] fifty-eight years after Elcano. In order to accomplish that feat, the sailor from Devon had the benefit not only of Spanish maps but also of two Spanish pilots he had taken prisoner: Alonso Sánchez Cordero and Martín de Aguirre. Despite all this, Queen Elizabeth saw fit to redesignate the title earned by Elcano, and Drake added to his coat of arms the words *Primus circumdedisti me*, although to be true to history it should have been *Primus anglorum circumdedisti me*. Drake wanted to take credit not only for the first circumnavigation but also for the second, that most eventful expedition in search of the Spice Islands that set out from Corunna in 1525. On this second voyage, in which the brave Elcano found the vast ocean discovered by Balboa a fitting grave for his greatness, Francisco de Hoces, aboard his caravel *San Lesmes*, discovered the Sea of Hoces, the passage between Antarctica and the continent of America. Fifty-four years later and, incredibly, without even sailing through it – since Drake navigated by way of the Strait of Magellan – the English mariner renamed this sea Drake Passage. To do so he used only Spanish cartography or maps derived from it. Although his claim to being the first to circumnavigate the globe was not recognized, to this day maps continue to name this stormy body of water after him.[49] The other *Golden Hind* was very small – Mattingly

---

[48] It is hard to establish when the *Pelican* was renamed as the *Golden Hind*. History tells us that it happened as it crossed the Strait of Magellan but there is nothing to confirm that this was the case and the ship's crew had no knowledge of it. It probably happened later in the context of Drake turning from 'a real man into a national legend'. On this subject, see Kelsey, *Sir Francis Drake*, pp. 113–16.

[49] Drake's voyage included a premeditated and well-orchestrated propaganda campaign designed to make the world believe that Drake had sailed the Sea of Hoces. Herrera himself believed the story, but in England Drake was found out. The maps presented by Drake were uncannily similar to the existing Spanish maps of the Straits area. Thus, Reverend Richard Madox wrote: 'I am convinced that Drake had probably found some Portuguese or Spanish map and added a few comments of his own.' Actually, the Spanish maps of this crucial area, the only passage to the Pacific Ocean and at that time a possession of Philip II, had been improved during three new expeditions following the discovery by Hoces up to 1560. The passage was then mapped once and for all although in an act of cartographical piracy Drake later renamed it. Ibid., pp. 124–36.

called it a bark[50]– and took part in the English fleet of 1588 as a surveillance ship. We should not confuse the two ships; the *Golden Hind* in the English expedition could not have been Drake's ship as it was in Deptford at the time, where the Queen had ordered that it be converted into a permanent reminder of the first English circumnavigation of the globe.

Returning to the numbers of losses from the expedition, we know that of the eighty-four ships listed as setting sail, fifteen were lost. But the number of those not listed and that failed to return is unknown. In addition to the sixty-nine that are known to have set sail and returned, another thirty-three also came back, most of them medium-sized. Considering the number of boats that set off, many of them small, it must be the case that the losses among these small craft were extremely high.

At Corunna, the English abandoned several vessels: 'Two half burnt, another damaged by the Fort of San Antón, and yet another in very bad condition from the storm they had on the fourth day of the siege that lasted for six hours.'[51] Probably, according to Duro, two ships and two boats,[52] although Mariano González-Arnao puts the losses at 'three large ships and several others destroyed'.[53] Martín de Padilla sank four and Alonso de Bazán at least three as the English Armada fled from Lisbon after the failure of the expedition.[54] Two later hit the rocks at Cangas and were then set alight by the Spanish and another ran aground in the Cíes Islands.[55] When they set sail from this estuary, Marcos de Aramburu captured another two and took them to Santander.[56] However, that is all we know. The great difference between the number of vessels that set sail from Plymouth and those that returned, plus the huge mortality rate among the crews, seems to point towards a regrouping of the survivors in the larger ships and the abandonment of the smaller vessels. If the mortality rate among the crew in the larger and better supplied ships (such as the *Dreadnought*) or in the medium-sized vessels (such as the *Gregory*) was so extreme that they could hardly sail – remember that the *Gregory* only made it back to England thanks to the transfer of men from the *Bark Bonner* – we can well imagine the fate of the smaller vessels. So, without any more precise information, a figure of seventy to eighty lost vessels does not seem exaggerated. However, as in the case of the Spanish Armada, losses in combat were relatively small.

Meanwhile, the recovery of the Spanish navy was now an incontrovertible fact. The large galleons had already been repaired and set sail from Santander towards the end of July. Each squadron went to its own port to overwinter, including Lisbon, Pasajes,

---

[50]   Mattingly, *The Defeat*, p. 241. Parker describes it as a fifty-tonne pinnace. Martin and Parker, *Spanish Armada*, p. 60.

[51]   *Relación Anónima*. BN mss 3790, p. 229.

[52]   Fernández Duro, *Armada española*, III, p. 48.

[53]   González Arnao, *Derrota y muerte*, p. 76.

[54]   Fernández Duro, *Armada española*, III, p. 48; González Arnao, *Derrota y muerte*, p. 93. This excludes the released *urcas* with captured crews.

[55]   William Fenner to Anthony Bacon, 1589. Wernham, *Expedition*, p. 241.

[56]   González Arnao, *Derrota y muerte*, p. 94.

Portugalete and the Cuatro Villas, while part of the armada assembled in Corunna.[57] In this way, the Spanish coast was protected once more and the opportunity that England had enjoyed during the early months of 1589 was dead and buried. However, this was not the end of the consequences of the failure of the English Armada. In a letter of 26 August, Alonso de Bazán, following orders from the King, sent a detailed report on the new Spanish Armada, which was designed to achieve what the original Armada could not. This new fleet would consist of 186 ships and vessels, allocated as follows: 100 large ships, 30 small *naos*, 20 *zabras*, 20 galleys, 12 pataches and 4 galleasses. It would transport 40,000 soldiers, '30,000 for landing and 10,000 to stay on board, fight the enemy and do whatever is required for the ships', 18,880 sailors and 5,000 sappers, a total of 63,880 men. It is interesting to see how Bazán applied the lessons of the failure of the Spanish Armada: in the first place, the large ships were galleons and *naos*, but there were no *urcas*, given their earlier disastrous performance. Also, 'thirty small ships should accompany the fleet to take part in skirmishing, since they are light, able to chase the enemy ships and board them'. The report also clearly emphasizes the reform of artillery planning, insisting on ships 'very well manned and armed with long-range artillery'. It also highlights that

> pinnaces are most useful as has been proven on many occasions, since they serve the same purpose as the enemy launches and to land men and artillery, and they can be armed with a couple of *versos* (light artillery pieces) on the bow. If necessary half a dozen can tow a *nao* to come in and out of port, and so every *nao* should have its own on the stern, to be manned by sailors from that same *nao*.

To sum up, the new armada would be made up of warships only, which were more seaworthy than transport ships. It would have a much higher percentage of smaller vessels, and it would have longer range artillery. In short, it was designed to fight in the same way as Howard's intercepting squadron, keeping its distance and relying on the lightness of its smaller ships and its long-range artillery. With the new Spanish approach, it would be much more difficult for English ships to keep their distance and avoid being boarded, and their merely artillery-based strategy would give them no advantage. Above all, and this is key, the new armada would not be hindered by the tiresome task of escorting Farnese's barges. Freed from this burden, it would be at liberty to head for the English coast and set about landing its men.

This armada would be considerably more powerful than its predecessor, both in numbers of ships and men. In his report, Bazán gives the specific name of every one of the vessels, which include those of the original Spanish Armada, as well as the twelve galleons whose construction Philip II had commissioned in January 1589 – the so-called Twelve Apostles, already being fitted out in Portugalete and Guarnizo. There were also

---

[57] *Relación de los navíos del Armada y el Repartimiento que dellos se ha hecho para ir a invernar en los puertos.* (Account of the ships of the Armada and the ports to which they were sent to overwinter.) Alonso de Bazán, Corunna, 14 August 1589. AGS. Guerra Antigua File 250, fol. 353.

another six galleons being built in Portugal, a number of vessels to be taken from the fleets and other vessels to be seized at several locations. The report also offers specific data on the exact composition and the places of origin of the armada's vessels. It also explained that

> since the armada must overwinter in a such scattered fashion and must come together from so many different places, a place should be appointed for ships to do so, and the best port for it is at Corunna, given its capacity for many ships and because supplies are more abundant in Galicia this year than in any other part of Spain.[58]

This project, as we shall see, would be completely altered and Bazán's plan for 1590 would not be put into effect. It illustrates, however, how right Elizabeth was – albeit in vain – to make the destruction of the restored Spanish fleet the primary objective of the English Armada. It also shows how significant was their failure to do so. The Spanish had realized the mistakes of the original Spanish Armada and were set on extending their control of the ocean routes for centuries to come in order to maintain their well-established empire. The danger of invasion was hovering over England once again and fear spread over the coastal towns, especially in Plymouth.[59]

Back in England, the pamphlets were published in August and a little later Drake and Norris made their inevitable appearance in London. After marathon sessions, nothing could prevent the commission charged with evaluating the outcome of the expedition from pronouncing its final verdict: the adventure had not only been a financial disaster but also a strategic one. The men responsible for this were Drake and Norris. However, the Queen did not amend the triumphalist letter of 17 June and the military leaders were not publicly admonished. They did fall out of favour, but at the same time the pamphlets circulated throughout Europe acclaiming their fictitious epic triumph. The limited bibliography that deals with this event was based upon these pamphlets and this is one of the main reasons why this vital episode has all but vanished from history, while another similar episode became one of its greatest legends.

---

[58] *Relación de las naos y otros bajeles que parece son menester para la jornada de el año que viene, los que hay en ser, y las partes donde se han de proveer los que faltaren, y la gente de guerra, y más que se ha de embarcar en ellos.* (Report on the *naos* and other vessels required for next year's expedition, those that already exist and where others need to be provided, and the fighting men and others who are to sail in them.) Alonso de Bazán, 26 August 1589. AGS. Guerra Antigua. File 250, fol. 536.

[59] During the spring of 1590, the news of preparations for a new armada caused many of Plymouth's inhabitants to flee from the town in high panic with their belongings. It was presumed the new attempted invasion would begin there. The old town's castle had its artillery strengthened and the roofs were covered with sheets of lead. Similar reinforcements took place on the Isle of St Nicholas and to pay for them a tax on sardines was authorized. In order to avoid it, the Cornish fishermen landed their catches at Cawsand Bay. Kelsey, *Sir Francis Drake*, pp. 370–1.

PART 3

The War Goes On

Chapter 32

A Glove, a Lion and El Dorado

From that moment on the war became even more cruel, producing many tales worthy of being told. We will deal with them only briefly, paying particular attention to the subsequent fate of those who took part in the great unsuccessful expeditions. The lesson was clear: the conditions on the seas, from the capabilities of the ships of the time to the limitations of medicine, militated against making long voyages, especially in the hostile waters of the English Channel. The imperatives of war, however, required the assembly of large fleets, and although operations on such a scale were not repeated, Philip II would be thwarted yet again by the stumbling block of the sea conditions surrounding the British Isles.

The English failure of 1589 and the uneventful arrival of the Spanish fleet from the West Indies gave Philip enough time for a vigorous resumption of the war and the opportunity to continue the massive naval construction plan that was soon to bear fruit. The failure of the Spanish Armada had caused Philip to abandon the age-old practice of *asentamiento*, the chartering and requisitioning of privately owned vessels designed for transport. Instead, he began to order the systematic building of galleons for his exclusive use. A number of towns on the northern Spanish coast were also fortified, among them Corunna and Ferrol.[1] Without wasting any time, a new expedition was prepared, due to leave from Corunna the following year. However, the struggle had become more complex due to the emergence of two clear-cut poles: the "Catholic Monarchy" and the powers that aimed to oppose it under the banner of a Protestant rebellion. The fact that France was embroiled in a war of religion, where the Protestant Huguenots seemed to have the upper hand, and the fact that Brittany was situated en route to England and Flanders – both hotbeds of the rebellion – powerfully shifted the theatre of operations in the direction of the Breton coast.

A new armada of thirty-seven ships and 6,470 men set sail to Brittany from Corunna in September 1590. The Spanish successfully landed there and consolidated their presence in the south of Brittany. Cristóbal de Rojas, one of the outstanding military engineers of the age, oversaw the construction of two modern forts in Blavet (Port Louis) built by soldiers and sailors. Blavet became a secure base for operations.[2]

Incursions on the English coast and the plunder of English and Dutch shipping by corsairs followed. The rearmament of the fleet began to show results. One hundred ships, either repaired or recently built and totalling 48,200 tonnes, were ready in the summer of 1590.[3] The Indies fleet continued operating undisturbed throughout the war,

---

[1]   Cerezo Martínez, *Las Armadas*, pp. 388–9.
[2]   Fernández Duro, *Armada española*, III, pp. 69–73.
[3]   Ibid., III, p. 79.

escorted by warships, although the English continued to be obsessed with trying to intercept it and its extraordinary treasures. Indeed, Cumberland was on the prowl in the spring, and was fought off by Don Francisco Coloma with five galleys, who captured a galleon, a large *zabra* and a caravel.

Thomas Howard, first Earl of Suffolk, was also out on the hunt off the Azores and got involved in a much more substantial challenge. He had the misfortune to run into a powerful fleet of fifty-five ships and 7,200 men under the command of Don Alonso de Bazán. The English had twenty-two ships, including six large galleons, and were intent on seizing the cargo of precious metals.[4] The English lay in ambush in the channel between the Islands of Corvo and Flores, which the fleet had to pass through, but themselves fell into the trap laid by Alonso de Bazán's larger fleet.

Then came one of the most poignant moments of the war for the Spanish. Martín de Bertendona saw his dream made reality. One of the English ships did not manage to escape and it was none other than Drake's *Revenge*. It was the same ship that had been the scourge of the Spanish Armada in the channel, the one that had witnessed the end of Recalde's legendary *San Juan* in Corunna. The *Revenge* had been responsible for the many acts of violence that had made the name of the most famous English pirate.[5] Like the *San Juan*, the *Revenge* went down bravely, having been hit repeatedly and boarded by several Spanish ships. One of them was Bertendona's, though the Spanish mariner must have felt bitterly disappointed when he found that on this occasion Drake was not the captain.

Drake had been demoted to supervising the coastal defences of Plymouth by Queen Elizabeth, who was furious with his behaviour in Corunna and Lisbon. But the *Revenge* did not suffer because Drake had been replaced. The new captain, brave Richard Grenville, was armed to the teeth with muskets, incendiary devices and forty-two magnificent bronze cannons (the best English ships, like the Spanish, were armed with bronze cannon; the supposed supremacy of English cast iron would have caused English captains of the period to blush).[6] With all that power, Grenville did not contemplate

---

[4]   Duro, *Armada española*, III, pp. 79–80.

[5]   Whether Drake should be referred to as a 'pirate' or a 'privateer' is a very difficult question. The term 'privateer' can be defended on the grounds that he was acting with licence from the Queen and on behalf of his country. But privateers operate in times of war, not in times of peace. Since the Queen allowed his activities in times of peace, he can also be considered to be a pirate, but a pirate of the Queen. Interestingly, this is the title of the book by Harry Kelsey, included in the bibliography: *Sir Francis Drake: The Queen's Pirate*. In any event, in Spanish eyes Drake is not only a pirate, but the most famous of all English pirates, which is no small matter.

[6]   Bronze was the alloy of preference for the manufacture of cannon. Those made of iron were viewed as weapons of the poor, and in addition they were also dangerous: 'In my opinion those made solely of iron should use casts, and if used with care can be put to good use and be safe, whereas all the rest are mortally dangerous.' Diego Garcia De Palacio, *Instrucción Náutica para el buen uso y regimiento de las Naos* (México, 1587). Bronze was more reliable than iron and had better physical properties. In addition, it was better at resisting corrosion from seawater and importantly it did not cause a spark when striking against other metals. Bronze cannon were also lighter than those made of iron, which needed to be thicker for the same calibre. But iron cannon had some advantages: they were a lot cheaper and they could fire up to five shots before they needed to be cooled, whereas bronze cannon had to be cooled after three. Hence, with lower thermal

surrender but defended every inch of the deck and later did the same from the aftercastle. His conduct was heroic and the Spanish suffered many casualties because of it. In its last stand, the *Revenge* was redeemed for the countless times that its regular captain had fled from a fight. Grenville, impractical in this regard, behaved rather as would have been expected from a Spanish captain. He only surrendered after the ship had sustained major damage, 150 men were out of action and he was seriously wounded. He was quickly taken to Bazán's flagship, where he was treated with the respect that his courage deserved, but there was nothing the surgeons could do about the harquebus shot that had wounded him in the head. And so the hunter – Drake's *Revenge* – became the hunted and Bertendona saw at least some of his hopes of revenge fulfilled. As for the ships that fled, they had been hit from short range under the waterline while their hulls had been tilted by the strong wind.[7]

A Spanish presence in the Azores was vital that summer, as the treasure fleet had to take that route. It was divided into two groups of eleven and forty-eight ships and had been badly battered by a hurricane. It would probably have been unable to withstand an English attack. A few days later, at anchor off Terceira, a new storm caused the loss of sixteen vessels, although their men and provisions were saved. Indeed, the sea itself was a much worse enemy than the pirates for the West Indies fleet, which was made up of transport and escort ships. Of its total losses throughout its history, only 10 per cent was accounted for by corsairs and buccaneers. The remaining 90 per cent was the work of the sea. In light of this, its success, in the face of the often terrible conditions for sailing ships in the sixteenth and seventeenth centuries, can only be described as outstanding.

The following year, 1592, four English squadrons under Raleigh, Hawkins, Frobisher and the Earl of Cumberland again tried to intercept the treasure fleet. Raleigh was hit by a storm in Finisterre that scattered his ships, six of which were captured by the fleet of Pedro de Zubiaur. The other three fleets won a great prize in the end as, after a stubborn defence lasting a night and a day by Captain Fernando de Mendoza and his men, the Portuguese *nao Madre de Dios* was captured, with a cargo valued at half a million pounds (although owing to irregularities in dividing up the booty, the Queen received only one hundred and fifty thousand). This was the most valuable prize seized thus far.[8] The determination of the English to charter vessels to intercept ships laden with treasure made a good deal of sense, since the profits they made could significantly enhance the crown's annual budget. In this regard, the flood of precious metals into the Spanish economy was so overwhelming that the inflation that it caused permanently destroyed the country's productive structure, simply because everything was so much cheaper abroad. Not only this, it also strengthened the production of Spain's enemies. So, paradoxically, the success of the treasure fleet brought about Spain's eventual collapse.

conductivity and a higher melting temperature, iron cannon were considered to be 'cold weapons' and could maintain a better firing rate once they were heated. On this subject see Antonio Luis Gómez Beltrán, *La invencible y su leyenda negra* (Málaga: Arin Ediciones, 2013), p. 228–31.

[7]   Fernández Duro, *Armada española*, III, p. 81.

[8]   Ibid., III, p. 82.

While this conflict took place at sea, the struggle continued in Brittany, but with a happy outcome for the Catholics who began to tip the balance in their favour in Craon. The town was under siege by Norris, who was back in active service after a period of suspension from duties by the Queen as punishment for his failures in Corunna and Lisbon. He was allied with French Huguenots who were reinforced by German troops. Together they had 6,500 infantry, 1,000 horses and twelve artillery pieces. Don Juan del Águila headed there with 2,000 Spaniards, eight hundred horses and five hundred Breton infantrymen. In spite of the superior numbers of the Protestant army, the experience of Don Juan del Águila and the bravery of his musketeers gave them a most notable victory. They killed 1,500 of the enemy, took many prisoners – among them two hundred knights for ransom – and seized artillery, munition carts, banners, baggage and provisions.

In reprisal for the inhuman cruelty shown by the English towards the shipwrecked men of the Spanish Armada, the Spanish gave no quarter and the death toll would have been even higher had the rye not grown so high, enabling many of the enemy to hide. A map and a description of the Battle of Craon was sent by Cristóbal de Rojas to the King.[9] The battle marked the start of a turning point in the war and was also important because it was the first time the famous Tercio regiments had fought on that front.

The time had come to march on Brest, a Huguenot bastion much supported by the English for its strategic location close to the English Channel. But this was when Philip made clear that it was the cause of religion that was paramount to him. The war against the United Provinces of the Netherlands and England took second place to the more pressing issue of preventing a French defection from the Catholic camp. Religious unity within Christianity was a key element in counteracting Ottoman and Islamic power and a Protestant France would align openly with Philip's enemies. Thus his efforts were devoted to the war against the French Huguenots with the sole aim, which was later made apparent, of preserving Catholicism in the neighbouring country. The Breton forces were ordered to head south to Guyenne where, after brilliant naval action, they lifted the siege of Bordeaux.

The war then became extraordinarily complex, with many different fronts and protagonists, and the Anglo-Spanish conflict was absorbed into a much wider struggle. Philip, who was focussed on France, had the Tercios regiments sent from Flanders to Paris, against the judgement of the Duke of Parma. Their absence in Flanders led to important losses on that front, such as Breda and Maastricht, which was taken by Maurice of Nassau. This absence, however, also made it possible for Henry of Navarre to undergo one of the most famous conversions in the history of religion. Henry, the belligerent Huguenot candidate to the French throne, was also a skilful politician. In July 1593 he allegedly made the famous statement 'Paris is well worth a Mass', embraced Catholicism and was crowned King of France. The focus of the war in France began to move away from religion and towards territorial matters.

---

[9] Fernández Duro, *Armada española*, III, p. 84.

To return to the Anglo-Spanish conflict, in 1594 there occurred one of its most epic episodes, that of fort Crozon, called by the Spanish *El León* (The Lion). In spite of his conversion to Catholicism the previous year in order to deprive Philip of the grounds to oppose him and seize the French crown, Henry of Navarre continued to support the Protestant cause. France was engaged in a complex struggle in which political affiliations or interests were superimposed upon religious ones and the result was a growing opposition to the power of Philip II. A good example of this was the role of the Duke of Mercoeur, ostensibly an ally of the Spanish in Brittany but secretly a supporter of the Huguenots and the Anglo-Dutch.

It was in these circumstances that Don Juan del Águila reached the Quélern peninsula, opposite the port of Brest, and there began work on a fascine fort made of wood and earth and designed by Rojas. Mercoeur protested and demanded that the fort be dismantled. Don Juan del Águila refused, on the grounds that English ships were in the area, and also that culverins had already been mounted on the fort. However, the Spanish were alone in Brittany by then and in open conflict with the French, English and Dutch. Don Juan del Águila detailed Captain Tomé Paredes and three hundred men to finish work on the fort and returned to Blavet. The Baron of Molac soon arrived with 3,000 Frenchmen, along with Norris with as many English soldiers, three hundred mounted harquebusiers, four hundred volunteer knights and René de Rieux, the Governor of Brest, with local militia and the artillery of the city castle.

The attackers opened up the trenches on 11 October and were supported by the constant fire from English and Dutch ships, but they suffered severe casualties because they were forced to use gabions (large cages full of earth used as a parapet for the men opening up the trenches). While they filled these up, they were exposed to gunfire from the fort, and later were subjected day and night to the frequent sallies of the Spanish. They finally managed to mount a battery of twelve heavy guns, which provided them with constant fire, and succeeded in breaking the fascines so the earth they contained began to spill into the moat. The French troops under the Baron of Molac then attacked the bulwark on the right, while Norris did the same on the left, in a competitive assault that lasted for three hours and ended with numerous casualties for both forces. The attackers had to wait for a convoy from Brest, giving Captain Paredes time to rebuild the stockade and repair the bulwarks.

The second assault was even more damaging to the Protestants, with the Spanish coming out of the bulwark and disabling three of the enemy cannon. Ammunition was running low at the fort, so they requested reinforcements from Don Juan del Águila, who was marching with 4,000 infantrymen. Águila had been stopped not only by enemy cavalry but also by their supposed ally. On 18 November, the Protestants attacked yet again with fresh columns, including one consisting of English sailors led by Frobisher, admiral of one of the squadrons that had pursued the Spanish Armada in the channel. With Don Juan only four leagues away from the fort, the Protestant forces redoubled their attacks with three more assaults. Paredes was killed during the last of these, in the thick of the fight and with pike in hand. At nightfall on 19 November, a mine was detonated and still the attackers were driven back. Once it became dark they used the stratagem of a flag of parley and took the bulwark, where there was only one officer left alive. The casualties acknowledged by the Protestants were around 3,000, among them many commanders and distinguished figures, including Frobisher himself.

They were utterly astonished to discover the small number of Spanish soldiers, most of whom had been killed. The English cut the throats of the surviving prisoners on account of the defeat at Craon, with as many women and children as soldiers. Only nine men hidden among the corpses survived, along with another four who managed to scramble down the rocks to the sea. Marshal d'Aumont, Supreme Commander of the French forces, had Paredes buried with full honours in Brest Cathedral and compared him to Achilles in his epitaph. French historians considered the resistance put up by the Spanish to be exceptional; Freminville stated that at fort Crozon the fundamental nature of each nation was made apparent: 'The Spaniard, cool, patient, daring and stubborn; the Englishman, brutally courageous and cruel in victory; the Frenchman, respectful, brave, generous towards the defeated enemy, whose courage he admires and whom he honours in his misfortune.'[10]

Don Juan del Águila arrived soon afterwards and razed the fort to the ground, as he knew the Protestants wanted to occupy it. Ever since then the place has been known as *Pointe des Espagnols*, and in Breton the word *real* continued to be used to mean 'small coins'. These coins were used as ammunition by the defenders, along with nails, stones and other hard objects. Juan del Águila informed the King that the loss of the fort was nothing to get upset about and that with men and money it could be finished off and made completely impregnable. However, the imperatives of war were heading in a different direction – towards maritime incursions. What stands out above all else is that Frobisher, one of the greatest English admirals to take part in the war, died at *Pointe des Espagnols*.

Once Henry, as King of France, had converted to Catholicism and was crowned – in spite of his new faith not being forced upon the nation as a whole – Spain focused on blockading England. To this end, numerous vessels were chartered for the purpose of privateering in the English Channel, causing serious damage to the English and Dutch seaborne trade. Not satisfied with this, Carlos de Amezola sailed from Blavet with four reinforced galleys on 26 July 1595 and, after seizing money and supplies from the Normandy Huguenots, he crossed the channel bound for Cornwall. On 4 August, he landed at Mount's Bay with four hundred harquebusiers and a few pikemen and marched on Mousehole. While three galleys bombarded the town, the *Peregrina* sailed out to Cape Cornwall to watch for enemy ships. The troops set fire to Mousehole and advanced to Penzance, taking the fort that protected the coast and three loaded ships, despite 1,200 men putting up a show of defending it. On their march they destroyed Penzance, Newlyn, Saint Paul, Church Town and a number of nearby villages. The following day, a Catholic mass was held within sight of the enemy and then the fort's

---

[10] Quoted in Fernández Duro, *Armada española*, III, p. 91.

artillery was dismantled and taken on board. On the third day of their stay on English soil, they learned that the governor of the region was coming to the rescue with several thousand men and, in anticipation of the fact that the English fleet based in Plymouth would cut off their retreat, Amezola released his prisoners and left the country. On his return journey he sighted a convoy of forty-six Dutch merchantmen escorted by four warships. These were attacked; two were sunk and the other two damaged. Amezola lost twenty men in the battle and his ships were hit repeatedly, but all four galleys made it back to Blavet two weeks after their departure.[11] Martín de Oleaga also landed in England with the aim of setting ships alight.[12]

The English were stung by these attacks and they precipitated Drake's final, ill-fated voyage. The Spanish, however, were merely satisfied at having done their duty without expecting any booty or recompense from a poor country. In aiming at a richer one, the English had logically been motivated more by temptation and self-interest. Preparations for privateering activities continued through personal initiatives. England had now become the base for countless such incursions rather than a country properly at war, and a single success among many setbacks made it all worthwhile. In 1593, the Earl of Cumberland embarked on his sixth expedition to the Azores, this time with twelve ships. Once again he failed.[13]

However, the fiasco of Richard Hawkins is better known. Richard, the son of John Hawkins, set sail from Plymouth on 22 June of the same year with three ships, the largest of which was the flagship, the *Dainty*, built by his father and armed with twenty guns. Adverse winds prevented him from approaching the Canary Islands, which had had their defences weakened by the attack of the Algerian Captain Xavan. After a long voyage in which Hawkins lost the other two ships, he managed to cross the Strait of Magellan, appearing by surprise in Valparaíso, Chile, where he captured five coastal vessels. He set four of them free for a ransom of 25,000 ducats and retained the fifth. This was a big mistake as one of the freed vessels set course for Peru, where it soon arrived and alerted the viceroy. A flotilla of three galleons was prepared and, although they found Hawkins, they did not manage to attack him and returned to Lima thwarted and damaged by a storm. In anticipation of this eventuality, however, Don García Hurtado de Mendoza had prepared a *galizabra* – a small vessel that was also strong

---

[11] Cerezo Martínez, *Las Armadas*, pp. 400–1. Amezola's adventure is recounted in *Relación de lo subçedido en el viaje que por orden de V. M. ha hecho el capitán Carlos de Amezola con las cuatro galeras de su cargo en la costa del reino de Inglaterra.* (Account of what happened on the voyage undertaken on the King's orders by Captain Carlos de Amezola with the four galleys under his command near the coast of the Kingdom.) Copied in the collection Sans de Barutell, art. 4, no. 1242. Larrey deals with it in his *History of England* and John Paine in *The Naval History of Great Britain*. References in Fernández Duro, *Armada española*, III, pp. 92–3.

[12] *Relación del desembarco que hizo en Inglaterra el capitán Martín de Oleaga y buques que incendió con los dos pataches de su cargo.* (Account of the landing of Captain Martín de Oleaga in England and the vessels that he set alight with the two *pataches* under his command.) Copied in the collection Sans de Barutell, art. 6, no. 142. References in Fernández Duro, *Armada española*, III, pp. 92–3.

[13] Ibid., pp. 95–6.

and light – and a brigantine. These two ships were accompanied by one of the hastily repaired galleons and set out to inspect every inlet of the coast until they found the English ship at Atacames, near Quito, on 1 July. After a bitter fight including hand-to-hand combat on the deck of the *Dainty*, Richard Hawkins surrendered on condition that their lives were spared. The noble knight Don Beltrán de Castro complied, giving him a glove as a pledge for his word.

The *Dainty* was a powerful, tastefully designed ship in which John Hawkins had invested his wealth and which boasted the coat of arms he had adopted when knighted. It was repaired in Panama and under the name *La inglesa* sailed for many years with the fleet of the South Seas. Don Beltrán de Castro forcefully defended his word and had the death sentence issued against the English by the Inquisition overturned. He had his glove considered by the council of the Indies and after a long trial Richard Hawkins finally managed to return to England.[14]

Cumberland did not sail on his annual Azores expedition in 1594, but three of his ships attacked a Portuguese *nao*, *Cinco Chagas*. The Portuguese put up such a fight – killing ninety men including the admiral and vice admiral and wounding one hundred and fifty – that the privateers let it burn with its crew on board. The Portuguese in the water begging for mercy were sent to the bottom, except for the thirteen who were seen wearing gold necklaces. Even the English historian John Barrow criticizes the cruelty of his countrymen.[15] Later, the English came upon the galleon *San Felipe* and invited it to surrender. Don Luis Coutiño answered that he was not a man given to surrendering without first trying out his weapons, as they should know from how Grenville's *Revenge* had fared. The English came off worse in the ensuing skirmish and fled with their wretched booty, with the *Cinco Chagas* already at the bottom of the sea. Cumberland, who was embittered by his repeated failures, returned in person for the next campaign in the Azores. In their only encounter with the Spanish, Captain Laughton was confronted by the Spanish flagship sailing apart from the rest of the fleet and was punished by the powerful galleon.

One of the most charged episodes in English history worth recounting is that of Antonio de Berrio y Oruña, a veteran soldier who inherited a large fortune and set out to find El Dorado, which had been forgotten about following the failed ventures

---

[14] The vicissitudes of Hawkins and his men were extremely complex and generated a great deal of correspondence. In Lima, 'Richarte Aquines' was reinstated and protected by Don Beltrán and became very popular. Nevertheless, nothing could stop the Inquisition from taking its own brand of interest in the English captives. Aside from the no small matter of their 'heresy', they were in possession of crucial knowledge about the South Seas that had to be kept from being spread to Europe, 'for information about navigation in this sea could be damaging there'. Don Beltrán struggled long and hard, going as far as writing to the King to justify having given his word. In 1597 Hawkins was sent to Spain and was not finally freed until 1602, on the grounds that 'the word of the King's captains must be kept, for otherwise he would not have surrendered'. The conditions of his captivity, however, were very benign. On this subject see José Toribio Medina, *Historia del Tribunal del Santo Oficio de la Inquisición en Chile*, Santiago de Chile, 1932, I, Chapter 15.

[15] John Barrow, *Memories of Naval Worthies*, cited in Fernández Duro, *Armada española*, III, p. 101.

of Orellana.[16] Berrio organized three unsuccessful expeditions in the Orinoco basin and news of his travels reached Walter Raleigh, who decided to try his luck where the Spanish had failed. Raleigh set sail in February 1595 with five ships and the same number of pinnaces in search of the lost city.

He reached Port of Spain in Trinidad and presented himself as a smuggler, landing on the beach in a barge bearing a white flag. He invited the sixteen Spanish soldiers put on watch by Berrio, governor of the island, to come aboard the flagship, fed them and then treacherously murdered them all. One hundred and twenty Englishmen marched from Port of Spain to San José, three leagues away, where Berrio had twenty-five Castilians. Eight of the Spanish were killed in the skirmish while seventeen were able to flee with their women folk. After setting fire to the barracks, the English moved on to Punta del Gallo on the coast of present-day Venezuela, where they built a wooden fort and equipped it with three cannon. They forced the elderly Berrio to be their guide and followed the course of the Orinoco. They soon came into contact with the Caribs and, according to the fantasy account written by Raleigh after he returned to England, they found a goldmine, a glass mountain and many other fabulous sites. Raleigh promised to deliver the natives from the Spanish yoke and even left two men with them to learn their language. One of them ended up in a Madrid prison after being handed over by the Caribs. The other was used for a cannibal feast once the English had left.[17]

It is important to highlight here the remarkable speed of the Iberian conquest of the Americas. This made it impossible for the English, Dutch and French to make a serious attempt to apply the strategy tried out by Raleigh, that is, using the indigenous peoples as allies to establish settlements and break up the Spanish Empire. By the time the other Europeans reached the continent, all they could do was rob and loot. The Dutch made a very earnest attempt to settle in Brazil during the seventeenth century and their defeat and expulsion was the last of the great efforts of a Spanish Empire that was well on the way to complete exhaustion. It would not recover until well into the eighteenth century.

Returning to the expedition, Raleigh headed next for Margarita Island, but the Spanish had been alerted so he sailed on to Cabo de la Vela in what is now Colombia. However, the news of his presence had spread all over the region and three of his men were taken prisoner. Later another seven were killed in the attack on Cumaná. There he let Antonio de Berrio go and would have ended the expedition had he not come across the mulatto Villalpando, who became an unexpected but valuable guide. Raleigh

---

[16] In 1541, in search of the supposed city of El Dorado, Francisco de Orellana accompanied Gonzalo Pizarro, half-brother of the *conquistador* Francisco Pizarro, as his lieutenant on an expedition down the Amazon in search of a valley to the east, purportedly rich in both cinnamon and gold. Gonzalo left the expedition but Orellana continued downstream, eventually reaching the Atlantic Ocean. The expedition found neither cinnamon nor gold, but Orellana is credited with mapping the Amazon River. See Buddy Levy, *River of Darkness: Francisco Orellana's Legendary Voyage of Death and Discovery down the Amazon* (Random House, 2011) [translator's note].

[17] Antonio Herrera y Tordesillas, *Historia general del Mundo* (Madrid, 1612), III, p. 585. Fernández Duro, *Armada española*, III, p. 104.

avoided the defences of La Guaira, crossed the Guaicamacuto Mountains and came upon Caracas whose only remaining inhabitant was the elderly Alonso Andrea de Ledesma. The old man – like Don Quixote on his steed Rocinante – rode a one-man charge against the English and lost his life in the process. Raleigh then asked for a ransom in return for not setting fire to the town, which Governor Garci González de Silva refused, so the town was burnt down. Raleigh withdrew to the ships empty handed but not before leaving their guide, the mulatto renegade Villalpando, hanging from a tree.

There is a tragic coda to the story. Raleigh wrote a fanciful tale which amazed Europe, despite the fact that in the opinion of the English historian Martin Hume it is full of scurrilous lies. Nevertheless, as a result, the agents of Antonio de Berrio gave more credit to Raleigh than to the explorers who had searched for El Dorado on so many previous occasions, and they prepared another expedition with four hundred families. In the end all of them, including Berrio, died of hunger or illness or were killed by the arrows of the Caribs.[18] It gives us pause to reflect that the myths created by the English had a great influence in Spain, even to the extent that they were believed without question. What could be called 'Berrization', in memory of the adventurer who was taken in by the myth of El Dorado, was a determining factor in Spain's obsession with the topics that would later transform Spanish historiography regarding the history of Spain itself. The replacement of twenty years of war by the 'defeat' of the 'Invincible' armada is the most striking example.

[18]   Fernández Duro, *Armada española*, III, p. 105.

Chapter 33

The End of Drake and Hawkins

Soon after the seafaring and literary endeavours of Raleigh and following the sacking of Mousehole, Newlyn and Penzance, Queen Elizabeth prepared a grand new expedition against Philip's empire. After the failure in Corunna and Lisbon, this time the target would be the Americas. The task was entrusted to the most high-ranking captains, Francis Drake and John Hawkins.[1] Never before had England put together such a large fleet bound for the New World. Drake declared to his men that this time he was going not 'as a thief in the night, but as a general in broad daylight', and he would demand submission from the Spanish and put thrones in the houses of the *Audiencias*,[2] which would bear the arms of the Queen for ever after. Elizabeth considered that the years spent by Drake overseeing Plymouth's defences had been punishment enough for the failure of 1589. Now he could return, at the height of his powers, to the sea where his escapades had begun. He was, however, heading for a sad end, for following his encounter with María Pita in Corunna, he never again enjoyed the sweet taste of success.

On 6 October 1595, twenty-eight ships preparing to attack were sighted from the town of Las Palmas in the Canary Islands. Fifteen took up positions opposite the castle of Santa Catalina, nine bombarded the castle of Santa Ana and the landing began with forty-seven barges. Don Alonso de Alvarado came out to prevent this landing with all the men available, including the bishop himself and a number of bellicose friars. With six small light cannon they sank four barges and in view of the way events were turning out, Drake gave the order to retreat, having been overwhelmed by heavy musket fire. He tried once more at the harbour of Arguineguín but again was met with resistance and so sailed on.[3]

Here we see the truth of the well-known adage that Man is the only creature that makes the same mistake twice, for this most famous of English pirates repeated the error he made six years earlier during his previous expedition: he stopped for supposedly easy booty on the way to his main goal, giving his foes the opportunity and the time

---

[1]   This was actually a plan announced at length by Drake and the Queen had authorized it months earlier. She even contributed £30,000 and six ships. For their part, Drake and Hawkins contributed £10,000 each. Amezola's action, however, incensed Elizabeth and was a factor in overcoming the delays and caution in the face of a possible Spanish attack in support of the Irish Catholics, which was keeping English ships on the English south coast. Cerezo Martínez, *Las Armadas*, p. 402.

[2]   The *Audiencias* in the Americas had the judicial functions of their counterparts in Spain but also legislative and executive ones [translator's note].

[3]   Fernández Duro, *Armada española*, III, p. 106. But before leaving he stopped to water and, in so doing, several Englishmen were killed and captured, among them the surgeon of the *Solomon*, who was forced to reveal the plans of the expedition. Kelsey, *Sir Francis Drake*, p. 382.

to prepare their defence, which would lead to a new and final failure.[4] A fast vessel was sent from the Canaries to alert both the Antilles and the South American mainland provinces.

That year, the flagship of Sancho Pardo, which belonged to the Indies' escort fleet, lost its mast during a storm at night. It had managed, albeit not without difficulty, to reach San Juan in Puerto Rico on its own and deposit its cargo of three million pesos at the fortress. Sancho Pardo sent a missive to Spain – where the intentions of the English were well known – and five light frigates were dispatched with the mission to bring Pardo and the treasure back straight away. When the frigates reached the island of Guadeloupe, they captured an English vessel and learned that Drake, who had found out about the treasure hidden in the Puerto Rican fortress, was assembling large launches that had been transported in pieces in his ships, for the assault on San Juan.

After careful deliberation, it was decided to defend the town, for apart from the seven hundred active local men available there were three hundred from the damaged flagship and five hundred from the five frigates. Governor Pedro Juárez used the ships' artillery to set up batteries at the entry to the port and atop various high places while the sailors sank the damaged flagship plus another merchant ship in the entry channel in order to block it. The frigates were then set in a row behind the obstacle, companies were deployed on the beaches and at inlets that were easily reached for landing, and there they waited for the enemy.

Here is a fine example of the difficulty involved in defending the vast empire, which was not yet populated by many Spaniards, for there was hardly any place where there was a sufficiently large concentration of forces capable of facing the timely attack of a large squadron of ships. By itself, the Spanish presence in the Americas was a very powerful one, but it was scattered over millions of square kilometres and consequently defending any given place from a powerful attack posed major problems.

For this reason, Philip II thought it more practical to concentrate his power in a decisive assault against the pirates' home territory than to attempt to fight a defensive war in the Americas. But the Spanish Armada had failed and although the King was preparing further expeditions with the same purpose, the attacks that year could not be avoided. In any case, not only had the plan for naval rearmament borne fruit by multiplying Spain's presence in the Atlantic, but the costly fortifications built across the Seven Seas must also be taken into account. In other words, the state of the defences of San Juan de Puerto Rico was no longer the same as Drake had known in his youth.

On Wednesday, 22 November, twenty-three large ships appeared in formation, preceded by a caravel and forty large landing launches. Some of these headed for the port under white flags, but the Spanish were well aware of such ruses, which had been used the year before by Raleigh, and opened fire from the forts of Morrillo and Boquerón. Having been driven back from there, the English headed for the small bay of El Cabrón,

---

[4]   It was Drake himself, after a bitter argument with Hawkins in which he threatened to go on his own with only half the fleet, who forced the expedition to deviate from the initial plan and attack the Canaries. Kelsey, *Sir Francis Drake*, p. 382.

unaware that one of the batteries strategically placed by Governor Pedro Juárez was waiting there patiently for them to come within range.

It was here that one of the most important English admirals lost his life. A cannon-ball from the tremendous barrage from the battery at El Cabrón that rained upon the invading fleet killed John Hawkins, although English historians maintain that he died of illness. One way or another, the privateer and admiral died there, while his old ship, the *Dainty* – converted in Panama into *La inglesa* – sailed the seas bearing the coat of arms of the unfortunate mariner. Above it was the wooden effigy of a beautiful black woman decorated with gold, a symbol of the greatness of the corsair who that day met a watery grave.[5]

The English fleet was forced to flee quickly from the coast and continue sailing nearby. During that night of mourning, the launches searched for an appropriate place to land. There was a light wind at dawn on 23 November and with the fleet sheltered close to an islet, their exploration of the coast continued. They made several dummy attacks, forcing the defenders to march back and forth. At 10.00 pm, twenty-five launches slipped under Morro castle, out of range of its artillery, and attacked the frigates with incendiary devices. In three of them they managed to put out the fire, but the *Magdalena* became a gigantic torch that lit up the entire bay. Thus the attackers' incendiary strategy worked against them, because the light from the burning frigate revealed their presence and they were fired on with harquebuses and cannon for an hour. Nine of their launches were sunk, with the loss of four hundred men. There were forty dead aboard the frig-ates, some of them burned alive. Drake's every attempt seemed to fail, but he would not give up, in the knowledge that behind the thick granite walls of the fortress there lay a fabulous amount of treasure.

On 24 November, he sailed close to the wind until he was windward of the port, so that it appeared that the fleet was about to attack. Another two ships were sunk to block the access and the townsfolk worked tirelessly to open new trenches. Drake, skilled seaman and a daring pirate in peacetime was, however, no war admiral, and just as he had failed to force his way into the Tagus estuary in 1589, he also did not attempt to attack San Juan de Puerto Rico six years later. He sailed to the other end of the island to get water and look for livestock. There he freed five prisoners with a courteous letter for the governor, requesting the same mercy for the English captives. Then he sailed south towards the continental mainland and dropped anchor at Riohacha (in modern-day Colombia). Pedro Juárez loaded the treasure aboard the frigates and Sancho Pardo set sail for Seville, where he arrived without further problems.

---

[5]   Fernández Duro, *Armada española*, III, p. 108. John Hawkins was the first Englishman in the slave trade and the initiator of the important Afro-American triangular trade route. He captured slaves in Africa and sold them, as a rule forcibly, in unsuspecting coastal Spanish American towns, that is if he did not sack the towns first. His cynical excuse for such behaviour was that he was thus delivering the captured Africans from the danger of falling victim to human sacrifices in their own land. Although approved by Queen Elizabeth, his activities in slavery and piracy were an infringement of the peace between Philip II and Elizabeth I and, as we have seen, one of the causes of the war.

Meanwhile, the Governor of Riohacha had asked for reinforcements and was trying to distract Drake by haggling over the amount to be paid to save the town from being torched. After two weeks, he told Drake that the colonists were unwilling to part with their pearls. So Drake went back to his old habits, burned down the town and kidnapped a few black pearl divers. Few men have so often had the smell in their nostrils of a fire burning. He passed by fortified Cartagena and, on 6 January 1596, arrived in Nombre de Dios on the Panama isthmus. This was the actual objective of the expedition, for Drake was familiar with this strategically located but undefended place from the time he had attacked it as a young man. He had dreamed of conquering the isthmus to gain access to both oceans and take control over Philip's main source of income.

It was impossible to defend the place. Alonso de Sotomayor, sent from Peru by the Marquis of Cañete with six cannon, harquebuses, powder and ammunition, commissioned the famous Italian engineer Bautista Antonelli to fortify the River Chagre with a bastion and trenches near Tornabellaco. This was the most logical option, since the English had shallow launches with which to go upriver. In case they chose the more tiring land route he had a wooden fort with a moat built on Capirilla hill, where he deployed seventy harquebusiers under Captain Juan Enríquez. The English were about to attack a strategic and vulnerable part of the empire and if they succeeded, not only could they literally cut it in half but they could also gain easy access to the Pacific Ocean, which was protected by the hellish Strait of Magellan. Drake decided on a two-pronged attack. By land he sent the Royal Infantry, while he personally led the advance of the launches upriver in the Chagre. This was an ideal waterway to use for invasion, since it flowed into the Atlantic and was navigable right up to the outskirts of the city of Panama on the Pacific coast.

At dawn on 8 January, the infantry, led by Baskerville, launched a furious attack against the fortification at Capirilla, but the harquebusiers, behind cover and not wasting a shot, resisted the attack until noon, by which time the English had suffered many casualties. With the news of the attack on Capirilla, Captain Hernando de Liermo Agüero came with fifty men as reinforcements and by sounding their trumpets and clarinets – just like the Drummer of El Bruc with his drum 212 years later during the Peninsular War[6] – they made the enemy believe that a large army was approaching. The English hurriedly retreated towards Nombre de Dios through hostile and unknown territory. The black slaves were given permission to rob those who were lagging behind; many English had their throats cut and Baskerville's losses grew to about five hundred men. When Drake heard of the disaster, he ordered his troops who were on the launches on the Chagre to land and, closing together to defend themselves from attack, they managed to return to the Atlantic coast.[7]

---

[6] The Drummer of El Bruc refers to a popular Catalan legend based on what happened during a skirmish at Bruc during the Peninsular War (part of the Spanish War of Independence) at the beginning of the nineteenth century. According to the legend, the sound of a young boy playing the drums echoed in the surrounding Montserrat mountains, convincing the French troops that they faced an army that was much larger than it really was and they decided to withdraw [translator's note].

[7] Fernández Duro, *Armada española*, III, p. 111.

Their attempt to reach the Pacific through the isthmus had been halted and the strategic location discovered eighty-three years earlier in September 1513 by Vasco Núñez de Balboa, the first European to set eyes upon the Pacific Ocean, was safe. Balboa himself, and later Álvaro de Saavedra and Hernán Cortés, had conceived a plan to connect the two oceans and the projects to make it feasible, involving a channel dug out through the isthmus, were considered by Charles I of Spain (Emperor Charles V) and his son Philip II. But the task was too complex for sixteenth-century technology, and it was not until 1914 that the work was undertaken by the United States, who schemed their way into annexing the Columbian province of Panama so that they could do with it as they wished. In any event, the isthmus was a strategic place for centuries, where significant riches were transported, attracting many bandits and causing many an ambush.

Going back to 1596 and having witnessed the courage of the men under Enríquez and Sotomayor – who were following in the footsteps of the Conquistadors – the English found themselves driven back in Nombre de Dios and took their leave in their usual fashion by burning the wooden houses. According to the testimony of prisoners, they had taken refuge in nearby Veragua and the necessary precautions were kept in place. Soon afterwards the locals of Santiago del Príncipe killed thirty-seven English who went to the River Fator for water, while others died attempting to seize supplies from a population that was armed and no longer afraid of them. The men of the expedition were utterly demoralized and Drake, scourge of the seas in times of peace but now an utterly dejected man, died on 28 January while the fleet continued to sail off the coast.[8]

England had lost the most famous mariner of the war, though his great fame had been earned in the incidents prior to the confrontation, during successful voyages as a pirate, for once the war had been declared his participation was actually quite modest. He did not venture to take on the few galleons of the Spanish Armada after its ships had been dispersed at Gravelines and, driven by his habit of looting, he committed the same mistake twice: he attacked Corunna instead of sailing straight for Lisbon in 1589, and he attempted to do the same in the Canary Islands rather than heading directly for the Americas in 1595. These episodes were at the root of the worst English disasters of the war. He was a great mariner, as well as a courageous pirate or privateer who as such did his country great service by seizing, sacking and burning. His undeniable daring was based essentially on the element of surprise, and the *coups de main* he managed to achieve were spectacular. He was also, as we have seen, the first English seaman who dared cross the Strait of Magellan, but as an admiral of large fleets and a war leader he was unimpressive.

Following the loss of their two leaders and the decisive failure of the expedition, there was nothing for it than for the English to return home. After much arguing, John Drake, brother of Francis, was appointed as commander. He regrouped the men in eighteen vessels for the return voyage. However, eight galleons and thirteen other vessels with 3,000 soldiers and seamen had been sent from Spain to protect the West Indies from

---

[8]   Fernández Duro, *Armada española*, III, p. 112.

Figure 33.1 Sir Francis Drake. By Marcus Geeraerts, National Maritime Museum.

attack. They were commanded by Don Bernardino de Avellaneda, with Juan Gutiérrez de Garibay as admiral. The fleet reached Cartagena in bad shape after a storm, but on learning that the English were on their way to Cuba, they put their pumps to work and set sail again immediately.

On 11 March they found the English taking on water at the Island of Pinos and attacked them straight away with only thirteen ships. The English fleet abandoned its launches and fled, heading for Cape San Antonio. Garibay's flagship took them on in an attempt to stop them. One of the larger ships, with three hundred men aboard, and a patache with thirty-five men, were captured. One of the Spanish vessels exploded during the encounter, leaving eighty dead and wounded. The chase continued, and the beleaguered English managed to escape by getting rid of what they could from their vessels, including their cannon. Only eight of the twenty-eight that had left Plymouth returned – and they suffered terrible losses. The Queen was in despair. At the same time, the Spanish treasure fleet arrived in Sanlúcar with one of the largest shipments ever brought in.

Chapter 34

Cádiz and the North Wind

After many disasters, the English found themselves close to achieving a great prize. To a large extent its origin lay in the wretched role of Philip's former secretary Antonio Pérez who, in revenge against the King, informed the English about where Spain was most vulnerable and encouraged them to attack Cádiz. Philip had paid particular attention to the fortification of the West and East Indian colonies, as well as the Italian and Flemish strongholds, all among the most distant parts of the empire. Unable to deal with every front, he neglected what he mistakenly considered to be the most secure, given that its possession was undisputed: the Spanish coast itself. The English were finally encouraged to go on the offensive by the Spanish conquest of Calais, right on England's doorstep, in April 1596. Hence an Anglo-Dutch fleet consisting of 150 vessels and 15,000 men set sail on 1 June under Lord Howard of Effingham, the same man who had commanded the English fleet in the channel eight years earlier.

When they reached as far south as Lisbon, two reconnaissance launches were sent to investigate the possibility of sacking the Portuguese capital. The launches were captured and so, faced with the eighteen ships under Don Diego Brochero that were preparing to defend the city, the English continued south towards the Algarve. This was in spite of having with them the son of the Prior of Crato, someone who might have incited the Portuguese to rebel against Philip II. The mighty Spanish fleet was in Cádiz. It consisted of eight galleons belonging to the escort of the treasure fleet, the five frigates which had brought in the treasure from San Juan de Puerto Rico under Sancho Pardo and the Tierra Firme fleet, which included the admiral's ship and the flagship – a total of between forty-three and fifty ships, plus eighteen galleys. It was a large contingent, though a number of its leaders were not there. It was decided to defend the entrance to the bay with a line blocking the channel and supported by the fort of San Felipe.

The English arrived on 30 June, stopped in front of the formation and sent skiffs out to their flagship to determine what to do against such a defensive line. If nothing had changed in this formation, they would probably have done the same as they did in Lisbon and headed for the Azores to intercept the treasure fleet. However, the Spanish fleet, lacking a unified command, made a crucial mistake: the shipowners of the Tierra Firme fleet, which was ready to sail for the Americas with cargo estimated to be worth over four million ducats, used their influence to have the loaded vessels withdrawn from the line, thus leaving the bay open to the enemy. The mistake turned out to be disastrous. Moreover, it showed the Spanish inability to appoint a supreme commander – in the absence of Francisco Coloma, general of the galleons, Sancho Pardo, general of the frigates, and the *Adelantado* of Castile – who could command ships with different functions and leaders in the face of that unexpected attack.[1]

Not only did the English have a gap through which to attack but the withdrawal of the Tierra Firme fleet was seen as a sign of fear that encouraged them to do so. Once the battle began, the galleons fought well and were supported in the rearguard by the galleys. They sank two English ships and set fire to another; among the casualties was Walter Raleigh who was wounded in the leg by a splinter. After four or five hours of bitter fighting, the galleons tried to withdraw further into the bay under pressure from the English fleet and cross the narrow strait of Puente Suazo, a manoeuvre that was difficult enough in favourable conditions. All they managed to do was to run aground in Los Puntales where the crew ended up setting all the ships on fire, with the exception of the *San Matías* and the *San Andrés*, which were the only ships the English captured. Later, the entire fleet followed suit, lighting up the Bay of Cádiz for three successive nights.

This only left the galleys, which had tried to refloat the stranded galleons before they were set alight. When they found this was impossible, they cut the wooden section of the bridge and went out to the open sea through the Boca de Sancti Petri. With the English in control of the bay, the resistance offered by Cádiz was, to say the least, shameful, the polar opposite of what had happened in Corunna. The fugitives from the stranded galleons knocked at the city gates but were told to go away, so they had to find a way to scale the walls. This showed the attackers how to get in, without anyone managing to stop them, for the men who were demanding weapons and ammunition had been abandoned by the mayor and wartime captain, who had shut himself in the castle. His name should only be remembered with contempt: Antonio Girón. Only the combative Franciscan friars stood up to the 'heretics', thereby enhancing the order's reputation for the aggressive defence of their faith. However, with neither resistance nor siege worthy of such a large city, it was not long before it fell into English hands.

It came as no surprise that the name of the Duke of Medina Sidonia was associated with such a disaster. When the English fleet was sighted he wrote to the King, assuring him that there was nothing the English could do to Cádiz. Later, though, he said nothing about his refusal to put four or five thousand men aboard the galleys, as had been proposed once it was known from the prisoners and the skirmishes that the English assault troops were not to be feared. He not only did nothing, but allowed no one else to do anything either. Girón and other nobles surrendered the castle, with the promise that no harm would come to them if they paid 120,000 ducats.

The invaders spent two weeks stealing absolutely everything they could lay their hands on: stored merchandise, clothes, furniture, jewels and other valuables including guns, bells and even grilles, doors and windows. As the ships sailed away, with the two Spanish galleons that had been spared the flames standing out among them, Medina Sidonia marched in with a large number of men and 'liberated' the city. Not content with calling him chicken – on account of Cádiz and his role in the channel – the Cordoban

---

[1]   Fernández Duro, *Armada española*, III, p. 122.

poet Góngora[2] referred to him as 'God of tuna'.[3] The satirical sonnet penned for him by Cervantes concluded with the lines:

> The earth trembled and the sky became dark
> Threatening total ruin,
> And into Cádiz, with great dignity,
> With the Count already departed, fearlessly,
> Marched the great Duke of Medina in triumph.[4]

It must be said in defence of the population that fear was still fresh in their memory following the sacking of the city by Drake in 1585. They must also have felt that all was lost when they saw the fleet on fire, but the shameful role of the leaders in charge of resistance was the decisive factor. Cádiz, a rich town, made it possible for these men to feel safe by paying their ransom. Such a disaster inflicted by pirates, of which there had been countless examples in the three thousand–year history of the city that had begun as part of the ancient civilization of Tartessos, would finally lead to its fortification being taken seriously. As a result, the English suffered serious losses in the attack in 1625, when with the same size fleet as in 1596, they made a surprise attack during the peace that followed the war. This was a most timely victory, since at that time much of the Spanish fleet was busy expelling the Dutch from Brazil. It is worth mentioning that on that occasion it was another Girón, Fernando, who more than restored the reputation of his family name. Later, the city would resist the wrath of Napoleon himself and Spain would recover the honour lost during that summer of 1596.

It was not all bad news for Spain at this time, however. Although the manoeuvrable galleys that began the pursuit the English only managed to capture a single 120-ton ship due to Howard's close formation, Pedro de Zubiaur took out six vessels carrying munitions for the English fleet, capturing four and sinking the other two. The English later landed in Faro, where an extraordinary episode took place. We know of this thanks to Bartolomé de Villavicencio, a Cádiz councillor, who was among those to be ransomed for 120,000 ducats and who was left in Corunna due to illness.[5]

Without orders from above, sixty Castilians on horseback arrived in Faro and challenged the English from the other bank of the river to do battle with an equal number of combatants, the number to be chosen by the English. The English decided to send just one man and he was defeated by a Spanish champion, but the English went back on the

---

[2] Luis de Góngora, a Spanish baroque lyric poet and probably the best known poet of the period [translator's note].

[3] An allusion to the rights of the House of Medina Sidonia over fishing with tuna nets in the Strait of Gibraltar.

[4] From Sonnet 136 (A la Entrada del Duque de Medina en Cádiz) by the poet and writer Miguel de Cervantes, author of *Don Quixote* [translator's note].

[5] On the English landing in Faro, see *Relaçao da desembarcaçao dos Ingreses na cidade de Faro, e de todo o mais sucesso*. BN. G 51, fol. 205. Bartolomé de Villavicencio's testimony in RAH. Col. Jesuitas, t. XXXVIII, fol. 241. References in Fernández Duro, *Armada española*, III, p. 128.

agreement and tore the winner to pieces. The remaining Spanish pulled back, staying within sight and later charged against the rearguard of the English as they re-embarked, taking twenty-seven prisoners whose noses, ears and hands were cut off before being set free. When Howard saw them, he vowed angrily that if he ever found out who had betrayed the Spanish, they would hang.

The English then approached Corunna, with the sole intention of dropping off the Cádiz councillor, Villavicencio. Their presence 'gave rise to unfavourable comparisons in the district governed by the Duke of Medina Sidonia'[6] for, as soon as their sails were sighted, the city prepared for battle, just as it had done seven years earlier. Although orders were given to remove the women to safe quarters, the women refused, arguing that they had already proven their worth by their work on the walls. In any event, after 1589 the English would never again make an attempt against the city.

As usual, Cumberland's fleet was lurking near the Azores that summer, but thirty-six armed supply ships that set sail from Seville under Luis Fajardo forced them to leave, inflicting twenty casualties and some damage. The treasure fleet reached Sanlúcar without incident and this time the riches encouraged an old and sick Philip II, who immediately went on the offensive and ordered a new expedition to aid the Irish insurrection against English occupation. To this end over 150 vessels, large and small, assembled in Corunna from Cádiz, Ferrol and Lisbon. The *Adelantado* of Castile, Don Martín de Padilla, set sail in October without waiting for the arrival from Cádiz of Marcos de Aramburu with another eleven galleons, which in turn brought munitions to arm eleven more that had been built in Guipúzcoa in the Basque Country. The large number of warships Spain had at the time indicates the size of the programme of naval rearmament commissioned by Philip II in the 1590s. However, brave Martín de Padilla – the same man who had punished Drake and Norris's fleet in 1589 – seemed to be jinxed from this point of the war. This misfortune would eventually lead to his being relieved of his duties.

Padilla set sail without waiting for Aramburu, in the belief that the stormy autumn weather made it too risky to wait a single day longer. Ironically, such reasoning led to a terrible shipwreck: thirty-two vessels – not counting the smaller ships – were driven by a violent storm on to the Costa de la Muerte between Corcubión and Finisterre, with the loss of nearly 2,000 men. A distraught Philip II might well have repeated the words attributed to him regarding the more famous armada of 1588, about not having sent his ships to fight against the elements, for once again they had turned out to be his worst enemy. The remaining ships were saved and preparations began immediately for a new expedition the following summer.[7]

Work progressed at a steady pace for the new attempt to invade England during the spring of 1597, while the Prudent King, as Philip was known, stoically suffered through a long illness that would eventually lead to his death a year later. Ships from Guipúzcoa,

6   Fernández Duro, *Armada española*, III, p. 128.
7   Ibid., p. 131.

Biscay, Lisbon, Andalusia and Italy arrived steadily in Ferrol, forming squadrons under Aramburu, Antonio de Urquiola, Villaviciosa, Oliste, Zubiaur and Martín de Bertendona, who nine years earlier had defended the castle of San Antón after putting the *San Juan* to the torch in the Bay of Corunna.

The head of this new Spanish Armada, as was the case the year before, was Martín de Padilla and the expert seaman Diego Brochero was appointed admiral. Although the fleet was not as large as that of 1588, it had the advantage of being able to use the ports of Blavet in Brittany and Calais, which had been conquered a year earlier, as we have seen. In addition, its objectives were less complex than those of the failed amphibious operation. The English, however, were also busy putting together a powerful fleet in order to prevent the invasion. As was often the case, they were quicker to complete their preparations and intrepidly left from Plymouth on 9 July determined to sail straight to Ferrol and attack the Spanish fleet before it was ready to leave port. The English had 120 vessels, large and small, commanded by the Earl of Essex, with Thomas Howard and the privateer and author Walter Raleigh as admirals. Twenty-five Dutch vessels also joined and strengthened the expedition. This time it was the northerners who were hit by a violent storm that damaged and scattered the ships, forcing them off course towards the Azores. These islands were the meeting point for the expedition's second objective which was, as ever, to intercept the treasure fleet.

When the King learned that the channel was clear of the English and Dutch who were on the lookout for silver in the Azores, he called for preparations to be hurried along. Martín de Padilla sent Carlos de Amézola, who had sacked the Cornish coast two years earlier, to Brittany with seven galleys and a thousand soldiers to continue helping the Catholics there. Padilla was finally able to sail on 19 October. He had 136 ships, 24 caravels, 4,000 mariners, 8,634 soldiers and 300 horses, which were joined by Aramburu from Andalusia with another thirty-two ships transporting men from the Tercios regiments brought over from Italy. It took them three days of easy sailing to reach the channel. Seldom had England's fate been as much in the balance as it was then, for the plan was to land in nearby Falmouth (the city where ninety-two years later the Anglo-Hispanic maritime mail service with Corunna would be set up).

The war had reached a tipping point and a moment of high interest: on the one hand we had the English and Dutch waiting, with a fleet the size of which had never been seen in the Azores, to finally realize their dream of seizing the vast riches of the Spanish treasure fleet. The Spanish, with a fleet that was no less powerful, were in search of their own dream: the conquest of the den of pirates that had done so much harm in the Americas.

It may be unfair to say that Martín de Padilla was jinxed. The historian Larrey preferred to believe that it was divine providence that saved England for the third time.[8] What is certain is that, with the English coast almost within sight, a powerful storm blew up with hurricane force gusts of wind from the north. It was so strong that, while

---

[8] Fernández Duro, *Armada española*, III, p. 167.

they tried to resist it by keeping the ship almost stationary with the prow facing the wind but without striking sails, a number of large vessels, several supply ships and Admiral Brochero's ship all lost their masts. The fleet then became scattered and only seven vessels made it to the Cornish coast. Four hundred men were landed, but after finding shelter they grew tired of waiting for the rest of the fleet and returned on board. A Spanish attack against England had once again come to naught, thanks to the strength of the north wind. The demoralized fleet, with its damaged ships, exhausted and hungry men and, above all, a crushing feeling of weariness after a year of strenuous preparations, slowly returned to its point of departure. Not only had pinnaces and boats in tow been lost, but some of the larger vessels also failed to make it back. But worse than these losses was the missed opportunity and the terrible sense of frustration among the men at the way in which events had unfolded.

Meanwhile, General Don Juan Gutiérrez de Garibay was heading for the Azores from Havana with forty-three fully laden ships and ten million pesos. Having been warned of the unusually large size of the enemy fleet waiting for him, he managed to take refuge in the anchorage of Angra in Terceira Island while the Anglo-Dutch were watching out elsewhere. He unloaded the treasure and left it in a safe place in the castle. With the heavier guns of the galleons he mounted a battery on the beach, then dug trenches and prepared to defend Angra.

Essex decided to test the effectiveness of these defences for himself at the expense of his flagship which had drawn up close by and was hit by two well-aimed shots in the stern gallery and the helm. This prompted him to keep his distance and to block the channel through which Garibay would have to leave sooner or later. Garibay consulted with his captains as to which was the lesser risk: staying in the bay and being exposed to the autumn storms or trying to break through the line of 150 enemy ships. In the end he chose the latter. The Indies' fleet took on William Monson's squadron, which proved unable to stop it. Before the rest of the enemy ships could close in, the Indies' fleet made it to the open sea and headed in close formation for Sanlúcar, where it safely arrived with the treasure.[9]

In 1598, after signing the Treaty of Vervins with France, which in the eyes of the dying monarch put paid to the Protestant threat in the neighbouring country, Philip II passed away. That summer, English privateers tried to intercept the treasure fleet for the umpteenth time and were again driven back in the Azores and Cape St Vincent. Spain also won victories in the Mediterranean against Turkish and Barbary corsairs, but from then on the fabulous riches of America would be used to defray the unbelievably high costs run up by Philip III's court from the very start of his reign.

As for an appraisal of Philip II's handling of the war, there is no denying that he conducted it with great vigour. He devoted to the conflict the attention it deserved, considering that it was in fact a war against England, the Dutch Republic and France. He made his worst mistakes before the war began, by turning a blind eye to the provocations of

---

[9]   Fernández Duro, *Armada española*, III, p. 165.

the English and ignoring the advice of his generals, in particular that of Don Álvaro de Bazán. He also failed to take decisive action in 1580, which gave the English time to form a navy, while leaving unpunished the activities of their pirates in times of peace. True to his sobriquet, Philip's failing was 'prudence' in giving preference to moral and religious considerations, in stark contrast to the radical Machiavellianism deployed by Elizabeth I. In light of this it is indeed striking that the 'black legend' that clouded his reputation should have acted as a smokescreen that obscured the reign of the English Queen.

Chapter 35

Crimson Taffeta

The reign of Philip III, who found himself at the head of a vast empire at the age of only twenty, was to be very different from that of his father and predecessor, and this also had its consequences for the final operations of the war. He was crowned and acclaimed on 13 September 1598 and this marked the start of the lavish festivities that lasted for a whole year, although it could be said that his entire reign was almost one long party. From the beginning he rejected the example given by his father, for if Philip II erred by not delegating anything and taking on himself a workload that was far too onerous, his son could hardly have delegated more, and thereby gave rise to the preponderance of the figure of the *valido* or King's favourite, which became such an ill-fated phenomenon in Spanish history.

Philip II had arranged two important royal marriages. The first was of his son Philip with the Archduchess Margaret of Austria, the second that of his favourite daughter, the Infanta Isabella Clara Eugenia, with Archduke Alberto, who was in charge of the defence of Lisbon in 1589. The latter couple became sovereigns of the Spanish Netherlands which, under official Spanish tutelage, enjoyed a large degree of autonomy and was intended by Philip II to release the Spanish crown from some of its responsibility. The lavishness of these weddings surpassed anything ever seen before. Alberto and Margaret took the Spanish Road from Brussels for their royal nuptials, and after the Pope had blessed the double wedding in Ferrara, they arrived in Genoa, where a magnificent squadron of forty powerful and richly adorned galleys under Martín de Padilla, Pedro de Toledo and Pedro de Leyva awaited them. They set sail on 18 February 1599 aboard the galley *Real*, which had been decked out for the occasion in the most exquisite fashion and whose oarsmen wore crimson taffeta dress coats. Escorted by this magnificent collection of warships, which patrolled the Mediterranean sector of the empire, they went on a luxury cruise, visiting frequent ports of call on the Italian, French and Spanish coasts and sailing only by day so that the future Queen of Spain and her mother, also present, would not get seasick. After forty days they reached Vinaroz.

Meanwhile, a splendid retinue left Madrid to accompany the late monarch's two children to their respective weddings. It was only the start of the unimaginable lavishness that defined the reign of what might be termed the Millionaire King. At the nuptials ratified in Valencia, the title of Duke of Lerma was bestowed upon Don Francisco de Sandoval, and the nobility received extraordinary gifts and favours, along with habits of the military orders 'that had not been given in ten years of the life of the King', according to Cabrera de Córdoba.[1] The new Spanish sovereigns then sailed with Alberto and Isabella Clara Eugenia from Valencia to Barcelona with a total of forty-five galleys.

---

[1] Fernández Duro, *Armada española*, III, p. 205.

In Barcelona, the newly married Philip III held *cortes* (a legislative assembly) with consequences for the final chapter of the war. The King agreed to a Catalan request to arm ten galleys to combat Mediterranean corsairs. This put an end to a tradition of restraint upheld since the time of Ferdinand the Catholic against fighting corsairs with corsairs, which had spelled the end of the glorious Catalan navy, famous for its incursions in the Mediterranean. But it also had repercussions in the Atlantic, as it marked the prelude to yet another crucial new development.

Federico Spinola, a wealthy Genoese aristocrat who had spent two years in the military campaigns of the Low Countries, did not waste the opportunity offered by the assembly in Barcelona to present an old project once more. His plan was to use galleys for privateering in the waters of the Low Countries, to harass the rebels of the United Provinces by disrupting their trading and fisheries and also to keep the sea routes open. Circumstances were favourable in the absence of Philip II, who had been sceptical regarding the role of galleys in those waters, and Spinola had the chance to put his case to both Philip III and Archduke Alberto personally. He succeeded in persuading both rulers, as in the case of the Catalans, by his commitment to finance the initiative and so they entrusted him with the six galleys that had served in Brittany, which were then in Santander under Carlos de Amézola. Once the *cortes* had ended, the two young royal couples 'parted most affectionately'.[2] The fleet then escorted the new monarchs of the Spanish Netherlands to Genoa, where they took the Spanish Road back to take possession of their new kingdom. This marked the birth of modern Belgium.

Meanwhile, in the Atlantic, the Dutch took over the role of the exhausted English. Thus a new struggle between Spain and the United Provinces was first superimposed upon the Anglo-Spanish war and then finally replaced it. The Dutch naval power had grown spectacularly thanks to their duplicity in continuing to trade with the naïve Philip II at the same time as waging war against him. On 11 June 1599, a powerful armed fleet of seventy-four vessels arrived at Corunna, which had strengthened its defences following the failed attack by the late Francis Drake. The castle of San Antón, which by then had been finished, and that of Santa Cruz, on which work had begun in 1594, sent a warning with heavy culverins, and the squadron of attackers, who were Flemish in this case, quickly got the message and left the estuary without delay. This was the first excursion of such size by the self-styled United Provinces of the Netherlands, hitherto despised in the early days of the rebellion as former herring fishers, as beggars of the sea turned small-time privateers. This began a new era in which the Dutch replaced the English, thereby achieving something that had seemed impossible: to become their equal, and often to surpass them, in the startling cruelty of their actions.

---

[2] *Jornada de Su Majestad Felipe III y Alteza la Infanta Doña Isabel, desde Madrid, a casarse, el Rey con la Reina Margarita y su Alteza con el Archiduque Alberto.* (Journey of His Majesty Philip III and Her Highness the Infanta Isabella from Madrid for the marriage of the King with Queen Margaret and Her Highness with Archduke Alberto). BN. H. 48. Reference in Fernández Duro, *Armada española*, III, p. 209.

The mighty fleet that had been turned back at Corunna succeeded in landing near Las Palmas in Gran Canaria, in spite of the death of brave governor Alonso de Alvarado – who had driven Drake back four years earlier – in the attempt to prevent it. The Flemish took the castle of La Luz, which they used to bombard the castle of Santa Ana, and the inhabitants of Las Palmas had to withdraw to defend themselves in the low hills near the town. The invaders attacked in well-ordered columns, but the Canary Islanders took advantage of the rough terrain, and drove them back, causing nine hundred casualties and forcing them back to the beach. The Flemish demanded the immediate payment of 400,000 ducats, recognition of the sovereignty of the United Provinces and an annual tribute of 10,000 ducats, on pain of the complete destruction of the city. They had been quick to learn from the English. They were told to do their worst and that is what they set out to do. The Canary Islanders, however, had entrenched themselves very near the town and as the invaders re-embarked they attacked their rearguard and frustrated the attempt to set the place alight. The result of the bravery of the Canary Islanders was that the admiral of the corsair fleet, Pieter Van der Does, went away with a pitiful booty of cannon, the church bells and a few casks of wine.

Knowing that the islands of Tenerife and La Palma had been alerted, he attacked Gomera, taking a small number of cannon along with objects belonging to the parish church. He then divided the fleet, sending Vice Admiral Jan Gerbrantsen with thirty-five ships to the Azores, where they would wait in vain, as the treasure fleet had been warned of the powerful threat and had decided to winter in Havana and wait for the new King to clear the seas of their new uninvited guests. In Spain, a war fleet was prepared that set sail from Corunna with fifty ships and 8,000 men. The fleet's only problem – though it was decisive – was that it was commanded by the unluckiest commander of that war, Martín de Padilla, the *Adelantado* of Castile. As a consequence, the fleet had to face a series of storms and a terrible gale off the Island of Flores towards the end of September …. The remnants of the crippled armada, without masts, sails or rigging, headed for Cádiz and the Galician coast. Some of the ships were never heard from again.

There was a general outcry at the bad luck of Padilla, whose vessels had already been dismasted before having a chance to fight in '96 and '97 and now again in '99. But the Count of Fuentes, defender of Lisbon in 1589, humiliated him by throwing in his face 'the loss of lives, armies, fleets, millions of ducats, galleons, galleys, supplies, artillery, ammunition, reputation, honour and opportunities'.[3] Although Padilla was a friend and in-law of the Duke of Lerma, who stood up for him, the young King had no choice but to remove him from his post. The decision brought relief to Spain – and there was no real cause for complaint – but in defence of the unlucky nobleman there is no denying that he fought bravely when he had the chance to do so, as in the Tagus against Drake in 1589. The cause of his misfortune was that he set sail at the wrong time, often well into the autumn, due to various delays or emergencies. One way or another, it was his fate to be remembered for his bad luck, not for any skill he may have had as a mariner.

---

[3]   RAH. Col. Jesuitas, t. CIV, fol. 114. Referenced in Fernández Duro, *Armada española*, III, p. 212.

Gerbrantsen also suffered a setback – though not to the same extent – on his way back to the Netherlands after his fruitless wait for the Spanish treasure fleet. Meanwhile, Van der Does headed for the most defenceless Spanish possessions in the Philippines with thirty-six large ships. He killed a considerable number of people on the island of São Tomé and burned what he could, but as far as booty was concerned he did not have much luck as all he got was salt and a tropical disease which reduced the northerners to a fraction of their number and killed the admiral himself. Economically the expedition was a failure but not so in the moral or political sense, since they had done harm to their powerful 'hereditary foe' and shown that there were vulnerable points in its vast possessions. As a result, they were ready to take over from the English as the parasites of the empire.

Thereafter Federico Spinola's strategy proved to be highly timely, for while Van der Does had his eventful and final summer, thus leaving the English Channel clear, Spinola sailed with his six galleys from Santander to Sluis, in the Netherlands, where he was able to establish an operational base. From the beginning he caused considerable disruption with this force, which was small in number but not in manoeuvrability and firepower. Sluis soon began to be filled with captured fishing vessels and merchantmen and the United Provinces were forced to devote a part of their naval forces and financial resources to the protection of their coasts that were no longer safe.

From then on, the Anglo-Spanish conflict began to take second place, though it remained active. After the winter had forced the West Indies fleet to stay in Havana, the following summer of 1600 it carried two years' worth of treasure safely back to Spain, escorted by Diego Brochero and Francisco Coloma.

The following year the fleet was attacked jointly by the squadrons of Richard Lewson and William Monson, who were seen off by Coloma. Also, in 1601, the new king was persuaded by his advisors and requested by the Irish Catholics to take up with renewed vigour the idea of establishing a Spanish presence in Ireland to help his fellow Catholics who were subjugated by the English. Don Diego Brochero was commissioned to prepare a new fleet for that purpose.

The armada set sail from Lisbon in early September 1601, taking with it the first army corps with some 4,000 soldiers. Its admiral was Diego Brochero, the vice admiral Pedro de Zubiaur and the army was commanded by Juan del Águila. When they were off Corunna they were joined by new contingents, although part of Zubiaur's squadron stayed at the Spanish port. Without the unfortunate Padilla, the expedition had an uneventful crossing and Juan del Águila landed in Kinsale on 8 October. There he read out a declaration explaining the reason for his arrival. The English Lord Deputy, Lord Mountjoy, marched against the Spanish with an army of eight or nine thousand men while Richard Levison blockaded them from the sea. The local Catholics, who were on the side of the Spanish, waited in expectation, given the small size of the Spanish army.

Shortly afterwards the ships that had stopped earlier in Corunna reached Baltimore with a further contingent of 2,000 men, led by second-in-command Alonso Docampo. Hugh O'Neill, the Earl of Tyrone, joined him with 4,000 men to form another Catholic front. However, the call for a general uprising in the island aimed at forming a larger army went unheeded although Pedro de Zubiaur had brought weapons, ammunition and equipment for this purpose. Docampo and O'Neill marched with their troops to join those of Juan del Águila. But as the letters that conveyed their plan had been intercepted, the Lord Deputy got there first, took up strategic positions and went out to meet them.

The battle took place on 3 January 1602, to the north-west of the walls of Kinsale, where Juan del Águila resisted the siege of the English. The lack of coordination between the Irish rebel leaders Hugh O'Neill and Red Hugh O'Donnell, the small number of Spanish troops, as well as the vigorous attack of the English infantry and cavalry gave the victory to Lord Mountjoy.

Docampo fought bravely in adversity, losing two hundred men, and along with several captains was taken prisoner himself. Meanwhile, the Spanish army successfully withdrew and went to ground in Baltimore. When Juan del Águila learned of what had happened, he concluded that the Irish emissaries had tricked Philip III into thinking that the Irish population would support the rebellion en masse. Under the circumstances, Águila saw that there was no chance of the Irish seceding from the Elizabethan crown, considering the ease with which the English could send more troops there, compared to the difficulty for Spain of doing the same because of the distance.

Although bitterly criticized for it later, the leader of the expedition decided to put an end to the Irish adventure. He began talks with Lord Mountjoy, offering the surrender of the strongholds that they occupied and the departure of the Spanish army from Ireland in exchange for a withdrawal with all the honours of war, weapons, ammunition and baggage. He also asked for immunity for the local population who had offered them refuge, and for the Spanish troops to be transported in English vessels, since the Spanish ships had returned to Spain to bring reinforcements. He added that if these conditions were not met, they would defend themselves, well equipped as they were, to the last man. The English nobleman did not take long to make up his mind. He had seen for himself how the Spanish had fought with inferior numbers on an open battlefield, and a Spanish withdrawal would put an end to the campaign and to the possible arrival of reinforcements. Above all, it offered the prize of keeping Ireland undivided, which was precisely his mission. So he accepted. Under persuasion from her advisors, Queen Elizabeth believed that Philip III's Irish policy was the same as her own. It was a fact that a rebellious Ireland, with Spain fanning the flames, forced her to keep an army of 20,000 men that cost £300,000 a year.[4] As in the case of English privateering and support for the Flemish rebels, the provision of escorts and troops required considerable expenditure by Spain.

It must be said that dealing with an English lord in the British Isles was in no way the same as dealing with a pirate – even if he bore the title of Sir – in the Caribbean. Mountjoy was true to the letter of his part of the agreement and the Spanish troops were taken to Corunna, where they arrived in April 1602. On this occasion, the English ships came in peace, or in the spirit of an agreed truce, which came as a prelude to the

---

[4] Fernández Duro, *Armada española*, III, p. 220.

welcome that would be given three years later in honour of Lord Howard of Effingham, as representative of a hard-earned peace between the two countries. The last days of an exhausted Juan del Águila were spent being reproached for abandoning what he had held without waiting for reinforcements or even orders. He died in Corunna not long after the Spanish troops returned to Spain.

The final point to mention is that in 1602 the English tried as usual to ambush the Spanish treasure fleet, this time with a fleet commanded once again by Monson and Lewson, but they decided against it in view of the sizeable escort. Elizabeth I died soon after, and with her went the implacable hatred of Spain, defender of the Catholic faith on whose behalf His Holiness had once declared that Henry VIII's daughter was the fruit of an adulterous marriage and was therefore unqualified to occupy the throne of England. Elizabeth's successor, James I, and the new Spanish King began peace talks. It was now the Dutch who would enthusiastically take over the waging of war once more. But that is another story.

As far as Elizabeth's role is concerned, she permitted and even sponsored the attacks by pirates against Spain in times of peace and in addition assisted the Flemish rebels against their legitimate king, Philip II. On that basis she was the instigator of the war. Once it had started, she came to realize the extent of the opportunity afforded by the failure of the Spanish Armada and she rightly embarked upon the general mobilization of her country in order to raise the English Armada. She clearly established her objectives, starting with the basics: the destruction of the Spanish Armada while it was being repaired in Santander. But Elizabeth's great mistake was to leave the ill-fated preparation of the fleet to private initiatives and in the hands of Drake and Norris. She would have done better to have invited to head the expedition some high-ranking courtier who would have sole command, not betray its objectives and not lead it to disaster. As for other matters, her prolonged strategy with piracy was no doubt beneficial for England while it lasted. But with it she ran the serious risk of being deposed and of witnessing the justified invasion of England by a foreign, Catholic army. The failure of the Spanish Armada, and the armadas of 1596 and 1597, indicated that she was a master at taking advantage of the natural protection of the English Channel.

Thus the peace that was achieved in 1604 made possible the first stable English settlement in America in 1607 and the birth of the United States 176 years later.

Chapter 36

Peace

In the evening of 26 April 1605, four large English galleons arrived in the bay of Corunna and lowered their banners before those of Castile and Leon, which were flying from the castle of San Antón. Salutes were fired from the castle, the city and the now-completed castle of Santa Cruz, and the English ships responded with their artillery. Lord Howard was then received with honours. The Count of Caracena, on a luxuriously decorated tender, was rowed up to the flagship and Howard came out to receive him on the ladder. At long last, after twenty years of the most brutal war ever known on the Atlantic Ocean, the people of England and Corunna made peace. Howard had been sent as the emissary of peace agreed in London a year earlier. Since it was late, it was decided that the English nobles would stay aboard the visiting ships until the following day and, as Caracena returned to port, their galleons fired their cannon in his honour. That night the Count sent Howard 'a huge salmon and other fish, savoury pies, turkeys, partridges, fruit, jams, fresh bread and wine'.[1]

The next day, amid a deafening thunder of salvoes both from the city and the English fleet, the admiral and his retinue disembarked at the Puerta de San Miguel, where they were received by the Count of Caracena, the members of the Real Audiencia, the council and the city's captains. An infantry squadron, deftly lowering their flags, made a striking passageway for them all. Then followed a solemn parade of musketeers and harquebusiers and, later, a gala dinner with dancing and music played on flutes, *vihuelas* and musical bows. The end of the war continued to be celebrated for days afterwards. The warmth of the hospitality of 1605 was equal to the ferocity of the resistance in 1589. Corunna, which had been victorious against Drake, was thus reconciled with England, which for many years would avoid meddling in Spanish affairs in both Europe and America.

It had not been at all easy to agree the peace. Negotiations lasted from May until 28 August 1604, when the armistice was signed in London. The most important demand from the English, relating to the commercial interests of Charles Howard and Robert Cecil, was for Spain to consent to English trade with the Americas and grant bases in the Caribbean for that purpose. Such ambitions, however, had to be put aside. Philip III, who was occupied in the war with the United Provinces, was also ready to make concessions.

---

[1] *Traslado y relación de lo sucedido en la celebración de las paces entre el rey católico de España, D. Felipe III, y el Srmo. Jacobo, rey de Escocia e Inglaterra, por medio de Juan Fernández de Velasco, condestable de Castilla.* (Notification and account of events at the peace celebrations between the Catholic King of Spain, Philip III, and HRH James, King of Scotland and England, via Juan Fernández de Velasco, *Condestable* of Castile.) Antwerp, 1603. Reference in Fernández Duro, *Armada española*, III, p. 226.

He allowed England to trade with wealthy Spain, and even turned a blind eye to the existence of fledgling English settlements in the remote areas of North America, relaxing his initial demand for them to be abandoned. He did, however, demand respect for the integrity of the empire and James I had to promise the application of the death penalty for any Englishmen who dared to challenge it.

> And thus ended the 'long and most cruel conflagration of war', in pursuit of a lasting peace and a general disregard for everything that had happened in the past, and it was understood that this would start from this very day; and that all actions shall be considered to be settled, with the exception of any captures taking place from 14 April 1603 onwards, for these will have to be accounted for; and from now on there shall be no theft, capture, attack, and looting of any kind.[2]

One of the fundamental elements of the treaty was that the King of England 'will order his garrisons not to serve the Dutch for any reason, nor aid them by providing victuals, cannon, powder, bullets or saltpetre, nor give them any other kind of weapons or help of any other kind whatsoever'. With this, plus the Treaty of Vervins signed six years earlier, Spain could now focus its efforts on strengthening its trade monopoly in America, completing the series of fortifications that would make it possible to retain its colonies until the independence of the American republics. It could also concentrate all its efforts on the only remaining war front: The United Provinces. Indeed, as all of the above was taking place, one of the most memorable sieges in the history of the war was in progress.

Stadtholder (Lord Lieutenant) Maurice of Nassau had strengthened his position in the large port city of Ostend and was threatening Spanish Flanders, especially after his great victory at Nieuwpoort, halfway between Dunkirk and Ostend. This victory gave him control of the coast and resulted in 6,000 Spanish casualties. In June 1601, the famous siege of Ostend began, in which Federico Spinola and his brother Ambrogio took part. The city was surrounded by a ring of fortifications, but not blockaded by sea. The siege became so intense that all the military techniques of the time had to be brought into play. The fortifications of Ostend were as renowned as the genius of Spinola's engineers who, after many ups and downs, managed to build a dyke and gradually dismantled the coastal defences.

One month after the signing of the peace treaty with England, in September 1604, Ostend surrendered. A quarter of a million bombs and cannonballs had rained on the town during a siege lasting three years and two months. The forces of the United Provinces and Spain had been so concentrated at that strategic point that there were some 18,000 dead among the besiegers, although the besieged suffered some 77,000.[3] The effect of the Spanish victory reverberated throughout Europe and prepared the way

---

[2] Ricardo De La Cierva, *Historia total de España* (Madrid: Fénix,1999), pp. 448–50
[3] Ibid., pp. 451–5.

for the Twelve Years' Truce signed with the United Provinces on 14 April 1609. This date marked the official birth of the Dutch Republic and a period of peace for Philip III, a *Pax hispanica* that can be considered the first high point of the Spanish Empire. The third King Philip of Spain celebrated it with a massive court extravaganza, until the inevitable discord unleashed the Thirty Years' War.

Epilogue

> The complete success of the propaganda campaign that followed the failure of the Spanish Armada is plain to see. Not so the actual military campaign. The English counterattack was a total disaster, and was also covered up by means of skilful propaganda.[1]

On the basis of the propaganda campaign that had already started at the time of the conflict and the well-worn notions repeated in so many books, articles, documentaries and films, especially in the last two hundred years, English historiography has reinforced a distorted view of what actually took place in 1588 and 1589 and the circumstances that surrounded it. Different clichés have been coined to explain the 'defeat of the Invincible Armada', but the minor premises are as false as the major ones. The defeat of the Armada has been explained by a lack of a Spanish naval policy. Nothing could be further from the truth for the sixteenth century when the first global empire was forged and several fleets were created, with many ships built for both trade and war. The English learned to sail the ocean, to some extent, by emulating the Spanish and by reading books on the art of sailing that they had written. One example is *Breve compendio de la esfera y del arte de navegar*, written in 1551 by Martín Cortés Albácar, which had nine editions in England as *The Arte of Navigation*, in the years 1561, 1572, 1579, 1584, 1589, 1596, 1609, 1615 and 1630.[2] Together with other books, it became the guide used by the English to learn advanced Spanish navigational techniques. It has been described as the use of Mediterranean strategies in an Atlantic war. As we have seen, the Spanish tactics of the treasure fleet and the Spanish Armada were copied by the English, who had never sailed with such large fleets. It has been suggested that Spanish ships were inferior in quality.

Criticisms of Spanish shipbuilding have been based on paintings and prints and have no scientific validity whatsoever. Spanish naval engineering was, in many respects, the most advanced of its time and this explains how the empire was forged and protected, as well as how the Indies' treasure fleet remained inviolable. It has been argued that English cast iron artillery was superior to the Spanish, which is also untrue – its only

---

[1] María José Rodríguez Salgado, 'La Guerra hispano-inglesa 1585–1589', *Memoria Centenario María Pita*, Corunna 1990, p. 25.

[2] Ricardo Cerezo Martínez, et al., *Carlos V. La náutica y la navegación* (Barcelona: Sociedad Estatal para la conmemoración de los centenarios de Carlos V y Felipe II and Lunwerg Editores, 2000), p. 219–20.

Figure 37.1 Book cover of *Breve compendio de la sphera y del arte de navegar*, first published in Seville in 1551. Naval Museum, Madrid.

This book was one of many 'best sellers' with which Spanish culture and science conquered Europe in the sixteenth and seventeenth centuries. It consists of three parts. The first deals with the configuration of the world and the universal principles of navigation. The second, with the sun, the moon, sundials, the causes of the tides and other matters. The third and most important is concerned with the workings and use of nautical instruments and the rules of navigation, as well as the winds, nautical charts, the compass, the astrolabe, how a seafarer determines his location in the sea, or how parallels must be separated when nearing the poles (a precursor of the cartographer Mercator), of magnetic declination and its influence on compasses, or the difference between the magnetic and geographic pole (a scientific breakthrough). It was a pioneering book that contributed to the advancement of nautical science and became indispensable for the other European nations that were to follow in the wake of the Iberian countries and expand across the world.

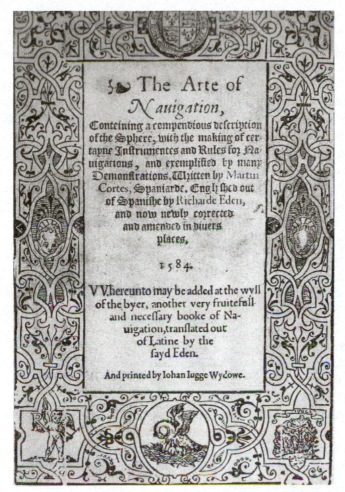

Figure 37.2 Book cover of the 1584 English translation of *Breve compendio* published under the title *The Art of Navigation*, Naval Museum, Madrid

This book became essential reading for English seafarers. Translated by Richard Eden, it was published by Iugge in 1561, 1572, 1579 and 1584, by Jeffes in 1589, by Allde in 1596, by Kingston in 1609, by Stansby in 1615 and by Fawcett in 1630. This case was by no means unique. *El Arte de Navegar*, written by Pedro de Medina in 1545, had an enormous impact internationally. It was translated into Italian (1553, 1554, 1555, 1569 and 1609), French (1554, 1561, 1569, 1577, 1579, 1583, 1615, 1618, 1628, 1633), Dutch (1580, 1589, 1592, 1598) and English (1581, 1595). However, it was not only works on navigation that were translated. José Acosta's *La historia natural y moral de las Indias* (Natural and Moral History of the Indies) went through thirty-two editions in six languages. In this work Acosta, three centuries before Darwin, argued among other things that American fauna had evolved from the European. We could mention many other examples, but the scientific text with the most editions in its day was probably *El examen de ingenios para las ciencias* (*The Examination of Men's Wits*) (1575) by Juan Huarte de San Juan, with eighty-two editions in seven languages up to the end of the eighteenth century. This was Spain's golden age.

advantage was that it was much cheaper. Much of the criticism of Spanish artillery is based on the discovery of short-range siege cannon in shipwrecks, but these guns were carefully loaded in the ships' hold for use in the conquest of English towns, not mounted on the decks for combat in the channel. Other minor historiographical errors include the belief that the preparation for the Spanish Armada caused problems of deforestation, which in Spain had other causes – such as the felling of trees for livestock and farming, for firewood and building – or the notion that the Spanish themselves had arrogantly called the Armada 'Invincible'.

Moreover, there is no hesitation in using these historical misrepresentations even in modern times, specifically around the number of lost ships. In 1988, José Luis Casado Soto, no doubt amazed at the inaccuracy and persistence of these errors, examined the fate of each ship, based on the records of the Spanish Armada and the management of later fleets, which provided precise data: there were twenty-eight shipwrecks in Scottish and Irish waters and the total losses were no more than thirty-five ships.[3] Most of these were *urcas*, transport and Mediterranean vessels. Only a single galleon, the *San Marcos* of Portugal, was wrecked on the return trip, which is of the greatest significance considering that they were the ships that did the fighting. In addition to the centuries-old notions derived from war propaganda and the blatantly biased works that were produced, there is another cause to consider while trying to explain such distortions. This is the tendency to impose the present onto the past or, to put it more precisely, to view earlier events in the light of much later ones. As a caricature of this tendency, we could say that Egyptian civilization carried within it the seed of its downfall, since it was defeated by the Romans. The same could be said about Ancient Greece. Rome, for its part, was the capital of a weak and corrupt empire, for it succumbed to the Barbarians. Al-Andalus was an incoherent entity, since it was defeated by the Christians. Similarly the Spanish Empire was a mere interlude, as proven by its irrecoverable collapse in the nineteenth century. According to this line of reasoning, all former empires were hollow veneers, apart from what we have today, which could be defined as Anglo-Saxon hegemony. And this in turn will be no more than a vague chimera in the future. Nothing could be further from the truth. The empires of Egypt, Greece, Rome, Cordoba and the Catholic Monarchy – without making any comparisons – no longer exist, but they really did exist and shone in the areas of politics, art, science and technology. The Spanish Empire currently comes off worst, for it is the penultimate great empire – in terms of both the time that it lasted and the extent of its territory – whose remains to a large degree provided the basis for the present one, which asserts itself by dismissing its immediate predecessor.

In this sense, there are paradigms that serve to define European historiography of the last two centuries. One of them, quite clearly, consists of ignoring or dismissing all things Hispanic.[4] Accordingly, books dealing with the period of Spanish dominance

---

[3] José Luis Casado Soto, *Los barcos españoles del siglo XVI y la Gran Armada de 1588* (Madrid: Editorial
       1988).
              digm has its origins in the so-called Black Legend. On this subject, see Julián Juderías, *La
              'a* (Salamanca: Junta de Castilla y León, 2003).

should be read bearing in mind the effect on such books of the historical reality of the time when they were written. We should not underestimate the influence of 'presentism', the view of historiography as a phenomenon always rooted in the present of the historian. This presentism has generated a body of well-worn expressions that have been very hard to demolish. Although we are aware of those who distort the most, we rely on others – who we are unaware of – to demolish them, but this paradoxically results in their consolidation. Dealing with such an inherited mixture requires a keen critical approach if the effects of 'historical presentism' are to be avoided.

In other words, historiography is not only the historical product of a particular society at a given moment in time, but this move from a particular present towards a presumed past is also subject to the intervention of other previous 'presents'. Barrow[5] and other authors who created the contemporary myth of the 'Invincible' Armada were conditioned by the England of their time: a society in a position of hegemony that was searching for its legendary origins, those heroic times to which its worthy lineage can be traced. For Victorian England, and for the England of previous decades, the sea was the stage where the nation's virtues, power and wealth were located. There was a massive programme of shipbuilding for war and trade. This was not surprising, since everything in England goes back to the sea, and its maritime presence has always determined its place as a nation among nations. Its careful focus on remaining superior to its competitors in this field has been quite apparent. The creators of England's imperial age, from that particular present, constructed the seafaring picture of sixteenth-century England. The resulting consumer product, aimed at a specific nineteenth-century society, was updated for the benefit of the West in the twentieth and twenty-first centuries.

We must therefore refute Ortega y Gasset's objection to Arnold Toynbee's thesis,[6] when the latter pointed out the nationalistic nature of historiography. Toynbee was correct in stating such intentionality in the field, which he very easily detected in the English-language historiography of his time. This is not in any way to support the oversimplification that such nationalistic influence is specific to Anglo-Saxon countries. It happens to be the case, however, that in the last two centuries English-speaking culture, and not just in Europe, has become overwhelmingly predominant to the point of hegemony, and this has a correlate in the power of its historiography. Therefore, it is not so much a question of a supposed nationalistic specificity in anglophone historiography, but simply a case of its overwhelming success.

There are, however, distinctive features attributable to England under Elizabeth I, such as the attention devoted to matters of propaganda, and to morals and to collective awareness. Unlike Philip II, Elizabeth did not have to bear the burden of a large-scale naval policy. A *laissez faire, laissez passer* approach was enough, with no need to be

---

[5]   John Barrow wrote *Memoirs of the Naval Worthies of Queen Elizabeth's Reign*, published in London in 1845 [translator's note].
[6]   See José Ortega y Gasset, *Una interpretación de la historia universal: en torno a Toynbee* (Madrid: Revista de Occidente, 1960). Translated as *An Interpretation of Universal History* (New York: W. W. Norton, 1984) [translator's note].

much concerned beyond getting whatever she could out of the actions of ships setting sail from England. She could rely on the irrepressible seafaring initiative of her people, which was linked to historical factors (such as the lure of the wealth that resulted from the discoveries of the Iberian nations); geographical factors, such as insularity; climatic factors and their consequences for agrarian poverty; or perhaps even the national character. Such factors amongst others meant that this social initiative was self-sustaining. The rewards obtained from the sea reinforced it in a 'virtuous circle' that led to further English involvement in seafaring, so that this self-sustainability was itself self-sustaining. The harder the living conditions became in England – even as a result of problems relating to the sea itself – the more urgent was the drive to go out to sea.

All of this gave rise to a very specific relationship between seafarers and the crown. The latter had its back more or less turned to the sea but it had its attention on those who sailed it. That is to say, the crown did not need to be on the lookout for maritime ventures to organize, but only to focus on monitoring the society from which such ventures arose spontaneously. The crown allowed such spontaneity to freely mould English history and society; it would go against Elizabeth's temperament to oppose it, for that would be to oppose the very essence of the nation, the goose that laid the golden egg. Englishness itself. Thus, the relationship between the crown and the maritime initiative was one of distance, and was schematic and extrinsic. For the Queen it was a matter of receiving what was her due and little else. What interested her was maintaining an oversight in order to exercise control over naval activity or organize it if it became necessary, but such a case was exceptional. The *laissez-faire* approach was the norm. Furthermore, this approach would play a fundamental role in English foreign policy, which in many cases was essentially a defence, justification or more or less veiled continuation of this *laissez-faire* policy.

Allied to this special relationship between the crown and maritime ventures is the particular nature of English documentation. The information about marine activities is written without any of the concerns of the accountant checking the accounts for the manager of a capitalist monopoly, in order to inform him of every penny spent, the occupation of every man employed and every occurrence. Quite the opposite: the aim was to deceive the crown, if possible, as to the value of goods seized, including those instances when knowledge of them would be detrimental to the purse, reputation or liberty of the person concerned to return to the sea when he wished to do so. Thus, the nature of this English documentation is self-congratulatory, self-exonerating, fictitious and full of praise for England, the crown, and the leaders of each voyage. It is not serious in relation to the actual events, and is emotionally exciting and delightful in the way it is written. It is this set of circumstances that affect the nature of English documentation, and therefore, inextricably, of its historiography – a certain amount of nationalistic specificity all its own that has to be taken into account when analysing the causes and effects of historical presentism.

In stark contrast we have the Spain of Philip II. Here was a king burdened by the task of organizing the first political structure in human history that spanned several continents. To manage the information received and sent daily from the capital of the Empire, Philip created a huge bureaucratic machine and became one of the greatest readers of documents in history. This is the context, so completely different from the English case, in which Spanish documentation must be considered. Reports aim to be accurate, detailed and descriptive; they are written with the intention of conveying precise information by each person depending on their specific responsibility, so that the King or those to whom he has delegated his power may have all the information they need on which to base their orders. It is a pyramidal structure in which there is no motive, place or opportunity for deception or distortion, since the many reports sent to the Court would make such behaviour easily detectable. The primary purpose of Spanish documentation is the conveying of information and any other aim is secondary. Consequently, what it gains in reliability as a source for the understanding of an actual event it loses in vividness and readability. Just as the most used source over the centuries regarding the story of the English Armada, Wingfield's pamphlet, is lively and pleasurable to read for anyone interested in its history, the much more copious, precise, reliable and dispersed Spanish documentation is not. Again, the main difference between them lies in their distinct purposes.

By themselves, however, these considerations are not enough to explain the unequal historiographical treatment of the Spanish Armada and the English Armada and it is important to bear in mind the differing historical development of England and Spain during the nineteenth and twentieth centuries. This was the period when Great Britain's power and influence reached its zenith. As a result, its historiography has established a number of well-worn notions regarding modern European history. At the opposite pole, nineteenth-century Spain was a society in a state of obvious decline. Although in military terms Spain achieved two of the greatest victories in its entire history in the early nineteenth century – the expulsion of the British from South America in 1806–7 and of France from Spain's own territory in 1808–14 – these were desperate defensive struggles in which the unyielding determination of the people had to compensate for the collapse and weakness of the State. Spain and the Hispanic presence in the world would survive these painful challenges, but finding themselves cast out of the mainstream of history[7] and powerless to undertake any greater endeavours, they faced a very long period of convalescence and a feverish Quixotic madness, in which they practiced futile sword-thrusts in the air against impossible enemies. Such was the nineteenth century for Spain. The country awoke from its slumber in 1898, when it lost the remains of its empire and was cast out of its bed of delusions to face the reality of a new period of destitution. In the twentieth century, its symptoms erupted into the worst of all wars.

---

[7] The independence of the Spanish-speaking states of the American continent was premature, in the sense that they were not yet prepared to control their commerce and the management of their wealth, which to a large extent ended up in the hands of the new colonial powers. As for Spain and its progress towards a New Regime, the damage done by the Napoleonic invasion left a profound and long-lasting mark.

Unlike English society during the last two centuries, Spain did not experience the need, the self-satisfaction, to look back to an idealized past as the cradle of its virtues of which it could feel proud. After the trauma of the last two centuries, however, a trauma which is in proportion to the vast dimensions of the lost empire in both space and time, Spain has reached the twenty-first century on a par with the wealth and the lifestyle of the other countries of old Europe. And it is now, from this present, that it is tempting to look back to the past, without suffering any signs of panic. And what does Spain find?

It finds that her past greatness has been buried by foreign historiography of the last two centuries. The reason is not any gratuitous ill will, but simply the need to give a degree of lustre to the historical image of the mainly English-speaking countries – whose greatness is more recent – who have produced much of this historical writing. Thus, we have a radical asymmetry between English-speaking and Spanish societies during the last two centuries, which have been the best in the history of the former and the worst for the latter. The projection of this asymmetry into the field of historiography has produced an asymmetric discourse and this in turn has given us a flagrant distortion of historical facts. The historian who sets out to study sixteenth-century Spain from his twenty-first-century present inevitably stumbles across nineteenth-century England and its consequences. Presentism thus acquires its full historical burden: the historiography is not only a bipolar entity that, positioned in the present, looks towards a past that becomes its object of study, but between the historiography and its subject there lies an earlier bibliography, previous presents, societies and moments whose study was not intended, and which may actually hinder the study of the period in question.

Hence a distorted picture has been constructed on the basis of the idealization of the failure of the Spanish Armada and the total concealment or ignorance of the later developments of the war. According to this picture, the failure of the Spanish Armada marked the end of Spain's presence in the Atlantic and the beginning of its decline, together with the rise of England as a power. In other words, the replacement of the old Spanish Empire by the new British Empire. This is clearly nonsense, since it would be centuries before the British Empire reached its height and the failure of the English Armada was one of the reasons, as well as one of the symptoms for the delay. The perpetuation of such nonsense meant ignoring the sixteenth, seventeenth and eighteenth centuries and even part of the nineteenth, removing that whole part of the historical process, performing a Victorian 'British ellipsis' and picking up the story once more from the Battle of Trafalgar. 'The Invincible Armada and Trafalgar as the greatest moments of Imperial Britain.' Such a distortion leads to a delusional view of history, in which too much has to be concealed, and indeed has been.

This distorted image has found expression in a number of historiographical clichés, of 'erudite syntheses' of 'conventional' (or 'Great') history. Their impact and validity can be seen by how often they are referred to in order to establish the importance of specific events. This practice is also to be found in Spanish historiography. One example is the appraisal of María Pita as a valid Spanish symbol for the English Armada, just as Drake is for that of the Spanish Armada. The concept was rejected in Corunna, of all places, in words that could hardly be any more illuminating. According to the official documents, the role of María Pita 'is fading with the passage of time and is reduced to a few brief lines in so-called 'great' history. Consider the amount of space in general histories given to the defence of Corunna in 1589 as proof of this.'[8] The reader may judge from this example the impact that a lack of awareness of the ways of historiographical process can have. The reification of erudite syntheses, the uncritical validation of them as references by which to assess new research findings, undermines the most valuable significance of research itself. These syntheses of 'great history', as basic structures that link the products of historical knowledge, would play a role similar to that reserved by Kuhn for 'paradigms'.[9] Paradigms are coherent sets of knowledge and values of a given age that inhibit the development of learning. Geocentrism, the notion that God created a world consisting of a motionless Earth with the celestial bodies revolving around it, and in which Man was at the centre of Creation, was a damaging impediment to the development of cosmology, until the facts accumulated against it became so overwhelming that it came crashing down and created the Copernican revolution. This concept can also be applied in a more restricted fashion to the history of Spain.[10] Weighing upon it is a paradigm of denial, and as long as we validate this paradigm as a reference for assessing new or forgotten historiographical findings, we will be unable to evaluate their true meaning.

In this sense, it is worth citing an article published in the summer of 2001 following the discovery of a vessel from the Spanish Armada that sank off the coast of Scotland:

> Immortalized in films, television documentaries and countless textbooks, the Spanish Armada is one of the most famous events in world history. But there was also an English Armada, sent by England to attack Spain, and this second armada has been almost completely erased from history. The English Armada was larger than the Spanish, and from many points of view it was an even greater disaster. This fact, however, is completely overlooked. It is never mentioned in the history courses taught in British schools and a majority of British history teachers have never even heard of it. In the view of the Chair of the Secondary Education Committee of the British Historical Association, Ben Walsh, 'The English Armada has never been taught in British schools, and the majority of history teachers may not be aware that it ever existed. Cultures tend to prize their victories. The Spanish Armada is seen as a victory and the English Armada is obviously not. The modern curriculum stems from these cultural values.' ... It may seem unfair that a disastrous attack by England against Spain is completely forgotten while a disastrous attack by Spain against England is universally remembered ... But specialists in the period need not feel disheartened, for the void of ignorance is

---

[8]   Xosé Ramón Barreiro Fernández, 'La iconología de María Pita: entre la realidad y la ficción' in *Memoria Centenario Maria Pita (1589–1989)* (Corunna: Ayuntamiento de La Coruña, 1989).

[9]   Thomas Kuhn, *The Structure of Scientific Revolutions* (Chicago: University of Chicago Press, 1962).

[10]   On this subject, see Philip Wayne Powell, *Tree of Hate: Propaganda and Prejudices Affecting United States Relations with the Hispanic World* (New York and London, 1971).

apparently being filled, even if for the wrong reasons. Although public knowledge of the English Armada is still practically zero, knowledge of the Spanish Armada is falling rapidly, and the likelihood is that it will fall even further as time passes. The reason is that in British secondary schools there is now such a full curriculum that teachers do not even have time to explain the Spanish Armada to the students. Twenty years ago the vast majority of secondary school students would have studied the Spanish Armada; nowadays it is only taught to between ten and twenty per cent. Therefore, the Spanish and English Armadas, four hundred years after the events, will achieve a kind of equality through ignorance. 'The curriculum today is broader than in the past. This has reduced the time devoted to the Spanish Armada, but has evidently made any mention of the English Armada even less likely,' said Ben Walsh, Chair of the Secondary Education Committee of the British Historical Association.[11]

The case in Spain is similar to that of Britain, although it should be remembered that the Spanish Armada is mentioned in every secondary school history textbook. However, it is hard to find any reference to the English Armada, even in higher education textbooks.

Nevertheless, just as it was impossible to deceive Elizabeth I for long that summer of 1589, as Lincoln said, you cannot fool all the people all the time. Inevitably, a new current of opinion and new avenues of research open up in search of historical truth. There are many honest British and Americans historians who have chosen to aim for objectivity in their research rather than defend biased stereotypes that flatter their self-image as a nation. Martin A. S. Hume heads the list with his magnificent work *The Year after the Armada*, published in London in 1896, during the heyday of the British Empire. Hume took issue with a number of well-established notions, such as the view that the Spanish Armada was an unjustified Spanish act of aggression – or justified only on religious grounds – by stating that the Spanish fleet was aimed at 'the Heretic Queen and her pirate countrymen, who for years had plundered and insulted with impunity the most powerful sovereign in Europe'.[12] Writing about those who were clamouring for revenge for the attack by the Spanish Armada, he adds:

> It mattered little to them that for a long course of years England had been the aggressor, and that Philip had exhausted all diplomatic and conciliatory means, including even secret murder, and the subornation of treason, in England, to arrive at a peaceful 'modus vivendi'. For thirty years he had suffered, more or less patiently, robbery, insult, and aggression in his own dominions at the hands of Elizabeth. The commerce of his country was well-nigh swept from the sea by marauders sallying from English ports or flying the English flag. His own

---

[11] David Keys, 'Gran Bretaña olvida su gran desastre naval mientras recupera restos de la Armada ', *ABC*, 6 August 2001, p. 38.
    The Year After, p. 3.

towns, both in the Spanish colonies and in old Spain, had been sacked and burnt by English seamen without any declaration of war; and rebellion in the ancient patrimony of his house had been, and was still, kept alive by English money and English troops.

Indeed, as we have seen, the reasons for sending the Spanish Armada were defence of American colonies from such attacks and also the defence of Flanders.[13]

Hume then concludes with gentle irony that 'Englishmen, then and now, had the comfortable and highly commendable faculty of believing their own side always to be in the right.'[14] It is not the intention here to put forward a moral disquisition on the past, but to establish the real lines of causality in the recounting of history. With Europe engaged in a war of religion, religious intolerance was obviously the order of the day, but Spain was not a special case in this sense and ecclesiastical zeal was not the driving force behind the Armada. To claim otherwise is to attempt to conceal the real motives. As far as the English Armada is concerned, Hume submitted an oft-repeated lament: 'The story of this ill-fated expedition is usually dealt with in a few lines by English historians, although if it had succeeded it would have changed completely England's status on the Continent.'[15]

It is no easy task to write about the importance of specific military actions, because their outcome is usually connected to prior circumstances of which they are only one aspect. However, it is possible to assess the historical importance of the failure of the English Armada, on account of the critical nature of the moment when Elizabeth decided to launch her attack. The men taking part in the Spanish Armada were aware from the outset of the serious risks involved in gambling everything on the Atlantic. Philip's gambit was a massive strike demanding the maximum concentration of naval forces in a single operation. Its destruction, therefore, would leave Spain seriously defenceless. Medina Sidonia clearly understood this when he warned that if the Armada failed, 'Portuguese possessions and the Indies would be in very great danger'.[16] Jorge Manrique was also aware that on the success of the operation 'all Christianity and the preservation of its states depended, for having devoted all the naval forces it was possible to use in these seas, with any misfortune in battle or storm everything was liable to be lost'.[17] Francisco de Bobadilla also accurately foresaw the danger when he stated that 'in the case of any adversity of war or storm, the Indies were lost, and Portugal and Flanders were at great risk of the same'.[18]

To sum up, the failure of the Spanish Armada not only meant the continuation of Elizabeth's reign, but also the risk of collapse for the Empire in the event of an

---

[13] See Chapter 1.

[14] Hume, *The Year After*, p. 8.

[15] Ibid., p. 10.

[16] Medina Sidonia to the King, Corunna, 24 June 1988. Fernández Duro, *La Armada Invencible*, II, p. 136.

[17] *Parecer de los generales de la Armada sobre la salida de ella del puerto de la Coruña*. Corunna, 27 June 1588; Ibid., p. 143.

[18] Ibid., p. 144.

Anglo-Dutch counterattack.[19] That Elizabeth should seize her great opportunity was part of the logic of war. And England made a huge effort to play her hand, by putting together the largest fleet that ever sailed from Britain. Its complete failure put an end to that historic opportunity and gave Spain the time, the strength and the will to establish conclusively its presence in the Americas. The success of the English Armada would have made it possible for the English and Dutch to find a way into Philip's American territories, and above all, in the short term, there would have been a great danger of Brazil ending up in English hands given the clauses agreed between Dom António and Elizabeth. The failure of that expedition, however, made it possible for the Iberian presence to survive in what we now call Latin America. The significance of the English Armada's defeat is therefore undeniable and palpable on a global scale, even in modern times.

So the amphibious operation of 1588 failed, but so did that of 1589. Considered together, the two disasters were not dissimilar. They both suffered enormous human losses. Between the time when forces began to assemble in Lisbon for the English Enterprise and the death of the last of the English Armada's men to return or who were infected once they were back on land, many thousands of men died for their country. The Spanish Armada suffered some 11,000 casualties, but in addition there were the 2,000 dead from disease in Lisbon, among them the commander of the expedition, Álvaro de Bazán.[20] Others also include the comparatively low number – less than 1,000 – of casualties in combat in Corunna and Lisbon. As for the English, their fleet no doubt suffered losses in combat in the channel in 1588, but the majority of their casualties by far were men who died from disease, especially during the time when they were ordered by the Queen to remain on board in port in case the Spanish Armada should return. These losses must have been at least 8,000 to 10,000 men, but the worst part of the tragedy for the English occurred during the expedition of 1589, especially while they were in Portugal and owing to virulent disease during the return journey. In total, the number of English casualties was probably over 20,000. It can therefore be said that the number who lost their life during the brief period of time that marked the height of the Anglo-Spanish conflict was not much less than 45,000. One-third of them were Spanish, the remaining two-thirds English. A large number of them left their bones at the bottom of

---

[19] 'The triumphalist tone of Wingfield's account is indisputable, but the actions that it celebrates – the attack against Galicia and Portugal in 1589 – are barely known today. They did not bring about the collapse of the Spanish monarchy as he predicted; on the contrary, it can be said that they were the salvation of Philip II's empire.' María José Rodríguez Salgado, 'La Guerra hispano-inglesa 1585–1589', *Memoria Centenario María Pita*, Corunna, 1990, p. 21.

[20] On this subject, see Gracia Rivas, *La sanidad*, pp. 104–12. The considerable means used in Lisbon to deal with disease should be noted: it was eventually contained, the ships were cleansed and strict health measures were taken. Thanks to this, even counting the losses due to shipwrecks on the return journey of the Spanish Armada, the death toll did not reach 50 per cent. In stark contrast, the lack of medical resources available on board the ships of the English fleet which were deployed against the Spanish Armada and which later became part of the English Armada – which was also deficient in medical resources – resulted in a death rate of over 75 per cent in the English expedition.

the sea, sowing the depths with the undoubted greatness of the intrepid men who dared to defy the oceans, even if it was just to fight among themselves.

What happened in 1588, though distorted, appears in the most basic of timelines, while the events of 1589 are passed over even in the most comprehensive of texts. May these words, in memory of those who fought and died, stand as a humble contribution towards a change in this state of affairs.

Bibliography

Abbreviations for Locations of Documents Consulted

AGS   Archivo General de Simancas, Valladolid.
BN   Biblioteca Nacional, Madrid.
MN   Museo Naval, Madrid.
RAH   Real Academia de la Historia, Madrid.

Adams, Simon. 'La estrategia isabelina y el desastre de la Armada'. *Historia 16*, No. 148. 1988.

Adams, Simon and M. J. Rodríguez Salgado (eds). *England, Spain and the Gran Armada, 1585–1604: Essays from the Anglo-Spanish Conferences, London and Madrid*, 1988. Edinburgh: John Donald Publishers, 1991.

Alcalá-Zamora y Queipo De Llano, José. *La Empresa de Inglaterra (La 'Armada Invencible': fabulación y realidad)*. Madrid: Real Academia de la Historia, 2004.

Anonymous. *Ephemeris expeditionis Norreysius et Drakus in Lusitaniam.* London: Thomas Woodcocke's Printing Press, 1589.

Apestegui, Cruz. *Piratas en el Caribe*. Barcelona: Lunwerg Editores, 2000.

Arquellada, Juan. *Sumario de prohezas y casos de guerra . . .* Jaén, 1999. (First published 1590).

Azcona Pastor, José Manuel, *Possible Paradises: Basque Emigration to Latin America*, Reno: University of Nevada Press, 2004.

Barreiro Fernández, Xosé Ramón. *Historia de la ciudad de La Coruña.* Corunna: Editorial La Voz de Galicia, 1986.

Barreiro Fernández, Xosé Ramón. 'La iconología de María Pita: entre la realidad y la ficción', in *Memoria Centenario Maria Pita (1589–1989)*, Corunna: Ayuntamiento de La Coruña, 1989.

Barrow, John. *Memoirs of the Naval Worthies of Queen Elizabeth's Reign.* London, 1845.

Barrow, John. *Life, Voyages and Exploits of Sir Francis Drake*. London, 1861.

Boxer, C. R.,*The Dutch in Brazil, 1624–1654*, Oxford: Clarendon Press, 1957

Breixo, Carlos, Emilio Ramil González and Emilio Grandío Seoane. *Historia de Ortigueira*. Corunna: Via Lactea, 1999.

Cabrera De Córdoba, Luis. *Historia de Felipe II Rey de España*. 4 vols. Salamanca: Junta de Castilla y León, 1998. Part One, first edition, Madrid 1619; Parts One and Two first published together Madrid 1877.

Calendar of State Papers and Manuscripts Relating to English Affairs Preserved in, or Originally Belonging to the Archives of Simancas, Vols I–IV: Elizabeth. London: H. M. Stationery Office, 1892–99.

Calendar of State Papers and Manuscripts Relating to English Affairs, Existing in the Archives and Collections of Venice and Other Libraries in Northern Italy, Vol. VIII. London: H. M. Stationery Office, 1894.

Calvar Gross, Jorge, María José Rodríguez Salgado, Simon Adams, José Luis Casado Soto. La Gran Armada. Simposio Hispano Británico. Londres junio 1988–Madrid noviembre 1988. *Cuadernos Monográficos del Instituto de Historia y Cultura Naval*, No. 3. 1989.

Cañete, Hugo A., *Los Tercios en América*. Málaga: Ediciones Platea, 2017.

Casado Soto, José Luis. *Los barcos españoles del siglo XVI y la Gran Armada de 1588*. Madrid: Editorial San Martín, 1988.

Cerezo Martinez, Ricardo. *Las Armadas de Felipe II*. Madrid: Editorial San Martín, 1989.

Cerezo Martínez, Ricardo et al. *Carlos V. La náutica y la navegación*. Barcelona: Sociedad Estatal para la conmemoración de los centenarios de Carlos V y Felipe II and Lunwerg Editores, 2000.

Cervera Pery, José. *La Estrategia naval del imperio*. Madrid: Editorial San Martín, 1982.

Corbett, Julian. *Drake and the Tudor Navy*. London: Longmans, Green, 1917.

Daviña Sáinz, Santiago. *La Coruña: Nuevos relatos sobre el cerco de 1589*. Corunna: Librería Arenas, 1997.

De La Cierva, Ricardo. *Historia total de España*. Madrid: Fénix, 1999.

Dictionary of National Biography, 1885–1900, Vol. 15 (for Sir Francis Drake), New York and London: Macmillan, 1888. Available online: https://archive.org/stream/dictionaryofnati15stepuoft#page/n10/mode/1up (accessed 2 February 2017).

Dictionary of National Biography, 1885–1900, Vol. 62 (for Anthony Wingfield), New York and London: Macmillan, 1900, pp. 182–3. Available online: https://archive.org/stream/dictionarynatio13stepgoog#page/n194/mode/2up (accessed 17 September 2017).

Domínguez Ortiz, Antonio. 'La Armada de Inglaterra en la política de Felipe II'. *Historia 16*, No. 148. 1988.

Douglas, Ken. *The Downfall of the Spanish Armada in Ireland*. Dublin: Gill & Macmillan, 2009.

Estrada Gallardo, Félix. 'Datos para la confección de un atlas histórico de La Coruña'. *Revista del Instituto José Cornide de Estudios Coruñeses*, No. V–VI. 1969–70.

Fernández Duro, Cesáreo. *Bosquejo Encomiástico de Don Pedro Enríquez de Acevedo. Conde de Fuentes*. Vol. X of the *Colección de Memorias de la Real Academia de la Historia*. Madrid, 1884.

Fernández Duro, Cesáreo. *La Armada Invencible*. 2 vols. Madrid, 1884.

Fernández Duro, Cesáreo. *Armada española*. Madrid: Museo Naval, 1972–73.

Fernández Duro, Cesáreo. *Disquisiciones náuticas*. Madrid: Ministerio de Defensa, 1996.

Fernández Fernández, Carlos M. *Antiguos Hospitales*. Corunna: Vía Láctea Editorial, 1995.

García Cárcel, Ricardo. *Las Culturas del Siglo de Oro*. Madrid: Biblioteca Historia 16. 1989.

Garcia De Palacio, Diego. *Instrucción Náutica para el buen uso y regimiento de las Naos*. México: Pedro Ocharte, 1587.

Garcia Oro, José. 'El Capitán Cristóbal Díaz y la invasión de La Coruña', *Anuario Brigantino*, Vol. 19 (1996), pp. 123–8.

Garcia Tapia, Nicolás. *Un inventor navarro: Jerónimo de Ayanz y Beaumont (1553–1613)*. Pamplona: Gobierno de Navarra, 2010

Gómez Beltrán, Antonio Luis. *La Invencible y su Leyenda Negra*. Málaga: Arin Ediciones, 2013.

Gómez-Centurión Jiménez, Carlos. *Felipe II. La Empresa de Inglaterra y el Comercio Septentrional (1566–1609)*. Madrid: Editorial Naval, 1988.

Gómez-Centurión Jiménez, Carlos. 'Los motivos de La Invencible'. *Historia 16*, No. 148. 1988.

González-Aller Hierro, José Ignacio. *España en la Mar*. Barcelona: Comisaría General de España en la EXPO de Lisboa '98 and Lunwerg Editores, 1998.

González-Aller Hierro, José Ignacio, et al. *La Batalla del Mar Océano*. Corpus of Documents. 10 vols. Madrid, 2014.

González-Arnao Conde-Luque, Mariano. 'La Aventura de La Armada'. *Historia 16*, No. 148. 1988.

González-Arnao Conde-Luque, Mariano. *Derrota y muerte de Sir Francis Drake.*Santiago de Compostela, 1995.

Gonzalez-Cebrian, Tello. *La ciudad a través de su plano*. Corunna: Ayuntamiento de La Coruña, 1984.

González Garcés, Miguel. *María Pita, Símbolo de Libertad de La Coruña*. Corunna: Fundación Caixa Galicia, 1989.

González López, Emilio. *La Galicia de los Austrias*. Corunna: Fundación Barrié de la Maza, 1980.

Gorrochategui Santos, Luis. 'Cañones de la Invencible a flor de agua', *Restauro. Revista Internacional del Patrimonio Histórico*, No. 2. Madrid, 2008

Gracia Rivas, Manuel. *La sanidad en la jornada de Inglaterra (1587–1588)*. Madrid: Editorial Naval, 1988.

Hemming, J. *The Conquest of the Incas*. New York: Harcourt Brace Jovanovich, 1970.

Herrera Oria, Enrique. *La Armada Invencible*. Madrid: Archivo Histórico Español, 1929.

Herrera Oria, Enrique. *Felipe II y el Marqués de Santa Cruz en la Empresa de Inglaterra*. Madrid: Instituto Histórico de Marina, 1946.

Herrera y Tordesillas, Antonio. *Historia general del Mundo*. 3 vols. Madrid, 1601–12. Available online: http://data.cervantesvirtual.com/person/7787 (accessed 9 February 2017).

Howarth, David. *The Voyage of the Armada: The Spanish Story*. London: Collins, 1981.

Hume, Martin A. S. *The Year After the Armada*. Dallas, 1970. (First edition 1896).

Hume, Martin A. S. *Calendar of Letters and State Papers Relating to English Affairs Preserved in, or Originally Belonging to the Archives of Simancas*, Vol. 4: Elizabeth, 1587–1603. London, 1899.

Juderías, Julián. *La Leyenda Negra*. Salamanca: Junta de Castilla y León, 2003. (First edition 1917).

Kamen, Henry. *Philip of Spain*. New Haven, CT and London: Yale University Press, 1997.

Kelsey, Harry. *Sir Francis Drake: The Queen's Pirate*. New Haven, CT and London: Yale University Press, 1998.

Keys, David. 'Gran Bretaña olvida su gran desastre naval mientras recupera restos de la Armada Invencible', *ABC*, 6 August 2001.

Knox Laughton, John (ed.) *State Papers Relating to the Defeat of the Spanish Armada, Anno 1588*. London: The Navy Records Society, 1894. Available online: https://archive.org/details/statepapersrela00lauggoog (accessed 9 February 2017).

Konstan, Angus. *The Spanish Armada*. Oxford: Osprey Publishing, 2009.

Kuhn, Thomas. *The Structure of Scientific Revolutions*. Chicago: University of Chicago Press, 1962.

Levy, Buddy. *River of Darkness: Francisco Orellana's Legendary Voyage of Death and Discovery down the Amazon*. New York: Random House, 2011.

López Ferreiro, Antonio, *Historia de la Iglesia de Santiago de Compostela*, Vol. VIII, Chapter XI, *La Iglesia compostelana en el siglo XVI,* Santiago de Compostela: Seminario Conciliar Central, 1905.

Luján, Néstor. *La vida cotidiana en el Siglo de Oro español*. Barcelona: Editorial Planeta,1992.

Manera Regueyra, Enrique et al. *El Buque en la Armada Española*. Madris: Sílex Ediciones, 1999.

Manzano Lahoz, Antonio and Luis Sorando Muzás. 'Las banderas de la capilla del Doncel de la catedral de Sigüenza'. *Banderas* (Boletín de la Sociedad Española de Vexilología), No. 44. 1992.

Martín, Colin and Geoffrey Parker. *The Spanish Armada*. London: Hamish Hamilton, 1988.

Martínez Salazar, Andrés. *El cerco de La Coruña en 1589 y Mayor Fernández Pita.* Corunna: Editorial La Voz de Galicia, 1988.

Mattingly, Garrett. *The Defeat of the Spanish Armada*. London: Jonathan Cape, 1983. (First edition 1959).

'The Miracle of Empel: An Astounding End to a Decisive Battle for the Spanish', *Ancient Origins*, 16 December 2015. Available online: http://www.ancient-origins. net/history-important-events/miracle-empel-astounding-end-decisive-battle-spanish-004943?nopaging=1 (accessed 17 September 2017).

Oliveira Martins, Joaquim Pedro. *Historia de Portugal*. Lisbon: Guimaraes Editores, 2004.

Ortega Y Gasset, José. *An Interpretation of Universal History*. London: W. W. Norton, 1984.

Parker, Geoffrey. 'Si la Invencible hubiese desembarcado ...' *Historia 16*, No. 140. 1987.

Parker, Geoffrey. 'Farnesio y el ejército de Flandes'. *Historia 16*, No. 148. 1988.

Parker, Geoffrey. 'Anatomy of Defeat. The Testimony of Juan Martínez de Recalde and Don Alonso Martínez de Leyva on the Failure of the Spanish Armada in 1588', *The Mariner's Mirror*, Vol. 90, August 2004, pp. 314–47.

Pires De Lima, Durval. *O ataque dos ingleses a Lisboa em 1589 contado por uma testemunha* in Lisboa e seu Termo: Estudos e Documentos, Associação dos Arqueólogos Portugueses, vol. I. Lisbon, 1948.

Rebello Da Silva, Luiz Augusto. *Quadro Elementar das relacoes políticas e diplomáticas de Portugal*. Lisbon, 1858.

Roca Barea, María Elvira. *Imperiofobia y Leyenda Negra. Roma, Rusia, Estados Unidos y el Imperio Español*. Madrid: Siruela, 2016.

Rodrígues De Oliveira, Chistovam. *Summario e que brevemente se contem alguas cousas (assi ecclesiasticas como seculares) que ha na cidade de Lisboa*. Lisbon, 1755 (First edition 1554).

Rodríguez Salgado, María José. 'La Guerra hispano-inglesa 1585–1589', in *Memoria Centenario María Pita*. Corunna: Ayuntamiento de La Coruña, 1989.

Ruela Pombo, Manuel. *Portugal 1580–1595*. Lisbon: Revista 1640, 1947

Russell-Wood, A. J. R. *The Portuguese Empire 1415–1808: A World on the Move*. Baltimore, Maryland: Johns Hopkins University Press, 1998.

Saavedra Vazquez, Maria del Carmen. *María Pita y la defensa de La Coruña en 1589*. Corunna: Ayuntamiento de La Coruña, 1989.

Saavedra Vazquez, María del Carmen. *La Coruña en la Edad Moderna*. Corunna: Vía Láctea Editorial, 1994.

Saavedra Vazquez, María del Carmen. *María Pita. Una aproximación a su vida y a su tiempo*. Corunna: Vía Láctea Editorial, 2005.

Salvá, Miguel, *Colección de Documentos Inéditos para la Historia de España*, Madrid 1879, Vol. 73.

Santiago y Gómez, José. *Historia de Vigo y su comarca*.Madrid: Impr. del Asilo de Huérfanos, 1919.

Soraluce Blond, José Ramón. *Castillos y fortificaciones en Galicia. La arquitectura militar de los siglos XVI–XVIII*. Corunna: Fundación Pedro Barrié de la Maza, 1985.

Stapleton, Jim, *The Spanish Armada 1588: The Journey of Francisco de Cuéllar*. Sligo, Ireland, 2001.

Tettamancy Gastón, Francisco. *Apuntes para la Historia Comercial de La Coruña*. Corunna: Ayuntamiento de La Coruña, 1994. (First edition 1900.)

Toribio Medina, José. *Historia del Tribunal del Santo Oficio de la Inquisición en Chile*. Santiago de Chile: Fondo Histórico y Bibliográfico José Toribio Medina, 1932.

Toynbee, Arnold. *A Study of History*. 2 vol. abridgement. Oxford: Oxford University Press, 1960. Available online: https://ia801508.us.archive.org/30/items/in.ernet. dli.2015.187403/2015.187403.A-Study-Of-History-Voll-I-vi.pdf (accessed 2 February 2017).

Ulm, Wes. 'The Defeat of the English Armada and the 16th-Century Spanish Naval Resurgence.' Available online: http://wesulm.bravehost.com/history/eng_armada. htm (accessed 17 September 2017).

Urgorri Casado, Fernando. 'Hombres y navíos de la Invencible. Los que volvieron a La Coruña'. *Revista del Instituto José Cornide de Estudios Coruñeses*, No. 23. 1987.

Vaamonde Lores, César. 'El capitán Colmelo', *Boletín de la Real Academia Gallega*, No. 36, 1910.

Vedia y Goossens, Enrique. *Historia y descripción de la ciudad de La Coruña*. Corunna: Instituto José Cornide de Estudios Coruñeses, 1975. (First edition 1845).

Velo Pensado, Ismael. *La vida municipal de A Coruña en el siglo XVI*. Corunna: Editorial Diputación Provincial, 1992.

Wayne Powell, Philip. *Tree of Hate: Propaganda and Prejudices Affecting United States Relations with the Hispanic World*. New York and London: Basic Books, 1971.

Wernham, R. B. (ed.) *The Expedition of Sir John Norris and Sir Francis Drake to Spain and Portugal*. London: Temple Smith for the Navy Records Society, 1988.

Index

Abd al-Malik I, Sultan of Morocco 33, 193
Abu Abdullah Mohammed II, Sultan of
    Morocco 33
Acapulco 10
Act of Supremacy 7
Acuña, Pedro de, captain 208
Africa, African 8, 33, 34, 162, 193, 265
Ágreda, Fernando de, captain 176, 190
Águila, Juan del, *Maestre de campo* of infantry
    203, 227, 256–8, 280–2
Aguirre, Martin, pilot who guided Francis Drake
    in his circumnavigation of the globe 247
Aid, ship, English Armada 42
Al-Andalus 290
Alarcón, Gaspar de, captain 125, 127–8, 135,
    138, 141–2, 153, 179, 186–7, 190, 195,
    221, 224
Alba, Duke of 8, 151
Albert, Archduke, Viceroy of Portugal 107, 125,
    133–4, 141, 181, 191, 199, 205, 209, 277–8
Alburquerque, Matías de 169, 200, 212
Alcántara, Lisbon 151, 185–7
Alcántara, Spanish military order 129
Aldana, Francisco de, general and poet killed in the
    battle of El-Ksar el Kebir on 4 August
    1578 34
Aldeburgh 247
Aldeia Galega 147
Alemparte, Rodrigo, archivist at the Cathedral of
    Santiago de Compostela 81
Alexander the Great 162
Alfândega (customs), Lisbon 155–6
Algarve 212, 269
Ali Pasha, Ottoman admiral at Lepanto 92
Almada 207
Almanzor 144
Almeida, Jorge de, Portuguese Archbishop 34
Almodóvar del Campo 233
Almonacir, captain 161–3, 171
Alonso Alfeirán, Rodrigo, Galician nobleman 85
Alonso de Aguilar, commander killed in the
    battle of El-Ksar el Kebir on 4 August
    1578 34

Altamira, Count of, Lope Osorio de Moscoso 56,
    71–2, 78, 79, 104, 105, 110
Alvalade, Lisbon 157–8, 163–4, 222
Alvarado, Alonso de, governor of Las Palmas,
    Canary Islands 263, 279
Álvarez, García, sacristan of the treasure of the
    Cathedral of Santiago de Compostela 81
Americas 8, 10, 37, 123, 261, 263–4, 267, 269,
    273, 283, 298
Amezola, Carlos de, sailor 258–9, 263
Ancora, river 229
Andalusia, Andalusian 14, 212, 273
Andrade, Count of, Fernando Ruiz de Castro
    70, 77–9, 81–2, 84–6, 101–7, 109–12,
    114, 115
  appointed as general of the Galician rescue
      troops 70
  appraisal of his performance 112
  battle of El Burgo 102, 103, 104, 105
  combat in Vilaboa 85
  defence plan for Santiago 110
  first combat in El Burgo 78
  reinforcements by sea unsuccessful 79, 82,
      101, 104
Andrade, Fernando de, Galician nobleman 110
Andrade, Lope de, Galician nobleman 85
Andrade, Manuel de, Philip II's secret agent
    239, 243
Andrade, Pedro de 70
Andrea de Ledesma, Alonso, nobleman killed in
    the defence of Caracas 262
Ángel, Francisco, captain 150, 198
Angra, Terceira Island, Azores 274
Antilles, Islands 264
Antonelli, Bautista, Italian engineer 266
Antonian 122, 137, 139, 151, 169, 173, 190,
    197, 201
António, Dom, Prior of Crato
  capture of his papers and letters 225
  clauses signed with Queen Elizabeth I 37, 298
  in Corunna 66
  Elizabeth refuses to allow him to sail with the
      English fleet in 1588 13

flees from Lisbon 184
illegitimate pretender 34
King of Peniche 129
murder attempt on his return 243
in Plymouth after the failure of the English
    Armada 243
his secret plan to take Lisbon 197
survivor in the battle of El-Ksar el
    Kebir 34
talks in London 35
'tyrant of the masses' 35
Antwerp 27, 283
Anunciada, convent, Lisbon 150, 173–4
Aramburu, Marcos de, sailor 48, 234, 240,
    248, 272–3
Aranda, Juan de, commander on Terceira,
    Azores 234
Araujo, Antonio de, head of the castle of Peniche
    125, 129
Arceo, Jerónimo de, secretary to Medina
    Sidonia 23
Archbishop of Santiago de Compostela 34, 38,
    43, 56–7, 65, 78, 80–1, 104, 106, 110–11
Arco da Rua Augusta, Lisbon 156
Arco dos Cregos, Lisbon 156
Ares de Galdo, Pedro, captain of the Galician
    rescue troops 85
Arguineguín, Canary Islands 263
Arias Maldonado, Francisco, judge of the
    Audiencia Real of Galicia 109
Ark Royal, ship, English fleet 1588 13
Arousa, estuary 201
Arquellada, Juan, historian 217
Arrepentidas, convent, Lisbon 150
artillery 254 .
Ashley, Anthony, member of the Privy Council
    241, 243
Asturias, Asturian 71, 82, 104
Atacames 260
Ataide, João González de, squire of Atouguía
    125–9, 160
Atienza, Andrés de, sailor 216
Atlantic 3, 16, 27, 43, 133, 261, 264, 266, 278,
    283, 287, 294, 297
Atouguia da Baleia, Peniche 125, 127, 130, 221
Aubrey, Dr, signatory to the report to the Privy
    Council on the plunder of supply ships
    captured by the English Armada 245
Aveiro, Duke of 224–5

Avellaneda, Bernardino de, sailor 268
Ayala, Martín de, Knight Commander of
    Puertomarín 70, 78, 105, 110
Ayanz, Jerónimo de, inventor 51
Azores 3, 10, 31, 35–6, 39, 211–12, 215, 225–6,
    228, 229–30, 234, 238, 254–5, 259, 260,
    269, 272–4, 279
the 'key to the New World' 35

Bacon, Anthony 88, 94, 96, 103, 105–6, 209–11,
    213, 216, 224–5, 235, 245, 248
Baeza 178
Bairro Alto, Lisbon 164, 180
Balboa, Núñez de, Vasco, discoverer of the
    Pacific Ocean 247, 267
Baltic 10, 45, 245
Baltimore, Ireland 280–1
Banners captured during the English withdrawal
    from Lisbon to Cascais on 5 June 1589
    186, 188–9
Baqueraña, Cascais 199
Barcelona 277–8, 287
Bark Bonner, ship, English Armada 230, 236,
    239, 248
Barrera, Antonio, ensign 70, 83
Barrow, John, historian 244, 260, 291
Bartholomew, lost ship, English Armada 247
Barton, captain, wounded at the bridge of El
    Burgo, Corunna 106, 225
Baskerville, captain 266
Bayona 19, 43–5, 48, 53, 70, 81, 112, 117, 122,
    124, 130–1, 135–6, 201, 220, 226, 231
Bazán, Alonso de, sailor 118–19, 121, 128, 133,
    163, 185, 190–2, 207, 209, 212–13, 216,
    227, 241, 248–50, 254
attack on the English Armada 216–17, 248
attack on the English army 190
capture of the *Revenge* 254–5
plan for a new Spanish Armada 249
plan to stop the English Armada in Lisbon
    118, 119
repairs to the Spanish Armada 241
Bazán, Álvaro, Son, Second Marquis of Santa
    Cruz 191
Bazán, Álvaro. First Marquis of Santa Cruz 9–
    10, 21, 23, 46–7, 87, 191
his plans for the Spanish Armada 9
Bazán, Diego de, captain 46, 53, 72, 87, 92, 113
Beamonde, Claudio de, commander 134

Beatriz, Portuguese Princess 34
Begoña, Santa María de, ship, Spanish Armada 131, 201
Belém, castle, Lisbon 118
Belgium 278
Benavente, Count of, Rodrigo Alonso Pimentel 114
Benavides, captain 126
Berbers 133, 205
Berbés, Vigo 232
Bergantiños, Corunna 54, 72
Berlengas, Islands 122, 125, 143
Bermúdez, commander 111, 228–9, 236
Berrio y Oruña, Antonio de, explorer and governor 260–2
Bertendona, Martín de, admiral 20, 48, 53, 59, 64, 99, 101, 111, 254, 255, 273
Betanzos 44–6, 48, 54–7, 61, 65, 69, 70, 82, 106, 110, 112
Bica, A, Lisbon 164
Bigbaque, Juan Antonio, merchant sailor 226, 239, 241, 243
Biscay 16, 26, 49, 273
Black Legend 275
Blankenberge, Flanders 25
Blavet (Port Louis) 253, 257–9, 273
Bobadilla, Francisco de, *Maestre de campo* of infantry 169
Bojador, Cape, Africa 162
Book of Matthew 59
Boquerón, castle, San Juan de Puerto Rico 264
Bordeaux 256
Bouzas, Vigo 231
Boyer, captain, wounded in Corunna 96
Bravo, Sancho, captain 129, 135, 142, 148, 153, 160, 165, 179, 186–90, 192, 206, 208, 224, 226
  seizes banners in combat 186
Brazil 33, 37, 201, 235, 261, 271, 298
Breda 256
Brest 256, 257–8
Brett, colonel, killed in the attack on 3 June Lisbon 176, 183, 190
British Empire 294, 296
  distorted image 294
Brittany 253, 256–7, 273, 278
Brochero, Diego, sailor 269, 273–4, 280
Brussels 277
Bugio, Fort, Lisbon 121

Burela 119
Burghley, William, Queen's adviser 2, 8, 31–2, 36, 214
  coins the term *Invincible* to refer to the Spanish Armada 2

Cabeça Seca, Lisbon 118
Cabo de la Vela 261
Cabrera de Córdoba, historian 23, 217, 277
Cádiz 219, 220, 222–3, 269, 270–3, 275, 279
Caesar, Dr, signatory to the report to the Privy Council on the plunder of supply ships captured by the English Armada 245
Calais 22–3, 25, 131, 208, 211, 269, 273
California 10
Calvinists 7
Camacho, Diego, captain 48
Cámara, prisoner 234
Caminha 229
Campello, Gaspar de 138–9, 160
Canary Islands 10, 259, 267, 279
Cangas 57, 131, 234–5, 238, 248
Cantabria, Cantabrian 14, 27, 39, 44, 122, 210
Canterbury Cathedral 239
Caparica, Lisbon 38, 117–8, 155, 165
Cape Roca 122, 212
Capirilla, Panama 266
Caracena, Count of 283
Caramanchón, Corunna 62–3, 65, 67, 69
Cárdenas, Francisco, head of the castle of Cascais 195, 197, 199, 201–3
Caribbean Sea 8, 162, 281, 283
Carmelites, monastery, Lisbon 150, 184
Carmona, Seville 46
Carrick na Spania (Rock of the Spaniards) 23, 25, 27–8
Cartagena de Indias 266, 268
Carvajal, Álvaro de, captain 186
Carvajal, Gómez de, captain 46, 62, 69–70, 83, 117, 124, 136
Casa de Paz Grande, ship 14
Casado Soto, José Luis, historian 290
Cascais 35, 38, 118, 128, 132, 134, 136, 139, 142–3, 149–51, 156–7, 159–60, 179, 181, 183–7, 190–2, 195, 198–200, 202, 205–12, 218, 220–2, 224–5, 229–31, 237, 240
Castelblanco, Manuel, *Maestre de campo* of infantry 156

Castile 7, 8, 10, 26, 36, 46, 48, 103, 180, 207, 215, 218, 222, 270, 272, 279, 283
Castillo, captain 126, 224
Castillo, sergeant, wounded in the attack on 3 June Lisbon 178, 180
Castiñeiras, Corunna 55
Castro, Beltrán de, admiral 260
Castro, Fernando de, Portuguese nobleman 115, 134, 152, 159
Casualties, total number on both sides 298
Catalan navy 278
Catherine of Aragon 7
Catherine of Medici 7
Catherine, Duchess of Braganza 34
Catherine, Portuguese Queen 34
Catholic Monarchs 114
Caverley, Captain, killed in the naval battle on 20 June 216
Cawsand Bay 250
Cayón 71
Cecil, Robert, First Earl of Salisbury 283
Cerralbo, Second Marquis of, Juan Pacheco
  building of the Castle of San Antón 43
  calm in the face of the arrival of the English 53
  deployment of the soldiers on the wall 70
  discipline 80
  first battles 54
  impossiblity of defending Vigo 231
  mystery of the galleys 101
  preparations for the defence of Corunna 43
  request for the infantry to remain in Corunna 44
  supplies for later fleets 43, 201
  supplies for the Spanish Armada 14, 119
Cervantes, Miguel de 271
Céspedes, Juan de, captain 48
Chacarreta, Sebastián de, sailor 171
Chafariz, Lisbon 155
Chagre, river 266
Charles I of Spain (Emperor Charles V) 7, 33, 103, 162, 174–5, 267
Chichester, captain, fatally wounded in the attack on 3 June 176
Church Town 258
Cid, El, Rodrigo Díaz de Vivar 48
Cíes, Islands 130, 226, 23–1, 234–6
Cinco Chagas, ship 260
Cock or Cope, captain, died when the ship Plaisir sank on 2 August 1588 20

Coimbra 38, 227
Collegiate Church of Santa María, Corunna 94
Collegiate Church, Vigo 232
Colmelo de Sevil, Jácome, captain 70
Coloma, Francisco 128, 156, 184–6, 201, 212, 215, 254, 269, 280
Columbus, Christopher 162, 168
Commission, the, an equivalent of the Inquisition 144
Concepción, ship 136
Consolação, beach, Peniche 125–6
Cook, captain, wounded in Corunna 96
Cooper, captain, killed at the bridge of El Burgo, Corunna 105–6
Corcubión 228, 272
Cornwall 213, 258
Corpo Santo, Lisbon 161, 169
Corrubedo 136
Corte Real, Lisbon 165
Cortés Albácar, Martín, author of Breve compendio de la esfera y del arte de navegar (1551) 287–9
Cortés, Hernán 267
Corunna
  actions of the womenfolk 68, 94, 96
  breaches in the walls 100
  celebrations on making peace 283
  coopers 14
  defence forces 51
  defended with stones 94
  incendiary attacks 111
  militia 96
  mined turret 83, 85–91, 96, 113
  oath of 73, 75–7, 83, 144
  pillage of Pescadería 65, 67
  total population 51
  walls of the high town 56, 58, 65, 67, 74, 102
  walls of the isthmus 5–5, 58, 63, 65, 67, 71–2, 84
Corvo, Island, Azores 254
Costa de la Muerte, Corunna 11, 12, 272
Cotrofe, Sánchez, Juan, captain 51
Coutiño, Luis 260
Coya, Vigo 232
Craon 256, 258
Crescent, lost ship, English Armada 247
Crisp, captain 130
Cristóvão de Távares, Portuguese counsellor 34
Cristóvão, son of Dom António, prior of Crato 36–7

Cross, Robert, captain 213, 214
Cuatro Villas (Santander, Castro, Laredo and San
    Andrés de la Barquera), Cantabria 249
Cuéllar, Francisco de, castaway on the Spanish
    Armada 27, 28
The de Cuéllar Suite, symphony 28
Culleredo 102
Cumaná 261
Cumberland, Earl of 254–5, 259–60, 272

D'Aumont, marshal 258
Dainty, ship, later called *La Inglesa* 259–60, 265
Daviña, Santiago, historian 56
Denmark, Danish 31, 210
Diana, ship 44, 53, 55, 58, 64
Dias Lobo, Rui 167–8, 190
Díaz, Cristóbal, captain 56
Dictionary of National Biography 3, 246
Docampo, Alonso, commander 280
Docwra, Francis, captain 235
Dominicans 16
Don Quixote 33, 262, 271, 293
Doncel of Sigüenza, Vázquez de Arce,
    Martín 186–8
Douro, river 227
Dover 24, 32–3, 39
Downs 32
Drake Passage 247
Drake, Francis
    agreement with investors 39
    argument with Hawkins 264
    argument with Norris in Peniche 122, 124
    argument with Norris in Plymouth 241
    attack on Las Palmas 263
    attack on Nombre de Dios 266–7
    attack on San Juan de Puerto Rico 264–5
    cartographical piracy 247
    in the Channel 21, 22, 24
    'cowardly knave or a traitor' 26
    disarray and dispersal of the English
        Armada 223
    dropping anchor in Cascais 143
    dropping anchor in Corunna 54
    dropping anchor in Vigo 230
    guilty for not having gone to Santander 132
    his death and appraisal of his performance 267
    hounding of *urcas* in Cascais 143, 150, 159
    in London 33, 35
    makes the same mistake twice 263
    overseeing Plymouth's defences 263

Primus circumdedisti me 247
    reserves food for seamen 200
    responsible of the disaster 250
    sets sail from Corunna 112, 117
Drake, John, brother of Francis Drake 267
Dreadnought, ship, English Armada 41, 238, 248
Drellet, Guillermo, prisoner 239
Drogheda 144
Drummer of El Bruc 266
Duarte, brother of Teodósio II of
    Bragança 198
Duarte, Francisco, general supplier 134, 160
Duarte, Portuguese Prince 34
Dunkirk 19, 23–4, 27, 122, 236–7, 284
Duquesa Santa Ana, lost ship, Spanish
    Armada 22

Eddystone 17
Egypt 290
Eirís, Corunna 54
El Burgo, Corunna 70, 77–9, 85–6, 96, 99, 101–
    7, 110–12, 115
El Cabrón, bay, Puerto Rico 264–5
El Dorado 253, 255, 257, 259–62
Elcano, Juan Sebastián, first man to
    circumnavigate the globe 247
Elizabeth I, Queen of England
    anti-Spanish Protestantism 1
    clauses signed with Dom António, *see* Dom
        António
    coalition with Islam against Spain 36
    collusion with Henry IV of France against
        Spain 133
    congratulations to Philip for the victory of
        Lepanto 8
    connivance with the pirates 7, 11
    deceived regarding the outcome of the English
        Armada 241, 243
    and her favourite Essex 121, 195, 209, 240
    financial problems 31, 32
    furious towards Drake 254
    hidden to public opinion the failure of the
        English Armada 32, 250
    lack of concern for her own men
        32, 275
    and her main objective for the English
        Armada 250
    naval policy 144, 291–2, 296
    preparations of the English Armada 39
    rearguard of the Flemish rebels 8

repatriation of her troops stationed in Holland
37, 282
use of war propaganda 2, 291
Elizabeth Jones, ship 26
El-Ksar el Kebir, battle (1578) 34–5
Elvas 147
Emmanuel Filiberto of Savoie 34
Emmanuel, lost ship, English Armada 247
Encamisada (Spanish night commando attack)
153–5, 157, 173
England
Englishness 292
its historical development 293
self-sustainability of the war for 292
English Armada
Anglo-Moroccan coalition 35
capture of two banners 186
cavalry 128
consequences of failure 297–8
demand of the Hanseatic League to return the
booty 245
deserters 213, 246
dispersion and return 238, 243
efforts to cover up its losses 1, 287, 290
English casualties among the local population
of Plymouth 245
English casualties at the Bridge of El Burgo
on 16 May Corunna 105
English casualties in the attacks of the walls
on 14 May Corunna 88
English casualties in the *Encamisada* on 1
June Lisbon 154
English casualties in the return trip 239
English casualties in the skirmish on 4 May
hill of Santa Lucía 55
English casualties on 22 June Peniche 225
English casualties on 3 June Lisbon 176
English casualties on 30 June-1 July Vigo
233, 234
English casualties on 5 June withdrawal
Lisbon Cascais 183, 186
English casualties until 5 June 246
English casualties, comparison with casualties
of Spanish Armada 246
English casualties, total number 245, 298
English drunkenness in Corunna 68, 73, 139
extreme conditions on the return trip 239
Hanseatic supply ships (hulks) captured by
159, 210, 226, 245

inability to pay to survivors and gallows for
seven of them 245
lack of siege artillery 143
lost ships, total number 248
new fears of invasion after its failure 250
objectives 2, 39
preparations 41
primary objetive 250
sacking of ships by survivors 245
seize 42
ships lost during return 238
ships lost in Corunna 248
ships lost in naval combat, Lisbon 219
ships lost in Vigo 235
Spanish casualties at the Bridge of El Burgo
on 16 May Corunna 106
Spanish casualties in the attack on castle of
San Antón on 14 May Corunna 100
Spanish casualties in the attacks on the walls
on 14 May Corunna 95
Spanish casualties on 3 June Lisbon 178
Spanish casualties, total number 298
Spanish ships lost in Corunna 59
struggle against peninsular union 35
supply flotillas 213, 214
survivors prohibited from going to London 244
two plans to take Lisbon 122
English Channel 7, 9, 16, 22–3, 27, 90, 175, 179,
253, 256, 258, 280, 282
English fleet 1588
attack with fireships 24
casualties in combat on 2 August Porland
Bill 20
casualties in combat on 3 August Isle of
Wight 22
casualties in combat on 31 July Eddystone 18
casualties in combat on 8 August
Gravelines 26
casualties, total number 33, 298
dangerous situation in Plymouth 13
infection 32
systematic concealment of casualties and
damage 20
Enríquez, Juan, captain 266
Enxara dos Cavaleiros, Lisbon 135, 141
Ephemeris expeditionis Norreysius et Drakus in
Lusitaniam, pamphlet 244
Epidemics, diseases and plagues 7, 31–2, 43, 62,
160, 229, 233, 236, 238–40, 244, 246

Esperança, convent, Lisbon 150, 162
Espichel, Cape 218, 224
Esposende 228
Esquibel, Miguel de 47
Esquivel, ensign 14
Essex, Earl of, Robert Devereux 42, 119, 121–2, 126, 132, 137, 195, 197, 199, 201, 203, 209, 211–12, 224, 227, 237, 240–1, 273, 274
  flight from England 121
Estaca de Bares, Cape 119
Estremoz 147
Europe 1, 7, 8, 33, 39, 123, 144, 149, 151, 162, 168, 172, 175, 233, 245, 250, 260, 262, 283–4, 288, 291, 294, 296–7
Evesham, John 103, 106, 119, 208–9, 212–13, 216–17, 220, 225, 229, 236, 239, 243
Évora 147
Exmouth 247
Extremadura 45–6

fascines (very tight bundles of twigs) 74, 85, 94, 96, 257
Fajardo, Luis, sailor 272
Falmouth 121, 273
Farnese, Alexander, Duke of Parma 8, 16, 18–19, 21–4, 26–7, 32, 39–40, 122, 165, 211, 249, 256
Faro 271
Fator, river 267
Fenner, Thomas, Vice Admiral of the English Armada, died of disease 41, 238
Fenner, William 42, 88, 94, 96, 103, 105–6, 209–10, 211, 213, 216, 219, 223–25, 235, 238, 245, 248
Feria, Duke of 150
Fernández Cid, Juan 233
Fernández de Aguiar, Juan, nobleman of the Galician rescue troops 85
Fernández de Córdoba, Antonio, gunner of Saô Jorge castle, Lisbon 164
Fernández de Velasco, Juan, *Condestable* of Castile 283
Fernández Duro, Cesáreo, historian 40
Fernández, Vasco, captain of militia in Corunna 61, 69
Ferrara 277
Ferreira, Luis, captain 71–2
Ferrol 45, 48, 58, 61, 64, 70, 101, 118, 253, 272–3
Fez 36, 205

Figueroa, Jácome de, lawyer of Vigo 231–3
Finisterre, Cape 11, 117, 119, 124, 136, 210, 228, 235–7, 255, 272
fireships 23–4, 119, 207–8, 211–12, 222
Fisher, John, cardinal 144
Flanders 1, 2, 7–9, 16–19, 23–4, 46, 56, 70, 133, 169, 253, 256, 284, 297
Flores, Diego, admiral 46
Flores, Island, Azores 279
Florida, ship, Spanish fleet 1589 216
Flushing 24, 26
Foley 247
food and drink
  bacon 11
  biscuit 62, 128, 148, 160, 200
  bread 16, 76, 160, 192, 211, 283
  cattle 14
  cheese 11, 14, 160, 192, 210
  chick peas 62
  chickens 14
  cod 12
  fish, fishermen 11, 16, 62, 76, 201, 237, 283
  flour 148
  hardtack (a type of long-lasting bread or biscuit and a fundamental part of any diet on sea voyages) 211
  honey 160
  lard 11
  meat 14
  olive oil 14
  rye 148
  salted meat 11
  sheep 14
  tuna 12, 46
  vegetables 12
  water 11–12, 51, 73, 96, 140, 160, 220, 224, 229, 232–3, 243, 263, 265, 267–8
  wheat 124, 128, 130–1, 148, 199–200, 210–11, 213, 220, 222
  wine 14, 43, 46, 62, 68, 69, 73, 76, 96, 132, 139, 160, 192, 196, 201, 237, 279, 283
Foresight, ship, English Armada 42
Fortune, lost ship, English Armada 247
France, French 2, 7, 21, 23, 35, 39, 118–19, 124, 131, 133, 196, 199, 203, 213, 215, 218, 221, 223, 253, 256–8, 261, 266, 274, 277, 289, 293
Francis I of France 156
Francis, lost ship, English Armada 247

Francisco de Sá, Portuguese counsellor 34

Freire, Gabriel, captain of the Galician rescue troops 85

Freminville, historian 258

Frobisher, Martin, sailor 17, 26, 255, 257–8

Fuentes, Count of, Pedro de Guzmán
accuses Padilla 279
appraisal of his performance 197
capture of the English garrison in Peniche 225
in Cascais 192
caution in the face of the withdrawal of the English 185, 187, 188, 189
harassment of Norris' army 129, 135, 157
obstructs landing in Peniche 126, 127, 134
organization of the external defence of Lisbon 133
sends caravels to spy on the English fleet 213, 227
a study of 125
suspects help given to Norris from António's supporters 151, 157, 167

Fulford, captain, wounded at the bridge of El Burgo, Corunna 106

gabions (large baskets full of earth used as a parapet for the men opening the trenches) 182, 257

Gaiteiro, bridge, Corunna 55, 58, 71

Galicia, Galician 11–12, 16, 19, 43, 45, 47, 50, 54, 56–8, 61–2, 65, 70, 77, 79, 81, 85, 94, 96, 104, 110–12, 115, 119, 124, 130–1, 135–6, 145, 165, 201, 209, 224, 226–9, 231–4, 237, 238, 250, 279, 298

Gandariña, Vigo 233

Garás, Corunna 55

García, Antonio, sacristan of the Cathedral of Santiago de Compostela 81

García, Pedro, captain 226

Garrard, William, author or the *Arte of War* (1591) 151

Genoa 277, 278

Gerbrantsen, Jan, admiral 279, 280

Germany, German 2, 10, 45, 199, 219, 256

Gift of Dover, lost ship, English Armada 247

Gift of Hampton, lost ship, English Armada 247

Gijón 14

Gil, Juan, ensign 16, 19

Girón, Antonio, mayor of Cádiz 270

Girón, Fernando, governor of Cádiz 271

Godspeed, lost ship, English Armada 247

Golden Hind, also named *Pelican* 247

Golden Hind, lost ship, English Armada 247, 248

Gomera, Canary Islands 279

Gómez de Medina, Juan, captain of the convoy of supply ships, Spanish Armada 13, 14, 21

Góngora, Luis de, Spanish poet 271

González de Silva, Garci, governor of Caracas 262

González, servant to Judge Luis de Padilla 61

González-Arnao, Mariano, historian 218, 246, 248

Good Hope, Cape of 162

Gracia, square, Lisbon 10, 11, 12, 16, 298

Gran Grifón, ship 21

Gravelines 25, 26, 196, 211, 267

Grecio, Eduardo, captain 216

Greece 175, 290

Gregorian calendar 239

Gregory, ship, English Armada 223, 225, 229, 236, 238, 239, 248

Grenville, Richard, last captain of the *Revenge* of Drake, captured by Alonso de Bazán, Azores, 1591 254, 255, 260

Greyhound, lost ship, English Armada 247

Griffin, ship 238

Guadeloupe, Island, Caribbean 264

Guadeloupe, monastery, Cáceres 34

Guaicamacuto 262

Guaira, La 262

Guarnizo 249

guerrilla 153

Guevara, Jerónimo de, captain 173, 190

Guild of fishermen, Corunna 69, 76, 114

Guipúzcoa 20, 272

Gutiérrez de Garibay, Juan, admiral 268, 274

Guyenne 256

Hampton 247

Hanseatic supply ship (hulks) captured by English Armada *see* English Armada

Harwich 32

Havana 274, 279, 280

Hawkins, John, admiral 17, 22, 24, 32, 217, 235, 255, 259, 260, 263, 264, 265, 267

Hawkins, Richard, admiral 20, 259, 260

Heneage, Thomas 153

Henry I of Portugal 34

Henry II of France 7

Henry III of Navarre 133, 25–7

Henry IV of France 133
Henry the Navigator, Portuguese Infante 144
Henry VIII of England 1, 7,
    144, 282
Herdan, captain, wounded at the bridge of El
    Burgo, Corunna 106
Herrera, Antonio de, ensign 44, 62, 69, 87,
    91, 113
Herrería, Corunna 90
historiography 4, 262, 287, 290–4
    anti-Spanish paradigm 290, 295
    asymmetric discourse 294
    British ellipsis 294
    clichés 2, 244, 287, 294
    English documentation, its nature 292
    Historical Presentism, Presentism 291–2, 294
    its nationalistic nature 291
    Spanish Berrization 262
    Spanish documentation, its nature 293
Hoces, Francisco de, discoverer of the passage
    between Antarctica and the American
    Continent, the Sea of Hoces 247
Hoces, Sea 247
Holland, Dutch 1, 2, 8, 16, 23, 25, 33, 36–7, 39–
    40, 130, 169, 201, 205, 210–12, 220, 224,
    228, 253, 257–9, 261, 269, 271, 273–4, 278,
    282, 284–5, 289, 298
Howard, Charles of Effingham, admiral of
    the English fleet 1588 2, 13, 16–22,
    24–7, 31–2, 198, 211, 223, 239, 249, 269,
    271–2, 282–3
Howard, Thomas, Earl of Suffolk 254, 273
Huarte de San Juan, Juan, author of *The
    Examination of Men's Wits* (1575) 289
Huguenots 124, 253, 256–8
Hume, Martin A. S, historian 174, 226, 245,
    262, 296–7
Huntington, Earl of 121
Hurtado de Mendoza, García, Viceroy of
    Peru 259

Ibarra, Esteban de, secretary to Philip II 134, 186
Iconoclasm 207–8
Idiáquez, Juan de, secretary Philip II 9
incendiary devices and 'right to burn' 74, 109
Indian Ocean 162
Inquisiçao, tower, Lisbon 174
Inquisition 260
Ireland, Irish 2, 27–8, 31–2, 36, 46–7,
    131, 280–1

legacy of gratitude to shipwrecked men of the
    Spanish Armada 28
Isabela, patache, Spanish Armada 45
Isabella Clara Eugenia, Spanish infanta 277
Isabella of Portugal, Queen of Spain 34, 134, 156
Isla, Nicolás de, *Maestre de campo* of infantry 47
Islam 8, 172
Italy 2, 273
Izquierdo, Miguel, soldier 79–80, 82

Jackson, captain, killed in action on 26 May
    1589 Peniche 126, 221
James VI of Scotland and I of England 283–4
Jerez, Blas de, captain 126, 173, 190, 199
Joanna of Austria, daughter of Charles I of Spain
    and mother of Sebastião I of Portugal 33
John II of Portugal 162
Jones, Antonio de, captain 129
Jonson, Thomas, captain, wounded in
    Corunna 96
Juan de Tassis, Spanish poet 35
Juárez, Pedro, governor of Puerto Rico 264–5

Kelsey, Harry, historian 217
Kent 1, 16, 23
Kinsale 280, 281
Klifford, lieutenant, wounded in Corunna 96
Knollys, Francis, courtier to Elizabeth I 121
Knollys, William 209
Kuhn, Thomas, philosopher 295

La Luz, castle, Las Palmas, Canary Islands 279
La Rochelle 212–13
Labañóu, Corunna 55
Labora, Jácome, canon, seized in the capture of
    Pescadería on 6 May 1589 63, 66
Lago, Pedro del, captain of militia in Corunna 51
Lamarinha, Lisbon 153–5
Lancastro, Dinis, mayor of Obidos 125, 127
Lane, Ralph, colonel 40, 126, 142, 153–4, 223
Laredo 14
Larrey, Isaac de, historian 259, 273
Las Palmas, Canary Islands 279
Latin America 8, 168, 298
Laughton, captain 260
León, (Fort Crozon) France 257
León, Luis de, sergeant major 48, 54, 57, 75, 90
Leona, ship, Spanish fleet 1589 216
Lepanto, naval battle 8, 16, 24, 92, 175
Lewson, Richard, sailor 280, 282

Leyva, Antonio de, admiral 17, 22, 26, 45, 47, 277
Liermo Agüero, Hernando de, captain 266
Lincoln, Abraham 296
Lisbon
  fear of its population 181
  fear of its womenfolk 150
  Fernandine wall 155, 163
  garrison of 145, 181
  population flees from 147
  weak spot 118, 155
Lobo, sergeant 70, 83
London 1, 3, 7, 9, 11, 14, 17, 21, 26–7, 31, 38, 89, 114, 121, 132, 171, 183, 209, 223, 229, 236, 243, 244–5, 250, 283, 291, 295, 296
Lopes, Diego, Portuguese governor 34
López de Almendras, Antonio, nobleman of the Galician rescue troops 85
López de Valladares, Martín, captain 70
Loreto, church, Lisbon 170, 173, 176, 190
Lourenço de Taide, Rui 157
Lourenço de Távora, Rui, captain 192
Loures, Lisbon 141, 143–4, 145, 148, 151, 153–4, 157, 222
Lourinha, Lisbon 130, 221
Low Countries 8, 278
Lübeck 226, 238
Lugo 61, 119
Luis César, house of, Lisbon 185, 199
Luis de Camões, Portuguese poet 167
Luis, Duke of Beja 34
Luna, ensign 70, 83
Luna, Juan de, captain 46, 53, 62, 67, 69, 82
Lutheranism 25, 191
Luzón, Diego, commander 14

Maas, river 169
Maastricht 256
Madeira, Islands 224, 225–7
Madox, Richard 247
Madre de Deus, convent, LIsbon 150
Madre de Dios, ship 255
Madrid 1, 2, 9, 10–11, 14, 19, 26, 38, 40, 44, 47, 114, 125, 162, 218, 232, 234, 261, 277–8, 284, 288–90, 291
Magdalena, hospital, Vigo 232
Magdalena, ship 265
Magellan, Ferdinand 162
Magellan, Strait of 247, 259, 266–7
Maghreb 34

Malo, Francisco Martínez, captain mortally wounded in the attack of 3 June Lisbon 129, 153, 173, 178, 180, 190
Malpica 12
Malta 44, 45
Malvecín, Corunna 53, 55, 58, 61, 63–4, 69, 72
Manila Galleon 10
Manrique, Jorge, *veedor* (inspector) of the Spanish Armada 297
Manrique, Juan de, captain general of artillery 117
Manrique, Pedro, captain 46, 53, 87, 113
Manuel, son of the Prior of Crato 66, 184–5, 269
Margaret of Austria 277
Mar da Palha, Lisbon 165
Margarita, Island 261
Margate 32
María Juan, lost ship, Spanish Armada 26
Mariñas, Diego de las, Galician nobleman 82
Mariño, Payo, captain of militia in Corunna 70, 83
Mascarenhas, João de, Portuguese counsellor 34
Mattingly, Garrett, historian 32, 247
Maurice of Nassau 256, 284
McClancy, Irish chieftan 28
Medina Sidonia, Duke of, Alonso Pérez de Guzmán 9–11, 13–7, 19–24, 26–7, 32, 47, 131, 165, 196, 211, 270–2, 297
  did not suffer from seasickness 11
  'God of tuna' 271
  improved the performance of the Spanish Armada 10
  very reluctant to command the Spanish Armada 11
Mediterranean Sea, Mediterranean 13, 16, 27, 48, 175, 214, 218, 274, 277, 278, 287, 290
Meiranes, Francisco de, captain of militia in Corunna 51, 54, 61, 70, 83, 99
Melo, Manuel de, Master of the Hunt in Portugal 138
Menchaca, Francisco de, squire of Cayón 71–2
Mendoza, Álvaro de, captain 156, 186
Mendoza, Bernardino de, Spanish ambassador to France 14, 21
Mendoza, Fernando de, captain 255
Mendoza, Rodrigo de, captain 110
Mendoza, Spanish agent in London 35
Mera, Corunna 54, 109
Mercoeur, Duke of 257
Mérida 45

Mérida, ensign 136
Mexía, Agustín, *Maestre de campo* of infantry 46
Minion, lost ship, English Armada 247
Ministerio das Finanzas, Lisbon 156
Miño, river 110
Minshaw, captain, killed in the naval battle of 20
    June 1589 216
Miracle of Empel 169
Molac, Baron of 257
Moluccas Islands' War 162
Moncada, Hugo de, captain of the squadron of
    galleasses in the Spanish Armada, killed on
    the attack to the *San Lorenzo* in Calais on 8
    August 1588 20, 25
Monroy, Jerónimo de, captain 44–5, 54, 99
Monsalve, Juan de, captain, killed in the attack
    on Corunna on 5 May 1589 47, 55–6,
    61, 65, 69
Monson, William, sailor 274, 280, 282
Montasique, pass, betwen Enxara and
    Lisbon 142
Monte de Arcas, Corunna 71, 77
Monterrey 81
Montoto, Lorenzo, captain of militia in Corunna
    51, 61, 69, 70, 83, 109
Monzón, captain 198
More, Thomas 144
Morocco 33, 35–7, 133, 175, 193
Morrillo, castle, San Juan de Puerto Rico 264
Morro, castle, San Juan de Puerto Rico 265
Moscow 149
Mount's Bay 258
Mountjoy, English Viceroy of Ireland 280, 281
Mousehole 258, 263
Mugía 14, 228
Mulay Ahmed, King of Morocco
    35, 36
Munguía, Cristóbal de, captain 208
Murad III, Ottoman Sultan 133
Muros 48
Museu Militar, Lisbon 156

Nabo, Cosme, soldier 207
Naples 45, 115
Napoleon 149, 153, 271
Nariga, Cape, Corunna 228
Nelle, Corunna 55
Newlyn 258, 263
Nieuwpoort 26, 284
Nightingale, lost ship, English Armada 247

Niño, Gabriel, *Maestre de campo* of infantry
    133, 134, 181, 186
Nombre de Dios, Panamá 266
Nonpareil, ship, English Armada 41
Normandy 258
Norris, Edward, colonel, wounded at the bridge
    of El Burgo, Corunna 42, 105, 106
Norris, John
    appraisal of his performance 242
    attempts to pay his men 245
    Battle of Craon 256
    capture of Fort Crozon 257
    makes a national pronouncement with the
        objective of covering up the English
        Armada 241, 243–4
    his plan 123
    recruitment problems 37
North Sea 10, 27, 245
Norway 31, 237
Nossa Senhora da Quietação das Flamengas,
    convent, Lisbon 150
Nossa Senhora da Luz, convent, Lisbon 141
Nuestra Señora del Rosario, captured ship,
    Spanish Armada 19

Obidos 125, 127
O'Donnell, Hugh, Irish chieftain 281
Oeiras, Lisbon 117–18, 134, 192–3, 196–9,
    207–8, 221
Oleaga, Martín de, captain 259
Oleiros, Corunna 70, 102
Oliste, sailor 273
Olivera, ensign 78
O'Neill, Hugh, Irish chieftain 280–1
Ons, Isle, Spain 119
Oporto 38, 112, 228
Oquendo, Miguel de, admiral 20, 22,
    26, 47
Orange, William of 1
Orejón, captain 186, 192
Orellana, Francisco 261
Orense 81
Orinoco, river 261
Orkney Islands 31
Oropesa, Count of 199
Orozco, Rodrigo de 229
Ortega y Gasset, José, philosopher 188, 291
Ortigueira 85, 86
Orzán, beach, Corunna 62, 65
Os Cardais, convent, Lisbon 165

Os Jerónimos, monastery, Lisbon 150
Ostend 284
Otalora, Juan de, judge of the *Audiencia Real* of
　Galicia 101
Oton, castle, Portugal 38
Ottoman Empire 33–4, 92, 133, 156, 175, 256
Oza, Corunna 54–5, 57–8, 106, 174

Pacheco, Juan, captain 186
Pacific Ocean 247, 260, 267
Paço de Arcos, Lisbon 118
Paços, Diego de, captain 233
Paços, Gregorio de, captain 233
Padilla, Luis, judge of the Audiencia Real of
　Galicia 61
Padilla, Martín de, *Adelantado* of Castile
　207–8, 215–16, 219–20, 222, 248, 272–3,
　277, 279–80
Palma, ship, Spanish fleet 1589 216, 279
Palmer, Edmund, English agent at Saint
　Jean-de-Luz 215
Palomino, galley captain 53, 58, 101, 104, 111
pamphlets 2–4, 244, 250, 293
Panama 168, 260, 265–7
Panama Canal, early plans for its
　construction 267
Panjón, Pontevedra 130
Pantoja, galley captain 53, 58–9, 101, 104, 111
Pardo de Cela, Bartolomé, sergeant major
　85, 106
Pardo, Pedro, captain 70, 81
Pardo, Sancho, admiral 264–5, 269
Paredes, Tomé, captain, killed in Fort Crozon on
　18 November 1594 46, 257–8
'Paris is well worth a mass', famous statement
　by Henry of Navarre, Huguenot, to accede
　to the throne of France 256
Parrote, Corunna 70, 99, 104
Pasaje, bridge, Corunna 102
Pasajes de San Juan 44, 248
Patrona, ship, Spanish fleet 1589　216
Payo-Mouro, Corunna 55
Peace of Cateau-Cambrésis (1559) 7
Peace of London (1604) 283–4
　celebrations in Corunna 283
Peace of Vervins (1598) 274, 284
Pedraza, Francisco de, captain, killed in the
　attack on 3 June Lisbon 173, 178,
　180, 190

Peniche 122–3, 125, 127–33, 136–7, 183, 195,
　197, 208, 211, 221, 224, 225, 226, 227,
　240, 242
Peninsular War 56, 153, 266
Penzance 258, 263
Peralta, Cristóbal de, captain 45
Peregrina, ship, Spanish fleet 1589 216, 258
Pereira, Antonio, captain 157
Pereira, Fernán, mayor of Vigo and captain 232
Pereira, Francisco, defender of Vigo 233
Peres de Távora, Rui, Portuguese nobleman
　134, 156
Pérez, Antonio, secretary to Philip II 269
Peru 168, 259, 266
Peto Burdelo, Corunna 111
Pew, Edward, captain, killed at the bridge of El
　Burgo, Corunna 106
pewter, zinc, lead, and tin alloy 96
Philip II, King of Spain
　appraisal of his performance 274
　arranges two marriages 277
　assists Sebastian, King of Portugal 34
　coalition against him 133
　death of 274
　defence of his inheritance 8
　dynastic rights to the Portuguese crown 34,
　　141, 156
　his Empire 8
　his errors 24, 274–5
　friendship with England 7, 8, 296
　his objetives 1, 9, 264
　old and sick 272
　as Philip I of Portugal 151, 181, 198, 205
　plans for Panama Canal 267
　his power 35
　preparation of coastal defences 39
　his prudence 8, 9, 296
　naval policy 3, 287, 291
　naval recovery 253
　repairs the Spanish Armada 201, 209
　second Armada 272
　sends the Duke of Alba to Flanders 8
　spies 239, 243, 246
　strategy in Lisbon 159
　unfounded criticism of 61
Philip III, King of Spain 115, 274, 277–8, 281,
　283, 285
　allows England to establish settlements in
　　America 284

authorizes corsair galleys 278
Irish policy 281
Millionaire King 277, 285
his *valido* (favourite) 277
his wedding 278
Phoenicians 162
Phoenix, lost ship, English Armada 247
Piew, Robert, captain, killed in Peniche on 26
    May 1589 221
Pimentel, Diego de, captain of *San Mateo*,
    captured ship, Spanish Armada 25,
    44, 45, 46
Pimentel, Rodrigo Alonso 114
Pinos, Island, Cuba 268
Pinzón brothers, Columbus' first voyage 168
pirates, piracy 1, 7, 10, 79, 144, 150, 161, 168,
    175, 211, 213, 223, 254–5, 263, 265, 267,
    271, 273, 275, 281–2, 296
Pita, María, heroine of Corunna 37, 45, 54, 57,
    59–60, 79, 81, 89, 91, 93–7, 104–5, 113–14,
    117, 231, 263, 294–5, 298
    as a symbol 114, 294
    her heroic action 93
Pizarro, Francisco, Spanish conquistador
    168, 261
Pizarro, Gonzalo, Spanish conquistador, half-
    brother of Francisco Pizarro 261
Plaisir, lost ship, English fleet 1588 20
Pliego, captain 129
Plymouth 14, 17, 19, 24, 40–1, 53, 119, 121,
    149, 166, 209, 216–17, 223, 226, 230, 238–
    9, 241, 243–8, 250, 254, 259, 268, 273
    death toll from plague brought by the English
        Armada 245
    fear of a new Armada 250
    Howard awaits the Spanish Armada 13
Pointe des Espagnols, France 258
Polo, Marco, Italian explorer 162
Ponce de León, Pedro 191
Ponce de Sandoval, Pedro, captain 48, 55, 61,
    69–70, 83, 87, 91, 113, 191
Pontevedra 119, 201, 228, 231, 237
Poole, William, captain, wounded in Corunna 96
Port of Spain, Trinidad 261
Porta da Cruz, Lisbon 156
Porta do Mar, Lisbon 156
Portland Bill 20
Porto da Arca, cove, Peniche 125, 127
Porto Santo, Island, Madeira 224

Portoalegre, Count of 227
Portobello, Panama 114
Portsmouth 243, 247
Portugalete 249
Portuguese Empire 127, 130, 162
Portuguese inflation 33
Poulo, Pontevedra 110
Praça do Comércio, Lisbon 156
Princesa, ship 44, 53, 55, 58, 64
Prioriño, cape, Corunna 53
Propaganda war 2–3, 21, 79, 90, 244, 247, 287
Protestantism, protestants 1, 8, 144, 152, 168,
    253, 256–7, 274
Puebla, Antonio de, captain 81, 111, 117,
    122, 124
Puentedeume 45, 70, 105
Puerta de Aires, Corunna 70, 74, 77, 79–80, 87,
    90–2, 99, 100–1, 113
Puerta Real, Corunna 65, 70, 79–80, 83
Puertocarrero, Juan, sailor 215–16
Punta del Gallo, Venezuela 261

Quélern 257
Quesada, Diego de, gunner at the castle of São
    Jorge, Lisbon 164, 186
Quintal, Lisbon 191
Quito, Ecuador 260

Ragazzona, ship, Spanish Armada 17, 48–9
Rainbow, ship 25
Raleigh, Walter, explored 255, 261, 262–4,
    270, 273
Rata Santa María Encoronada, lost ship,
    Spanish Armada 17
Recalde, Juan Martínez de
    arrives in Corunna 45
    his death and appraisal of his performance 47
    the heaviest artillery on the lower decks 22
    first encounter in the Cannel 17, 18
    managed to weigh anchor again 25
    men saved in the *San Juan* 46
    his ships dispersed by the storm in Corunna 13
    surrounded by English ships 20
    took out the main mast of *Revenge* 21
    unequal combat 26
Redondela 238
Regueras, Juan de, Spanish prisoner 233
Relief, lost ship, English Armada 247
Religious intolerance 144, 297

Restoration of the Spanish Navy (1590) 249, 253
Revenge, ship 17, 20–2, 26, 41, 54, 66, 226, 229, 254–5, 260
  becomes detached from the other ships 229
  goes down 254, 255
  sets sail with the English Armada 41
Rías Altas, Galicia 227
Rías Bajas, Galicia 124, 130, 136
Ribadavia 201
Ribadeo 119
Ribeira das Naos, Lisbon 155
Ribeira, palace, Lisbon 155
Rieux, René, governor of Brest 257
Riohacha, river 265, 266
Roberts, Henry, English agent in Morocco 36
Robles, ensign 70, 83
Rocha, Juan da, Portuguese nobleman 139
Rochester 33
Rodrígues de Távora, Álvaro, captain 212
Rodríguez Muñiz, Pedro, superintendent of fortifications 89
Rodríguez Suárez, Juan, councillor of Betanzos 57, 70
Rodríguez, Bernardino 228
Rodríguez, Juan, captain of the ship *Trinidad* 231, 235
Rojas, Cristóbal de, military engineer 253, 256–7
Rome 290
Rooney, Michael, musician 28
Rosclogher, castle 28
Rossio, square, Lisbon 171
Rouen 21
Rua dos Bacalhoeiros, Lisbon 156
Ruiz, Juan, captain 177, 219

Saavedra, Álvaro de, Spanish explorer 267
Sada 70, 84, 104
Saint Bartholomew's night in 1572 slaughter of Huguenots in France 8
Saint James on horseback or 'Santiago Matamoros' ('the Moorslayer') 153
Saint Nicholas, Isle of, Plymouth 250
Saint Paul 258
Saint-Jean-de-Luz 215
Salazar, Pedro de, captain 156
Saldanha, Lisbon 164
Salvatierra, Pontevedra 61, 81, 233
Sampson, John, colonel, wounded in Corunna 96, 153–4

San Andrés, hospital, Corunna 112
San Antón, castle 9, 15, 43, 49, 50, 53–5, 57–9, 61, 62, 64, 71, 74, 77–8, 80, 97, 99–101, 103, 105, 107, 114, 116, 118, 168, 174, 248, 273, 278, 283
San Antonio, cape, Cuba 268
San Antonio, monastery, Cascais 143, 183, 195, 198, 202, 207, 222
San Bartolomé, ship, Spanish Armada 44–5, 54–5, 64, 101
San Bernardo, ship, Spanish Armada 45, 58, 70
San Diego, castle, Corunna 118
San Esteban, patache, Spanish Armada 45, 47
San Fausto de Chapela, Vigo 233
San Felipe, castle, Setúbal 207
San Felipe, fort, Cádiz 269
San Felipe, lost ship, Spanish Armada 25
San Francisco, monastery, Corunna 113
San Jorge, Corunna 63, 66
San José, Trinidad 261
San Juan Bautista, lost ship, Spanish Armada 46
San Juan de Sicilia, lost ship, Spanish Armada 25
San Juan of Portugal, ship, Spanish Armada 17, 20, 21, 25–6, 28, 45–7, 53–5, 59, 61, 64, 76, 99, 101, 132, 254, 273
San Lesmes, caravel in which Francisco de Hoces discovered the passage that separates America from Antarctica 247
San Lorenzo, lost ship, Spanish Armada 25, 102
San Luis, ship, Spanish Armada 22
San Marcos, lost ship, Spanish Armada 25–6, 290
San Martín, ship, Spanish Armada 2, 11, 16–17, 19–20, 22, 24–6, 44, 131, 290
San Mateo, lost ship, Spanish Armada 25
San Matías, Spanish ship captured in Cádiz 270
San Pedro de Cardeña, monastery 48
San Pedro Mayor, ship, Spanish Armada 14
San Pedro Menor, ship, Spanish Armada 47
San Roque, Lisbon 176, 180–90
San Salvador, church, Vigo 233
San Salvador, lost ship, Spanish Armada 19
San Saturniño, Corunna 70
San Sebastián 47
Sánchez Cordero, Alonso, pilot who led Francis Drake in his circumnavigation of the globe 247
Sancti Petri, Cádiz 270

Sandoval, Francisco de, Duke of Lerma, *valido* of Philip III 277, 279
Sandwich 238
Sanlúcar de Barrameda 11, 268, 272, 274
Sansón, ship, Spanish Armada 45, 55, 64, 70, 101
Santa Ana, castle, Las Palmas, Canary Islands 263, 279
Santa Ana, convent, Lisbon 150
Santa Bárbara, convent, Corunna 67
Santa Catalina, castle, Las Palmas, Canary Islands 263
Santa Catalina, Lisbon 119, 150, 159, 164–5, 167–8, 170, 176, 183, 189, 190, 192, 196, 200
Santa Catalina, ship, Spanish Armada 19
Santa Clara, convent, Lisbon 150
Santa Clara, Lisbon 148
Santa Compaña, mythical belief 226
Santa Cristina de Lavadores, Vigo 233
Santa Cruz, castle, Corunna 278
Santa Cruz, Corunna 57
Santa Lucía, Corunna 55, 57, 71, 72
Santa María de la Rosa, lost ship, Spanish Armada 15
Santa María de Oza, Corunna 54, 58
Santa María, gate, Lisbon 169
Santa Marta, monastery, Vigo 232
Santander 2, 14, 122, 143, 209, 210–11, 235, 237, 243, 248, 278, 280, 282
Santarém 139, 143
Santiago de Compostela 38, 49, 54, 56, 62, 65, 71, 73, 77–9, 81, 88, 100, 102–7, 109–12, 114, 133, 153–4, 186, 228, 231–4, 237, 260, 267
  Archbishop letter 80
  assistance for those returning from the Spanish Armada 43
  fears 79, 102
  reinforcements from Galicia converging on 81
  relics attributed to the Apostle hidden when faced with the threat from the English Armada 81
Santiago del Príncipe, Panama 267
Santiago y cierra España!, Spanish battle crie 153
Santo Adrião, Lisbon 144
Santo Amaro, hill, Lisbon 160, 165, 187, 189–90
Santo Antón, gate, Lisbon 173

Santo Domingo, monastery, Corunna 68–9, 73–7, 79, 82, 86–8, 90–1, 93, 100, 102–3, 170
Santoña 14
São Jorge, castle, Lisbon 121, 134–5, 155, 161, 163–5, 172–3, 177, 182, 190, 199–200
São Julião, castle, Lisbon 117–21, 123, 128, 134, 143, 155–6, 161, 163, 186, 191–2, 195, 197–8, 202, 207–8
São Tomé, island 280
Sarmiento, Diego, son of García Sarmiento 81
Sarmiento, García, squire of Salvatierra 61, 233
Sarmiento, Luis, son of García Sarmiento 233–4
Scilly, Isles of 13–14
Scotland, Scottish 2, 27, 31, 44, 119, 136, 239, 283, 290, 295
Seagar, captain, wounded in Corunna 96
Sebastião I, King of Portugal 33–4, 184, 193
Second Crusade 172
Seixo Branco, Corunna 101
Serena, ship, Spanish fleet 1589 216
Servido, Gregorio, prior of Vigo 233
Sesimbra 224
Setúbal 203, 211, 224
Seville 36, 115, 129, 160, 186, 265, 272, 288
Seymour, captain 25
Sharif 222
Shrewsbury, Earl of, George Talbot 106, 210
Sicily 44, 46
Sidney, Thomas, colonel, wounded at the bridge of El Burgo 40, 105
Sierpe, fountain, Corunna 63, 75
Sigüeiro 110
Sigüenza 186–90
Silva, Diego da, Portuguese nobleman 138
Silva, Fernando da, Portuguese nobleman 138
Sinos, tower, Lisbon 174
Sintra, mountains, Cascais 195, 206–7
Sisargas, Islands 11, 12, 228
slavery, the Afro-American triangular trade route 265
Sligo 27
Sluis 280
Soares, Martiño, mayor of Peniche 125, 127, 224–5
Solomon, ship 263
Somers, lieutenant, killed in Corunna 96
Soto, Juan, captain 46
Sotomayor, Alonso de, Spanish conquistador and Real Governor 266

Sotomayor, Pedro de 71, 101, 110, 112, 231
Sousa, Diego de, Portuguese nobleman 138
Spain, its historical development 293
Spanish Armada
  already repaired, sets sail from Santander 248
  casualties in combat on 2 August Portland
    Bill 20
  casualties in combat on 3 August Isle of
    Wight 22
  casualties in combat on 8 August
    Gravelines 26
  casualties in combat on 31 July Eddystone 18
  casualties in the explosion of the nao *San
    Salvador* on 31 July near Plymouth 19
  casualties, total number 33, 246, 298
  end of its repair 241
  lessons from its failure 249
  lost ships, total number 27, 290
  motives 9, 297
  re-establishment in Corunna 16
  repairs in Corunna 15
  risk of concentrating the naval force 297
Spanish Empire 122, 175, 261, 285, 290, 294
  causes of its neglect 290
  danger of collapse 36
  difficulty of defending it 264
  distorted image 294
  expulsion of Dutch 261
  first high point 285
  speed of the Iberian conquest 261
Spanish infantry 1, 63, 114, 123, 126, 133, 145,
    176, 182, 188, 197, 200
  Tercio, a former unit of Spanish infantry 1, 3,
    8–9, 16, 18–19, 23–4, 26, 44–8, 96, 103,
    129, 133, 156, 169, 174, 186, 192, 200,
    256, 273
Spanish inflation 10, 210, 255
Spanish Road 277
Spanish shipbuilding 287
Spanish treasure fleet 268, 273, 280, 282
Spanish-Portuguese rivalry 161
Spanocchi, Tiburzio, royal engineer, Spain 77
Spencer, captain, artillery lieutenant, killed in
    Corunna 95, 100, 183
Spigott, captain, killed at the bridge of El
    Burgo 106
Spinola, Ambrogio 284
Spinola, Federico, Italian nobleman in the
    service of Philip II 278, 280, 284

State of Andrés Soares, Lisbon 165, 173, 176–7
Streedagh, beach, Sligo 28
Suárez, Diego, captain 47
Suárez, Lope, soldier 155
Suazo, bridge, Cádiz 270
Suffolk 254
Suleiman 175
Sumiel, Felipe, captain 173, 190
Sussex, Earl of 104
Swallow, ship, English fleet 1588 20
Swiftsure, ship, English Armada 41, 119,
    121, 127
Sydenham, captain, killed in Corunna 96

Tagus, river 10, 51, 117, 122, 155, 265, 279
Talbot, Lord 106, 210
Tambre, river, Galicia 110
Tartessos 271
Távares, Cristóvão de, Portuguese counsellor 34
Teis, Vigo 231–2
Tello, Rodrigo, captain 23
Tenerife 279
Teodósio II of Bragança, Duke 198, 201, 207
Terceira, Island, Azores 35, 234, 255, 274
Terreiro do Trigo, Lisbon 155–6
Thames, river 9, 21, 23, 171, 175
Thirty Years' War 285
Thomas, lost ship, English Armada 247
Todos os Santos, hospital, Lisbon 171, 179, 180
Toledo, Francisco de, captain of *San Felipe*, lost
    ship, Spanish Armada 25, 129, 134, 186,
    192, 226
Toledo, Luis de, cavalry general 227
Toledo, Pedro de, captain general of the galleys
    of Naples 277
Tomar, Parliament of 129, 181
Torbay 19, 243
Tornabellaco, Panama 266
Torres Vedras 125, 127, 128–9, 135, 137–9, 141,
    221, 224, 225
Torres, Antonio de, captain 148
Torres, ensign, killed in the attack on 3 June
    Lisbon 178
Torres, Juan de, captain, fatally wounded in
    the attack of 1 June near Lisbon 147–8,
    151, 153–5
Touriñán, Cape 228
Tower of Abajo, Corunna 61
Tower of Hercules, Corunna 67

Toynbee, Arnold, historian 175, 291
Trafalgar, naval batle 114, 294
Trafaría, Lisbon 117, 118
Treaty of Medina del Campo, between England and Spain, 1489 7
Trigueros, Juan, captain 45, 70
Trinidad 261
Trindade, monastery, Lisbon 190
Triumph, ship, English fleet 1588 17
Troncoso, Álvaro, captain 16, 51, 54–5, 57, 61–2, 69–70, 74, 83, 87, 88–9, 113
A True Discourse, English pamphlet about the English Armada 3, 130–4, 106, 130, 183, 216, 224–5, 293, 298
Twelve Apostles, twelve galleons 249
Twelve Years' Truce, between the United Provinces and Spain, 1609 285

United States of America 267, 282, 295
Urdaneta, Andrés de, sailor and explorer 10
Urquiola, Antonio de, sailor 273

Vaamonde Lores, Cesar, historian 70
Valdés, Pedro, admiral 17
Valencia 277
Valparaíso, Chile 259
Van der Does, Pieter 279–80
Varela, Juan, captain 49, 54, 55–9, 61–3, 65, 67–8, 70–2, 82, 84, 101
Vargas, Alonso, of the Council of War 200–1, 206
Vázquez de Neira, Juan, mayor of Betanzos 61
Veamonte, Claudio de, captain, wounded in the attack on 3 June Lisbon 173, 178, 180, 190
Velasco, Bernardino de, captain 133–4, 173, 179, 186, 190, 192
Velasco, Francisco de 199
Venegas de Córdoba, Pedro, governor of São Julião castle 134
Venegas, captain 18
Venezuela 261
Venice 19, 48
Vera, Fernando de, captain 45
Veragua, Panama 267
Viana do Castelo 228–9
Victoria, Queen of England 244, 291, 294
Victoria, ship in which Juan Sebastián Elcano first circumnavigated the globe 247
Victory, ship, English fleet 1588 17

Vienna 175
Vigo 46, 48, 57, 131, 227–9, 231–41
Vila do Conde 228
Vila, Luis da, servant of García Sarmiento, squire of Salvatierra 61
Vilaboa, Corunna 85, 86, 102
Villadorta, Count of, general of the Portuguese cavalry 157, 182, 189, 205–7, 224
Villalpando, mulatto guide and renegade 261–2
Villavicencio, Bartolomé de, mayor of Cádiz 271
Villaviciosa, captain 273
Vinaroz 277
Vivero 14, 44, 85, 238

Walsh, Ben, Chair of the Secondary Education Committee of the British Historical Association 295–6
Walsingham, Francis, secretary to Queen Elizabeth I 13–14, 27, 31–2, 36–7, 104, 209, 211, 215, 239, 241
Wernham, R. B., historian 246–7
Weymouth 213
Wight, Isle of 22
William, ship sunk in naval battle on 20 June English Armada 217
Williams, Roger, soldier and military theorist 8, 40, 42, 89, 119, 121–2, 126, 128, 132, 137, 161, 174, 240
Winall, John, captain, wounded in Corunna 96
Wingfield, Anthony, *see A True discourse*
Woodcocke, Thomas, publisher of the pamphet *Ephemeris expeditionis Norreysius et Drakus in Lusitaniam* about the English Armada 244
www.celticfringefest.com 28

Xavan, Algerian captain 259
Xuarez Tandil, Diego, archivist of the Cathedral of Santiago de Compostela 81

Yeguas, Gulf 10
Yepes, Pedro de, captain 177
Young, captain, killed in Corunna 74

Zapateira, Corunna 71–2, 78
Zealand, Denmark 220
Zubiaur, Pedro de, sailor 255, 271, 280–1
Zúñiga, Bernardino de, captain 186